Parking and ''

Donald Shoup brilliantly overcame the ch
ing without being boring in his iconoclasti
of Free Parking. Easy to read and often er   ....к snowed
that city parking policies subsidize cars, encourage sprawl, degrade
urban design, prohibit walkability, damage the economy, raise housing
costs, and penalize people who cannot afford or choose not to own a
car. Using careful analysis and creative thinking, Shoup recommended
three parking reforms: (1) remove off-street parking requirements, (2)
charge the right prices for on-street parking, and (3) spend the meter
revenue to improve public services on the metered streets.

Parking and the City reports on the progress that cities have made in
adopting these three reforms. The successful outcomes provide convincing evidence that Shoup's policy proposals are not theoretical and
idealistic but instead are practical and realistic. The good news about
our decades of bad planning for parking is that the damage we have
done will be far cheaper to repair than to ignore. The 51 chapters by 46
authors in *Parking and the City* show how reforming our misguided and
wrongheaded parking policies can do a world of good.

Donald Shoup, FAICP, is Distinguished Research Professor of Urban
Planning in the Luskin School of Public Affairs at the University of
California, Los Angeles, USA.

"Don Shoup has done more to revolutionize the way we think about parking than anybody else on the planet. His latest book tells the story of the impact his ideas are having on the subject. It is a must read for anybody who cares about the future of our cities."

Michael Dukakis, Distinguished Professor of Political Science, Northeastern University, USA

Parking and the City

Edited by
Donald Shoup

Routledge
Taylor & Francis Group

NEW YORK AND LONDON

First published 2018
by Routledge
711 Third Avenue, New York, NY 10017

and by Routledge
2 Park Square, Milton Park, Abingdon, Oxon, OX14 4RN

Routledge is an imprint of the Taylor & Francis Group, an informa business

Library of Congress Cataloging-in-Publication Data
Names: Shoup, Donald C., editor.
Title: Parking and the city / edited by Donald Shoup.
Description: First edition. | New York, NY : Routledge, 2018.
Identifiers: LCCN 2017057741 | ISBN 9781138497030 (hardback) | ISBN
9781138497122 (pbk.)
Subjects: LCSH: Automobile parking. | City and town life--Parking. |
Parking meters.
Classification: LCC HE336.P37 P36 2018 | DDC 388.4/74--dc23
LC record available at https://lccn.loc.gov/2017057741

ISBN: 978-1-138-49703-0 (hbk)
ISBN: 978-1-138-49712-2 (pbk)
ISBN: 978-1-351-01966-8 (ebk)

Typeset in Palatino
by Servis Filmsetting Ltd, Stockport, Cheshire

Table of Contents

List of Figures

List of Figures **xi**

List of Tables

Notes on Contributors

Carol Atkinson-Palombo is associate professor in the Department of Geography at the University of Connecticut.

Paul Barter is adjunct associate professor in the LKY School of Public Policy at the National University of Singapore.

Leah M. Bojo is an urban-planning and land-use policy professonal in Austin, Texas.

Bill Chapin is an urban planner in Michael Baker International's Oakland, California, office.

Dan Chatman is associate professor of city and regional planning at UC Berkeley.

Mikhail Chester is associate professor in the Department of Civil, Environmental, and Sustainable Engineering at Arizona State University.

Amélie Davis is an assistant professor at Miami University in Oxford, Ohio, with a dual appointment in the Department of Geography and the Institute for the Environment and Sustainability.

Elizabeth Deakin is Professor Emerita at the University of California, Berkeley.

Andrew Fraser is research assistant professor in the Department of Civil, Environmental, and Sustainable Engineering at Arizona State University.

C.J. Gabbe is assistant professor in the Department of Environmental Studies and Sciences at Santa Clara University.

Norman Garrick is associate professor in the Department of Civil and Environmental Engineering at the University of Connecticut.

Rodrigo García Reséndiz holds a Master's degree in Urban and Regional Planning from the University of California, Los Angeles, with a concentration in transportation.

Peer Ghent has been the project manager of LA Express Park since October 2008.

Seth Goodman is an architectural designer and an activist for sustainable transportation and urban design.

Zhan Guo is an associate professor in the Wagner School of Public Service at New York University.

Robert Hampshire is research assistant professor in the University of Michigan's Transportation Research Institute.

Daniel B. Hess is professor and chair in the Department of Urban and Regional Planning at the University of Buffalo, State University of New York.

Arpad Horvath is professor in the Department of Civil and Environmental Engineering at the University of California, Berkeley.

Maria Irshad, CAPP, is the assistant director for ParkHouston, the on-street parking operations for the City of Houston.

Wenyu (Wendy) Jia is the manager of systems and capital planning at the Washington Metropolitan Area Transit Authority.

Emma Kirkpatrick is a planner and GIS technician at the Maumee Valley Planning Organization in Defiance, Ohio.

Michael Klein, CAPP, is the founder and CEO of Klein & Associates. He was previously the executive director of the Albany Parking Authority.

Douglas Kolozsvari is a principal at Solutions 2050, which provides consulting services in the areas of air quality, climate change and parking.

Samer Madanat is dean of Engineering and Xenel Distinguished Professor of Civil and Environmental Engineering at New York University, Abu Dhabi.

Josiah Madar is an attorney at the Massachusetts Housing Finance Agency and a research affiliate at the New York University Furman Center for Real Estate and Urban Policy.

Michael Manville is associate professor in the Department of Urban Planning at the University of California, Los Angeles.

Juan Matute is associate director of the Institute of Transportation Studies at the University of California, Los Angeles.

Chris McCahill is an associate researcher with the State Smart Transportation Initiative at the University of Wisconsin, Madison.

Simon McDonnell is the director of research and strategic analysis at the New York State Homes and Community Renewal (NYSHCR) and a research affiliate at New York University Furman Center for Real Estate and Urban Policy.

Thomas Mericle is the city transportation manager for Ventura, California.

Adam Millard-Ball is assistant professor in the Department of Environmental Studies at the University of California, Santa Cruz.

Ram Pendyala is professor in the Department of Civil, Environmental, and Sustainable Engineering at Arizona State University.

Gregory Pierce is adjunct assistant professor of urban planning and senior researcher in the Luskin Center for Innovation in the Luskin School of Public Affairs at the University of California, Los Angeles.

Bryan Pijanowski is a professor in the Department of Forestry and Natural Resources at Purdue University and is the director of the Discovery Park Center for Global Soundscapes.

Jay Primus works as a transportation consultant. Previously, he led parking management for San Francisco, including the planning, delivery, operation, and evaluation of the federally-funded SFpark pilot project.

Andrés Sañudo Gavaldón was the parking policy coordinator at Mexico City's Institute for Transportation and Development Policy from 2011 to 2015.

Patrick Siegman is founding principal of Siegman and Associates. He also as an advisor to San Francisco's SF*park* program.

Fernando Torres-Gil is Professor of Social Welfare and Public Policy and Director of the UCLA Center for Policy Research on Aging.

Martin Wachs is distinguished professor emeritus of Civil and Environmental Engineering and of City and Regional Planning at the University of California, Berkeley.

Rachel Weinberger is a transportation consultant in New York City.

Jonathan Williams, AICP, is a strategic adviser in the City of Seattle's Department of Transportation.

Hank Willson is the parking policy manager in San Francisco's Municipal Transportation Agency.

Richard Willson, FAICP, is a professor in the Department of Urban and Regional Planning at California State Polytechnic University, Pomona.

Quan Yuan is a Ph.D. candidate in Planning and Policy Development at the Sol Price School of Public Policy, the University of Southern California.

Dan Zack, AICP, was the downtown development manager for Redwood City, California, from 2003 to 2014. He is now assistant planning director for Fresno, California.

Preface to *Parking and the City*

The American Planning Association published *The High Cost of Free Parking* in 2005. Surprising everyone, this 750-page book on parking was popular enough to reprint, with additions, as an 800-page paperback in 2011. Since then, many people have asked for a shorter version of the book to appeal to general readers who are concerned about the future of cities but don't want to buy or read an 800-page book about parking.

The Introduction to *Parking and the City* is this shorter, updated version of *The High Cost of Free Parking*. The following 51 chapters then report on the subsequent flowering of research and action on three recommended parking reforms: (1) remove off-street parking requirements, (2) charge the right prices for on-street parking, and (3) return the revenue to pay for local public services.

Writing about parking without being boring presents quite a challenge. *Parking and the City* is based on my experience as the Editor of *ACCESS*, a magazine that bridges the gap between academic research and practicing planners. Academic research often requires years of work before the author eventually publishes the results. Developing a theory, collecting data, and conducting rigorous statistical tests are necessary before an academic journal will accept an article for publication. Then what happens? A few fellow academics and their students might read the article and discuss it. But city planners and elected officials who can use the results to improve public policy will probably never see the article or even hear about the research.

ACCESS offers academics an opportunity to reach a wider audience. I invite the authors of policy-relevant research on transportation to write condensed versions in plain and even lively English. I have used this same editorial policy for *Parking and the City*. I invited the authors of academic research on parking to write shorter versions for a general audience with high standards for clarity, readability, and even humor. The goal is to take the vital last step in research: make the information accessible. By connecting scholars with practicing planners and elected officials, I hope *Parking and the City* can catapult academic research into public debate and convert knowledge into action. I also have invited local officials who have implemented parking reforms in their cities to write original chapters that explain their methods and the benefits.

I have accumulated many intellectual debts while assembling this book. First, I want to thank my wife Pat, who is the best editor any writer ever had. I also want to thank the many UCLA graduate students who have worked on editing all the chapters. If you find the book easy to read, you can thank, as I do, Eve Bachrach, Sam Blake, Katherine Bridges, Anne Brown, Kevin Carroll, Jordan Fraade, Cally Hardy, Dylan Jouliot, David Leipziger, Rosemary McCarron, Lance McNiven, Evan Moorman, Taner Osman, Heidi Schultheis, Ryan Sclar, Andrew Stricklin, Jacqueline Su, Ryan Taylor-Gratzer, Trevor Thomas, Zoe Unruh, Julie Wedig, and Warren Wells. Easy reading is hard writing, and I hope these student editors have learned from me as much I have from them. Nancy Voorhees and the Alan and Nathalie Voorhees Fund generously contributed financial support to employ the long parade of brilliant student editors. Krystal LaDuc and Edward Gibbons at Routledge skillfully and patiently converted the manuscript into this book.

Finally, I would especially like to thank the talented, dedicated, and wise James Hecimovich, formerly the editor of the Planning Advisory Service Report series at the American Planning Association. Jim was also the editor of *The High Cost of Free Parking,* and I have greatly enjoyed working with him again.

Both *The High Cost of Free Parking* and *Parking and the City* severely criticize current planning policies. Condemning the way many cities now plan for parking is an indictment of strategy and tactics, not of motives. Whatever our differences, I am sure all planners share the same goal of improving city life. How to go about this task is the enduring question of our profession, and I hope this new book will spur a debate that brings us to a better answer. After all, that is why we are city planners.

Introduction

He told the truth, mainly.
There was things which he stretched,
but mainly he told the truth.

Mark Twain, *Huckleberry Finn*

At the dawn of the automobile age, suppose Henry Ford and John D. Rockefeller had asked how city planners could increase the demand for cars and gasoline. Consider three options. First, divide the city into separate zones (housing here, jobs there, shopping somewhere else) to create travel between the zones. Second, limit density to spread everything apart and further increase travel. Third, require ample off-street parking everywhere so cars will be the default way to travel.

U.S. cities have unwisely adopted these three car-friendly policies. Separated land uses, low density, and ample free parking create drivable cities but prevent walkable neighborhoods. Although city planners did not intend to enrich the automobile and oil industries, their plans have shaped our cities to suit our cars. Cars themselves have also reshaped our cities. As John Keats (1958, 13) wrote in *The Insolent Chariots*, "The automobile changed our dress, manners, social customs, vacation habits, the shape of our cities, consumer purchasing patterns, and positions in intercourse." Many of us were probably even conceived in a parked car.

Parking requirements in zoning ordinances are particularly ill advised because they directly subsidize cars. We drive to one place to

1

do one thing, and then to another place to do another thing, and then finally drive a long way back home, parking free almost everywhere. Off-street parking requirements are a fertility drug for cars.

In *The High Cost of Free Parking,* which the American Planning Association published in 2005, I argued that parking requirements subsidize cars, increase traffic congestion, pollute the air, encourage sprawl, increase housing costs, degrade urban design, prevent walkability, damage the economy, and penalize people who cannot afford a car. Since then, to my knowledge, no member of the planning profession has argued that parking requirements do *not* cause these harmful effects. Instead, a flood of recent research has shown they *do* cause these harmful effects. Parking requirements in zoning ordinances are poisoning our cities with too much parking.

On average, cars are parked 95 percent of their lives and driven only 5 percent (*The High Cost of Free Parking,* Appendix B). As a result, cities require an enormous amount of land for parking. In Los Angeles County, all the parking spaces that cities require cover at least 200 square miles of land, equivalent to 14 percent of the county's incorporated land area and 1.4 times larger than the 140 square miles dedicated to the roadway system (see Chapter 14 below).

Ultimately, parking requirements can make driving more difficult because all the cars engendered by the required parking spaces clog the roads and congest traffic. Los Angeles has more parking spaces per square mile than any other city on earth (*The High Cost of Free Parking,* 161-65), and, according to the INRIX 2016 Global Traffic Scorecard, Los Angeles also has worse traffic congestion than any other city on Earth.

Despite all the harm off-street parking requirements cause, they are almost an established religion in city planning. One should not criticize anyone else's religion, but when it comes to parking requirements I'm a protestant and I believe city planning needs a reformation.

THREE PARKING REFORMS

Reform is difficult because parking requirements don't exist without a reason. If on-street parking is free, removing off-street parking requirements will overcrowd the on-street parking and everyone will complain. Therefore, to distill 800 pages of *The High Cost of Free Parking* into three bullet points, I recommend three parking reforms that can improve cities, the economy, and the environment:

- **Remove off-street parking requirements**. Developers and businesses can then decide how many parking spaces to provide for their customers.

- **Charge the right prices for on-street parking**. The right prices are the lowest prices that will leave one or two open spaces on each block, so there will be no parking shortages. Prices will balance the demand and supply for on-street parking spaces.
- **Spend the parking revenue to improve public services on the metered streets.** If everybody sees their meter money at work, the new public services can make demand-based prices for on-street parking politically popular.

Each of these three policies supports the other two. Spending the meter revenue to improve neighborhood public services can create the necessary political support to charge the right prices for curb parking. If cities charge the right prices for curb parking to produce one or two open spaces on every block, no one can say there is a shortage of on-street parking. If there is no shortage of on-street parking, cities can then remove their off-street parking requirements. Finally, removing off-street parking requirements will increase the demand for on-street parking, which will increase the revenue to pay for public services.

Right pricing is also called demand-based pricing (because the prices are based on parking demand), performance pricing (because the parking performs better), variable or dynamic pricing (because the prices vary), and market-rate pricing (because prices balance the demand and supply for curb parking). I will use these five terms interchangeably.

THE GOALS OF PARKING AND THE CITY

Parking is the Cinderella of transportation. Universities preach equality but they have a rigid internal status hierarchy, including the status of research topics. Global and national affairs have the most prestige, state government is a big step down, and local government seems parochial. Even within the unglamorous world of local government, parking occupies the lowest rung on the status ladder. Because most academics cannot imagine anything less interesting to study than parking, I was a bottom feeder with little competition for many years. But there is a lot of food down there, and many other academics have joined in what is now almost a feeding frenzy. Parking is far too important not to study.

The 51 chapters in this book summarize recent academic research on parking. Several practitioners have also contributed chapters that explain their experience with charging market prices for on-street parking, dedicating the meter revenue to pay for public services, and removing off-street parking requirements. The results show that parking is an important policy issue, not merely a regulatory detail. Parking affects almost everything and almost everything affects parking.

THE MOST EMOTIONAL TOPIC IN TRANSPORTATION

Most people consider parking a personal issue, not a policy question. When it comes to parking, rational people quickly become emotional and staunch conservatives turn into ardent communists. Thinking about parking seems to take place in the reptilian cortex, the most primitive part of the brain responsible for making snap judgments about urgent fight-or-flight issues, such as how to avoid being eaten. The reptilian cortex is said to govern instinctive behavior involved in aggression, territoriality, and ritual display—all important issues in parking.

Parking clouds the minds of reasonable people. Analytic faculties seem to shift to a lower level when one thinks about parking. Some strongly support market prices—except for parking. Some strongly oppose subsidies—except for parking. Some abhor planning regulations—except for parking. Some insist on rigorous data collection and statistical tests—except for parking. This parking exceptionalism has impoverished our thinking about parking policies, and ample free parking is seen as an ideal that planning should produce. If drivers paid the full cost of their parking, it would seem too expensive, so we ask someone else to pay for it. But a city where everyone happily pays for everyone else's free parking is a fool's paradise.

Daniel Kahneman, who won the Nobel Prize in economics in 2002 for his research integrating psychology and economics, summarized some of this research in *Thinking, Fast and Slow*. He examined two modes of thought. Fast thinking is instinctive, emotional, and subconscious, while slow thinking is logical, calculating, and conscious. It's hard to be rational about an emotional subject, but when thinking about parking, we should slow down.

I hope *Parking and the City* will convince readers that parking is worth taking seriously. Few people are interested in parking itself, so I always try to show how parking affects whatever people do care strongly about, such as affordable housing, climate change, economic development, public transportation, traffic congestion, and urban design. For example, parking requirements reduce the supply and increase the price of housing. Parking subsidies lure people into cars from public transportation, bicycles, or their own two feet. Cruising for underpriced curb parking congests traffic, pollutes the air, and creates greenhouse gases. Do people really want free parking more than affordable housing, clean air, walkable neighborhoods, good urban design, and a more sustainable planet? Recognizing that our misguided parking policies block progress toward many goals that people care deeply about—from providing affordable housing to slowing global warming—may spark a planning reformation. Reforms in planning for parking may be the simplest, cheapest, quickest, and most politically feasible way to achieve many important policy goals.

After this introduction, the following 51 chapters are divided into three parts that correspond to three recommended reforms. Part I focuses on removing off-street parking requirements; Part II focuses on charging the right prices for on-street parking; Part III focuses on spending the resulting revenue to improve public services. In the rest of this introduction I will use material from both *The High Cost of Free Parking* and the chapters in this book to show why these reforms are necessary and how they work.

I. REMOVE OFF-STREET PARKING REQUIREMENTS

City planners set the parking requirements for every art gallery, bowling alley, dance hall, fitness club, hardware store, movie theater, night club, pet store, tavern, and zoo without knowing the demand for parking at any of them. Despite a lack of both theory and data, planners have set parking requirements for hundreds of land uses in thousands of cities—the Ten Thousand Commandments for Off-Street Parking (*The High Cost of Free Parking*, Chapter 3). To paraphrase Charles Darwin, there is grandeur in the array of parking requirements that planners originally created for a few land uses or only one. From so simple a beginning, endless forms of complex parking requirements have been, and are being, evolved.

Although planners have adopted a veneer of professional language to justify the practice, planning for parking is learned on the job and is more a political activity than a professional skill. Consider all the information planners do not know when they set parking requirements:

- How much the required parking spaces cost.
- How much drivers are willing to pay for parking.
- How parking requirements increase the price of everything except parking.
- How parking requirements affect architecture and urban design.
- How parking requirements affect travel choices and traffic congestion.
- How parking requirements affect air and water pollution.
- How parking requirements affect fuel consumption and CO_2 emissions.

Cost is an especially important unknown. For example, without knowing how much the required parking spaces cost to build, planners cannot know how parking requirements increase the cost of housing.

Small, spartan apartments cost less to build than large, luxury apartments, but their parking spaces cost the same. Because many cities require the same number of spaces for all apartments regardless of their size or quality, the required parking disproportionately increases the cost of low-income housing. Minimum parking requirements show that cities care more about free parking than about affordable housing.

Parking requirements reduce the cost of owning a car but raise the cost of everything else. For example, the parking spaces required for shopping centers in Los Angeles increase the cost of building a shopping center by 67 percent if the parking is in an aboveground structure and by 93 percent if the parking is underground (see Chapter 3 below). This increased cost is then passed on to all shoppers. Parking requirements raise the price of food at grocery stores for everyone, regardless of how they travel. People who cannot afford to own a car pay more for their groceries to ensure that richer people can park free when they drive to the store. Parking requirements also help to explain why the rent is "too damn high." Chapter 11 estimates that parking requirements increase the rent carless households pay for their apartments by 13 percent.

Drivers have to pay market prices for their cars, fuel, tires, maintenance, repairs, insurance, and registration fees, but no one argues that all these should be free because charging for them would hurt the poor. People who don't own cars don't pay any of these costs. Nevertheless, cities require people who can't afford a car or choose not to own one to pay for parking.

America is a free country and many people seem to think that means parking should be free. Parking requirements enable everyone to park free at everyone else's expense, and no one knows that anyone is paying anything. Parking is free, however, only because everything else costs more. Parking requirements are well intentioned, but good intentions don't guarantee good results or compensate for unintended harm.

In astronomy, dark energy is a force that permeates space and causes the universe to expand. Similarly, in urban planning, parking requirements are a force that permeates space and causes cities to expand. The higher the parking requirements, the stronger the dark energy that spreads cities out and rips them apart. Parking requirements are an unnecessary evil.

The Pseudoscience of Parking Requirements

When I am invited to a city to speak about parking, I usually start with an aerial view of a site in that city with too much parking, such as this view of an office park in San Jose (Figure I-1). Off-street parking requirements require this pattern of development.

Figure I-1   Office park in San Jose

Too much of suburban America looks like this view of San Jose. We tend to ignore this asphalt blight in our daily life, especially when we park free in it. Parking is only free to us in our role as motorists, however, because we pay for it dearly in every other aspect of our lives. The cost of parking doesn't go away just because the driver doesn't pay for it. In trying to avoid paying for our own parking, we end up paying for everyone else's parking.

I then show a page from San Jose's parking requirements, such as the one in Figure I-2, which shows the city's parking requirements for entertainment and recreation. The many pages of parking requirements illustrate the New Urbanists' complaint that conventional zoning is all about numbers and ratios, with little thought given to how the resulting city will look.

Parking requirements are so precise and so specific for so many land uses that most people probably assume planners carefully study parking. Instead, planners are winging it.

Planners are not oracles who can divine the demand for parking. More often, they act as mediators between opposing political interests. I have never met a city planner who could intelligently explain why any parking requirement should not be higher or lower. The demand for parking is not only more complicated than planners think, but it's also more complicated than planners *can* think (*The High Cost of Free Parking*, Chapters 2 and 3). To set parking requirements, planners usually take instructions from elected officials, copy other cities' parking requirements, or rely on unreliable surveys of the peak parking occupancy

Entertainment and Recreation	
Arcade, amusement	1 per 200 sq. ft of floor area
Batting cages	1 per station, plus 1 per employee
Bowling establishment	7 per lane
Dancehall	1 per 40 sq. ft. open to public
Driving range	1 per tee, plus 1 per employee
Golf course	8 per golf hole, plus 1 per employee
Health club, gymnasium	1 per 80 sq. ft. recreational space
Miniature golf	1.25 per tee, plus 1 per employee
Performing arts production per rehearsal space	1 per 150 sq. ft. of floor area
Poolroom	1 per 200 sq. ft. of floor area
Private club of lodge	1 per 4 fixed seats on the premises, or 1 per 6 linear feet of seating, plus 1 per 200 square feet of area without seating but designed for meeting or assembly by guests, plus 1 per 500 sq. ft. of outdoor area developed for recreational purposes
Recreation, commercial (indoor)	1 per 80 sq. ft. of recreational area
Recreation, commercial (outdoor)	20 per acre of site
Skating rink	1 per 50 sq. ft. of floor area
Swim and tennis club	1 per 500 sq. ft. of recreation area

Figure I-2 Parking requirements in San Jose, California

observed at a few suburban sites with ample free parking and no public transit. Parking requirements are closer to sorcery than to science.

Because cars must park somewhere, many people think parking behaves like a liquid. If the parking supply is squeezed in one place, cars will park somewhere else. But parking behaves more like a gas; the number of cars expands and contracts to fill the available space. More parking leads to more cars. Nevertheless, planners base parking requirements on the assumption that cars and people come in fixed proportions, and they often state the requirements in parking spaces per person: per beautician, dentist, mechanic, nun, student, teacher, or tennis player. This assumed ratio between cars and people is in turn based on the assumption that all parking is free. If parking were priced to cover its cost, the ratio of cars to people would be lower.

Next, I show the size of the parking lots resulting from San Jose's parking requirements for a few land uses. When you take into account the individual spaces and add the access aisles to that calculation, each

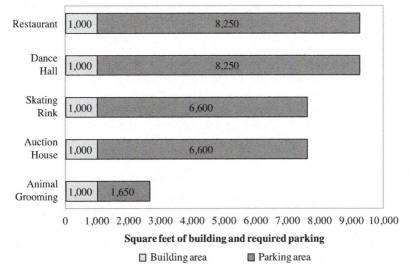

San José's minimum parking requirements

Figure I-3 Size of buildings and the required parking in San Jose, California

parking space typically requires about 330 square feet of land. For many land uses, the parking lots are bigger than the buildings they serve (Figure I-3). There is more space for parking than for people.

The light gray bar on the left represents 1,000 square feet of the building, and the darker gray bar on the right shows the size of the required parking lot. For example, San Jose requires 25 parking spaces per 1,000 square feet of dining area in a restaurant, and 25 parking spaces occupy 8,250 (25 × 330) square feet. The parking lot for a restaurant is thus more than eight times the size of the restaurant itself. Parking requirements provide parking everywhere anyone wants to go, but they also create many places where few people want to be. Furthermore, some of this expensive parking is rarely used. Underused parking has even inspired an annual photo contest showing half-empty parking lots at shopping centers on the day after Thanksgiving, one of the busiest shopping days of the year (Schmitt 2014).

Parking requirements make the city friendly to cars but not to people—drivable but not walkable. As Jane Jacobs (1962, 19) wrote, "The more downtown is broken up and interspersed with parking lots and garages, the duller and deader it becomes, and there is nothing more repellent than a dead downtown." We want more out of our streets than just traffic and free parking. We also want prosperity, safety, health, walkability, and pleasure.

If citizens demand off-street parking requirements, however, I think the right ones are the lowest ones that are politically possible after planners have made a strong case for low or no parking requirements. Planners can suggest many ways to reduce parking requirements. For example, developers can include bicycle parking spaces and on-site parking spaces for shared cars, offer cash-out programs for commuter parking, and offer free transit passes to all residents of an apartment building (see Chapters 19, 20, and 43, and *The High Cost of Free Parking,* Chapter 10). These programs can justify targeted reductions in parking requirements even where political concerns do not allow removing them.

The High Cost of Parking Requirements

Parking requirements resemble what engineers call a *kludge*—an awkward but temporarily effective solution to a problem, with many moving parts that are clumsy, inefficient, redundant, hard to understand, and expensive to maintain. Microsoft users will easily understand this concept. Planners should recognize that off-street parking requirements are a kludge designed to prevent a shortage of free on-street parking. Parking requirements are superficially plausible but fundamentally wrong. To paraphrase Anthony Downs (2004), using parking requirements rather than prices to balance the supply and demand for parking is like adjusting the position of a picture on the wall by rebuilding the wall rather than by shifting the picture.

Parking requirements are like barnacles on a ship, accumulating one at a time and slowing the ship's progress. These requirements have severed the link between the cost of providing parking and the price that drivers pay for it. They increase the demand for cars, and when citizens object to the resulting traffic congestion, cities respond by restricting development to reduce traffic. In sum, cities require parking and then limit the density of people to limit the density of cars. Free parking has become the arbiter of urban form, and cars have replaced people as zoning's real density concern.

In disputes about exactly how many parking spaces a city should require for every land use, each side makes solemn claims backed by dubious evidence. Parking requirements may look scientific, but compared with the current science behind parking requirements, Scientology is science and the Wizard of Oz was a scientist. Parking requirements are a step up from astrology, but they are several steps short of the Farmers' Almanac. They give pseudoscience a bad name.

Planners often use "motivated reasoning" to justify the parking requirements required by elected officials who want enough parking to ensure they won't be yelled at about parking shortages. Planners must create arguments for conclusions already reached. Assumptions are the starting point of most parking requirements, and the person who makes the assumptions determines the outcome. Instead of reasoning about parking requirements, planners are forced to rationalize them and must feign expertise they don't have. Setting the parking requirement for any land use is like searching in a dark room for a black cat that isn't there and claiming that you have found it.

Planners typically assume that all residents come with a car and require enough off-street parking to house the cars. Most residents usually do come with a car, but that is only because requiring plenty of off-street parking ensures that most residents will own a car. Parking requirements thus result from a self-fulfilling prophecy that everyone needs parking. Everyone needs parking because parking requirements engender an oversupply of cars that are then used to justify the need for parking requirements.

Urban planners cannot say how many parking spaces every apartment building needs any more than they can say how many cars every family needs. Because the number of available parking spaces affects the number of cars a family will own, the number of cars a family owns cannot predict the number of parking spaces that planners should require. The supply of parking creates its own demand, and planners estimate the demand for free parking as the way to require supply. It's as if planners required storage space in every residence based on their estimate of all the stuff they think people will store in the required space. Requiring every building to provide ample parking encourages everyone to buy a car.

All the required parking takes up a lot of space. Each off-street parking space typically occupies about 330 square feet (half for the parked car, and half for the access aisles). Because there are at least three off-street parking spaces per car in the United States (Chapter 8), and three parking spaces occupy about 990 square feet (330 × 3), there are at least 990 square feet of off-street parking space per car. In comparison, there are about 800 square feet of housing space per person in the United States (Moura, Smith, and Belzer 2015, 11). The area of parking per car in the United States is thus larger than the area of housing per human. Most of this parking is free to motorists because its cost is bundled into higher prices for housing and everything else.

Parking requirements result from complex political and economic forces beyond the control of city planners, such as demands for high parking requirements from residents who oppose nearby development. Nevertheless, planners enable the pseudoscience of parking requirements and the public bears the cost. When it comes to parking requirements, planners have used Pandora's box as a toolkit.

Evidence from In-Lieu Fees

Off-street parking requirements are counterproductive because cities can't fix traffic congestion and air pollution by subsidizing cars. We can use cities' in-lieu parking fees to suggest the subsidy for cars. Some cities allow developers to pay a fee in lieu of providing the off-street spaces required for a new building; the cities then use the revenue to provide public parking spaces (*The High Cost of Free Parking*, Chapter 9). The willingness to pay in-lieu fees rather than provide parking spaces shows that a developer wants to provide less parking.

To justify their in-lieu fees, some cities calculate the cost per parking space added by new public garages (*The High Cost of Free Parking*, Chapter 6). For example, in 2016 Palo Alto, California, calculated that its public parking garages cost $67,429 for every parking space added. Palo Alto therefore charges developers $67,429 for every required private parking space not provided.

This in-lieu fee reveals the cost of parking requirements. Palo Alto requires four parking spaces per 1,000 square feet for commercial uses. Because the in-lieu fee is $67,429 per space, the in-lieu fee is $269,716 (4 × $67,429) per 1,000 square feet of commercial area. The in-lieu fee thus adds almost $270 ($269,716 ÷ 1,000) per square foot to the cost of a new building that doesn't provide parking. This added cost is like an impact fee to pay for parking (impact fees on new development pay for the costs of providing public services to the new development). The in-lieu fee hides the cost of parking by bundling it in the cost of development. In-lieu fees unveil the high, hidden cost of parking requirements.

Palo Alto also levies impact fees on new buildings to pay for parks, libraries, and public safety facilities: $5.04 per square foot of building area for parks, $0.27 per square foot for libraries, and $0.58 per square foot for public safety facilities (City of Palo Alto 2016). Palo Alto's in-lieu parking fee of $270 per square foot thus dwarfs the impact fees that it imposes for all other public purposes combined. If impact fees reveal a city's priorities among public services, Palo Alto's highest priority is free parking.

America's Report Card

Every four years, the American Society of Civil Engineers issues its Report Card for America's Infrastructure showing the condition of 16 infrastructure categories. Figure I-4 shows the Report Card for 2017. The grade point average was D+.

If the civil engineers included parking in their Report Card, it would probably earn an A+. The Good Intentions Paving Company

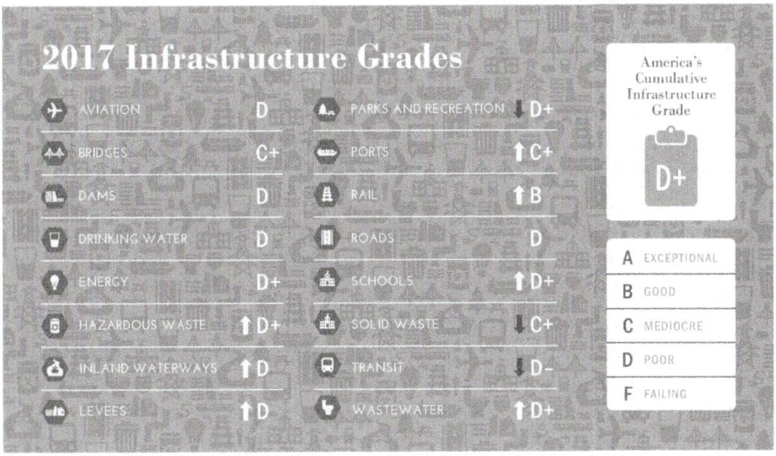

2017 Infrastructure Grades

America's Cumulative Infrastructure Grade

D+

AVIATION	D	PARKS AND RECREATION	↓ D+	
BRIDGES	C+	PORTS	↑ C+	
DAMS	D	RAIL	↑ B	
DRINKING WATER	D	ROADS	D	
ENERGY	D+	SCHOOLS	↑ D+	
HAZARDOUS WASTE	↑ D+	SOLID WASTE	↓ C+	
INLAND WATERWAYS	↑ D	TRANSIT	↓ D-	
LEVEES	↑ D	WASTEWATER	↑ D+	

A EXCEPTIONAL
B GOOD
C MEDIOCRE
D POOR
F FAILING

Figure I-4 American Society of Civil Engineers Report Card for America's Infrastructure

has produced great parking, and off-street parking requirements have hidden its cost in higher prices for everything else.

Although public infrastructure is an essential input for all economic activity, the U.S. probably spends more to subsidize parking than for all the rest of its transportation infrastructure combined. The estimated total subsidy for off-street parking in the U.S. in 2002 was between $127 billion and $374 billion (*The High Cost of Free Parking*, 205–208). In comparison, the total public infrastructure spending (capital, operation, and maintenance) for transportation by federal, state, and local governments in 2002 was $190 billion (Congressional Budget Office, 2015). Therefore, the total subsidy for off-street parking was somewhere between 67 percent and 197 percent of total public infrastructure spending for highways, mass transit, rail, aviation, and water transportation in the U.S. Users pay for much of the public spending for highways, mass transit, rail, aviation, and water transportation through gasoline taxes and other fees, but parking fees paid by drivers pay for less than 4 percent of the cost of parking (*The High Cost of Free Parking*, 208–210).

The Unequal Burden of Parking Requirements

Cities require parking for every building without considering how the required spaces place a heavy burden on poor people. A single parking space, however, can cost more than the net worth of many U.S. households. Table 3-1 shows an estimate that the average construction cost (excluding land cost) for parking structures in 12 U.S. cities in 2012 was $24,000 per space for aboveground parking and $34,000 per space for underground parking.

By comparison, in the U.S. in 2011, the median net worth (the value of assets minus debts) was $7,700 for Hispanic households and $6,300 for Black households (see Figure 4-1). One space in a parking structure therefore costs at least three times the net worth of more than half of all Hispanic and Black households in the country. Because cities require parking spaces at home, work, stores, restaurants, churches, schools, and everywhere else, there are several required parking spaces for every household, and the costs are passed on to all consumers.

Off-street parking requirements have produced an environment where most people feel they need a car to get a job, go to school, and shop. In a misguided attempt to provide free parking for everyone, cities force poor people to pay for parking spaces they can ill afford and often don't use. Free parking has the veneer of equality, but it increases inequality. It is wasteful *and* unfair.

Cities have a limited amount of money to spend on helping poor residents, and subsidizing parking is not the best way to spend this money. Free parking has two grave flaws as a way to aid poor people. First, free parking will not aid the poorest residents who cannot afford to own a car. Second, free parking will mainly aid the richer residents who own most of the cars. Nevertheless, cities seem willing to pay any price, bear any burden, and meet any hardship to ensure the survival and success of free parking. Cities have expensive housing for people but at least three parking spaces for every car (see Chapters 6, 13, and 14).

Parking requirements may seem fair, but they produce unfair results. To assess the financial reserves available to households, in 2015 the Federal Reserve Board (2016, 22) conducted a survey asking respondents how they would pay for a $400 emergency expense. Forty-six percent said that they would have to cover the expense by selling something, or borrowing the money, or would not be able to come up with the $400 at all. Although almost half of all families live from hand to mouth, parking requirements compel every household to pay for several off-street parking spaces even if they don't own a car.

City planners cannot do much to counter the inequality of wealth in the U.S., but they can help to reform their cities' off-street parking requirements that unfairly place heavy burdens on the poor (see Chapter 4). The planning profession should issue a recall for parking requirements.

Every Sin Is Forgiven If It Is Done with Our Permission

Removing off-street parking requirements has yet another advantage: It reduces the opportunities for corruption. When cities require off-street parking, they can issue planning variances that grant exceptions from parking requirements; that is, the city can allow a business to provide fewer than the required number of parking spaces because of a special circumstance, which is sometimes a donation to influence a bureaucrat or politician. When cities establish parking requirements, city officials have something to sell—a reduction in the parking requirement.

Just as the medieval Catholic Church sold indulgences for the remission of sins, cities can sell planning variances. In Dostoyevsky's *The Brothers Karamazov*, the Grand Inquisitor of Seville explained why the Church was popular even though it threatened Hell as the punishment for minor sins: "Every sin will be forgiven if it is done with our permission." Similarly, if cities require off-street parking, officials can forgive the sin of providing fewer than the required number of parking spaces.

Seeking a parking variance from city hall resembles buying an indulgence from the medieval church. Money goes in; favors come out. Removing the parking requirements will remove the temptation for elected officials to sell variances that allow sinfully few parking spaces.

Beyond saving money, removing the parking requirements will reduce the risk of development. Requiring developers to *ask* for a parking variance increases the risk of their projects because everyone has the legal right to oppose the variance and extract concessions, even when parking is not the opposition's real concern. Opposition to a parking variance makes it appear that everyone wants–demands–more parking when parking is only a pretext and what the opponents really want is to stop development. If a city allows development without parking, the objections to granting a parking variance will vanish and developers can propose financially viable projects.

Maximum Parking Limits

We often recognize the fine line between sensible planning and a foolish blunder only after we have crossed it. In the future, I think planners will look back at our predatory parking requirements the way we now look back at the urban renewal programs of the 1960s—they seemed like a good idea at the time but they created a disaster.

Some prescient critics foresaw the grave consequences of parking requirements. In 1927, Hawley Simpson, who was a founding member and then president of the Institute of Transportation Engineers, predicted that requiring off-street parking would create many problems (*The High Cost of Free Parking*, 279–80). He wrote, "Rather than assisting in solving the street traffic problem, it may very probably have the opposite effect by inducing a large amount of unnecessary vehicle usage. Free storage is an economic fallacy." Lewis Mumford (1963, 23) warned, "The right to have access to every building in the city by private motorcar, in an age when everyone possesses such a vehicle, is actually the right to destroy the city." Unfortunately, city planners ignored these warnings. Parking requirements were not just a misguided step onto the slippery slope toward command-and-control planning. Many cities have landed in the ditch at the bottom of the hill.

In the aftermath of urban renewal programs and minimum parking requirements, some U.S. cities' downtowns began to resemble images of medieval Romans camping in the ruins of an ancient and superior civilization. Fortunately, many cities have reversed course. San Francisco now has maximum parking limits with no minimum requirements in its downtown, while Los Angeles has minimum parking requirements with no maximum limits. Someone has to be wrong.

Maximum parking limits are justified if the traffic is so congested and the air is so polluted that a neighborhood can't safely handle any more cars. But a problem with maximum parking requirements is how to set them. The simplest reform of U.S. zoning would be to declare that all the existing off-street parking requirements are maximums rather than minimums, without changing any of the numbers. If minimum requirements specify what a city considers enough parking spaces, what is the harm in prohibiting more than enough parking spaces?

The successful experience of cities that do have maximum parking limits in their Central Business Districts (such as Boston, Chicago, New York, and San Francisco) is clear evidence that bankers will lend and developers will build in areas with parking maximums. The CBDs in these cities have much more development than the CBDs in cities that still have minimum parking requirements, such as Detroit and Phoenix. One banker told me he was willing to lend for a building with limited parking if it is in a district where all the other buildings also have limited parking. Maximum parking limits mean that bankers and developers have a city-imposed disarmament treaty in their competition to woo tenants with free parking.

Removing minimum parking requirements is much easier than reducing them or imposing maximum parking limits because planners don't have to invent the lower minimums or new maximums, justify them, and then administer them. In many cities, removing minimum parking requirements will also probably be much more important and much less controversial than imposing maximum parking limits. Zhan Guo studied what happened when London replaced parking minimums with maximums in 2004 (see Chapter 16). Before the change most developments provided no more parking than the minimum required, whereas after the change most developments provided much less than the maximum allowed. After the change, the parking supply in new buildings was only 68 percent of the new maximum allowed and only

52 percent of the previous minimum required. The new maximum limits caused only 2 percent of the decline in the parking supply; almost all the benefits of shifting from minimum requirements to maximum limits resulted simply from removing the minimum requirements.

Pretextual Parking Requirements

Some planners say that minimum parking requirements are needed because they enable cities to reduce the parking requirements in exchange for community benefits, such as affordable housing. For example, California requires cities to reduce the parking requirements for residential developments that include a specific share of affordable housing units (see Chapter 17). Reducing parking requirements as an inducement to provide affordable housing shows how unnecessary the parking requirements are in the first place. Cities would never reduce the code requirements for safe electrical wiring or fire escapes in exchange for affordable housing units in a development, but parking can easily be bargained away because it is obviously not necessary.

Reducing the parking requirements for developments that include affordable housing, however, has led affordable housing advocates in California to oppose any general reduction in parking requirements, even if this would increase the supply of housing and therefore make all housing more affordable. Affordable housing advocates would lose a bargaining chip they now use to secure a few dedicated affordable units in new developments. In this case, parking requirements are used as a *pretext*; their stated goal is to increase the parking supply but the real goal is to place a heavy burden on developers that the city can reduce in exchange for whatever it really wants (Manville and Osman 2017). This pretext is largely futile because developers usually provide the required parking and the city ends up with expensive housing and too much parking.

How can cities remove their minimum parking requirements and still have the bargaining power that the parking requirements provide? They can establish maximum parking limits and allow developers to provide more spaces if they pay a fee for every space they provide above the limit (*The High Cost of Free Parking*, Chapter 9). Mexico City adopted a version of this policy when it changed from minimum parking requirements to maximum parking limits in 2017 (see Chapter 15). Mexico City charges developers a fee for every space provided above half the maximum number allowed. I do not recommend establishing pretextual parking maximums to use as a bargaining tool with developers. Nevertheless, if cities want to use parking as a bargaining tool, it is much better to bargain from the starting point of low maximum limits than of high minimum requirements.

The Upside of Minimum Parking Requirements

If cities tried to micromanage other parts of our lives the way they micromanage off-street parking, everyone would join the Tea Party. Nevertheless, the upside is that removing the parking requirements can do so much good. Figure I-1 showed the asphalt desert created by excessive parking in Silicon Valley. Many spaces around the periphery of the parking lots remain vacant all the time. What would happen if San Jose removed off-street parking requirements, charged demand-based prices for on-street parking, and used the resulting revenue to improve neighborhood public services? Property owners might decide their land is more valuable for housing than for parking. If a city wants more housing and less traffic, removing off-street parking requirements will help.

Everyone in Silicon Valley complains about expensive housing, long commutes, traffic jams, polluted air, and the difficulty of attracting employees. Figure I-5 suggests what could happen to the scene in Figure I-1 if San Jose removed its off-street parking requirements. Housing could be built on the periphery of parking lots. A large parking lot can easily be redeveloped because it has a single owner, has no demolition costs, does not require new infrastructure, and is near both jobs and shopping. If apartment buildings were built on the parking lots next to the sidewalks, anyone walking, biking, or driving by would see a real city. The smartest way to travel is to be near your destination already, and this job-adjacent housing would give commuters out-of-car experiences while walking to work.

Figure I-5 An office parking lot lined with apartment buildings

The housing can be built without new parking because the existing spaces can be shared between office buildings and apartments. To avoid a parking shortage, the cost of parking will have to be separated from the rent for apartments and offices, so only drivers will pay for parking (*The High Cost of Free Parking*, Chapter 20). Residents who work in a nearby office building may find they can live with only one or even no car. They will have the option to rent an apartment without paying for two parking spaces, an option that parking requirements now prohibit. The new housing can't cause gentrification or displacement because no one lives on the parking lots now. The acres of surface parking offer the possibility of something much better, but parking requirements make the vision in Figure I-5 impossible. If cities remove the parking requirements at office parks, shopping malls, and big box stores, the peripheries of their parking lots can become sites for infill development.

Converting parking spaces into housing sites can reduce traffic congestion because more people could walk, bike, or ride transit to their destinations. Some of the remaining automobile travel could be in shared cars or through Lyft and Uber. The asphalt landscape in too much of America is not walkable, beautiful, or sustainable, but it can be reformed and transformed. Removing parking requirements can produce a cascade of benefits: shorter commutes, less traffic, a healthier economy, a cleaner environment, and more affordable housing. And the benefits don't stop there. If we reform our misguided planning for parking, and therefore our overreliance on the personal car, vast parking lots can evolve into real communities. Economic objectives are often said to conflict with environmental objectives, but parking reforms can easily serve both objectives at once. Parking reforms that make sense on economic grounds also make sense on environmental grounds.

The money now spent on cars and fuel can be spent on other things. Cars and fuel are often imported, but we cannot import apartment buildings. Spending less for cars, fuel, and parking, and spending more for housing will increase the demand for labor in a host of professions, such as architects, carpenters, electricians, engineers, gardeners, glaziers, lawyers, locksmiths, painters, plumbers, real estate agents, roofers, surveyors, and even urban planners. Parking lots employ few people but building on parking lots will boost the whole economy.

Parking requirements make U.S. cities look different from the European cities that many Americans admire. Most U.S. cities put a floor under the number of parking spaces to satisfy the peak demand for free parking, and then put a ceiling on development density to limit vehicle trips. Many European cities do the exact opposite; they put a ceiling on the number of parking spaces to avoid traffic congestion and put a floor under allowed development density to encourage walking, cycling, and public transport. In sum, many European cities limit parking and require density, whereas most U.S. cities limit density and require parking. U.S. buildings are now connected more closely to their parking than to the cities around them. Unfortunately, city planners have ignored the Hippocratic oath "First, do not harm" as a guiding principle in planning for parking.

Many successful business districts were built before cities began to require every business to have its own off-street parking. In cities that do require off-street parking, some business districts succeed if the city uses in-lieu fees to finance public parking structures so that businesses do not have to provide their own on-site parking (*The High Cost of Free Parking*, Chapter 10). Developers pay a fee for every required parking space they do not provide. Beverly Hills, Old Pasadena, and the Third Street Promenade in Santa Monica (all in California) are good examples. Try to think of any successful shopping street where every store has its own on-site parking.

Off-street parking requirements without the option to pay in-lieu fees leave no way to develop a successful group of stores except as a shopping mall. No one can build a street of shops of the sort that was common before cities began to require each building to provide its own parking. Only inside the better malls can most Americans find the dense, pedestrian-friendly shops that off-street parking requirements have made impossible everywhere else. Off-street parking requirements promote malls and devitalize cities. Parking requirements favor cars, and removing those requirements will level the playing field.

Some critics argue that removing an off-street parking requirement amounts to "social engineering" and a "war on cars." Instead, parking requirements are the social engineering and a war on walking. All the required parking spreads buildings apart so people need cars to get around. Removing a requirement that restaurants must provide 10 parking spaces per thousand square feet of floor area, for example, is no more a war on cars than removing a requirement that everyone must eat 10 hamburgers a month would be a war on hamburgers. Removing a parking requirement does *not* interfere in the market, and it is *not* a war on cars.

When it comes to off-street parking, I'm pro-choice. Cities should not require developers to give birth to unwanted parking spaces. Parking requirements were a bad idea, poorly executed, and it is easy to see the disastrous results—asphalt everywhere and a lack of life on the streets. It is hard to see the good results that parking requirements prevent but Figure I-5 shows how cities might look without parking requirements. The upside of the mess we have made is that we have an accidental land reserve available for job-adjacent housing. If cities remove their unwise parking requirements, we can reclaim land on a scale that will rival the Netherlands.

Parking requirements are a top-down decision by city planners and elected officials to replace many independent decisions by residents, developers, lenders, buyers, and travelers. Zoning now forces cities to gorge on parking. Stopping this force feeding is not the same thing as putting the city on a parking diet.

Even President Obama weighed in against off-street parking requirements because they "impose an undue burden on housing development.... These requirements have a disproportionate impact on housing for low-income households because these families tend to own fewer vehicles but are nonetheless burdened by the extra cost of parking's inclusion in the development" (The White House 2016, 16). And as Joseph Stiglitz, who won the Nobel Prize in Economics in 2001, has argued, reforms in land and housing are the key to a fairer economy. Because parking requirements commit so much land to cars and raise the cost of housing so much for people, reforms in parking requirements may be the most politically feasible way to reduce inequality (*The High Cost of Free Parking*, Chapter 19).

Cities have three good reasons to remove minimum parking requirements: We can't afford them, we don't need them, and they do immense harm. Wishing that parking requirements did not exist, however, is not a strategy for removing them. Parking requirements respond to a real problem but they are the wrong solution, and cities cannot remove their parking requirements without also better managing on-street parking. Cities require off-street parking so they won't have to manage on-street parking. The chapters in Part II focus on charging the right prices for on-street parking to prevent congestion at the curb without requiring off-street parking.

II. CHARGE THE RIGHT PRICES FOR ON-STREET PARKING

Many people think that parking is like sex—if you have to pay for it, it's just not right. It's also easy to think that parking is like oxygen, so essential that it's a human right and should be free for everyone. Free parking almost *is* a human right in the U.S. because drivers park free at the end of 99 percent of their trips (*The High Cost of Free Parking*, Appendix B). But even if parking is necessary, it doesn't have to be free. Food and housing are also necessary, but we don't assume they should be free.

Charging too much or too little for on-street parking can cause a lot of harm. If the price is too high and many curb spaces are vacant, adjacent businesses will lose customers, employees will lose jobs, and cities will lose tax revenue. If the price is too low and no curb spaces are vacant, drivers searching for a place to park will congest traffic, waste fuel, and pollute the air. Consequently, the right price for curb parking is the *lowest* price that can keep a few spaces open to allow convenient access. This is the Goldilocks principle of parking prices—not too high, not too low, but just right.

With conventional parking meters, the price stays the same throughout the day but the occupancy rate varies. With dynamic parking meters, the prices vary but the occupancy rate stays the same—one or two spaces are open. Goldilocks prices will give all drivers great parking karma and will guarantee front-door access to all businesses.

The curb lane may be much more productive in uses other than parking. For example, in dense neighborhoods a bike station can serve many more people than the same length of curb used for parking. In a study comparing a bike station on one side of a street with three curb parking spaces occupying the same length of curb on the other side of the street in Manhattan, Metcalf (2017) reported that during an hour almost 200 people arrived or departed from the bike station while only 11 people arrived or departed from the three parking spaces.

Wherever the curb is used for parking, it is important to price the parking properly to make sure it is being used properly. Market prices for curb parking will then help cities compare the value of parking spaces with the value of wider sidewalks, bike stations, or loading zones, and better judge the highest and best use of their valuable real estate.

The High Cost of Free Curb Parking

Underpriced curb parking creates an incentive to cruise in already-congested traffic. Cruising creates a moving queue of cars that are waiting for curb vacancies, but no one can see how many cars are in the queue because the cruisers are mixed with other cars that are actually going somewhere. Nevertheless, a few researchers have attempted to estimate the share of traffic that is cruising and the time it takes to find a curb space. They have analyzed videotapes of traffic flows, interviewed drivers who park at the curb or are stopped at traffic lights, and have themselves cruised for parking.

Table 25-1 shows the results of 22 studies of cruising for parking. Between 8 and 74 percent of the traffic was cruising, and the average time to find a curb space ranged between 3.5 and 14 minutes. These results are selective because researchers study cruising only where they expect to find it: on downtown streets where traffic is congested and all the curb spaces are occupied. On streets where open curb spaces are readily available, no one needs to cruise for parking. Because curb parking is underpriced and overcrowded in the busiest parts of most of the world's big cities, however, the sun never sets on cruising.

Newspapers often report on cruising. For example, consider this report in the *Los Angeles Times* (October 13, 2014): "In Los Angeles, parking your car on the street can be almost as stressful as driving it in traffic. Day after day, motorists repeat the same drill in the congested neighborhoods of the city: They weave up and down the streets, eyes peeled for an empty spot or a driver sitting in a parked car. (Is he maneuvering out or angling his way in?) Then they circle the block again and maybe again, getting sadder and madder with each loop." Drivers may begin to think the only way to find a parking space is to buy a parked car.

On-street parking is the most contested public land outside the Gaza Strip, and the competition for space can be fierce. In one study, the German Automobile Club set up video cameras at each intersection in central Freiburg and used them to follow randomly selected cars traveling from one intersection to another. The researchers estimated that 74 percent of the 800 cars followed on camera were cruising for parking and would have parked immediately had they found a space. The cameras revealed another notable finding: cruising, the researchers reported, produces psychological changes as drivers creep along in search of a parking space:

> This fixation on a parking space turns many drivers into unscrupulous maniacs. When all else fails, they will pull into any available space in a no-stopping zone, on the sidewalk, or even in an intersection (*The High Cost of Free Parking*, Chapter 11).

Closer to home, consider parking at a local farmers market. Drivers aggressively compete for the nearby on-street parking. But in the farmers market itself, everyone is considerate, trying not to get in each other's way, waiting patiently when someone else is blocking them, and saying "after you" when two people get to the counter at the same time. People's personalities don't change in the few minutes it takes to walk from their cars to the market. Instead, what changes is the transition from competing for parking in an overcrowded commons to cooperating in a market where everyone pays for what they buy.

Having an open parking space available on the street is like having an open pump space available at a gas station. When the government capped gas prices at the pump in 1979, long lines immediately formed at gas stations. Drivers had to wait for their turn to fill up. The lines of idling cars spilling onto the streets showed the mistake of setting below-market prices for gasoline, and the price caps were removed in 1981. When cities charge below-market prices for curb parking, drivers have to cruise in search of an open space but we can't see the lines of cars waiting for parking. We know some cars are cruising because we have done it ourselves.

Suppose we had two kinds of gas stations, private and public. The private stations sell gas at market prices, but the public stations sell gas at heavily subsidized prices. The market-priced private stations won't have any lines at the pump, but the underpriced public stations will have long lines at the pump, with engines idling, drivers fuming, and time being wasted, as with underpriced curb parking.

For each hour that an additional car is parked on a crowded street, other drivers will have more difficulty finding an open space and will spend more time cruising for parking. Inci, Ommeren, and Kobus (2017) estimate that for each extra hour that a car parks at a crowded curb, the total extra time that other drivers waste while cruising for parking is worth about 15 percent of what an average worker earns in an hour. This external cost is only for the additional time spent by drivers who are cruising, and cruising does far more than waste the cruisers' time. Cruising also congests traffic, pollutes the air, endangers pedestrians and cyclists, and creates CO_2 emissions. All these extra costs show that underpriced parking costs a lot more than right-priced parking.

The U.S. spends about as much to subsidize the parking-industrial complex as on Medicare, and the parking subsidies encourage additional driving (*The High Cost of Free Parking*, Chapter 7). To fuel this extra driving, the U.S. imports oil and pays for it with borrowed money. Just as we now look back at gas price controls in 1979–1981 as a well-intended disaster, we will eventually look back at underpriced curb parking as a far greater man-made disaster that has lasted far longer.

Some critics may say that using market-clearing prices to allocate curb parking amounts to rationing. We already ration parking now, but we don't do it rationally. Drivers who cruise for free curb parking pay with time rather than money. Their cruising congests traffic, pollutes the air, and wastes energy. If drivers pay for curb parking with money, that money can then pay to clean the sidewalks and repair streets. Cities that underprice their curb parking are telling drivers to foul the environment and starve public services.

The Cumulative Costs of Cruising

The driver who occupies the last open parking space on a street creates a cascade of costs for everyone else because cruising for parking is nonlinear. There is no problem finding a curb space if one space is open on a block. When that last space is filled, however, there is no place to park, and new arrivals have to circle the block in their air-conditioned or heated cocoons with seats as soft as a caramel mousse. The cruising cars increase the traffic flow as they troll for open spaces. So filling the last curb space on a block quickly creates a problem.

Traffic congestion is also nonlinear. If the traffic flow increases past a critical point where cars are bunched too close together, suddenly all the cars and buses are mired in stop-and-go traffic. The cars' fuel consumption in traffic is also nonlinear. When traffic becomes stop-and-go, the cars' fuel consumption, pollution emissions, and greenhouse gas emissions per mile quickly increase. And drivers who are distracted while hunting for parking increase the accident risks for pedestrians, cyclists, and other drivers. So the car that fills the last open curb space on a block creates a domino effect of damaging consequences. The maddening shortage of on-street parking also leads to political demands for off-street parking requirements that have further consequences throughout the housing and transportation markets. Cruising for free curb parking is individually rational but collectively insane.

Filling the last open parking space on a block has consequences similar to those in the proverb about the lack of a single horseshoe nail:

> For want of a nail the shoe was lost.
> For want of a shoe the horse was lost.
> For want of a horse the rider was lost.
> For want of a rider the message was lost.
> For want of a message the battle was lost.
> For failure in battle the kingdom was lost.
> And all for the want of a horseshoe nail.

The lack of an open parking space may seem as minor as the lack of a horseshoe nail, but the unfolding chain of consequences is similarly disastrous. Failing to charge the right prices for curb parking can lead to widening dysfunctions in related markets and produce grave results that few people will trace back to the lack of an open curb space. By the same reasoning, charging the right prices can produce a cascade of benefits that few people will trace back to an open parking space. An open parking space helps everyone, not just drivers. And there is yet another benefit. Every year, Americans waste 3.14159 billion hours complaining about parking, and getting the prices for parking right will save all this lost time.

Now, the mark of a great city is that there are never enough places to park. With demand-based prices for curb parking, great cities will have enough places to park and more money to pay for public services. A few vacant spaces on a crowded street may look underused or even wasted, but the vacant spaces are valuable *because* they are vacant.

Debating the Doubters

Despite all the damage done by cruising, convincing cities to charge market prices for curb parking is hard. I know because I have tried for many years in many cities to make the case for market-priced curb parking. Drivers who want to park for free tend to shout and they dominate most public debates.

In 2009 I was invited to make a presentation in Santa Rosa, in the wine country of Northern California. Santa Rosa has a lively downtown with many good restaurants and a parking problem. I was pleased to see the large auditorium in city hall packed to hear a professor talk about parking. I spoke for an hour and explained why I thought Santa Rosa should charge market prices for its scarce curb parking and spend the revenue to improve the metered areas.

I pointed out that the city's parking meters operated from 8 a.m. to 6 p.m., but almost all the curb spaces were empty before 10 a.m. and full after 6 p.m. I suggested that the city should begin to operate the meters at 10 a.m. so more customers might come to the coffee shops that were open early and instead operate the meters longer in the evening to prevent a shortage of curb spaces for diners. If the meters create a few open spaces in the evening, people will find it easier to drive to the many restaurants. Anyone who doesn't want to pay for curb parking can park free in Santa Rosa's municipal garages. If the meters are priced right, cars will fill most of the curb spaces, leaving only one or two vacant spaces on each block. If the curb spaces are almost but not quite full all the time, parking meters can't be chasing many customers away.

The audience seemed to agree, but the first question came from an angry man in the top row of seats. He wasn't foaming but people nearby seemed to recoil from bits of saliva. He shouted that if the city ran the parking meters in the evening, he would never come to a restaurant downtown again. He seemed to think that settled the question.

Elected officials and city planners can't argue in a public meeting with an angry citizen about parking because his anger might be the tip of an iceberg of popular opposition. But I responded that if this guy didn't drive downtown, someone who was willing to pay for parking would take his place. And I asked, who do you think will leave a bigger tip in a restaurant? Someone who will come downtown only if he can park free after driving for 20 minutes hoping to see a car pulling out, or people who are willing to pay for parking if they can easily find a curb space near the restaurant? I also suggested that if he didn't want to pay for parking downtown, he might get a better deal in the food court of a suburban mall with ample free parking. The audience began to cheer and clap, no longer the silent majority.

I had dined in restaurants in Santa Rosa the previous two evenings, and I asked the waiters—as I do whenever I visit a restaurant—where they park. If the restaurant is in a part of town with parking meters that stop operating at 6 p.m., the waiters almost always say that they try to arrive before 6 p.m. when there are a few metered spaces available, pay for the short time until 6 p.m., and then they can park free for the rest of the evening. That seems good for the waiters, but they occupy parking spaces that customers could have used. That means fewer customers for the restaurants and also fewer tips for the waiters.

Waiters who park at the curb will probably be solo drivers, but two, three, or four diners may arrive in one car. If a metered curb space turns over twice during the evening, each space can deliver two groups of diners to a restaurant rather than one waiter. With more customers, the restaurants can expand and hire more waiters. It seems counterintuitive that waiters will be better off if the parking meters operate in the evenings, but waiters and everyone else involved will benefit. Some waiters can move to garages or more distant on-street parking, and restaurant customers will take their place. The on-street parking will be well used but the parkers will be different—they will be customers, not waiters. Business will improve even if the parking occupancy doesn't look much different.

One argument against operating meters in the evening is that the conventional one- or two-hour time limits are inconvenient for customers who want to spend more time at a restaurant or theatre. For this reason, cities should remove the time limits at meters in the evening and allow prices alone to create turnover.

A stronger argument against operating meters in the evening is that waiters and other service staff who work late hours and earn low wages cannot afford to pay for parking. For this reason, some cities offer free or discounted parking passes in municipal garages for evening and night workers rather than keep the on-street parking free. Because nights are usually a time of low demand in downtown garages, there are plenty of off-street parking spaces available. When Santa Fe, New Mexico, extended its meter hours into the evening, it also began to offer "social equity" parking passes in municipal garages at half the usual price for drivers who work for downtown business and have wages of $15 an hour or less. Portland, Oregon, and Sacramento, California, have similar programs. Shifting workers to off-street spaces can make the most convenient on-street spaces available for customers.

Finally, to shorten any debate about how much to charge for on-street parking, I sometimes ask critics of demand-based prices what principle they would use to set the prices for parking on every block at every time of day. Asserting that demand-based prices are unfair is much easier than coming up with a logical alternative.

It took longer than I expected for Santa Rosa to adopt any of the parking reforms I had proposed. In 2017 Santa Rosa decided to operate the parking meters from 10 a.m. to 8 p.m. and to increase the meter prices in the high-demand areas to $1.50 an hour. As reported in the city's newspaper, *The Press Democrat,*

The city has been considering progressive parking policies since 2009, when Donald Shupe, an influential academic on the subject, visited Santa Rosa and outlined his views. He is the author of a book called "There Ain't No Such Thing as Free Parking." Shupe argued that a community should shoot for 85 percent occupancy of its parking spaces, and adjust rates to hit that level if possible (McCallum 2017).

The author misspelled my name and garbled the book's title, but he nailed the policy proposal: "a community should shoot for 85 percent occupancy of its parking spaces and adjust rates to hit that level if possible."

Perishable Goods

Although perishable may seem a strange word to describe parking, a parking space is what economists call a perishable good. A perishable good has fixed costs and cannot be stored. Airline seats and hotel rooms are examples of perishable goods—an empty seat on an airplane or an empty hotel room cannot be stored and sold later. Therefore, like effective management for airlines and hotels, effective management for parking requires ensuring that the spaces are used efficiently.

Private operators adjust prices of perishable goods to maximize revenue, but a city's goal for curb parking should be different. Full occupancy of curb parking produces unwanted cruising, while low occupancy means the curb spaces are not delivering customers to the adjacent businesses. A city must balance the competing goals of reliable availability (one or two spaces are open on each block) and high occupancy (most of the spaces are occupied by customers). If parking demand varies greatly over time, pricing curb parking to balance supply and demand creates a conflict between the two goals of ready availability and high occupancy. The key measure in setting prices should focus on the arriving drivers' ability to find an open space.

When Seattle began to base parking prices on demand, the city council directed the Seattle Department of Transportation (SDOT) to "set rates to achieve approximately one or two open spaces per block face throughout the day. The policy objective is to ensure that visitors to neighborhood business districts can find a parking spot near their destination. SDOT may both *raise* and *lower* rates in different areas as appropriate to meet the occupancy target" (City of Seattle 2011). After the first occupancy counts in the city's 22 meter districts in 2011, SDOT increased meter rates in four districts, left them unchanged in seven, and reduced them in eleven.

Business groups supported the city council because the city switched from a revenue goal to an outcome goal for setting meter rates. The city continues to earn revenue but revenue is no longer a justification for raising meter rates. The goal of one or two open spaces per block is an easy way to explain that the purpose is to guarantee parking availability and reduce cruising. Because some blocks are short and have few spaces, while others are long and have many spaces, the goal of one or two vacant spaces on every block cannot be applied rigidly.

Given the random nature of arrivals and departures, cities will need to accept some time during which a street has two or more vacancies so there will be less time with no vacancies. Instead of aiming for an average occupancy, a city can aim to keep at least one vacant spot on every block for at least a certain share of every hour. A city will have three goals in setting a target occupancy rate for curb parking:

1. *Ready availability.* Availability can be defined as the share of an hour (e.g., 50 minutes) with at least one vacant space on the block. Ready availability means that drivers can usually find a convenient open space.
2. *High occupancy.* Occupancy can be defined as the average share of spaces that are occupied during the hour. High occupancy means that the curb spaces are well used and serve many customers.
3. *Revenue.* Revenue depends on both the meter price and the occupancy rate. Revenue should not be the primary goal, but there will be revenue if the program is managed well.

Cities face a trade-off between ready availability and high occupancy. These two goals conflict because raising the meter rates to ensure at least one vacant space will reduce the average occupancy rate. Suppose, for example, a city sets prices to ensure a vacant space on each block for at least 50 minutes during each hour. If at least one vacant space is available on that block for only 30 minutes in an hour, the availability target is not met, and the price should increase. This price increase, however, means that the average occupancy during the hour will decline.

San Francisco and Los Angeles are the first two cities to set parking prices by time of day and location, and they adjust these prices every two or three months in response to the observed occupancy, although by different rules. During each time period on each block, San Francisco sets the prices to achieve an average target occupancy rate on each block, while Los Angeles sets the prices to achieve a target share of the time with at least one open space on each block.

San Francisco

In 2011, San Francisco adopted SF*park*, a pricing program that aims to solve the problems created by charging too much or too little for curb parking. In seven pilot zones across the city, with a total of 7,000 curb spaces, San Francisco installed sensors that report the occupancy of curb spaces on every block and parking meters that charge variable prices according to location and time of day. The meters were also the first in San Francisco to accept payment by credit cards, and this convenience provided good publicity for SF*park*.

SF*park* adjusts parking prices every six weeks in response to the average parking occupancy during the previous six weeks. If the occupancy rate on a block was higher than 80 percent during a time period (such as from noon to 3 pm), the hourly price of parking increases by 25 cents. If the occupancy rate was below 60 percent, the hourly price of parking decreases by 25 cents. Consider the resulting prices of curb parking on a weekday at Fisherman's Wharf, a popular tourist and retail destination, after almost two years of price adjustments (see Figure 37-1).

Before SF*park* began in August 2011, the price for a space was $3 an hour at all times. With SF*park*, each block can have different prices during three periods of the day—before noon, from noon to 3 pm, and after 3 pm. By May 2012, most prices had decreased in the morning hours. Some prices increased between noon and 3 pm—the busiest time of day—and most prices declined after 3 pm. Prices changed every six weeks, never by more than 25 cents per hour.

SF*park* based these price adjustments purely on observed occupancy. City planners cannot reliably predict the right price for parking on every block at every time of day, but they *can* use a simple trial-and-error process to adjust prices in response to past occupancy rates. The only way to tell whether the price is right is to look at the results. The right price for curb parking is the price that leads to the right occupancy rate, and it is like the Supreme Court's definition of pornography: "I know it when I see it." I won't know the right price for curb parking until I see the right occupancy.

Did these small changes in parking prices change many drivers' behavior? Only a few drivers have to change their behavior to produce the right parking occupancy because most drivers are not trying to park, and many drivers who do want to park will park off street. Of those few drivers who want to park at the curb, even fewer will have to change their behavior to create one vacant space on each block. Therefore, SF*park* does not have to change many drivers' behavior to improve parking availability and reduce traffic congestion. If only a few drivers change their behavior, finding a curb parking space will no longer resemble winning the lottery.

Where the meters are priced correctly, drivers will not need information about parking availability on every block because an open space will be available almost everywhere. Drivers will only need information about parking prices to choose the best place to park.

Demand-based parking prices are efficient, but are they fair? Thirty percent of households in San Francisco don't own a car, so they don't pay anything for curb parking. San Francisco uses all its parking meter revenue to subsidize public transit, which helps everyone who can't afford a car. SF*park* further aids bus riders, cyclists, and pedestrians by reducing the traffic caused by cruising for underpriced and overcrowded curb parking. So it's hard to argue that SF*park* is unfair.

If the price of parking is the same everywhere, no one can save money by parking in a cheaper space and walking farther. Suppose you want to park on a street at Fisherman's Wharf, where prices shifted from $3 an hour all day to different prices on different blocks at different times of day, ranging from 25 cents an hour on many blocks to a maximum of $3.75 an hour on one block (see Figure 37-1). Would you rather face the previous price of $3 an hour on every block, or the prices after 10 adjustments in the first two years of SF*park*? If you walk a few blocks you can pay only 25 cents an hour. That seems like a big improvement for low-income drivers. People can now walk to save money on curb parking.

Suppose you are not short of money and you want to park in front of the address you are visiting. Would you prefer to pay $3 an hour for a parking spot after cruising several blocks to find it, or would you prefer the SF*park* prices that ensure a vacancy on every block? SF*park* can help everyone, rich or poor.

SF*park* also helps to depoliticize parking because transparent, data-based pricing rules can bypass the usual politics of parking. Demand dictates prices and politicians cannot simply raise prices to gain revenue. SF*park*'s goal is to optimize occupancy, not to maximize revenue, and prices can go down as well as up. Because most prices had been too high in the mornings, the average price of curb parking fell by 4 percent during SF*park*'s first two years.

Before SF*park* began, skeptics worried that variable parking rates would create uncertainty and confuse customers. SF*park* changed more than 5,000 prices at the 7,000 SF*park* meters in the first year, but there were no complaints about uncertainty. If inching prices up or down every six weeks really did confuse drivers, one would expect someone to complain. Available parking is more important than fixed prices.

Because parking is more readily available, San Francisco issues fewer tickets for illegal parking in the SF*park* zones. Variable prices, more availability, and fewer tickets are far more customer-friendly than fixed prices, parking shortages, and more tickets. SF*park* could also encourage merchants to post the maps of parking prices in their stores as a way to improve the drivers' knowledge about prices and show them how to take advantage of the price differences to save money.

In preparing for SF*park*, San Francisco conducted a census of its parking spaces and found 275,450 on-street spaces (San Francisco Municipal Transportation Agency 2014). If laid end-to-end, San Francisco's on-street parking would stretch about 1,000 miles, which is longer than California's 840-mile coastline. San Francisco has one on-street parking space for every three people in the city, but only 10 percent are metered. Expanding SF*park* into more areas that have a shortage of curb parking can better manage this valuable public space and also yield revenue for public services. In January 2018, San Francisco expanded SF*park* to include all of the city's 28,000 metered parking spaces and to all city-owned garages and lots.

SF*park* will always be a work in progress because the right price for curb parking is always a moving target and the parking technology is improving rapidly. Chapters 36–40 analyze the results of SF*park*.

Los Angeles

In 2012, Los Angeles launched LA Express Park (see Chapter 41), which resembles SF*park* except for one key difference. In Los Angeles, the price adjustments are based not on average occupancy during a time period, but rather on parking availability, measured by the share of each hour in which a block is overused (over 90 percent occupancy), underused (below 70 percent occupancy), or well used (between 70 and 90 percent occupancy).

Los Angeles contracts with the Xerox Research Centre in Grenoble, France, to analyze the parking occupancy data and recommend the price changes. If the block is overused a large fraction of the time and underused a small fraction of the time, the price increases. If the block is underused a large fraction of the time and overused a small fraction of the time, the price decreases. If the occupancy is neither overused nor underused most of the time, the price does not change.

A difficult decision arises, however, when there are spikes in demand at some times but demand is low most of the time. Xerox devised an algorithm that compares the fractions of time that are overcrowded, underused, or just right to recommend price changes (Zoeter et al. 2014). One way to deal with the problem of both congestion and underuse of parking during the same time period is to divide the day into shorter time periods that will allow more price changes in response to the varying demand.

LA Express Park has aroused almost no political opposition. Most drivers don't even seem to notice that prices are changing. LA Express Park began with 6,300 meters downtown, and the city has extended the program to Hollywood, Westwood Village, and Venice.

The technology used for demand-based pricing in Los Angeles and San Francisco is getting both cheaper and more sophisticated. Other cities will therefore find it easier to mount similar programs. Baltimore, Berkeley, and Oakland have begun to charge demand-based parking prices with simple technology (see Chapter 35). Boston and Washington, D. C., have also begun to charge demand-based parking prices with more advanced technology.

The results in Los Angeles and San Francisco show that cities can make huge improvements even without frequently adjusting prices in response to demand. Simply extending the operating hours for existing meters into the evening in places with high demand rather than turning the meters off at 6 p.m. is a demand-based strategy, and it does not require any new investment. The meters are already there, so they will reduce parking and traffic congestion and bring in new revenue without any new cost.

People who beg for a living work until midnight in many cities but the parking meters quit work at 6 p.m. Why not run the meters during the times of high parking demand in the evening and use some of the money to help the homeless? Similarly, cities can operate their meters during times of high demand on Sundays. If cities carry the argument for demand-based pricing to its logical conclusion, they can extend the hours of meter operation for as long as needed to manage demand, and thus provide large benefits where meters already exist. If cities put their meters to sleep at 6 p.m. and on Sunday, they have learned little about demand-based prices for curb parking.

After several years of experience, cities may be able to shift from reaction to prediction when adjusting prices, such as with seasonal adjustments. Like hockey players who skate to where the puck will be, cities can base parking prices on expected future demand, not simply on past occupancy. Parking prices will never be a simple joystick that planners can use to manipulate precise outcomes because it's almost impossible to get the price of parking exactly right all the time. Nevertheless, cities can do a far better job than they do now to balance supply and demand. When parking is overcrowded, it is underpriced, not undersupplied.

Equity

A final question about demand-based prices for curb parking is whether they will penalize the poor. Although the lion's share of parking subsidies go to people who are not poor, drivers who don't want to pay for parking often push poor people out in front of them like human shields, claiming that charging market prices for curb parking will hurt the poor. This objection is either misguided altruism or disguised self-interest.

Are flexible parking prices really unfair to poor people? Let's look at the bigger picture. The prices for fresh fruits and vegetables vary to balance supply and demand according the season. The prices for hotel rooms vary to balance supply and demand according to location and time of year. The prices for theater seats vary to balance supply and demand by location and day of the week. The price of gasoline varies from place to place and from day to day. Are all these and many other price variations unfair to poor people? If not, why would parking prices that vary to balance supply and demand be unfair to poor people? And how much money are we really talking about here? It's only curb parking. Drivers should expect to pay for parking if they take two tons of metal with them wherever they go.

Admittedly, some drivers do prefer to spend their time circling the block, congesting traffic, wasting energy, polluting the air, slowing public transit, endangering pedestrians and bicyclists, causing accidents, and contributing to climate change rather than pay to park. But faster and cheaper public transit, cleaner air, and safer walking and biking will help everyone who is too poor to afford a car. The public services financed with parking revenue will also help the poor. On balance, right-priced curb parking can help the poor and everyone else.

Disabled Placard Abuse

California may have been the wrong place to test demand-based prices for curb parking because the state requires all cities to allow cars with disabled placards to park free at meters, with no time limit. The placards are thus permits to park free at any meter for an unlimited time. Because controls on obtaining or using a disabled placard are lax, 9 percent of registered drivers in California now have a disabled permit, and evidence of placard abuse is everywhere. Because of the widespread abuse, disabled placards do not guarantee a physical disability. Instead, they often signal a desire to park free and a willingness to cheat the system. Placard abusers learn to live without their scruples but not without their cars.

Because many people with disabilities are too poor to own a car, the all-placards-park-free policy delivers an unnecessary benefit to placard abusers and to people with disabilities who are not poor. Far worse, the all-placards-park-free policy has created a culture of corruption. More of the subsidy for placards probably goes to morally handicapped placard abusers than to low-income drivers with serious physical disabilities. The rampant abuse encouraged by free parking for all placards has made life even harder for everyone with impaired mobility.

If disabled placard abuse is common on a block that is fully occupied, raising the price will not affect placard abusers, but it will reduce the number of paying parkers at the curb and make even more spaces available to placard abusers. Therefore, revenue will decline but availability will not increase. Placard abuse throws sand in the gears of LA Express Park and SF*park* and helps to explain why they were much less effective in reducing occupancy on congested blocks than in increasing occupancy on underused blocks. Increasing the price of curb parking drives away paying parkers and allows placard abusers to take their place. Disabled placard abuse is the Achilles heel of demand-based parking pricing.

Michigan and Illinois have adopted a two-tier system that takes into account different levels of disability. Drivers with disabilities that seriously limit mobility can park free at meters, and drivers with less serious disabilities must pay. Enforcement is simple: drivers without serious mobility impairment who use the special serious-disability placard to park free at meters are obviously breaking the law as soon as they step out of a car and stride away. Other states require all placard holders to pay at meters. Demand-based prices for curb parking will produce far greater benefits in states that do not invite placard abuse by treating placards as permits to park free at any meter for an unlimited time. Chapters 30–32 analyze the problems caused by meter exemptions for placards and propose ways to solve the problem.

Progressive Parking Prices and Fines

Demand-based parking prices can create curb vacancies but cities may also want to ensure steady turnover. To encourage turnover, a city can charge progressively higher parking prices for successive hours. Table 28-1 shows the progressive rate structure in Albany, New York. The hourly price for the first two hours is $1.25, and the price of each subsequent hour increases by 25 cents, with no time limit.

Some cities charge progressive prices on game days near stadiums that generate periodic peak demands. Brookline, Massachusetts, charges special prices at meters on Beacon Street close to Fenway Park: $1 an hour for the first two hours and $10 an hour for the third and fourth hours, with a maximum of $22 for the day. Washington, D.C., has similar progressive parking rates around the Nationals baseball stadium. Washington also dedicates the extra revenue from the game days to pay for added public services in the area, such as cleaning and repairing the sidewalks. If cities charge progressive parking prices on game days and spend the revenue on public services, stadiums can help rather than harm the surrounding neighborhoods.

Progressive parking prices are appropriate where a city wants to encourage turnover, but they are not appropriate at times when the demand for parking is declining. For example, if the demand for parking is declining during the evening, higher prices per hour for longer parking durations will be counterproductive. The price may have to decline over time to keep the spaces occupied during the time of lower demand.

Some cities have also adopted progressive parking fines to deter repeat violators who often account for a large share of all violations (Chapter 29). In Los Angeles, for example, 8 percent of the license plates that received tickets in 2009 accounted for 29 percent of all the tickets in that year. Most drivers rarely or never receive a parking ticket, and for these drivers modest fines are a sufficient deterrent. But the many tickets for a few repeat offenders suggest that modest fines will not deter drivers who view parking violations as an acceptable gamble or just another cost of doing business. If cities raise parking fines high enough to deter the few chronic violators, they unfairly penalize many more drivers for occasional, often inadvertent violations.

Progressive parking fines deter repeat violators without unfairly punishing anyone else. Progressive fines are lenient for the many cars with one or two tickets a year but punitive for the few cars with many tickets. In Claremont, California, for example, the first ticket for overtime parking in a calendar year is $35, the second $70, and the third $105. For illegally using a disabled parking space, the first ticket is $325, the second $650, and the third $975.

Progressive parking prices encourage turnover without overcharging the short-term parkers, and progressive parking fines encourage compliance without penalizing the occasional offenders. Recent advances in parking technology now make it possible for any city to use these progressive parking prices and fines.

Sophisticated Parking Technology

Parking was for many years the most stagnant industry outside North Korea. Now, however, nothing in parking is the last word for long. The parking industry is taking advantage of everything Silicon Valley has to offer, and the humble parking meter has improved rapidly in recent years. Meters now accept payment by credit cards and cell phones. They can charge different prices by time of day or day of the week, depending on demand. Parking officials can remotely reconfigure the price schedule in any neighborhood, and the new rates are sent wirelessly to all the meters in the neighborhood. They can be multilingual and guide the users through transactions, displaying messages such as "Please insert your card other side up."

Parking occupancy sensors have also evolved rapidly. The first generation of sensors used in San Francisco and Los Angeles were embedded in the pavement and had to be dug up or abandoned when the batteries needed replacement, but new forms of occupancy sensing have developed. Some single-space meters have occupancy sensors embedded in the meter heads, which lower the power requirements and simplify the battery replacement. Parking enforcement vehicles equipped with cameras to record license plate numbers can also count the number of parked cars. Fixed-mount cameras can also analyze parking occupancy.

The technology of metering and occupancy sensing is becoming cheaper and better so fast that programs like SF*park* and LA Express Park will be much easier for other cities to adopt. We may soon consider coin-in-the-slot parking meters as primitive as the Wright brothers' first airplane at Kitty Hawk.

Two new technologies—occupancy sensors and variably priced parking meters—may change parking and transportation as profoundly as the invention of the cash register in the nineteenth century changed retail commerce. They can unlock the immense value of land now devoted to free parking and bring transportation into the market economy. The adage that "You can't manage what you can't measure" fits parking perfectly. Setting the right price for on-street parking is much cheaper than requiring developers to supply ample off-street parking. Only on-street parking management can solve on-street parking problems.

Performance pricing requires surprisingly little information. Planners compare the actual parking occupancy with the desired occupancy and nudge prices up or down accordingly. Because free parking is the perfect medium for political pandering, politicians are not the right people to set parking prices. An impersonal rule to seek the optimal occupancy becomes the new apolitical way to set prices. Cities can depoliticize parking by combining new technology with the old law of supply and demand.

Performance pricing for curb parking is not a simple plug-and-play operation, but most cities will soon have the technical capacity to charge prices that ensure one or two open curb spaces most of the time on every block. The new parking technology makes smart parking policies possible, and the new smart policies increase the demand for the new technology. Intelligent transportation technology is the key to intelligent parking management.

Technology will continue to change the way we park. Finding and paying for parking is migrating to the internet and the dashboards of connected cars. Just as drivers now expect their navigation systems to choose the best routes for trips, they may soon expect these systems to give them turn-by-turn directions to the closest and cheapest parking available at their destinations, and to pay for parking automatically with bits rather than quarters. Before cars learn to drive themselves, they should be able to find and pay for parking. When cars learn to find and pay for parking, parking demand will respond to parking prices more accurately and drivers will be able to save money by parking a few blocks from their destination and walking the rest of the way (*The High Cost of Free Parking*, Chapter 18).

License plate recognition systems may become the future of parking management as cities move toward virtual payments by cell phones or connected cars, and doing away with on-street meters may completely change the parking game for governments (Chapter 34). Wireless payments for parking are also more resilient after natural disasters, like a flood, because there is no on-street meter hardware to repair.

Better technology can also reduce the hassle in paying for parking, which is often as important as the price of parking. A friend once told me that she avoids going downtown because of the difficulty of finding a parking spot, estimating how long she'll be there, preparing beforehand by making sure she has coins, and having to leave after an arbitrary time limit. Anywhere else in the city, she can give no thought to the logistics of parking. It's not so much the cost of parking (because it's not expensive), it's the bother and threat of a costly ticket if she lingers too long at a store or a restaurant. Getting the prices right and making payments simple are both important in parking management. Parking should be friendly but not free.

If curb parking isn't properly priced, it won't be properly used. With performance parking prices, drivers will find convenient places to park just as easily as they find convenient places to buy gasoline. Before they buy a car, people will have to consider how much they will have to pay for parking, just as they now consider the costs of the car itself, gasoline, insurance, registration, and repairs. And anyone who thinks about driving a car will have to consider the cost of parking at the destination. Parking will become a natural part of the market economy.

Transportation network companies (Uber and Lyft) and driverless cars are two new technologies that can reduce the demand for parking.

Reduced car ownership will reduce the political support for off-street parking requirements, and a reduced parking supply can increase the price of all parking. Shifting toward market-priced parking will therefore hasten the shift toward shared and driverless cars.

Any shift from privately owned cars to shared and driverless cars will convert the fixed costs of ownership (including parking) into marginal costs of driving or being driven. If driverless and shared cars increase vehicle travel, however, they will increase traffic congestion and thus make it even more important to charge the right price for using the roads—the lowest price that will prevent traffic congestion. The technology for congestion pricing is already here, and cities such as London, Singapore, and Stockholm already use it. As with charging for parking, the problem of charging for roads is not technical but political. To solve the political problem, cities might consider Traffic Benefit Districts, which are similar to Parking Benefit Districts, except the revenue comes from congestion tolls rather than from curb parking (*The High Cost of Free Parking*, Appendix G; King, Manville, and Shoup 2007).

Price Therapy

If performance prices for on-street parking don't work well, a city can easily revert to fixed prices, but off-street parking requirements have major, almost irreversible, effects. To use a medical analogy, performance prices resemble physical therapy while parking requirements resemble major surgery. Because physical therapy is much cheaper and does much less damage if it turns out to be the wrong choice, many physicians first recommend physical therapy to see if it can resolve a problem before they resort to drugs or surgery. Planners should try price therapy first before they require asphalt and concrete to solve parking problems.

City planners have diagnosed a shortage of free parking as a failure of the market to supply enough parking spaces. Their recommended remedy has been to require more off-street parking, which has a high cost in money, distorted land use, and disfigured cities. Because the demand for free parking is so much higher than the demand for market-priced parking, cities must require many more off-street spaces than the market would provide if the scarce on-street spaces were priced properly. The ample supply of required off-street parking then leads to more cars and driving, which increase traffic congestion and create the demand for wider roads. The original misdiagnosis of too few off-street parking spaces rather than a failure to price on-street parking properly has weakened cities and harmed the environment. The resulting traffic congestion has led many people to blame cars as the source of the problem. Cars can produce many more private benefits, far fewer social costs, and much more public revenue if cities price driving and parking properly.

Converting Free Private Parking into Paid Public Parking

If cities remove off-street parking requirements, drivers who visit a new business without free parking will be tempted to park in the lot of another nearby business that does provide free parking. Most businesses with free parking do not want to police their lots and chase away drivers who are not their customers, so they understandably want cities to require new businesses to provide ample off-street parking.

Preventing unauthorized drivers from parking in a free lot is difficult, but businesses in some cities have found a new way to solve the problem without off-street parking requirements. They contract with commercial parking operators to manage their lots as paid public parking and split the resulting revenue (*The High Cost of Free Parking*, 700–701). Customers and employees continue to park free, but noncustomers must pay, and the formerly free-for-everyone lot begins to earn revenue. When a business is closed, all its parking spaces are available to the public. This arrangement generates revenue and increases the supply of public parking available for drivers who want to visit nearby businesses (Figure I-6).

Figure I-6 Private parking converted to public parking

A major difficulty with metering the spaces in private lots has been the difficulty of enforcing the drivers' responsibility to pay at the private meters. If private operators cannot issue enforceable tickets for violations, the only legal way to ensure compliance is to boot or tow the violators, which is expensive, inconvenient, and unpopular with both drivers and merchants. Toronto has solved this problem by allowing private parking operators to issue municipal parking tickets for meter violations in private parking lots (Toronto By-Law No. 725-2004). The private operators must send their staff to complete a required private parking enforcement course, and the city then deputizes these staff to issue municipal tickets. The city specifies the required signage, sets the fines for violations, and receives all the ticket revenue. The private operators therefore issue tickets to secure compliance, not to profit from the ticket revenue. Drivers can contest the municipal tickets issued in private lots in the same way they contest tickets at on-street meters. As another solution, a city's parking enforcement officers can give tickets for violations at off-street meters in the same way they enforce on-street meters, and the city keeps the revenue. Extending municipal enforcement to formerly free private parking takes advantage of the existing public protocol for enforcement and creates a new public-private partnership that benefits both parties.

One big advantage of converting free private parking into paid public parking is that drivers demand fewer spaces when parking is priced. If cities remove off-street parking requirements, large free parking lots can morph into smaller paid parking lots, releasing valuable land for infill development. The market will slowly reclaim land from free parking and people will displace cars.

Everybody wants something for nothing, but we should not promote free parking as a principle for urban planning, transportation, or public finance. Using prices to manage parking can produce a host of benefits for cities, transportation, and the environment. The right prices can produce the best parking for the most people at the lowest possible cost. Information wants to be free but parking wants to be paid for.

We now have the right technology to charge the right prices for parking. Part III of the book focuses on using Parking Benefit Districts to get the right politics.

III. PARKING BENEFIT DISTRICTS

Elected officials may know that charging market prices for curb parking is the right thing to do, but they don't know how to get reelected after they do it. Market-priced parking looks like an expensive way to commit political suicide. Because people are so used to free parking, the notion that there might be something wrong with it sounds crazy. And if market prices for curb parking work so well, why haven't more cities tried them? When it comes to parking, many people don't like the way things are but they also don't like change. What can create the desire for change?

The money fed into a parking meter seems to disappear into thin air, and no one believes the revenue will benefit them personally. There is pain but no gain. Politically, it is as if the meter money were incinerated. Most drivers will place a higher value on the immediate, tangible benefit of free parking than on the possible long-run benefits of better public services or lower taxes that would be made possible by charging higher prices for curb parking. Cities can transform the politics of parking, however, by using the curb parking revenue to pay for public services in the neighborhoods that generate it. If each neighborhood keeps its curb parking revenue to pay for local public services, residents may support desubsidizing curb parking because they want a safer and cleaner neighborhood.

To create local support for user-paid parking in commercial areas, some cities have created Parking Benefit Districts that spend the meter revenue for public services in the metered areas. These cities offer each district a package that includes both priced parking and better public services. Everyone who lives, works, visits, or owns property in a Parking Benefit District can see their meter money at work, and the package is much more popular than the meters alone. Localizing the parking revenue will generate local support for the parking meters.

Parking Benefit Districts are a form of "political engineering," a term coined in the 1970s to describe the practice of spreading the contracts for a military project, such as a new fighter plane, to as many congressional districts as possible to maximize the number of Congress members who support the project. Parking Benefit Districts resemble political engineering because they spread the cost of paying for parking among a dispersed array of drivers and concentrate the public benefits within the metered districts (*The High Cost of Free Parking*, Chapter 17). The right parking policies require the right parking politics.

The pain of paying for parking is individual but many of the benefits are collective. The best way to show these collective benefits to local stakeholders is to spend the revenue for added public services on the metered streets. If each neighborhood keeps the parking revenue it generates, a powerful new constituency for market prices can emerge—the neighborhoods that receive the revenue. These stakeholders who benefit from the public services paid for by parking meters will know who they are, and they will see a good reason to support the meters. These same stakeholders will lose something they value if the city doesn't charge for curb parking, so they may support operating the meters as long as needed to manage the demand for parking.

If drivers from outside the neighborhood pay for curb parking and the revenue benefits the residents, charging for curb parking can become a popular policy rather than the political kryptonite it is today. Rather than an eat-your-spinach edict that drivers must pay for parking, Parking Benefit Districts can persuade residents that they want to charge for parking. Some people will always object to any new policy, especially those who think that cities should never do anything for the first time, but the new revenue for local public services can change minds.

To explain this proposal, I will summarize how it can work in two settings: commercial areas and residential neighborhoods. Chapters 16 and 17 in *The High Cost of Free Parking* explain the proposal in full.

Parking Benefit Districts in Commercial Areas

The best way to recommend parking reforms may be not to mention parking at all. It's not enough to say the city got parking wrong because cities get a lot of things wrong. Instead, planners can ask the stakeholders in a district what new services they want the government to provide. For example, their highest priority may be to repair broken sidewalks. After the stakeholders have identified their highest priorities but have no way to pay for them, planners can suggest a Parking Benefit District as a way to finance the public services. The stakeholders can then decide whether to install parking meters to pay for the public services they want. For the stakeholders, parking reform is the means, not the end.

I am not saying that putting parking revenue into a city's general fund won't produce public benefits. The important political issue is the *perception* of benefits. Residents won't *see* any benefits if the revenue goes into the general fund, but they can easily see the benefits if the revenue stays on the metered streets. If meter money pays for sidewalk repairs the stakeholders want, for example, they may recommend meters they previously opposed when they thought the money would disappear into a black hole. This scenario describes what happened in 1992 when Pasadena, California, installed parking meters and dedicated the revenue to pay for public services on the metered streets.

Pasadena's original business district, Old Pasadena, had become a commercial Skid Row, with wonderful historic buildings in terrible condition. The city proposed installing meters to regulate curb parking, but the merchants opposed them. They knew their employees occupied many of the most convenient curb spaces but feared that meters would drive away the few customers they had. To defuse opposition, the city offered to spend all the meter revenue to pay for public investments in Old Pasadena. The business and property owners quickly agreed to the proposal because they saw the direct benefits, and the desire for public improvements soon outweighed the fear of meters.

Businesses and property owners began to see the parking meters in a new light—as a source of revenue. They agreed to the then high rate of $1 an hour for curb parking and to operating the meters in the evenings and on Sunday. The city also liked the arrangement because it wanted to improve Old Pasadena. The city needed $5 million to finance an ambitious plan to invest in Old Pasadena's streetscape and to convert its alleys into walkways with access to shops and restaurants, and the meter revenue would pay for the project. In effect, Old Pasadena became a Parking Benefit District. The business and property owners bought into parking meters because they were bought off with the resulting revenue.

The city worked with Old Pasadena's Business Improvement District to establish the boundaries of the Old Pasadena Parking Meter Zone (PMZ) where the parking meters were installed. Only the blocks with parking meters benefit directly from the meter revenue. The city also established the Old Pasadena PMZ Advisory Board, consisting of business and property owners who recommend parking policies and set spending priorities for the zone's meter revenues. Connecting the meter revenues directly to added public services and providing for local control are the two elements largely responsible for the parking program's success.

The city installed the parking meters in 1993 and borrowed $5 million to finance the Old Pasadena Streetscape and Alleyways Project, with the meter revenue dedicated to repaying the debt. The bonds paid for new sidewalks, street furniture, trees, and lighting throughout the area. The city turned dilapidated alleys into safe, functional walkways with access to shops and restaurants. Old Pasadena boomed and sales tax receipts shot up. Two other business districts in Pasadena then petitioned the city to install parking meters with revenue return to pay for public improvements (Chapter 44, and *The High Cost of Free Parking*, Chapter 16).

Parking meters have two natural sources of opposition—the drivers who park at the curb and the businesses these drivers patronize. That's why it is important to create support for the meters by localizing the revenue. If residents, merchants, and property owners can see the public improvements, they are more likely to support the meters. Without this local public spending financed by the meters, it is hard to see the benefits of meters. Drivers who have an easier time finding a curb space don't know it's because of the meters. Drivers who suffer less traffic congestion don't know it's because there is less cruising for free parking. People who breathe cleaner air don't know it's because less cruising produces less pollution. A city has to show direct local benefits to convince most people that they want parking meters. To paraphrase William Butler Yeats, advocates for parking meters lack all conviction while the opponents are full of passionate intensity. Parking Benefit Districts can create the conviction to charge for curb parking and deflate the opposition's passionate intensity.

Performance pricing converts the costs of cruising into public benefits. People can see some of the benefits, such as clean sidewalks and trimmed street trees. Other benefits—reductions in traffic congestion, air pollution, and carbon emissions—remain invisible. The visible benefits of parking-financed local public services will create popular support for parking reforms that also have widespread invisible benefits. When it comes to political support for priced parking, merchants are far more interested in a sustainable business district than in a sustainable planet.

Doing the right thing is more important than doing something for the right reason, and the best way to get people to do what's right collectively is to make it right for them to do it individually. Parking Benefit Districts can give individuals a personal incentive to do what's right for society. I do not mean to advocate or celebrate self-interest, but rather to recognize it and take advantage of it. Cities can let the market some work for the public good—the approach that Brookings Institution economist Charles Shultze termed "the public use of private interest."

Parking Benefit Districts are multiplying. Chapters 44–50 describe the great range of public improvements funded by Parking Benefit Districts in Austin and Houston in Texas, in Pasadena, Redwood City, and Ventura in California, and in Mexico City. Pasadena uses meter money to clean the sidewalks every night and to pressure wash them twice a month (see Chapter 44). Ann Arbor, Michigan, and Boulder, Colorado, use meter money to provide free transit passes for all workers in the central business district. (It's hard to believe these cities would be better off with hard-to-find free curb parking and expensive public transit rather than free public transit and easy-to-find priced curb parking.) Ventura uses the parking meters to provide free Wi-Fi for all the residents, businesses, and visitors on the metered streets. Neighborhoods with parking meters have free Wi-Fi and neighborhoods with free curb parking don't (see Chapter 46). If parking meters become synonymous with free Wi-Fi in cities around the world, Parking Benefit Districts may spread quickly.

Parking Benefit Districts and Business Improvement Districts

Curb parking revenue is a benefit in search of a beneficiary; the funds need the right recipient to generate political support for market prices. In commercial areas, Business Improvement Districts (BIDs) are logical recipients. In a BID, property owners tax themselves to pay for supplemental public services beyond the level provided citywide. In essence, BIDs are a form of cooperative capitalism, and they provide public services that cities either do not provide (such as sidewalk cleaning) or do not provide at a satisfactory level (such as security). BIDs have a good track record, their legality is well established, and their operating principles are familiar to public officials and business owners. BIDs are therefore ready-made recipients for curb parking revenue.

Earmarking curb parking revenue to fund BIDs and giving the BIDs a say in setting the parking prices for their area will encourage business-like management of the parking supply. Each district can examine how other districts deal with curb parking, and they can weigh the benefits and costs of alternative policies. BIDs can recommend the parking meter rates because their members observe the meter occupancy every day on every block, and they see the effects of occupancy on their businesses. BIDs have every incentive to get the prices right because their members will be the first to benefit from good decisions and the first to suffer from bad ones.

Cities can even give BIDs full responsibility for managing the parking meters, setting the prices, and collecting the revenue. Bangalore, India, adopted this strategy in its Brigade Road business district (Center for Science and the Environment 2016, 31). The Brigade Shops Establishments Association paid for installing parking meters for 85 spaces. Half the meter revenue goes to the city government and the other half remains in the district to pay for managing the system. Business leaders have strong incentives to charge appropriate prices at the meters. If the price is too high and there are many open parking spaces, the empty spaces fail to deliver customers to the shops. If the price is too low and there are no open spaces, customers will complain about a parking shortage and the district could earn more revenue by charging higher parking prices. Allowing BIDs to manage on-street parking may be especially appropriate in cities where inefficiency or corruption have blocked managing on-street parking properly.

Equity Concerns

An equity problem arises if business districts with higher parking demand have higher parking prices and therefore earn more money for public services. One way to avoid this inequity is to use what in public finance is called "power equalization." The city can return equal revenue per parking meter to every Parking Benefit District.

Suppose the average citywide meter revenue is $2,000 per meter per year. In this case, the city can offer to spend $1,000 a year per meter for added public services in every Parking Benefit District and spend the other $1,000 a year for citywide public services. All neighborhoods with Parking Benefit Districts will therefore receive equal revenue per meter for added public services and all neighborhoods without Parking Benefit Districts will receive better public services. The federal and state governments use similar formulas to distribute gasoline tax revenues among lower levels of government. For example, the federal government distributes most federal gasoline tax revenue to the states that generate it (return to source) and distributes the rest to fund special projects throughout the country.

Parking Benefit Districts that earn more revenue will subsidize those that earn less, and they will also subsidize the rest of the city. This sharing arrangement retains the local incentive to install parking meters but distributes the revenue equally, which seems fairer than the usual policy of installing parking meters in the parts of the city that have parking problems and spending the revenue everywhere else.

There are also worldwide equity concerns. When I was speaking in Florida recently, residents told me they worry that rising sea levels caused by global warming will flood their cities (the highest point in the state is only 345 feet above sea level). I said that free parking is a subsidy for burning fossil fuels. I then asked whether they thought global warming would be a smaller problem if cities around the world charged market prices for curb parking and eliminated off-street parking requirements. Or should all cities instead adopt Florida's policies of free curb parking and high off-street parking requirements? If Floridians won't reform their own parking policies to help forestall global warming, why should the rest of the world worry about flooding in Florida?

Florida is strengthening its coastal defenses to protect against rising sea levels. Charging for parking can generate the needed funds and also reduce carbon emissions. It's much easier to price curb parking than to price carbon emissions, so advocates for carbon pricing should also advocate parking reforms. Climate change's potential to harm everyone on Earth makes underpriced curb parking and off-street parking requirements unwise not only locally but also globally.

Parking requirements reflect planning for the present but not for the future (*The High Cost of Free Parking*, 171–73). They are politically desirable in the short term but the opposite of what cities need in the long term. Parking requirements create great places for cars but not great cities for people or a great future for the Earth.

Religious Concerns

Beyond equity concerns about dedicating revenue to pay for public services on the metered streets, there are also religious concerns (*The High Cost of Free Parking*, 494–95). San Francisco provides an important lesson. In January 2013 the city began to operate its parking meters on Sunday from noon to 6 p.m. Previously, it was hard to find an open curb space on Sunday in almost every commercial area in the city. Some drivers would park in metered spaces on Saturday afternoon and not move their car until Monday morning. After the meters began operating on Sunday, it became much easier to find curb parking near neighborhood businesses on Sunday.

Nevertheless, responding to complaints that church members had to "pay to pray," in April 2014 the city resumed free parking on Sunday. If San Francisco had shared some of the Sunday meter revenue to improve public services in the metered neighborhoods, the prospect of losing public services could have generated political support for the Sunday metering. Merchants and residents who benefited from the public services might have insisted on the separation of church and parking. The laws of supply and demand do not miraculously stop operating on Sunday.

Some pastors may fear that charging for parking on Sunday will reduce church attendance, which it can. In his book, *Going Clear*, about the links between Scientology and Hollywood, Lawrence Wright related how L. Ron Hubbard recruited movie stars to publicize the church. One recruitment strategy was to establish the Celebrity Center in Hollywood, where notable actors and musicians had their own private entry. A few celebrities did join, but one got away:

> Rock Hudson visited the Celebrity Center but stormed out when his auditor had the nerve to tell him he couldn't leave until he finished his session, although the matinee idol had run out of time at his meter. The exemplary figure that Hubbard sought eluded capture (Wright 2013, 140).

An Enabling Act for Parking Benefit Districts

If state legislation does not authorize Parking Benefit Districts, some cities may hesitate to establish them. In 2016, the Massachusetts legislature passed the Parking Advancements for the Revitalization of Communities (PARC) Act, which explicitly authorizes cities to charge market prices for on-street parking and to establish Parking Benefit Districts to spend the revenue (Section 22A of Chapter 40 of Massachusetts General Laws).

[Parking] fees shall be established and charged at rates determined by the city or town. Rates may be set for the purpose of managing the parking supply. The revenue therefrom may be used for acquisition, installation, maintenance and operation of parking meters and other parking payment and enforcement technology, the regulation of parking, salaries of parking management personnel, improvements to the public realm, and transportation improvements including but not limited to the operations of mass transit and facilities for biking and walking.

A city or town may establish one or more parking benefit districts, as a geographically defined area, in which parking revenue collected therein may be designated in whole or in part for use in said district through a dedicated fund. ... A parking benefit district may be managed by a body designated by the municipality, including but not limited to a business improvement district or main streets organization.

The act's language is simple. Cities can charge demand-based prices for curb parking and spend the revenue to improve public services in the metered districts. Other states could adopt similar legislation that will encourage cities to establish Parking Benefit Districts.

The PARC Act took effect in October 2016. In January, 2017, Boston launched two performance parking pilot programs. The meter rates are based on parking demand, and the city will reinvest a share of the revenue increase in the metered districts (City of Boston 2017).

Cities in Massachusetts now have a great opportunity to create Parking Benefit Districts because the state had previously prohibited cities from using meter revenue to fund general public services. The new Parking Benefit Districts will therefore not take meter revenue away from other public services, which should simplify the politics of establishing them.

The Massachusetts legislation combines San Francisco's demand-based pricing policy and Pasadena's revenue-return spending policy. This combination can depoliticize curb parking in two ways. First, the pricing policy relieves the city council of voting on every price change. The city council sets policy by choosing an occupancy goal, and then gives the parking authority the responsibility to set prices to achieve this goal. Parking demand then sets the prices, without political intervention. Second, dedicating meter revenue to paying for public services on the metered streets relieves the city council of voting whether to install every new meter. If the city council returns all or a share of meter revenue to pay for services on the metered blocks, neighborhoods can decide for themselves whether they want parking meters and added public services. Parking Benefit Districts are a bottom-up rather than a top-down policy.

Parking Benefit Districts in Residential Neighborhoods

Cities have established Parking Benefit Districts in commercial areas but have not yet done so in residential neighborhoods. Most on-street parking spaces are in residential neighborhoods, however, and the greatest opportunities for public improvement may lie in these neighborhoods (see Chapter 51).

In residential neighborhoods, Parking *Benefit* Districts resemble conventional Parking *Permit* Districts except for three features. First, the number of permits is limited to the number of curb spaces. Second, drivers pay market prices for the permits. Third, the permit revenue pays for neighborhood public services. In neighborhoods where most residents park off-street or do not own a car, the prospect of better public services—a cleaner and greener neighborhood—may persuade a majority to support charging market prices for on-street parking.

On-street parking revenue can pay to clean and repair sidewalks, add security, bury overhead utility wires, and provide other public services. Few residents will pay for curb parking but everyone will benefit from the public services. Because cities do not now charge for on-street parking in residential neighborhoods, Parking Benefit Districts will not take any existing revenue away from other public services. Money will come right out of the ground.

Richer neighborhoods that have higher parking prices will earn more money for public services. Cities can avoid this inequality and still provide the local incentive to charge for parking permits by using power equalization as proposed earlier for commercial Parking Benefit Districts. All neighborhoods that charge market prices for their curb parking will receive equal revenue for public services (see Chapter 50).

If a block has 20 parking spaces that can each earn $2,000 a year to pay for public services, for example, free parking subsidizes parking on the block by $40,000 a year. If the city already charged market prices for curb parking on a block and spent an extra $40,000 a year to improve public services, few would say the city should spend $40,000 a year less on public services in order to subsidize hard-to-find parking for 20 cars. Some activities justify public subsidies, but parking a car is not one of them.

If laid end to end, the 3 million curb parking spaces in New York would stretch almost halfway around the Earth and would cover about 17 square miles of land, 13 times the size of Central Park. Because 97 percent of New York's on-street parking is unmetered, the parking subsidy must be astronomical. If only half of New York's 3 million on-street spaces were in Parking Benefit Districts and they earned an average revenue of $2,000 per space per year (that's only $5.50 per day), the total revenue would amount to $3 billion per year. Half of that could go to improve neighborhoods, and the other half could pay for citywide services, such as renovating the subway system (see Chapter 51).

Many people seem to think the best reason to do anything is that it's best for them individually. Planners should therefore be realistic about devising policies so the stakeholders receive personal benefits. Parking Benefit Districts can produce many social benefits, ranging from less traffic to less global warming, but these benefits alone will not persuade many people that they ought to pay for parking. The narrow local benefits like cleaner and safer sidewalks in front of their homes can persuade self-interested residents to support market prices for curb parking. The streets will be paved with possibilities.

Parking Benefit Districts are evolutionary, not revolutionary, and they require little change in the way cities conduct business. In commercial areas, they combine Business Improvement Districts and parking meters. In residential areas, they combine Parking Permit Districts and market prices. Parking Benefit Districts combine familiar institutions in a new way, and they are bold but understandable. The more they look like what cities already do, the more they can make a radical change. And they can be tried out a few blocks at a time.

Some critics may complain that charging for curb parking will privatize public land, but the government owns the land, uses a market to set the prices, and spends the revenue on public services. Parking Benefit Districts are markets without capitalism, more like market socialism than privatization, and they are small scale and democratic (*The High Cost of Free Parking*, 447–450). Market prices can't solve every problem, but they can solve the parking problem.

Parking Benefit Districts won't be necessary if a city's public infrastructure is in good shape, public transport works well, traffic is not congested, the air is safe to breathe, housing is affordable, and neighborhoods are walkable. But many cities do have serious problems that we have been trying to fix for decades, and we are now on the sixth or seventh generation of fixes. We have tried every silver bullet: urban renewal, high-rise public housing, rotating restaurants, world fairs, public parking structures, development banks, and light rail. Parking Benefit Districts are modest and cheap in comparison to previous fixes and are worth a try.

Residential Parking Benefit Districts and Affordable Housing

Almost every proposal for new housing in an old neighborhood now comes bundled with a dispute over scarce curb parking. Current residents fear that new residents will compete for the free on-street parking and make their already difficult parking situation worse. As a result, cities require new housing to provide enough off-street parking to prevent crowding the curb. But if parking permits restrain parking demand to fit the available curb supply, new housing will not crowd the curb. Cities will then be able to eliminate their off-street parking requirements and allow developers to provide less parking and more housing.

Most residents probably won't ask for a PBD because they want to increase the supply of affordable housing, but they may ask for a PBD because they want to improve their neighborhood. As a byproduct, removing off-street parking requirements will remove a major barrier to affordable housing. Granny flats (also called second units and backyard cottages) are an especially promising form of housing that can flourish if cities remove off-street parking requirements in residential neighborhoods. Second units provide a simple, relatively inexpensive, and nearly invisible way for homeowners to create additional housing.

On-street parking congestion is not the only reason why neighbors may object to second units, but it is a major reason and a politically powerful one. If cities can remove parking as an objection to second units, the other issues (such as concerns about noise or attracting low-income residents to high-income neighborhoods) can be discussed more openly. Parking Benefit Districts that mitigate the parking concerns of neighbors can thus reduce the political opposition to second units (*The High Cost of Free Parking* 462–64; Brown, Mukhija, and Shoup, 2018).

CONCLUSION

Charging market prices for curb parking makes perfect economic sense, but politics are even more important. John Kenneth Galbraith warned about the danger of focusing on the economics and neglecting the politics:

> In making economics a non-political subject, neoclassical theory destroys the relation of economics to the real world. In that world, power is decisive in what happens. And the problems of that world are increasing both in number and in the depth of their social affliction. In consequence, neoclassical and neo-Keynesian economics regulates its players to the social sidelines. They either call no plays or use the wrong ones. To change the metaphor, they manipulate levers to which no machinery is attached (Parker 2005, 616).

Parking Benefit Districts combine economics and politics in a new way to gain popular support for parking reforms.

Assembling support for parking reform is like opening a combination lock: each small turn of the dial seems to achieve nothing, but when everything is in place the lock opens. Diverse interests across the political spectrum can support a combination of three reforms: (1) remove off-street parking requirements, (2) charge market prices for on-street parking, and (3) spend the revenue for neighborhood public services.

On-street parking is a missing market in the economy, and neighborhoods are a missing level of government. Charging the right prices for on-street parking can fill the gap in the market, and Parking Benefit Districts can fill the gap in government (*The High Cost of Free Parking*, Chapter 17). Conservatives often want more markets, while liberals often want more government. Parking Benefit Districts give both more markets and more government, but a new kind of both: market prices for on-street parking and parking-financed public services.

Conservatives sometimes underestimate how individual choices have collective consequences, and liberals sometimes underestimate how economic incentives affect individual choices. Parking Benefit Districts can mediate between these two views. Charging market prices for curb parking will lead drivers to make travel choices that benefit society, and the parking-financed public services will benefit everyone in the neighborhood.

Repealing off-street parking requirements and replacing them with market prices for on-street parking may at first glance seem a herculean task, almost like Prohibition or the Reformation, too big an upheaval for society to accept. Nevertheless, the repeal-and-replace strategy should attract voters across a wide political spectrum. Conservatives will see that it reduces government regulations and relies on market choices. Liberals will see that it increases spending for public services. Environmentalists will see that it reduces energy consumption, air pollution, and carbon emissions. New Urbanists will see that it enables people to live at higher density without being overrun by cars. Developers will see that it reduces building costs. Drivers of all political stripes will see that it guarantees convenient curb parking. Residents will see that it improves their neighborhoods. Elected officials will see that it depoliticizes parking, reduces traffic congestion, allows infill development, and provides public services without raising taxes. Finally, urban planners can devote less time to parking and more time to improving cities.

The following 51 chapters explain how repealing off-street parking requirements, replacing them with the right prices for on-street parking, and spending the resulting revenue to improve neighborhood public services may be the cheapest, fastest, and simplest way to improve cities, the economy, and the environment, one parking space at a time.

REFERENCES AND FURTHER READING

Board of Governors of the Federal Reserve System. 2016. Report on the Economic Well-Being of U.S. Households in 2015. Washington, DC: Board of Governors of the Federal Reserve System. http://www.federalreserve.gov/2015-report-economic-well-being-us-households-201605.pdf

Brown, Anne, Vinit Mukhija, and Donald Shoup. 2018. "Converting Garages into Housing," *Journal of Planning Education and Research.*

Centre for Science and Environment. 2016. *Parking Policy for Clean Air & Liveable Cities: A Guidance Framework.* New Delhi: Centre for Science and Environment. http://www.cseindia.org/userfiles/parking-report-dec27.pdf

City of Palo Alto, California, Development Impact Fees, August 15, 2016. http://www.cityofpaloalto.org/civicax/filebank/documents/27226

City of Seattle, Statement of Legislative Intent, Neighborhood Paid Parking Rates, 2011. http://clerk.seattle.gov/~public/budgetdocs/2011/2011-118-3-A-1-145-Desc.pdf

Congressional Budget Office. 2015. *Public Spending on Transportation and Water Infrastructure, 1956 to 2014.* https://www.cbo.gov/publication/49910

Downs, Anthony. 2004. *Still Stuck in Traffic.* Washington, D.C.: Brookings Institution.

Inci, Eren, Jos van Ommeren, and Martijn Kobus. 2017. "The External Cruising Costs of Parking," *Journal of Economic Geography.* https://doi.org/10.1093/jeg/lbx004

Jacobs, Jane. 1962. "Downtown Planning," in Max Allen (ed.). 1997. *Ideas That Matter, the Worlds of Jane Jacobs,* Owen Sound, Ontario: The Ginger Press, pp. 17–20.

Kahneman, Daniel. 2011. *Thinking, Fast and Slow.* New York: Farrar, Straus and Giroux.

Keats, John. 1958. *The Insolent Chariots.* New York: J. B. Lipincott Company.

King, David, Michael Manville, and Donald Shoup. 2007. "For Whom the Road Tolls," *ACCESS,* No. 31, Fall, pp. 2–7. http://www.accessmagazine.org/wp-content/uploads/sites/7/2016/02/Access-31-02-For-Whom-the-Road-Tolls.pdf

McCallum, Kevin. 2017. "Santa Rosa Considering 'Progressive' Parking Downtown," *The Press Democrat,* March 15, 2017. http://www.pressdemocrat.com/news/6784389-181/santa-rosa-considering-progressive-parking?artslide=0

Manville, Michael and Taner Osman. 2017. "Motivations for Growth Revolts: Discretion and Pretext as Sources of Development Conflict," *City and Community,* March.

Metcalfe, John. 2017. "Stark Comparison of Parking vs. Bike-Share Spaces," CityLab, June 29. https://www.citylab.com/transportation/2017/06/bike-share-dock-parking-space-citi-bike-new-york/531936/

Moura, Maria Cecilia, Steven Smith, and David Belzer. 2015. "120 Years of U.S. Residential Housing Stock and Floor Space," *PloS One,* Vol. 10, No. 8. http://journals.plos.org/plosone/article?id=10.1371/journal.pone.0134135

Mumford, Lewis. 1963. *The Highway and the City,* New York: Harcourt, Brace & World.

Parker, Richard. 2005. *John Kenneth Galbraith: His Life, His Politics, His Economics,* New York: Farrar, Straus and Giroux.

Pierce, Gregory, and Donald Shoup. 2013. "SF*park*: Pricing Parking by Demand," *ACCESS*, No. 43, Fall, pp. 20–28. http://www.accessmagazine.org/wp-content/uploads/sites/7/2015/10/SFpark.pdf

San Francisco Municipal Transportation Agency. 2014. "On-street Parking Census Data and Map." http://sfpark.org/resources/parking-census-data-context-and-map-april-2014/

San Francisco Municipal Transportation Agency. 2014. "Pilot Project Evaluation: The SFMTA's Evaluation of the Benefits of the SF*park* Pilot Project." http://sfpark.org/wp-content/uploads/2014/06/SFpark_Pilot_Project_Evaluation.pdf

Schmitt, Angie. 2014. "The Spectacular Waste of Half-Empty Black Friday Parking Lots,"*Streetsblog*, December 1. http://usa.streetsblog.org/2014/12/01/the-spectacular-waste-of-half-empty-black-friday-parking-lots/

Shoup, Donald. 2011. *The High Cost of Free Parking*. Revised edition. Chicago: Planners Press.

Shoup, Donald. 2014. "The High Cost of Minimum Parking Requirements," in *Parking: Issues and Policies*, edited by Stephen Ison and Corinne Mulley. Bingley, United Kingdom: Emerald Group Publishing, pp. 87–113.

The White House. 2016. "Housing Development Toolkit," September 2016. https://www.whitehouse.gov/sites/whitehouse.gov/files/images/Housing_Development_Toolkit%20f.2.pdf

Williams, Jonathan. 2010. "Meter Payment Exemption for Disabled Placard Holders as a Barrier to Manage Curb Parking." Master's thesis, University of California, Los Angeles. http://shoup.bol.ucla.edu/MeterPaymentExemptionForDisabledPlacardHolders.pdf

Wright, Lawrence. 2013. *Going Clear*. New York: Knopf.

Zoeter, Onno, Christopher Dance, Stéphane Clinchant, and Jean-Marc Andreoli. 2014. "New Algorithms for Parking Demand Management and a City-Scale Deployment," Proceedings of the 20th ACM SIGKDD International Conference on Knowledge Discovery and Data Mining. Pages 1819–1828. http://www.xrce.xerox.com/Our-Research/Publications/2014-026

Part I

Remove Off-Street Parking Requirements

Paul had noticed already that in Los Angeles automobiles were a race apart, almost alive. The city was full of their hotels and beauty shops, their restaurants and nursing homes—immense, expensive structures where they could be parked or polished, fed or cured of their injuries. They spoke, and had pets—stuffed dogs and monkeys looked out of their rear windows, toys and good-luck charms hung above their dashboards, and fur tails waved from their aerials. Their horns sang in varied voices ... few people were visible. The automobiles outnumbered them ten to one. Paul imagined a tale in which it would be gradually revealed that these automobiles were the real inhabitants of the city, a secret master race which only kept human beings for its own greater convenience, or as pets.

—ALISON LURIE, *THE NOWHERE CITY*

CHAPTER

1

Truth in Transportation Planning

By Donald Shoup

It ain't what you don't know that gets you into trouble.
It's what you know for sure that just ain't so.

MARK TWAIN

How far is it from San Diego to San Francisco? An estimate of 632.125 miles is precise—but not accurate. An estimate of somewhere between 400 and 500 miles is less precise but more accurate because the correct answer is 460 miles. Nevertheless, if you had no idea how far it is from San Diego to San Francisco, which would you believe: a manual published by the National Geographic Institute that reports the distance to be 632.125 miles, or someone who tentatively says somewhere between 400 and 500 miles? Probably the first, because institutional prestige and extreme precision imply certainty.

Although reporting estimates with extreme precision implies confidence in their accuracy, transportation engineers and urban planners often use extremely precise numbers to report highly uncertain estimates. To illustrate this practice, I will draw on two manuals published by the Institute of Transportation Engineers (ITE)—*Parking Generation* and *Trip Generation*. Urban planners rely on parking generation rates to establish off-street parking requirements, and transportation planners rely on trip generation rates to predict the traffic effects of proposed developments. Unwarranted trust in these precise but uncertain estimates of travel behavior lead to bad policy choices for transportation, parking, and land use.

TRIP GENERATION

Trip Generation reports the number of vehicle trips as a function of land use. The 6th edition of *Trip Generation* describes the database used to estimate trip generation rates:

> This document is based on more than 3,750 trip generation studies submitted to the Institute by public agencies, developers, consulting firms, and associations. ... Data were primarily collected at suburban localities with little or no transit service, nearby pedestrian amenities, or travel demand management (TDM) programs (ITE 1997, vol. 3, pp. ix and 1).

ITE says nothing about the price of parking, but the 1990 Nationwide Personal Transportation Survey found that parking was free for 99 percent of vehicle trips in the U.S., so the surveyed sites probably offer free parking. Of the 1,515 trip generation rates reported in the 6th edition, half were based on five or fewer studies, and 23 percent were based on a single study. Trip generation rates thus typically measure the number of vehicle trips observed at a few suburban sites with free parking but no public transit, no nearby pedestrian amenities, and no TDM programs. Urban planners who rely on these trip generation data as guides when designing transportation systems are therefore skewing travel toward cars.

Figure 1-1 is a facsimile of a page from the 4th edition of *Trip Generation* (1987). It shows the number of vehicle trips to and from fast-food restaurants on a weekday. Each point in the figure represents a single restaurant, showing the number of vehicle trips it generates and its floor area. Dividing the number of vehicle trips by the floor area gives the trip generation rate for that restaurant. The rates ranged from 284.000 to 1,359.500, with an average of 632.125 trips per 1,000 square feet of floor area.

A glance at the figure suggests that vehicle trips are unrelated to floor area in this sample, and the equation at the bottom of the figure confirms this impression. The R^2 of 0.069 implies that variation in floor area explains less than 7 percent of the variation in vehicle trips. The correlation between trips and floor area is not significantly different from zero, but ITE reported the sample's average trip generation rate (which urban planners normally interpret as the exact relationship between floor area and vehicle trips) as precisely 632.125 trips per day per 1,000 square feet. The trip generation rate looks accurate because it is so precise, but the precision is misleading. Few planning decisions would be changed if ITE reported the trip generation rate as 632 rather than 632.125 trips per 1,000 square feet, so the three-decimal-point precision serves no purpose except to falsely suggest that the estimate is accurate.

Average Vehicle Trip Ends vs: **1,000 Square Feet Gross Floor Area**
On a: **Weekday**

TRIP GENERATION RATES

Average Weekday Vehicle Trip Ends per 1,000 Square Feet Gross Floor Area

Average Trip Rate	*Range of Rates*	*Standard*	*Number of Studies*	*Average 1,000 Deviation Square Feet GFA*
632.125	284.000–1359.500	*	8	3.0

DATA PLOT AND EQUATION

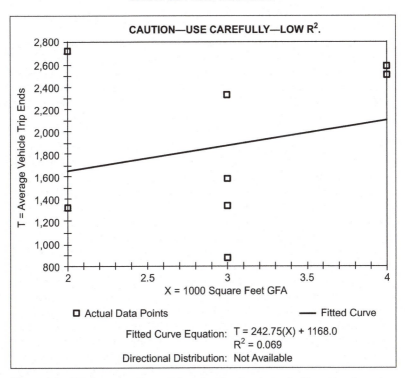

Figure 1-1 ITE trip generation rate for a fast-food restaurant with a drive-through window, 1987

Source: ITE, 1987, p. 1199

Figure 1-1 suggests that larger restaurants generate more vehicle trips but the smallest restaurant generated the most trips, and a midsize restaurant generated the fewest. The page does contain the warning, "Caution—Use Carefully—Low R^2," which is good advice because the data show no relationship between vehicle trips and floor area. Nevertheless, the average trip generation rate is reported at the top of the page as if it were accurate. Despite its precision, the number is far too uncertain to use in transportation planning.

PARKING GENERATION

Parking generation rates suffer from similar uncertainty. *Parking Generation* reports the average peak parking occupancy as a function of land use. The 2nd edition of *Parking Generation* (ITE 1987, p. vii and xv) explained the survey process:

> A vast majority of the data … is derived from suburban developments with little or no significant transit ridership. … The ideal site for obtaining reliable parking generation data would … contain ample, convenient parking facilities for the exclusive use of the traffic generated by the site. … The objective of the survey is to count the number of vehicles parked at the time of peak parking demand.

Half the 101 parking generation rates in the 2nd edition were based on four or fewer surveys, and 22 percent were based on a single survey. Therefore, parking generation rates measured the peak parking demand observed at a few suburban sites with ample free parking and no public transit. Urban planners who used these rates to set off-street parking requirements were therefore planning a city where people drive wherever they go and park free when they get there.

Figure 1-2 shows the page for fast-food restaurants from the 2nd edition of *Parking Generation* (1987). The equation at the bottom again confirms the visual impression that parking occupancy is not related to floor area in this sample. The R^2 of 0.038 implies that variation in floor area explains less than 4 percent of the variation in parking occupancy. The largest restaurant generated one of the lowest peak parking occupancies, while a midsize restaurant generated the highest peak parking occupancy. ITE reported the average parking generation rate for a fast-food restaurant as precisely 9.95 parking spaces per 1,000 square feet of floor area although it is not significantly different from zero.

I am not saying that vehicle trips and parking demand are unrelated to a restaurant's size. Common sense suggests some correlation. Nevertheless, Figures 1-1 and 1-2 do not show a statistically significant relationship between floor area and either vehicle trips or parking demand. It is misleading and irresponsible to publish precise average trip and parking generation rates based on these data.

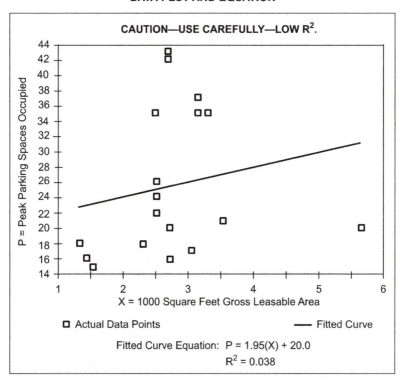

Peak Parking Spaces Occupied vs: **1,000 Square Feet Gross Floor Area**
Leasable Area
On a: **Weekday**

PARKING GENERATION RATES

Average Rate	Range of Rates	Standard Deviation	Number of Studies	Average 1,000 SFG Leasable Area
9.95	3.55–15.92	3.41	18	3

DATA PLOT AND EQUATION

CAUTION—USE CAREFULLY—LOW R^2.

□ Actual Data Points   —— Fitted Curve

Fitted Curve Equation: P = 1.95(X) + 20.0
$R^2 = 0.038$

Figure 1-2 ITE parking generation rate for a fast-food restaurant with a drive-in window, 1987

Source: ITE, 1987, p. 146

ITE's stamp of authority relieves planners from the obligation to think for themselves about parking demand—the answers are right there in the book. ITE offers precise numbers about parking demand, although it does warn, "Users of this report should exercise extreme caution when utilizing data that is based on a small number of studies." Nevertheless, many planners recommend the parking generation rates as minimum parking requirements because they are the only data available. For example, the median number of parking spaces required for fast-food restaurants in U.S. cities is 10 spaces per 1,000 square feet—almost identical to ITE's reported parking generation rate. After all, planners expect minimum parking requirements to meet the peak demand for free parking, and parking generation rates seem to predict this demand precisely! When ITE speaks, urban planners listen.

STATISTICAL SIGNIFICANCE

The breathtaking combination of extreme precision and statistical insignificance in parking and trip generation rates at fast-food restaurants raises an important question: How many of the rates for other land uses are statistically insignificant? ITE first stated a policy regarding statistical significance in the 5th edition of *Trip Generation* (1991):

Best-fit curves are shown in this report only when each of the following three conditions is met:

- The R^2 is greater than or equal to 0.25.
- The sample size is greater than or equal to 4.
- The number of trips increases as the size of the independent variable increases.

The third criterion is egregiously unscientific, even antiscientific. For example, suppose the R^2 is greater than 0.25 (which means that variation in floor area explains more than 25 percent of the variation in vehicle trips), the sample size is greater than four, and vehicle trips decrease as floor area increases. The first two criteria are met but the third is not. In this case, ITE would report the average trip generation rate (which states that vehicle trips increase as floor area increases), but not the equation (which would show that vehicle trips decrease as floor area increases). ITE's stated policy is to conceal evidence that contradicts expected relationship.

Figure 1-3, from the 5th edition, shows how this policy affects the report on fast-food restaurants. It showed the same eight data points as the 4th edition, but omitted the regression equation and the R^2, as well as the warning "Caution—Use Carefully—Low R^2." The 5th edition was, however, cautious about needless precision: it truncated the average trip generation rate from 632.125 to 632.12 trips per 1,000 square feet.

ITE revised its reporting policy in the 6th edition of *Trip Generation* (1997). It showed the regression equation only if the R^2 is greater than

Average Vehicle Trip Ends vs: **1,000 Square Feet Gross Floor Area**
On a: **Weekday**

Number of Studies: 8
Average 1000 Square Feet GFA: 3
Directional Distribution: 50% entering, 50% exiting

TRIP GENERATION RATES

Trip Generation per 1000 Square Feet Gross Floor Area

Average Rate	Range of Rates	Standard Deviation
632.12	284.00–1359.50	266.29

DATA PLOT AND EQUATION

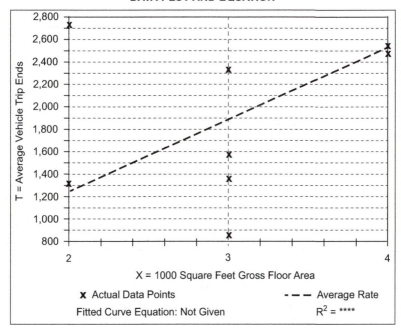

x Actual Data Points   − − − Average Rate
Fitted Curve Equation: Not Given $R^2 = $ ****

Figure 1-3 ITE trip generation rate for a fast-food restaurant with a drive-through window, 1991

Source: ITE, 1991, p. 1308

or equal to 0.5, but the other two criteria remained the same. Figure 1-4 shows the trip generation report for a fast-food restaurant from the 6th edition. The number of studies increased to 21, and the average trip generation rate fell to 496.12 trips per 1,000 square feet. Since the previous edition's trip generation rate was 632.12 trips per 1,000 square feet,

Average Vehicle Trip Ends vs: **1,000 Square Feet Gross Floor Area**
On a: **Weekday**

Number of Studies: 21
Average 1000 Square Feet GFA: 3
Directional Distribution: 50% entering, 50% exiting

TRIP GENERATION RATES

Trip Generation per 1000 Square Feet Gross Floor Area

Average Rate	Range of Rates	Standard Deviation
496.12	195.98–1132.92	242.52

DATA PLOT AND EQUATION

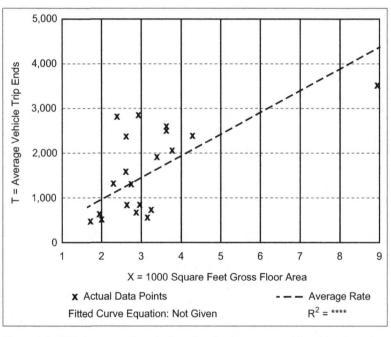

Figure 1-4   ITE trip generation rate for a fast-food restaurant with a drive-through window, 1997

Source: ITE, 1997, p. 1401

anyone comparing the two editions might conclude that vehicle trips to fast-food restaurants declined 22 percent in the six years between 1991 and 1997, perhaps because of a recession in the fast-food industry. But both the 5th edition rate (632.12) and the 6th edition rate (496.12) were derived from data that do not show a statistically significant relation between floor area and vehicle trips, so this 22 percent decline is spurious. The 9th edition of *Trip Generation* (2012) showed the same 21 trip generation studies shown in the 6th edition (1997), and the same trip generation rate (496.12) reported 15 years earlier.

The 6th edition (1997) showed regression equations for only 34 percent of the 1,515 trip generation rates. Although 66 percent of the rates failed to meet at least one of the three significance criteria, ITE nevertheless published a precise rate for every land use no matter how small the sample or how unrelated vehicle trips are to floor area. Consider, for example, the report of trip generation at a fast-food restaurant with a drive-through window and no indoor seating, a new land use that was reported for the first time in the 7th edition in 2003 (Figure 1-5). Two sites were surveyed, and the larger site generated fewer vehicle trips. Nevertheless, ITE reported the average trip generation rate at the two sites and plotted a line suggesting that larger sites generate more vehicle trips. The precision defies common sense, but there it is: 153.85 vehicle trips per 1,000 square feet during the peak hour of adjacent street traffic on a weekday. Two observations were thus sufficient to launch this new land-use category, even though both its precise trip generation rate and the plot are absurd.

The 9th edition of *Trip Generation* (2012) continued the unscientific practice of concealing evidence that contradicts expected relationships. It showed the fitted curve equation and R^2 for only 38 percent of the 1,725 reported trip generation rates, which means that 62 percent of them failed to meet at least one of the three criteria that must be met before ITE shows the R^2.

The large share of trip generation reports showing no R^2 is explained in part by the large number of specialized reports for each land use. For example, pages 1910 to 1931 in the 9th edition showed 20 different trip generation reports for fast-food restaurants with a drive-through window. Nine trip generation rates were expressed as the number of trips per 1,000 square feet of floor area, in nine time periods:

1. A weekday
2. A weekday during the peak hour of adjacent street traffic in the morning
3. A weekday during the peak hour of adjacent street traffic in the evening
4. A weekday during the peak hour of trip generation in the morning
5. A weekday during the peak hour of trip generation in the evening
6. A Saturday
7. A Saturday during the peak hour of trip generation

Average Vehicle Trip Ends vs: **1,000 Square Feet Gross Floor Area**
On a: **Weekday**
**Peak Hour of Adjacent Street Traffic,
One Hour Between 4 and 6 p.m.**

Number of Studies: 2
Average 1000 Square Feet GFA: 0.35
Directional Distribution: 54% entering, 46% exiting

Trip Generation per 1000 Square Feet Gross Floor Area

Average Rate	Range of Rates	Standard Deviation
153.85	124.37-191.56	*

DATA PLOT AND EQUATION

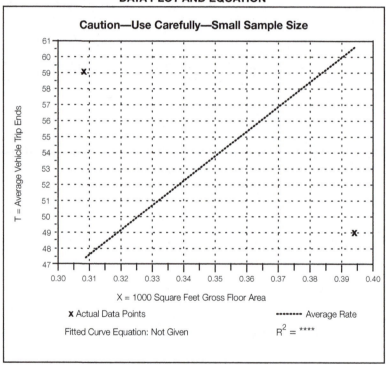

Caution—Use Carefully—Small Sample Size

X = 1000 Square Feet Gross Floor Area

x Actual Data Points   ▪▪▪▪▪▪▪▪ Average Rate

Fitted Curve Equation: Not Given $R^2 = ****$

Figure 1-5   ITE trip generation rate for a fast-food restaurant with a drive-through window and no indoor seating, 2003

Source: ITE, 2003, p. 1773

8. A Sunday
9. A Sunday during the peak hour of trip generation

The 11 other trip generation rates were expressed as the number of trips per seat in the restaurant during various time periods, or as the number of trips divided by the volume of traffic on the adjacent street during the morning and evening peak hours.

Despite the heroic attempt to find a relationship between the number of trips and some factor at fast-food restaurants with a drive-through window, the 9th edition showed the R^2 for only one of the 20 trip generation reports—the number of peak-hour trips per 1,000 square feet of floor area during the peak hour on Sunday—and that R^2 was only 0.63 with a sample size of five observations.

ITE reported its policy regarding statistical significance for *Parking Generation* in the 4th edition, published in 2010: "For data sets with at least four study sites, a linear regression equation and line are presented if the coefficient of determination (R^2) is greater than or equal to 0.60" (ITE 2010, 14). How did this new policy affect the report of parking generation for fast-food restaurants? The parking generation rate was 9.98 vehicles per 1,000 square feet of gross floor area in 4th edition in 2010, almost identical to the 9.95 reported in 2nd edition in 1987 (Figure 1-2 above). The 2010 edition, however, omitted the fitted curve equation and the R^2 shown at the bottom of the data plot in the 1987 edition. As in 1987, the largest restaurant generated one of the lowest peak parking occupancies, while a midsize restaurant generated the highest. Omitting the R^2 and the regression line in 2010 implies that the R^2 is less than 0.60, which is no surprise since the R^2 reported in 1987 for a similar graph was only 0.038.

Not showing the regression equation is ITE's subtle way of pointing out that the information is flawed and irrelevant. Continuing to report misleadingly precise parking and trip generation rates, however, creates serious problems. Many people rely on ITE manuals to predict how urban development will affect parking and traffic. When estimating traffic impacts, for example, developers and cities often battle fiercely over whether a precise trip generation rate or parking generation rate is correct; given the uncertainty involved, the debates are ludicrous. But few seem to pay any attention to the statistical insignificance of this rigorous pseudoscience.

Many cities base their parking requirements on ITE's parking generation rates, and some cities base their zoning categories on ITE's trip generation rates. Consider the zoning ordinance in Beverly Hills, California:

The intensity of use will not exceed either sixteen (16) vehicle trips per hour or 200 vehicle trips per day for each 1,000 gross square foot of floor area for uses as specified in the most recent edition of the Institute of Traffic Engineers' publication entitled "Trip Generation."

The precise but highly uncertain ITE data thus govern which land uses a city will allow. Once they have been incorporated into municipal codes, parking and trip generation rates are difficult to challenge. Planning is an uncertain activity, but it is difficult to incorporate uncertainty into legal regulations. Admitting the flimsy basis of zoning decisions would also expose cities to countless lawsuits. It's easier to ignore the uncertainty and rely on the precise but statistically insignificant ITE numbers.

PLANNING FOR FREE PARKING

Not only are most ITE samples too small to draw statistically significant conclusions, but ITE's method of collecting data also skews observations to sites with high parking and trip generation rates. Larger samples might solve the problem of statistical insignificance, but a basic problem would remain: ITE measures the peak parking demand and the number of vehicle trips at suburban sites with ample free parking.

Consider the process of planning for free parking:

1. Transportation engineers survey peak parking demand at suburban sites with ample free parking, and ITE publishes the results in *Parking Generation* with misleading precision.
2. Urban planners consult *Parking Generation* to set minimum parking requirements. The maximum observed parking demand thus becomes the minimum required parking supply.
3. Developers provide all the required parking. The ample supply of parking drives the price of most parking to zero, which increases vehicle travel.
4. Transportation engineers survey vehicle trips to and from suburban sites with ample free parking and little or no transit ridership, and ITE publishes the results in *Trip Generation* with misleading precision.
5. Transportation planners consult *Trip Generation* to design the transportation system that brings cars to the free parking.
6. Urban planners limit density so that new development with the required free parking will not generate more vehicle trips than nearby roads can carry. This lower density spreads activities farther apart, further increasing vehicle travel and parking demand.

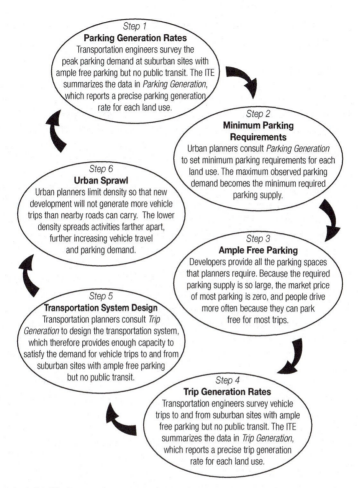

Figure 1-6 Six-step process

The loop is completed when transportation engineers again survey the peak parking demand at suburban sites that offer free parking and—surprise—find that more parking is needed. Misusing precise numbers to report uncertain data gives a veneer of rigor to this elaborate charade, and the circular logic explains why planning for transportation and land use has gone subtly, incrementally wrong.

The belief that minimum parking requirements are based on rational city planning resembles the belief that the earth is flat and balanced on the back of a giant turtle. In a debate between a scientist and a flat-earth-on-a-turtle believer, the scientist asked, what the turtle stands on.

The flat-earther replied that the turtle stands on the back of a far larger turtle. What does this second turtle stand on? The reply came, "You're very clever, young man, very clever. But it's turtles all the way down!" (Hawking 1988, 1).

Minimum parking requirements are also based on turtles all the way down. Cities require off-street parking without considering parking prices, the cost of parking spaces, or the wider consequences for transportation, land use, the economy, and the environment. Misinterpreting the peak demand for free parking as *the* demand for parking and then requiring that amount of parking everywhere has led to a planning disaster of epic proportions.

ITE manuals do not cause this circular and cumulative process, and ITE of course deplores any misuse of its parking and trip generation rates. In the early editions of *Parking Generation* and *Trip Generation*, ITE warned users to be careful when the R^2 is low (see Figures 1-1 and 1-2) but removed this advice from the data plots in recent editions (see Figures 1-3, 1-4, and 1-5).

The users of any data should always ask themselves whether the data are appropriate for the intended purpose. Only users can misuse data, but ITE invites misuse. The spurious precision of ITE data has helped to establish parking requirements and trip generation rates as dogma in the planning profession.

Parking requirements assume that everyone is parked at home, everyone is parked at work, everyone is parked at school, everyone is shopping on the day after Thanksgiving, and so on for every land use, simultaneously. If parking requirements do not meet the peak demand for free parking everywhere, there may be a shortage of parking somewhere, sometime, which is intolerable.

Parking requirements in zoning ordinances stem from the delusion that urban planners can estimate the right number of parking spaces needed at every site without considering the price that drivers pay for parking, the cost of providing the required spaces, or the wider consequences for transportation, land use, and the environment.

Parking requirements are closer to astrology than to astronomy and planners might just as well base parking requirements on signs of the zodiac. I have tried for years to let the theoretical hot air out of the tires of *Parking Generation* and *Trip Generation*, but the tires seem designed to run well even while flat.

LESS PRECISION AND MORE TRUTH

Parking and trip generation estimates respond to a real demand for information. Citizens want to know how development will affect their neighborhoods. Developers want to know how many parking spaces to provide for their customers. Planners want to regulate development. Politicians want to avoid complaints about too little parking and too much traffic. These are all valid concerns but false precision does not resolve them. To unsophisticated users, the precise parking and trip generation rates look like constants similar to the boiling point of water or the speed of light, and the ITE data look like scientific observations. But parking and trip generation are poorly understood phenomena, and they both depend on the price of parking. Demand is a function of price, and this does not cease to be true merely because transportation engineers and urban planners ignore it. Cities are planned on the unstated assumption that parking should be free—no matter how much it costs to provide.

ITE's parking and trip generation rates illustrate a familiar problem with statistics in transportation planning. Placing unwarranted trust in the accuracy of precise but highly uncertain data leads to bad policy choices. Being roughly right is better than being precisely wrong. We need less precision and more truth in transportation planning.

REFERENCES AND FURTHER READING

Hawking, Stephen. 1988. *A Brief History of Time*. New York: Bantam Books.

Institute of Transportation Engineers. *Parking Generation*. Second Edition. Washington, D.C.: 1987.

Institute of Transportation Engineers. *Parking Generation*. Fourth Edition. Washington, D.C.: Institute of Transportation Engineers. 2010.

Institute of Transportation Engineers. *Trip Generation*. Fourth Edition. Washington, D.C.: Institute of Transportation Engineers. 1987.

Institute of Transportation Engineers. *Trip Generation*. Fifth Edition. Washington, D.C.: Institute of Transportation Engineers. 1991.

Institute of Transportation Engineers. *Trip Generation*. Sixth Edition. Washington, D.C.: Institute of Transportation Engineers. 1997.

Institute of Transportation Engineers. *Trip Generation*. Ninth Edition. Washington, D.C.: Institute of Transportation Engineers. 2012.

Planning Advisory Service. *Off-Street Parking Requirements: A National Review of Standards*. Planning Advisory Service Report Number 432. Chicago: American Planning Association. 1991.

Shoup, Donald. 2003. "Truth in Transportation Planning." *Journal of Transportation and Statistics*, 6, no. 1: 1–16.

This chapter first appeared in ACCESS, *Spring 2002. The* ACCESS *article was condensed from "Truth in Transportation Planning," which was published in the* Journal of Transportation and Statistics *6, no. 1 (2003): 1–16.*

2

People, Parking, and Cities

By Michael Manville and Donald Shoup

What a man had rather were true he more readily believes.

FRANCIS BACON

The pop culture image of Los Angeles is an ocean of malls, cars, and exit ramps dotted with drab tract homes and populated by isolated individuals whose only solace is aimless driving on endless freeways. From Joan Didion to the Sierra Club, Los Angeles has been held up as a poster child of sprawl. This is an arresting and romantic narrative; it is also largely untrue.

To the extent that anyone has a definition of sprawl, it usually revolves around the absence of density, and Los Angeles has since the 1980s been the densest urbanized area in the U.S. This would make it the *least* sprawling city in the U.S. Compared to other cities, Los Angeles also does not have inordinately high rates of automobile ownership.

These facts strike some as hard to believe, or perhaps false, and they haven't made much of a dent in the Los Angeles-as-sprawl idea. Clichés about Los Angeles-style sprawl die hard, partly because the definition of sprawl is so malleable (urbanist William Fulton now simply calls Los Angeles "dense sprawl") and partly because the anti-urban stereotype about Los Angeles contains its own kernels of truth. After all, if density is a barometer for healthy urbanism, and Los Angeles is denser than cities like New York or San Francisco, then why are Manhattan and downtown San Francisco such vibrant places, and why is downtown Los Angeles comparatively lifeless?

Obviously there's no single answer to those questions. But we think the differences between Los Angeles, New York, and San Francisco stem in part from the different ways they regulate downtown development and, in particular, the way they regulate parking. Los Angeles is an example of density as a dilemma rather than a solution. Planners and urban critics who regularly call for increased density as a salve for city life should realize that without corresponding changes in parking requirements, increased density will compound, rather than solve, the problems we associate with sprawl.

DENSITY WITHIN REGIONS AND BETWEEN THEM

Before opening this discussion, we should make an important distinction. We are referring to the U.S. Census Bureau's definition of "urbanized areas" rather than to the political boundaries of cities. So when we say that Los Angeles is denser than New York, we are actually saying that the Los Angeles urbanized area, which is Los Angeles and its suburbs, is denser than the New York urbanized area.

Without doubt, the *cities* of New York and San Francisco are denser than the city of Los Angeles. But sprawl is a regional attribute, and Los Angeles has much denser suburbs than New York or San Francisco. Indeed, the Los Angeles region's distinguishing characteristic may be the uniformity of its density; its suburbs have 82 percent of the density of its central city. In contrast, New York's suburban density is a mere 12 percent of its central-city density, and San Francisco's suburban density is only 35 percent of the city's. New York and San Francisco look like Hong Kong surrounded by Phoenix, while Los Angeles looks like Los Angeles surrounded by, well, Los Angeles.

In other words, Los Angeles is a dense area without an extremely dense core, while New York and San Francisco are less dense overall but enjoy the benefits of very dense core areas. It's worth asking why that is. It may be that uniform density across an urbanized area is a result of the inability to have a very dense core. Or it may be that high uniform density precludes having a lively downtown. We don't have definitive answers to these questions, but we can highlight the tremendous deadening effect that parking regulations have on Los Angeles's Central Business District.

PARKING AND THE CENTRAL BUSINESS DISTRICT

A successful Central Business District (CBD) combines large amounts of labor and capital on a small amount of land. CBDs thrive on high density because the prime advantage they offer over other parts of a metropolitan area is *proximity*—the immediate availability of a wide variety of activities. The clustering of museums, theaters, restaurants, and offices is the commodity a downtown can offer that other areas cannot. Yet downtowns have long been plagued by questions about access because they can either thrive on or be destroyed by congestion. In order to thrive, a CBD must receive a critical mass of people every day but do so without clogging itself to the point of paralysis. One way to do this is to require off-street parking spaces. Off-street parking can reduce the cruising for parking that often strangles the streets of CBDs, but parking requirements have high costs.

It's not hard to see how a conventional parking lot can undermine a CBD's success; a downtown surface lot often has a very high and very visible opportunity cost. Instead of a building teeming with activity, there is an expanse of asphalt with one employee manning a booth; where there could be something, there is instead not much. But even when off-street parking is dressed up or hidden—when it is placed underground or in a structure that has retail uses at the street level—it is inimical to density. Because land is most expensive in the CBD, off-street parking is also most expensive there, and constructing it uses up capital that could otherwise be invested more productively. More important, if off-street parking is *required*, as it is in many cities, then it becomes rational for firms to locate in places where land is less expensive, meaning it becomes rational to locate outside the CBD. A parking requirement applied uniformly across a city implicitly discriminates against development in the CBD because the burden of complying with the requirement is greater in the CBD than almost anywhere else.

A TALE OF TWO PARKING REQUIREMENTS

The impact of parking requirements becomes clearer when we compare the parking requirements of our three cities. New York and San Francisco have strict limits on how much parking they allow in their CBDs; Los Angeles, however, pursues a diametrically opposing path—where the other two cities limit off-street parking, Los Angeles requires it. This requirement not only discourages development in downtown Los Angeles relative to other parts of the region, but also distorts how the downtown functions.

Take, for example, the different treatment given by Los Angeles and San Francisco to their concert halls. For a downtown concert hall, Los Angeles requires, as a minimum, *50 times* more parking than San Francisco allows as its maximum. Thus, the San Francisco Symphony built its home, Louise Davies Hall, without a parking garage, while

Disney Hall, the new home of the Los Angeles Philharmonic, did not open until seven years after its parking garage was built.

Disney Hall's six-level, 2,188-space underground garage cost $110 million to build (about $50,000 per space). Financially troubled Los Angeles County, which built the garage, went into debt to finance it, expecting that parking revenues would repay the borrowed money. The garage was completed in 1996, and Disney Hall—which suffered from a budget less grand than its vision—became knotted in delays and didn't open until late 2003. During the seven years in between, parking revenue fell far short of debt payments (few people park in an underground structure if there is nothing above it), and the county, by that point nearly bankrupt, had to subsidize the garage even as it laid off employees.

The county owns the land beneath Disney Hall, and its lease for the site specifies that Disney Hall must schedule at least 128 concerts each winter season. Why 128? That's the minimum number of concerts that will generate the parking revenue necessary to pay the debt service on the garage. And in its first year, Disney Hall scheduled exactly 128 concerts. The parking garage, ostensibly designed to serve the Philharmonic, now has the Philharmonic serving it; the minimum parking requirements have led to a minimum concert requirement.

The money spent on parking has altered the hall in other ways too by shifting its design toward drivers and away from pedestrians. The presence of a six-story subterranean garage means most concert patrons arrive from underneath, rather than outside, the hall. The hall's designers clearly understood this, and so while the hall has a fairly impressive street entrance, its more magisterial gateway is a vertical one: an "escalator cascade" that flows up from the parking structure and ends in the foyer. This has profound implications for street life. A concertgoer can now drive to Disney Hall, park beneath it, ride up into it, see a show, and then reverse the whole process—and never set foot on a sidewalk in downtown Los Angeles. The full experience of an iconic Los Angeles building begins and ends in its parking garage, not in the city itself.

Visitors to downtown San Francisco are unlikely to have such a privatized and encapsulated experience. When a concert or theater performance lets out in San Francisco, people stream onto the sidewalks, strolling past the restaurants, bars, bookstores, and flower shops that are open and well lit. For those who have driven, it is a long walk to their cars, which are probably in a public facility unattached to any specific restaurant or shop. The presence of open shops and people on the street encourages other people to be out as well. People want to be on streets with other people, and they avoid streets that are empty because empty streets are eerie and menacing. Although the absence of parking requirements does not guarantee a vibrant area, their presence certainly inhibits it. "The more downtown is broken up and interspersed with parking lots and garages," Jane Jacobs argued in 1962, "the duller and deader it becomes ... and there is nothing more repellent than a dead downtown" (Jacobs 1997, 19).

THE DENSITY OF PARKING

In the end, what sets downtown Los Angeles apart from other cities is not its sprawl or its human density. Rather, it is its high human density combined with its high *parking* density. If you took all of the parking spaces in the Los Angeles CBD and spread them across a surface lot, they would cover 81 percent of the CBD's land area. We call this ratio—of parking area to total land area—the "parking coverage rate," and it is higher in downtown Los Angeles than in any other downtown on earth. In San Francisco, for instance, the coverage rate is 31 percent, and in New York it is only 18 percent.

The density of parking depends on both the density of jobs and the number of parking spaces per job. Consider the CBDs of Phoenix, San Francisco, and Los Angeles, which are roughly the same size. Why does Phoenix, which most people would consider the most auto-oriented of the three cities, have the lowest parking coverage rate, at 25 percent? Phoenix has the highest number of parking spaces per job, but also by far the fewest jobs. It has a lot of parking for not many people, and for that reason many commuters to the Phoenix CBD drive alone to work. San Francisco, by contrast, has a lot of people and very little parking—a function of its ordinances that limit parking spaces. This helps explain why many commuters to downtown San Francisco walk, carpool, or ride transit—and contribute to a vibrant CBD by doing so. Although San Francisco has over eight times as many jobs as Phoenix, its parking coverage rate is only slightly higher, at 31 percent.

And what about Los Angeles? Downtown Los Angeles has more than three times as many parking spaces as Phoenix, but it also has five times as many jobs. Compared to San Francisco, Los Angeles has fewer jobs but more than twice as many parking spaces. As a result, its parking coverage rate, at 81 percent, is higher than both of the other cities combined. Los Angeles is both car-oriented *and* dense; it approaches the human density of San Francisco but dilutes it with the parking supply of a suburb. Any benefits Los Angeles might derive from its density are offset by its relentless accommodation of the automobile.

This car-oriented density creates something different from plain old sprawl. Los Angeles is dense and getting denser, but so long as its zoning assumes that almost every new person will also bring a car—and requires parking for that car—it will never develop the sort

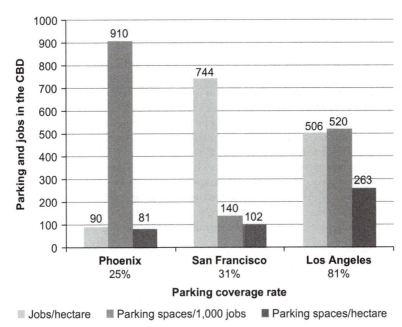

Figure 2-1 Parking and jobs in the Phoenix, San Francisco, and Los Angeles central business districts

Source: ACCESS, Fall 2004

of vital core we associate with older urban centers. The need to house humans might push toward an increasingly dense center, but the zoning requirement to house cars pushes back, sending development outward. With off-street parking requirements, higher density simply brings more cars and more congestion, as well as increased disruptions in the urban fabric, with money directed away from buildings and toward parking lots.

CONCLUSION

"The right to access every building in the city by private motorcar," Lewis Mumford wrote in 1961, "in an age when everyone owns such a vehicle, is actually the right to destroy the city." Mumford meant not physical destruction, of course, but loss of the cohesion that can make a CBD more than the sum of its parts. Parking requirements go a long way toward making downtown Los Angeles little more than a group of buildings, each a destination in its own right, to be parked at and departed from, and not part of some larger whole. This missing sense of urbanity—subjective though that term may be—might explain why people often react with disbelief when they are told Los Angeles sprawls less than New York or San Francisco.

So what should we do? We could start by admitting that there is such a thing as too much parking. So long as we continue to make minimum parking requirements a condition of development, we subordinate almost every other function of our cities to the need for free parking. But free parking—indeed, parking in general—is not what makes cities great. It doesn't create Manhattan, and it doesn't make downtown San Francisco. Urbanists who admire these cities should call for other areas to mimic not simply their density, but also their willingness to limit rather than require parking. Perhaps the simplest and most productive reform of American zoning would be to declare that all existing off-street parking requirements are maximums rather than minimums. From that point, we could let the market take care of parking and let city planners take care of the many vital issues that really demand their attention.

REFERENCES AND FURTHER READING

Jacobs, Jane. 1997. "Downtown Planning," in *Ideas That Matter, the Worlds of Jane Jacobs,* edited by Max Allen. Owen Sound, Ontario: The Ginger Press, pp. 17–20.

This chapter first appeared in the Journal of Urban Planning and Development *131, no. 4 (December 2005).*

CHAPTER

3

The High Cost of Parking Requirements

By Donald Shoup

This chapter examines how parking requirements can dramatically increase the cost of constructing new buildings. If planners do not know how much required parking spaces cost, they cannot know how much the parking requirements increase the cost of development.

THE COST OF REQUIRED PARKING SPACES

Off-street parking requirements have put a cloak of invisibility over the cost of parking spaces. If most parking is free, how could parking spaces cost very much? Because construction costs vary by location, there is no single measure of how much a parking space costs, but we can estimate the price tag in different locations by using published estimates of local construction costs. Rider Levett Bucknall (RLB), an international consulting firm that specializes in estimating real estate construction costs, publishes quarterly cost estimates for several real estate categories in cities around the world, including 12 cities in the United States. Table 3-1 presents RLB's estimates of the average cost of parking spaces in these 12 American cities in 2012. Even within the same city, the cost can vary according to the soil conditions, the height of the water table, the shape of the site, and many other factors. RLB therefore reports both a low and a high construction cost; for simplicity, I have used the average of these two costs for each city.

Columns 1 and 2 show the average cost per square foot to build underground and aboveground parking structures. The average parking space, including the access aisles, occupies about 330 square feet

Table 3-1 The Construction Cost of a Parking Space

City	Construction Cost per Square Foot		Construction Cost per Space	
	Underground	Aboveground	Underground	Aboveground
	$/sq ft (1)	$/sq ft (2)	$/space (3)=(1)x330	$/space (4)=(2)x330
Boston	$95	$75	$31,000	$25,000
Chicago	$110	$88	$36,000	$29,000
Denver	$78	$55	$26,000	$18,000
Honolulu	$145	$75	$48,000	$25,000
Las Vegas	$105	$68	$35,000	$22,000
Los Angeles	$108	$83	$35,000	$27,000
New York	$105	$85	$35,000	$28,000
Phoenix	$80	$53	$26,000	$17,000
Portland	$105	$78	$35,000	$26,000
San Francisco	$115	$88	$38,000	$29,000
Seattle	$105	$75	$35,000	$25,000
Washington, DC	$88	$68	$29,000	$22,000
Average	$101	$71	$33,000	$24,000

(31 square meters). Given this size, Column 3 shows the cost per parking space for an underground garage. For example, the average cost of constructing an underground garage in Boston is $95 per square foot, and the average space occupies 330 square feet, so the average cost of a parking space is $31,000 ($95 × 330). Across the 12 cities, the average cost per space ranges from a low of $26,000 in Phoenix to a high of $48,000 in Honolulu, with an overall average of $34,000 per space. For an aboveground garage, the cost per space ranges from $17,000 in Phoenix to $29,000 in Chicago and San Francisco, with an average of $24,000.

These estimates refer to the cost of *constructing* a parking space. For an aboveground garage, the land beneath the garage is another cost. Underground garages also occupy space that could be used for other purposes, such as storage and mechanical equipment, and the opportunity cost of this space has been called the underground land value. Because numbers in Table 3-1 do not include the cost of land, they underestimate the total cost of parking spaces (*The High Cost of Free Parking*, Chapter 6).

To put the cost of parking spaces in perspective, we can compare this cost with the value of the vehicles parked in them. In 2009, the U.S. Department of Commerce estimated that the total value of the nation's 246 million motor vehicles was $1.3 trillion (Tables 723 and 1096 in the 2012 Statistical Abstract of the United States). The average value of a motor vehicle was therefore only $5,200. (This average value is low because the median age of the fleet was 10.3 years in 2009.) Because the average cost of an underground parking space is $34,000, the average vehicle is therefore worth only 15 percent of this cost

($5,200 ÷ $34,000). And because the average cost of an aboveground garage space is $24,000, the average vehicle is worth only 22 percent of this cost ($5,200 ÷ $24,000).

Parking spaces outnumber cars, and each space can cost much more than a car parked in it, but planners continue to set parking requirements without considering this cost. If I own the average American car worth $5,200, cities require someone else to pay many times more than that to ensure that a parking space will be waiting for me whenever and wherever I drive. Minimum parking requirements amount to an Affordable Parking Act (APA). They make parking more affordable by raising the costs for everything else. So who does pay for all these required parking spaces?

THE COST OF PARKING REQUIREMENTS
FOR OFFICE BUILDINGS

Most cities require parking in proportion to the size of a building, such as 4 spaces per 1,000 square feet of building area. We can use the RLB data on the cost of parking spaces to show how parking requirements increase construction costs. Eight of the 12 cities in Table 3-1 require parking in direct proportion to the size of an office building. We can calculate the cost of required parking per 1,000 square feet of building area in these eight cities by combining the parking requirements with the cost of constructing a parking space.

Table 3-2 shows how the cost of satisfying the parking requirement increases the total cost of constructing an office building. Column 1 shows the minimum parking requirement in each city, although certain areas of the city may have higher or lower requirements according to their specific area plans. Las Vegas, for example, requires 3.3 spaces per 1,000 square feet. Because the average size of a parking space is 330 square feet, this translates to 1,100 square feet of parking per 1,000 square feet of office building (Column 3). Thus, Las Vegas requires parking structures that are bigger than the buildings they serve.

Columns 4 and 5 show the cost per square foot for a Grade A office building and an underground garage. Column 6 shows the cost of constructing 1,000 square feet of an office building, and Column 7 shows the cost of constructing the required parking. Finally, Column 8 shows that the required parking increases the cost of an office building in Las Vegas by 78 percent. Because most developers will provide some parking even if the city does not require it, the parking requirements are not responsible for all the money spent on parking. Nevertheless, Columns 7 and 8 show the minimum cost of the required parking for buildings with underground garages.

Table 3-2 The cost of parking requirements for office buildings—underground parking structure

City	Parking Requirement	Building Area	Parking Area	Construction Cost		Building Cost	Parking Cost	Cost Increase
				Building	Parking			
	Spaces/1,000 sq ft (1)	Sq ft (2)	Sq ft (3)=(1)×(2)×0.33	$/sq ft (4)	$/sq ft (5)	$ (6)=(2)×(4)	$ (7)=(3)×(5)	% (8)=(7)/(6)
Las Vegas	3.3	1,000	1,100	$148	$105	$148,000	$116,000	78%
Phoenix	3.3	1,000	1,100	$128	$80	$128,000	$88,000	69%
Honolulu	2.5	1,000	825	$233	$145	$233,000	$120,000	52%
Portland	2.0	1,000	660	$138	$105	$138,000	$69,000	50%
Los Angeles	2.0	1,000	660	$158	$108	$158,000	$71,000	45%
Denver	2.0	1,000	660	$125	$78	$125,000	$51,000	41%
Seattle	1.0	1,000	330	$138	$105	$138,000	$35,000	25%
New York	1.0	1,000	330	$225	$105	$225,000	$35,000	16%
Average	2.1	1,000	708	$161	$104	$161,625	$73,125	47%

The high cost of structured parking gives developers a strong incentive to build in low-density areas where cheaper land allows surface parking, thus encouraging sprawl. Surface lots cost developers less money, but they cost the city more land that could have better uses.

Table 3-2 ranks cities by how much the required parking increases the cost of office buildings (Column 8). Las Vegas and Phoenix have the highest parking requirements (3.3 spaces per 1,000 square feet) and the highest cost increases (78 percent and 69 percent). Seattle and New York have the lowest parking requirements (1 space per 1,000 square feet) and the lowest cost increases (25 percent and 16 percent). The last row shows that the required parking increases the average cost of an office building by 47 percent.

Table 3-2 shows the results for underground parking. Table 3-3 shows the same calculations for an aboveground garage. On average, the cost of providing the required parking in an aboveground structure adds 30 percent to the cost of an office building. Figure 3-1 compares these results from Tables 3-2 and 3-3. The higher the parking requirement, the more it costs to construct an office building.

The average parking requirement for office buildings in these eight cities is only 2.1 spaces per 1,000 square feet, which is lower than in most American cities. One survey of 117 cities, for example, found that the median parking requirement for office buildings was 4 spaces per 1,000 square feet, which is almost double the average requirement in Tables 3-2 and 3-3. Some planners call this requirement of 4 parking spaces per 1,000 square feet for office buildings the "golden rule" or "magic number" (*The High Cost of Free Parking*, 612–13).

THE COST OF PARKING REQUIREMENTS FOR SHOPPING CENTERS

Because RLB also provides data on the cost of building shopping centers, we can use the method described above to estimate how parking requirements increase the cost of building a shopping center. Tables 3-4 and 3-5 and Figure 3-2 show these estimates for underground and aboveground parking structures.

Cities usually require more parking for shopping centers than for office buildings. Los Angeles's requirement of 4 spaces per 1,000 square feet, for example, leads to parking lots that are 32 percent larger than the shopping centers they serve. For underground parking, this requirement increases the cost of building a shopping center by 93 percent; for an aboveground garage, the cost increase is 67 percent. In contrast, New York City's requirement of 1 space per 1,000 square feet increases the cost of a shopping center by only 18 percent for underground parking

Table 3-3 The cost of parking requirements for office buildings—aboveground parking structure

City	Parking Requirement	Building Area	Parking Area	Construction Cost		Building Cost	Parking Cost	Cost Increase
				Building	Parking			
	Spaces/1,000 sq ft	Sq ft	Sq ft	$/sq ft	$/sq ft	$	$	%
	(1)	(2)	(3)=(1)×(2)×0.33	(4)	(5)	(6)=(2)×(4)	(7)=(3)×(5)	(8)=(7)/(6)
Las Vegas	3.3	1,000	1,100	$148	$68	$148,000	$74,000	50%
Phoenix	3.3	1,000	1,100	$128	$53	$128,000	$58,000	45%
Portland	2.0	1,000	660	$138	$75	$138,000	$50,000	36%
Los Angeles	2.0	1,000	660	$158	$78	$158,000	$51,000	32%
Honolulu	2.5	1,000	825	$233	$83	$233,000	$68,000	29%
Denver	2.0	1,000	660	$125	$55	$125,000	$36,000	29%
Seattle	1.0	1,000	330	$138	$75	$138,000	$25,000	18%
New York	1.0	1,000	330	$225	$85	$225,000	$28,000	12%
Average	2.1	1,000	708	$161	$71	$161,625	$48,750	30%

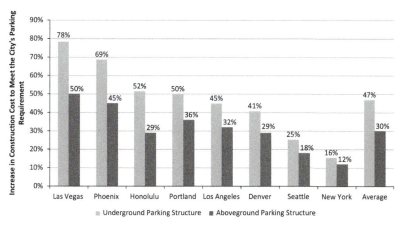

Figure 3-1 How parking requirements increase the cost of constructing office buildings

and 14 percent for an aboveground garage. On average, the required off-street parking increases construction costs by 53 percent if underground and by 37 percent if aboveground.

The average parking requirement for shopping centers in these eight cities is only 2.8 spaces per 1,000 square feet, which is lower than in most American cities. The Urban Land Institute recommends at least 4 spaces per 1,000 square feet for small shopping centers, and 5 spaces per 1,000 square feet for large shopping centers (*The High Cost of Free Parking*, 84–87). Five parking spaces per 1,000 square feet would increase the cost of constructing a large shopping center by 95 percent if underground, and by 66 percent if aboveground.

THE COST OF PARKING REQUIREMENTS FOR APARTMENT BUILDINGS

City planners cannot predict how many parking spaces an apartment needs any more than they can predict how many cars a family needs. But the parking requirements for apartments help to predict how many cars a family will own. Even when planners try to measure the "need" for parking by observing the number of cars parked at existing buildings, they often require too much. Seattle's Right Size Parking Project, for instance, surveyed occupancy at over 200 apartment buildings in the region in 2012. The parking requirements in suburban Seattle were, on average, 0.4 spaces per dwelling unit greater than the observed parking occupancy (King County Metro 2013, 11). Table 3-1 shows

Table 3-4 The cost of parking requirements for shopping centers–underground parking structure

City	Parking Requirement	Building Area	Parking Area	Construction Cost		Building Cost	Parking Cost	Cost Increase
				Building	Parking			
	Spaces/1,000 sq ft	Sq ft	Sq ft	$/sq ft	$/sq ft	$	$	%
	(1)	(2)	(3)=(1)x(330)	(4)	(5)	(6)=(2)x(4)	(7)=(3)x(5)	(8)=(7)/(6)
Los Angeles	4.0	1,000	1,320	$153	$108	$153,000	$142,000	93%
Phoenix	3.3	1,000	1,100	$135	$80	$135,000	$88,000	65%
Honolulu	3.3	1,000	1,100	$255	$145	$255,000	$160,000	63%
Denver	2.5	1,000	825	$105	$78	$105,000	$64,000	61%
Las Vegas	4.0	1,000	1,320	$298	$105	$298,000	$139,000	47%
Portland	2.0	1,000	660	$153	$105	$153,000	$69,000	45%
Seattle	2.0	1,000	660	$158	$105	$158,000	$69,000	44%
New York	1.0	1,000	330	$195	$105	$195,000	$35,000	18%
Average	2.8	1,000	914	$181	$104	$181,500	$95,750	53%

Table 3-5 The cost of parking required for shopping centers—aboveground parking structure

City	Parking Requirement	Building Area	Parking Area	Construction Cost		Building Cost	Parking Cost	Cost Increase
				Building	Parking			
	Spaces/1,000 sq ft	Sq ft	Sq ft	$/sq ft	$/sq ft	$	$	%
	(1)	(2)	(3)=(1)×(2)×0.33	(4)	(5)	(6)=(2)×(4)	(7)=(3)×(5)	(8)=(7)/(6)
Los Angeles	4.0	1,000	1,320	$153	$78	$153,000	$102,000	67%
Phoenix	3.3	1,000	1,100	$135	$53	$135,000	$58,000	43%
Denver	2.5	1,000	825	$105	$55	$105,000	$45,000	43%
Honolulu	3.3	1,000	1,100	$255	$83	$255,000	$91,000	36%
Portland	2.0	1,000	660	$153	$75	$153,000	$50,000	33%
Seattle	2.0	1,000	660	$158	$75	$158,000	$50,000	32%
Las Vegas	4.0	1,000	1,320	$298	$68	$298,000	$89,000	30%
New York	1.0	1,000	330	$195	$85	$195,000	$28,000	14%
Average	2.8	1,000	914	$181	$71	$181,500	$64,125	37%

Source: Rider Levett Bucknall, Quarterly Construction Cost Report, Fourth Quarter 2012

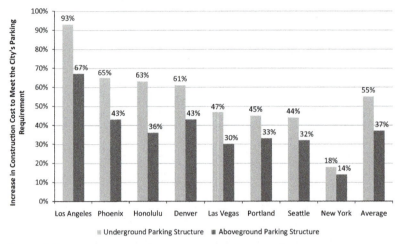

Figure 3-2   How parking requirements increase the cost of shopping centers

that underground parking costs $35,000 per space in Seattle, and aboveground parking costs $25,000 per space. These figures suggest that the parking requirements in suburban Seattle require developers to spend between $10,000 (0.4 × $25,000) and $14,000 (0.4 × $35,000) per apartment to provide *unused* parking spaces.

The typical requirement of two spaces per apartment forces developers to spend at least $70,000 per dwelling unit for parking if the spaces are underground, or $50,000 per dwelling unit if the spaces are in an aboveground structure. These estimates refer to the *average* cost of building a parking space. The *marginal* cost of a parking space, however, can be far higher due to natural break points in the cost of building a parking structure. For example, a dramatic break point occurs with the construction of a second level of underground parking because it requires removing several spaces on the first level to provide a ramp to the lower level. Therefore, the marginal cost of the first space on the second level can be far higher than the average cost of the spaces on the first level. This high marginal cost of excavating a second parking level severely limits what developers can build on a site.

To demonstrate how break points in the cost of building a garage affect development decisions, Figure 3-3 shows a four-story apartment building in Los Angeles on a typical lot that is 50 feet (15 meters) wide and 130 feet (40 meters) deep. The city's R3 zoning allows eight apartments on the site, and the city's parking requirement is 2.25 spaces per unit. Eight apartments would therefore require 18 parking spaces (8 × 2.25), but only 16 spaces could be squeezed onto one level of underground parking (Figure 3-4 shows how tightly the spaces are packed).

Figure 3-3   Seven-unit apartment building on a 50 × 130 foot lot (47 units per acre)

Photo credit: Donald Shoup

Figure 3-4   Tandem compact parking space in underground garage

Photo credit: Donald Shoup

In response, the developer built only seven apartments on the site, rather than excavate a second level of parking to provide two additional spaces for the eighth apartment (Shoup 2008).

In this case, the parking requirement, not the limit on density, constrained the number of apartments. If the city had allowed the developer to provide only two parking spaces per apartment, the developer could have built eight apartments and 16 parking spaces. The prohibitively high *marginal* cost of two more spaces on a second underground level, however, reduced the feasible number of dwellings from eight to seven, or by 13 percent.

Where land is expensive and the parking is underground, the high cost of the required parking per apartment creates an economic incentive to build larger and more expensive apartments than they would without parking requirements. In the example above, *adding* another apartment requires building another 2.25 parking spaces, but *enlarging* an apartment does not.

Because land values are higher in the center of the city, parking requirements create an economic incentive to build larger apartments in the city center. By increasing the construction cost per square foot, and also increasing the number of square feet per apartment, parking requirements increase both the size and cost of apartments in the center of the city (*The High Cost of Free Parking*, 143–45). In a housing market without parking requirements, higher land values would produce smaller, not larger, apartments in the center of the city.

Repealing or reducing a city's parking requirement does *not* mean that developers won't provide parking. Even without parking requirements, the developer in the example above would probably have built a garage with 16 spaces because the site told the developer that 16 spaces were feasible. With parking requirements, however, the 16-car garage told the developer that only seven apartments were feasible. More parking for cars means less housing for people.

By increasing the cost of development, parking requirements can reduce the supply and increase the price of real estate in two ways. First, parking requirements can reduce the density of what gets built, as in the 13 percent reduction in apartments in the example above. Parking requirements increase the density of cars but reduce the density of people (Manville, Beata, and Shoup 2012). Because parking requirements reduce the supply of apartments, they increase the price of housing. On some days, planners think about housing affordability, but on most days they think about parking requirements and forget about housing affordability.

Second, parking requirements not only reduce the density on sites that are developed, but also reduce the number of sites that are developed. If the required parking spaces increase the cost of constructing a building by more than they increase the market value of the building, they will reduce the residual value of land (the market value of the most profitable development that could be constructed on a site minus the cost of constructing it). For example, if the best choice for development on a site would cost $750,000 to construct and would have a market value of $1 million, the residual value for the land is $250,000. If $250,000 is not enough to pay for buying and demolishing an existing building on the site, redevelopment won't happen. The residual land value of a site for redevelopment must be greater than the value of the land and existing building on the site before a developer can buy the building, clear the site, and make a profit on a new development. Therefore, if minimum parking requirements reduce residual land values, they make redevelopment to increase the housing supply less likely.

Cities discourage historic preservation if they require additional parking when a rental apartment building is converted to condominium ownership. Los Angeles requires at least 1.5 spaces per unit before an apartment building can be converted to owner-occupancy (*The High Cost of Free Parking*, 157). Because most old buildings do not have 1.5 parking spaces per apartment, the solution is often to reduce the number of apartments to match the number of parking spaces available, either by combining small apartments to create fewer but larger and more expensive ones, or by demolishing some apartments and converting the land to parking. More commonly, developers demolish the rental apartment house and build a new condominium with all the required parking. Many residents of historic buildings would prefer to own rather than to rent their apartments, but parking requirements preclude this opportunity. In practice, the law discriminates against tenants who would like to own their housing but have only one car or none.

CIRCULAR PARKING REQUIREMENTS

Off-street parking requirements are a strong planning intervention based on scant, unreliable evidence. Planners who do not know how many cars every family needs cannot know how many parking spaces every residence needs. And because the number of available parking spaces affects the number of cars a family will own, the number of cars a family owns cannot predict the number of parking spaces to require. Parking requirements increase the demand for cars, and then the number of cars increases the parking requirements. It's like requiring closet space in every residence based on how much stuff planners think people will want to store, and then using the amount of stuff stored in the required closets to set the minimum closet requirements.

Because city planners and elected officials don't know how much it costs to construct a parking space, they can't take this cost into consideration when deciding how many spaces to require. Instead, they often use the occupancy of parking spaces at existing buildings to estimate the "need" for parking spaces at new buildings, as though the cost of a space was irrelevant. Since most drivers park free at existing buildings, parking requirements based on existing occupancy at sites with free parking will therefore reflect the demand for *free* parking, no matter how much the required spaces cost. To use a familiar analogy, if pizza were free, would there ever be enough pizza? Charging drivers a price for parking that is high enough to cover the cost of constructing and operating a garage would reduce the parking occupancy rates that planners use to estimate parking requirements.

The required parking spaces are cemented into each new development and thus force up the supply of parking for long into the future. The demand for parking, however, may be declining. Transportation network companies (Uber and Lyft) and driverless cars are two technologies that can reduce the demand for parking. Conversely, market-priced parking can increase the demand for shared and driverless cars, because high parking prices at destinations increase the desire to rideshare. By reducing the market price of parking and ignoring the role of future technology, parking requirements blunt the economic incentive to adopt new technology that reduces the demand for parking.

MINIMAL PARKING REQUIREMENTS

Minimum parking requirements often force developers to provide more parking than the market demands or to construct smaller buildings than the zoning allows. Parking requirements promote an unsustainable city. If cities require ample off-street parking everywhere, most people will continue to drive everywhere, even if Santa Claus delivers a great transit system. Cities get the traffic they plan for and the behavior they subsidize.

City planners should begin to consider minimal, not minimum, parking requirements. "Minimal" means barely adequate, or the smallest possible number, depending on the context. A minimal parking requirement would thus require planners to estimate an adequate number of parking spaces after taking all the costs into account. For example, can the adjacent roads handle all the additional traffic caused by the cars that will park in the required spaces? Can the city's air safely absorb all the additional vehicle emissions? Can the earth's atmosphere safely absorb all the additional carbon emissions? How will the required parking spaces increase the cost of housing and all other real estate? And who will pay for all the required parking spaces?

If planners are faced with the impossible task of calculating the costs and benefits of parking spaces required for every building in every location, they will appreciate the idea of going Dutch on parking: Each driver can pay for his or her own parking, and planners should abandon the idea of parking requirements. If you pay for your parking and I pay for mine, someone who does not own a car will not pay anything for parking. Paying for parking should be the driver's responsibility, not the government's.

If cities don't want to abandon parking requirements altogether, they can start by reducing the minimum number of spaces required until they reach a minimal number that seems reasonable. Eventually, they might reinterpret this to mean the maximum number of spaces allowed, not the minimum number required. With only a slight change in terminology, cities can require developers to provide no more than an adequate number of parking spaces.

As Zhan Guo (Chapter 15) found in London, removing the minimum parking requirements will greatly reduce the supply of new parking spaces, even without imposing a maximum parking limit. Removing a minimum parking requirement can be far important than imposing a maximum parking limit, and politically easier. If cities do impose maximum parking limits, however, they can offer developers the option to pay per-space fees if they want to exceed the maximum number of spaces allowed, just as cities already offer developers the option to pay in-lieu fees if they want to provide fewer than the minimum number of parking spaces required.

CONCLUSION

The politics that produce parking requirements are understandable, but their high costs are indefensible. Irrefutable evidence on the health cost of smoking eventually led many people to kick their addiction to tobacco. I hope evidence about the high cost of required parking spaces will eventually lead cities to kick their addiction to parking requirements.

REFERENCES AND FURTHER READING

King County, Washington, Metro. 2013. "King County Parking Requirements and Utilization Gap Analysis," July 12. metro.kingcounty.gov/up/projects/right-size-parking/pdf/rsp-pricingpilotrfi-080613.pdf

Manville, Michael, Alex Beata, and Donald Shoup. 2013. "Turning Housing into Driving: Parking Requirements and Density in Los Angeles and New York." *Housing Policy Debate* 23, no. 2: 350–75.

Shoup, Donald. 2011. *The High Cost of Free Parking*. Revised edition. Chicago: Planners Press.

Shoup, Donald. 2008. "Graduated Density Zoning." *Journal of Planning Education and Research* 28, no. 2: 161–79.

This chapter was condensed from "The High Cost of Minimum Parking Requirements," in Parking Issues and Policies, *edited by Stephen Ison and Corinne Mulley. Bingley, United Kingdom: Emerald Group Publishing Company, 2014.*

4

The Unequal Burden of Parking Requirements

By Donald Shoup

Cities require off-street parking for every building without considering how the parking requirements place a heavy burden on poor people. A single parking space can cost far more than the net worth of many American households. Table 3-1 in Chapter 3 shows that the average construction cost (excluding land cost) for parking structures in 12 American cities in 2012 was $24,000 per space for aboveground garages, and $34,000 per space for underground parking.

By comparison, in 2011 the median net worth (the value of assets minus debts) was only $7,700 for Hispanic households and $6,300 for African-American households in the U.S. (Figure 4-1). One space in a parking structure therefore costs at least three times the net worth of more than half of all Hispanic and African-American households in the country. Because cities require parking spaces at home, work, stores, restaurants, churches, schools, and everywhere else, there are several required parking spaces for every household.

Group	Median Net Worth
All Households	$68,828
White	$89,537
Hispanic	$7,683
Black	$6,314

Figure 4-1   Median net worth of U.S. households, 2011

Source: U.S. Census Bureau, Net Worth and Asset Ownership of Households, 2011, Table 4.

Much of household net worth comes from equity in owner-occupied housing, which is illiquid. Excluding home equity, the median net worth in the U.S. was much lower: $16,900 for all households, $4,000 for Hispanic households, and $2,100 for African-American households.

Many families have a negative net worth because their debts exceed their assets: 18 percent of all households, 29 percent of Hispanic households, and 34 percent of African-households had zero or negative net worth in 2011 (Figure 4-2). The only way most of these indebted people can navigate through the parking-induced sprawl where they live is to buy a car, which they then often must finance at a high, subprime interest rate. In a misguided attempt to provide enough parking for everyone, cities have inadvertently created a serious economic injustice by forcing poor people to pay for parking spaces they can ill afford.

This low or negative net wealth suggests that many families live from paycheck to paycheck. To assess households' financial reserves, in 2015 the Federal Reserve Board (2016, 22) conducted a survey asking respondents how they would pay for a $400 emergency expense. Forty-six percent said that they would have to cover the expense by selling something, or borrowing the money, or would not be able to come up with the $400 at all. Although one parking space costs more than many drivers are worth, and almost half of all families are living hand to mouth, cities compel every household to pay for several off-street parking spaces even if they are too poor to own a car.

Table 4-1 shows another way to look at America's ability to afford all the parking cities require. Column 1 ranks 24 countries according to their median net wealth per adult in 2014. The U.S. is in 23rd place.

Column 2 shows the *mean* wealth per adult. The U.S. jumps to fifth place because the top half of the U.S. population includes many people with very high wealth. Only Switzerland, Australia, Iceland, and Norway have a higher mean wealth per adult.

Finally, Column 3 divides the mean wealth by the median wealth to get a rough measure of inequality in each country, and the U.S. climbs to number 1. Because the top half in the U.S. are much richer than the

Group	Share with Negative Net Worth
All Households	18%
White	16%
Hispanic	29%
Black	34%

Figure 4-2 Share of U.S. households with zero or negative net worth, 2011

Source: U.S. Census Bureau, Net Worth and Asset Ownership of Households, 2011, Table 4.

Table 4-1 International data on mean and median net wealth per adult

Median Net Wealth per Adult			Mean Net Wealth per Adult			Mean ÷ Median		
(1)			(2)			(3)		
1	Australia	$225,337	1	Switzerland	$580,666	1	United States	6.5
2	Belgium	$172,947	2	Australia	$430,777	2	Switzerland	5.4
3	Iceland	$164,193	3	Iceland	$362,982	3	Sweden	5.2
4	Luxembourg	$156,267	4	Norway	$358,655	4	Norway	4.1
5	Italy	$142,296	5	United States	$347,845	5	Germany	3.9
6	France	$140,638	6	Luxembourg	$340,836	6	Israel	3.3
7	United Kingdom	$130,590	7	Sweden	$332,616	7	Taiwan	2.8
8	Japan	$112,998	8	France	$317,292	8	Canada	2.8
9	Singapore	$109,250	9	Belgium	$300,850	9	Qatar	2.7
10	Switzerland	$106,887	10	United Kingdom	$292,621	10	Singapore	2.7
11	Canada	$98,756	11	Singapore	$289,902	11	New Zealand	2.5
12	Netherlands	$93,116	12	Canada	$274,543	12	Netherlands	2.3
13	Finland	$88,130	13	Italy	$255,880	13	France	2.3
14	Norway	$86,953	14	Japan	$222,150	14	United Kingdom	2.2
15	New Zealand	$82,610	15	Germany	$211,049	15	Finland	2.2
16	Spain	$66,752	16	Netherlands	$210,233	16	Iceland	2.2
17	Taiwan	$65,375	17	New Zealand	$204,401	17	Luxembourg	2.2
18	Sweden	$63,376	18	Finland	$196,621	18	Greece	2.1
19	Malta	$63,271	19	Taiwan	$182,756	19	Spain	2.0
20	Qatar	$56,969	20	Israel	$169,064	20	Japan	2.0
21	Germany	$54,090	21	Qatar	$156,096	21	Australia	1.9
22	Greece	$53,365	22	Spain	$134,824	22	Italy	1.8
23	United States	$53,352	23	Malta	$113,724	23	Malta	1.8
24	Israel	$51,346	24	Greece	$111,405	24	Belgium	1.7

Source: Credit Suisse Global Wealth Databook, 2014

bottom half, the U.S. mean is 6.5 times the median, a higher ratio than in any other country in this list. Among the most prosperous nations, the U.S. has the greatest inequality because it has an unusually rich top half and an unusually poor bottom half.

When we focus on the ranking in Column 1, our median net wealth is quite low compared to many other countries. The U.S. has more cars per capita than all other countries in large part because our cities require so many parking spaces (*The High Cost of Free Parking*, Chapter 1). For example, the median net wealth per adult in the United Kingdom ($139,590) is 145 percent greater than the median net wealth per adult in the United States ($53,352). Nevertheless, the U.S. (806 vehicles per 1,000 persons) has 54 percent more vehicles per capita than the UK (519 vehicles per 1,000 persons). Our wealth does not explain our greater number of cars. Instead, our high parking requirements help to explain our greater number of cars. We have strip-mined our cities to provide free parking. America may the first nation to drive to the poorhouse, but we will park free when we get there.

City planners cannot do much to counter the inequality of wealth, but they can help to reform off-street parking requirements that unfairly place heavy burdens on minorities and the poor.

REFERENCES AND FURTHER READING

Credit Suisse Global Wealth Databook. 2014. http://economics.uwo.ca/people/davies_docs/credit-suisse-global-wealth-report-2014.pdf

Shoup, Donald. 2011. *The High Cost of Free Parking*. Revised edition. Chicago: Planners Press.

U.S. Federal Reserve Board of Governors. 2016. *Report on the Economic Well-Being of U.S. Households in 2015*. Washington, DC: Board of Governors of the Federal Reserve System. https://www.federalreserve.gov/2015-report-economic-well-being-us-households-201605.pdf

5

Parking Mismanagement: An R$_X$ for Congestion

By Rachel Weinberger

It was once believed that the main cause of urban congestion was a lack of available parking. As early as the 1920s, Bostonians battled over the question of whether more road space or tighter rules on parking would better solve their congestion problem. By the 1960s, the question seemed settled; most cities in the U.S. decided that more abundant parking would be the best way to reduce congestion, and they enshrined minimum parking requirements for new development in their zoning and building codes.

But, like the proverbial chicken and egg, it turns out that parking begets driving, and driving demands parking. In the 1980s, Portland, Oregon, Boston, Massachusetts, and New York, New York, running afoul of the Clean Air Act, determined that limiting parking would decrease driving and congestion; they made parking maximums on new construction a central element of their efforts to comply with the law. And while on-street parking is still a hotly contested commodity in many cities, the preponderance of evidence suggests that off-street parking is oversupplied far more frequently than it is undersupplied. In San Francisco, the perceived parking shortage seemed so acute that in 2008 the Federal Highway Administration assisted the city with an experiment to adjust meter prices up and down to push demand away from the busiest locations and attract it to the areas of excess supply. During the experiment, city officials found they consistently had to drop meter prices to attract more parkers to underused—that is, oversupplied—off-street municipal lots.

In spite of opposing evidence, many cities cling tenaciously to the belief that they can reduce congestion by building new municipal lots and garages in their commercial districts and by requiring developers to include off-street parking in new developments. Little do they realize that adding parking spaces, without managing the parking system, is itself a potential cause of the very problem they seek to fix. And, as if the decisions of whether to own a car and then whether to use that car were independent of the supply characteristics of the overall transportation system, policymakers often ask, what is the right amount of parking for any given building? But the decisions to own and use a car are not independent of the broader transportation system. The "right" amount of parking thus depends on how many cars, how much driving, and how much congestion the community wants.

In this chapter, I make the case that parking is a critical component of automobile-enabling infrastructure. I explain, in terms of basic microeconomics, why more parking would lead to more driving. Then I present empirical evidence of this relationship from a study conducted in New York City. Previous research shows that limited parking supply at "destinations," like central business districts, is associated with higher transit and reduced car use; conversely, increasing the parking supply results in lower transit use and more driving. This study is focused on the impact of parking availability at the "origin" or residential end of a trip.

PARKING AS AUTOMOBILE-ENABLING INFRASTRUCTURE

Though some argue that parking supply is, or should be, a function of land use—and, indeed, cities typically regulate it as such—here I argue it is a fundamental element of the transportation system. Transportation systems are made up of rights-of-way, vehicles, and terminals, and these components must be coordinated to work effectively. Bus stops, docks, and airports are obvious terminals for transit, ferries, and planes, respectively. Parking, though seldom considered as such, is the "terminal" for cars in the automobile/highway system. A parking space is where the passenger boards or alights the vehicle; it is where trips begin and end. These elements, rights-of-way, vehicles, and terminals, represent the system supply. How users respond to this supply constitutes demand on the system. As a key element of transportation supply, parking influences individual decisions to drive or own a car. Parking supply affects the demand for *driving* by changing the cost structure of mode-choice decisions. Minimum parking requirements also affect demand for auto ownership by shifting some of the cost of auto ownership from the auto onto the home, thus changing the underlying cost structure of owning a car. Parking policy can be a powerful tool for traffic management; understanding these two effects on demand is critical to leveraging that tool. Regulating off-street parking as a land use without regard to the transportation system creates a devastating mismatch in the transportation-policy sphere.

PARKING INDUCES DRIVING AND DISTORTS MARKETS (IN THEORY)

In spite of (or perhaps because of) a sustained, decades-long policy approach to make both auto use and ownership easier by increasing the capacity of rights-of-way and terminals through the use of zoning, public expenditure, and minimum parking requirements, congestion remains an issue of great concern. Simply put, congestion occurs when the demand for a facility exceeds its capacity. Though intuition suggests that adding capacity (new infrastructure) would reduce congestion, research has repeatedly shown the fallacy of that intuition. Downs (1992 and 2004) shows how building more transportation infrastructure results in greater congestion. Likewise, Mogridge (1997) describes the history of road-capacity policy and how it has achieved the opposite results of those intended.

The principal reason that cities cannot build their way out of congestion is explained by the concepts of latent and induced demand. When capacity is added to relieve congestion, two important effects result: the direct effect of adding more capacity serves latent demand, and the secondary effect of reducing the cost (via faster travel) attracts more users, thus inducing demand. Increasing supply in congested conditions invariably leads to greater demand.

Requiring parking with housing increases the price of housing by adding construction costs, thereby shifting part of the cost of car ownership onto the house. While the effects of required parking on higher housing costs are well documented, much less considered is how bundling parking reduces the marginal cost of car ownership. Anyone who purchases or rents a home that includes an off-street parking space is *de facto* making a pre-payment toward car ownership. The payment is not toward the car directly but toward the expense of owning and operating a car, which includes the cost of storage. Compared with a market where parking is unbundled from housing, the bundle decreases home-ownership (as it is made more expensive) and increases car ownership (as it is made less expensive).

Cities are faced with managing the conflict between two seemingly "normal" goods that may be fundamentally incompatible with one another. Demand for car ownership and use increases with income, but in recent years, so too has the desire for urban living. Wealthier households are bidding for urban living, yet increased car ownership may be impossible to achieve in an environment dense enough to accommodate the variety of amenities that make urban environments most attractive. The conflict between selecting urban living (potentially preferred with rising income) and transit (less preferred with rising income) as a bundle may cause some discomfort among those able to choose, but selecting urban living and car ownership may be impractical if not infeasible—physics seems to preclude it. However, the fact that only 22 percent of households in Manhattan—home to many of that region's wealthiest residents—own cars certainly suggests that many households are willing to trade car ownership for dense urban environments.

PARKING INDUCES DRIVING AND DISTORTS MARKETS (IN PRACTICE)

In a 2006 study, I looked at two similar neighborhoods in New York City: Jackson Heights in Queens, and Park Slope in Brooklyn (Table 5-1). I ran a simulation based on the usual correlates of car use: household income, car ownership, density, employment, and quality of transit connectivity at the trip origin and destination. (In the case of New York City, employment in the government sector is also important, as many government workers are entitled to a parking placard that allows for fairly unrestricted parking across the city.) The simulation results were opposite the expected outcome: Jackson Heights residents, who are on average lower income, own fewer cars, and have similar public-transit connectivity compared to Park Slope, were 45 percent more likely to commute by car to destinations that are well served by transit. Tellingly, the primary difference between the neighborhoods is that in Jackson Heights, a more recently developed area, homes are six times more likely than Park Slope homes to have an on-site driveway or garage (Table 5-2).

In the next phase, I abstracted this finding to the Bronx, Brooklyn, and Queens, systematically examining all neighborhoods in the three New York City boroughs for which residential, off-street parking is possible but potentially scarce. I excluded Manhattan, where only 22 percent of households report having a vehicle available, and Staten Island, which is extremely low-density by New York City standards, where 80 percent of households have one or more vehicles available, and where residential parking abounds.

Lacking data on individuals, the analysis is based on aggregate characteristics and travel behavior at the census tract level. To best control

Table 5-1 Neighborhood characteristics

	Jackson Heights	Park Slope
Demographics		
Occupied housing units	24,900	24,360
Average household size	2.9	2.2
Household per square mile	34,110	26,194
Median household income	$39,566	$60,711
Home ownership (% of households)	27%	34%
Vehicle ownership		
Vehicles per employed resident	0.37	0.38
Households with at least one vehicle	39%	42%
Commuting behavior		
Employed residents	31,190	31,619
Drive or carpool to work	7,029	5,300
Percent auto share	23%	18%
Residents employed in CBD	12,824	16,481
Drive or carpool to CBD	1,004	885
Percent auto share to CBD	7.80%	5.40%

Source: Weinberger, R., M. Seaman, and C. Johnson (2009) Residential Off-street Parking Impacts on Car Ownership, Vehicle Miles Traveled, an Related Carbon Emissions: New York City Case Study. *Transportation Research Record: Journal of the Transportation Research Board.* No. 2118 pp24–30.

Table 5-2 Off-street parking spaces in Jackson Heights and Park Slope

	Jackson Heights	Park Slope
Type of parking		
Spaces in parking lots	605	883
Number of driveways and garages	3,028	533
Total	3,633	1,416
Spaces per Dwelling Unit		
Off-street parking space per Dwelling Unit	0.14	0.06
Off-street space per car owner	0.31	0.12
"On-site" off-street per car owner	0.26	0.05

Source: Weinberger, R., M. Seaman, and C. Johnson (2009) Residential Off-street Parking Impacts on Car Ownership, Vehicle Miles Traveled, and Related Carbon Emissions: New York City Case Study. *Transportation Research Record: Journal of the Transportation Research Board.* No. 2118 pp24–30.

for transportation alternatives at both ends of the trip, I limited the analysis to include only commuters to areas of Manhattan south of 96th Street (an area known as the Manhattan Core) that lie within one-quarter mile of a subway stop. Tract data on income, journey to work, and other characteristics were combined with the New York City's tax-lot data, which allowed me to estimate parking availability.

I posit that the percentage of workers who commute by car from a given census tract in the outer boroughs to a Manhattan work destination is a function of built environment characteristics (such as transit accessibility), socioeconomic characteristics (income), and available off-street parking. I hypothesize that car ownership is a function of available parking and control for it by using a two-stage model. The first stage estimates auto ownership and the second stage estimates auto use.

Satellite imagery from Google Earth, Google Maps, and Bing Maps was used to survey one-, two-, and three-family houses in the Bronx, Queens, and Brooklyn. Using these data, I developed a binary logit model to predict the likelihood of a garage or driveway on the property. I paired the data with information contained in New York's Primary Land Use Tax-lot Output (PLUTO) database, which reports the square footage devoted to parking for residential buildings of four families or greater (parking is summarized in Table 5-3). Using this information, I estimated the amount of parking per dwelling unit for each census tract and regressed parking against propensity to drive to work reported in the Census Transportation Planning Package.

In the two-stage model, I first estimate auto ownership using an array of socio-economic and built environment variables. In addition, I use the percent of population who have moved from other metropolitan statistical areas and those who have moved from other central cities. Variables that are positively correlated with tract-level auto ownership are income, age, household size, home ownership, white population, and off-street parking per dwelling unit. Variables that depress auto ownership are transit accessibility, Black population, and, curiously, percent of government employees. This last observation potentially underscores the effect of "free-parking" on the choice to drive: Although government employees are less likely than others to own a car, they are more likely to *use* their cars to drive to work because many of them have parking permits that allow fairly unrestricted parking across New York City.

Variables in the second stage that depress auto commuting are higher income, median age, household size, transit accessibility, and higher percentage of population reporting Black alone as their race. Increased levels of auto and home ownership, higher percentages of government employees, and more off-street parking contribute to increased auto commuting, even after the question of co-determined commute mode and auto ownership is addressed.

Controlling for median tract income, median age, household size, age of housing stock, vehicle availability, tract-level transit accessibility, transit service, auto ownership, percentage government employees, auto ownership, and race, I find that tracts with higher levels of

Table 5-3   Variables affecting auto ownership and the decision to drive to work

Variable	Auto Ownership	Drive to Work
Average household size	+	−
Percent housing owner occupied	+	+
Median age	+	−
Median income	+	−
Percent population reporting race "White Alone"	+	+
Percent population reporting race "Black Alone"	−	−
Transit accessibility	−	−
Percent government employees	−	+
Off-street parking per dwelling unit	+	+

on-site parking have higher levels of auto commuting to the transit-rich Manhattan Core. The results are summarized in Table 5-3; as noted, all variables are measured at the census tract level.

CONCLUSION

While a true behavioral study with disaggregate data could make a stronger case, the ecological study performed here provides important insights of how parking at home affects auto ownership and commute mode choice. The model demonstrates a clear relationship between increased access to guaranteed parking at home and the propensity to drive to work in the Manhattan Core. Off-street parking correlates to driving to work both indirectly (by easing car ownership) and directly (by easing car use). Guaranteed parking at home contributes to a worker's decision to drive to work.

In dense neighborhoods where on-site parking is relatively scarce, competition for curb space implies search costs and additional effort to walk from the parking spot to home or other destinations. With private on-site parking, the search costs and additional effort are eliminated; travelers who have access to such parking face a different utility constellation than travelers without access to such parking at home. The guaranteed spot makes auto use a more attractive option.

City planning departments across the U.S. make decisions about parking supply in order to mitigate potential local spot shortages. Such policy considerations do not take into account induced behaviors demonstrated in this research. With the exception of most of Manhattan and a small part of Queens, where parking provision is highly restricted as part of the city's effort to maintain compliance with the Clean Air Act, off-street parking is required for all parcels in the city. Minimum parking requirements are supported by the logic: if current residents *believe* parking demands from new development will not create additional shortages, they will find new development less objectionable. To the extent that additional driving is the product of increased parking supply, however, more parking produces more traffic congestion.

An important question that is not addressed in this model is location self-selection. It is highly conceivable that people who prefer to drive will self-select into districts that provide a high level of service for auto use—including ample protected parking. For precisely this reason, this research demonstrates that parking should be further restricted in transit-rich zones. From a policy perspective, people with a strong preference to drive should be discouraged from living in transit-rich areas because they potentially "waste" the transit resource.

The idea that reducing minimum parking requirements, and, indeed, implementing parking maximums, has the effect of reducing auto use is well established. The rationale behind implementing parking maximums is to reduce emissions and comply with Clean Air Act requirements. Armed now with empirical knowledge that minimum parking requirements will lead to additional driving, cities should consider these facts when crafting their residential parking policies.

REFERENCES AND FURTHER READING

Downs, Anthony. 1992. *Stuck in Traffic*. Washington, D.C.: Brookings Institution.

Downs, Anthony. 2004. *Still Stuck in Traffic*. Washington, D.C.: Brookings Institution.

Mogridge, Martin. 1997. "The Self-defeating Nature of Urban Road Capacity Policy: A Review of Theories, Disputes and Available Evidence." *Transport Policy* 4: 5–23.

Weinberger, Rachel. 2012. "Death by a Thousand Curb-Cuts: Evidence on the Effect of Minimum Parking Requirements on the Choice to Drive." *Transport Policy* 20: 93–102.

Weinberger, R., M. Seaman, and C. Johnson. 2009. "Residential Off-street Parking Impacts on Car Ownership, Vehicle Miles Traveled, an Related Carbon Emissions: New York City Case Study." *Transportation Research Record: Journal of the Transportation Research Board* 2118: 24–30.

6

The United States
of Parking

By Seth Goodman

Residents of the U.S. generally expect to pay for the food they eat, the clothing they wear, and the homes they live in, but when looking for a parking spot, they usually expect to find one for free. Parking is the exception because it is typically not supplied in response to market consumer demands, but rather is required by mandate. Minimum requirements ensure that parking accompanies nearly every new building constructed across the country, giving rise to huge expanses of asphalt and supersized garages. This chapter will shed light on the prevalence, scale, and inconsistency of parking requirements in the U.S. by comparing the code minimums for five common land uses in the 50 largest cities in America.

THE MADNESS IN THE METHOD

Every zoning code uses a similar formula to calculate required parking. Planners start with an attribute that they think best predicts parking demand, such as the building's area or the number of seats it contains. They then decide how many spaces should be required per unit of that attribute. The formulas look like "three spaces per thousand square feet of professional office" or "one space per dwelling unit." Cities often disagree, however, on which attributes best predict parking demand for the same building use. Figures 6-1 and 6-2 show the various features considered when determining minimum parking for high schools and restaurants among the cities studied.

METRIC USED TO CALCULATE MINIMUM PARKING REQUIREMENTS FOR **HIGH SCHOOLS**

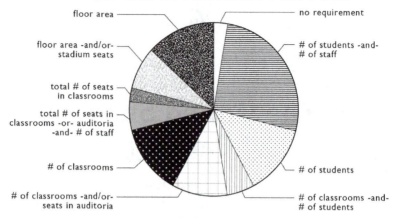

Figure 6-1   Metric used to calculate minimum parking requirements for high schools

METRIC USED TO CALCULATE MINIMUM PARKING REQUIREMENTS FOR **RESTAURANTS**

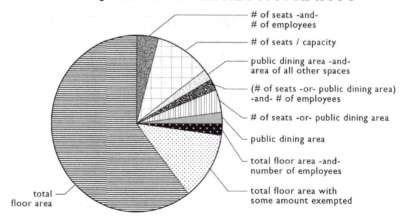

Figure 6-2   Metric used to calculate minimum parking requirements for restaurants

If these requirements were based on a solid understanding of which factors best predict parking demand, we would expect to see a consistent method, even if the ratio varied between cities to account for different driving rates. Instead, cities use many methods that fail to inspire confidence in the integrity of parking minimums. For example, a restaurant with a large footprint but relatively few seats will face a higher parking burden if requirements are based on the building's floor area as opposed to the number of seats it contains. Arbitrary one-size-fits-all minimums prevent builders from assessing the particular needs of each building and providing the appropriate amount of parking on a case-by-case basis.

City codes presume that the type and size of a building are the strongest—sometimes the only—indicators of parking demand, and routinely fail to consider a building's *location* as an equally significant factor. Some cities offer reductions in denser urban zones or near frequent transit, but these remedies are often weak and still do not account for the multitude of ways location choices affect transportation choices. Take for example two schools, one located at the center of its neighborhood and the other placed on the edge and separated by a busy, high-speed road. Both neighborhoods might be low-density suburbs with poor transit, but the school built at the core of its community would allow more students to safely bike or walk to class than the one built on the other side of a dangerous thoroughfare. The former would generate far less demand for parking than the latter.

Sidewalks, street trees, and bike lanes may also have a strong effect on parking demand, in some cases even more than transit availability. A neighborhood corner store or coffeehouse might see most of its patrons arrive by foot or bicycle where high-quality active transportation amenities make the short journey easy and pleasant. There is no accounting for these kinds of details in the majority of zoning codes, which creates a disadvantage for businesses that would choose proximity and walkability over parking.

City zoning codes also ignore the potential for parking fees to moderate demand. It is unsurprising that where parking is given away for free, there are often apparent shortages. Charging a market price for parking is one way to handle the problem, but minimum parking requirements rarely, if ever, account for whether nearby street parking is managed with meters or permits. Some codes even forbid buildings from charging for privately owned parking to manage demand. There is a largely unspoken assumption that city governments have an obligation to ensure parking is cheap, plentiful, and convenient at most destinations. In order to realize effective parking reforms and the associated benefits, cities must dispense with this assumption.

MAPPING PARKING REQUIREMENTS ACROSS AMERICA

While the process of calculating minimum parking requirements is unscientific and narrowly focused, the results are disastrous and immense. Parking spaces require between 300 to 400 square feet of pavement each (that calculation includes the circulation aisles). Cumulatively, the land set aside for parking spreads out and isolates communities, reduces walkability, and degrades the quality of public space. In the following pages, maps of the requirements highlight the scale of required parking in each city and show regional differences. Floor plans illustrate the median requirement for each kind of building, revealing that the minimum space required for car storage often exceeds the space allocated for people. Finally, bar graphs illuminate the idiosyncrasies in the calculations for each land use.

To account for the variety of methods used to calculate parking requirements, this chapter makes comparisons between cities by assuming a model set of attributes for each of the five building types. These are depicted on the corresponding maps and plans. A few cities are omitted from some sections where they could not be reasonably compared; the graphics show the standard requirements as of 2013. The relevant code sections can be found at graphingparking.com/sources. In rare cases where there is no baseline standard, the highest commonly applied requirement is used.

High Schools

Only two generations ago it was commonplace to walk or bike to school. Now, most cities expect high school upperclassmen to drive. Parking minimums compel schools to spend money on extra land and asphalt, taking away funds that could otherwise provide students with higher-quality facilities and education. Free or subsidized parking benefits only wealthier students who choose to drive. Those who either choose not to drive or are unable to afford a car gain nothing. In an era of budget cuts and overcrowded classrooms, one wonders if subsidized parking for teenagers is the best use of a community's limited resources.

The graphics below are based on a model high school that corresponds to national facilities, staffing, and enrollment averages cited at graphingparking.com. As seen in Figures 6-3 and 6-5, the amount of space devoted to parking usually exceeds the amount of classroom space and sometimes exceeds the area of all buildings on campus combined, including gymnasiums and auditoriums. Figure 6-4 shows that while cities employ a wide variety of metrics to calculate parking minimums for high schools, there is little correlation between the metric used and the resulting number of spaces required. The minimums span such an enormous range that they defy plausible differences in culture, density, and transportation options

Figure 6-3   Parking requirements for high schools

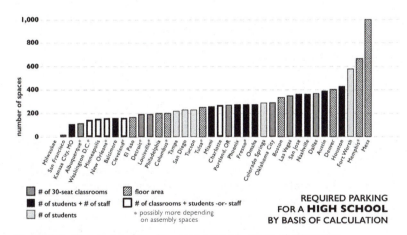

Figure 6-4   Required parking for a high school by basis of calculation

between cities. For example, it seems very unlikely that the travel habits of high school students in Memphis really differ from teenagers in Kansas City to the extremes suggested by their cities' parking requirements.

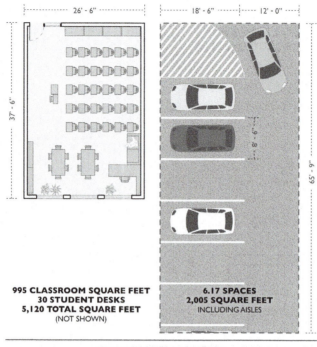

995 CLASSROOM SQUARE FEET
30 STUDENT DESKS
5,120 TOTAL SQUARE FEET
(NOT SHOWN)

6.17 SPACES
2,005 SQUARE FEET
INCLUDING AISLES

MEDIAN REQUIRED PARKING
FOR A **HIGH SCHOOL**
AMONG LARGE U.S. CITIES

Figure 6-5 Median required parking for a high school among large U.S. cities

Places of Worship

Benjamin Franklin said that the only things certain in life are death and taxes. Places of worship are tax exempt and usually offer some promise of eternal life, but even they cannot escape minimum parking requirements. In places where pastors preach humility and frugality, parking minimums for worship spaces are often extravagant, consuming many times the area of the sanctuary. Bustling plazas and grand stairs filled with spectacle and pageantry have given way to isolating deserts of required parking. Processions have been replaced with traffic jams.

Assembly spaces, including places of worship, exemplify the effect that parking minimums have on our lives. On the one hand, they follow a certain logic: many people will be packed into a small space, so many cars need to be accommodated. On the other hand, they put the startling excess of car-centric planning into clear perspective. This waste is certainly not lost on some religious leaders. In his encyclical *Laudato Si,*

Pope Francis himself has decried "parking areas which spoil the urban landscape." At most, these required spaces are filled for a few hours per week. If the work of religious organizations is important enough to merit tax-exempt status, surely underused parking is not the best use of those tax-exempt dollars.

Parking minimums for places of worship are commonly based on the number of seats in the sanctuary, but where fixed seating is not provided, many cities have a backup requirement that is usually stated in terms of square footage in the main assembly space. Interestingly, cities do not come close to agreeing on how many square feet equals one seat. Each seat is equivalent to 25 square feet in Las Vegas, 16.67 square feet in Louisville, 8 square feet in Houston, and only 7 square feet in Washington D.C. These differences mean that the installation of fixed seats will increase the parking burden in some cities while decreasing it in others.

Perhaps the best example of how divorced parking minimums are from actual demand comes from Baltimore where, "for places of worship whose worshipers are required to walk to worship because of religious tenet" (Zoning Code of Baltimore City, Table 16-406), one space is required for every eight persons. No one belonging to these congregations can arrive to services in a car without violating the very beliefs that brought them there, yet the best Baltimore could do is to halve its standard requirement.

Figure 6-6 Parking requirements for places of worship

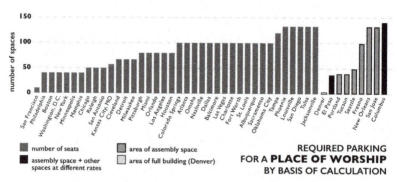

Figure 6-7 Required parking for a place of worship by basis of calculation

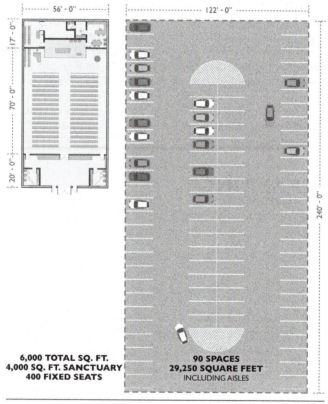

MEDIAN REQUIRED PARKING
FOR A **PLACE OF WORSHIP**
AMONG LARGE U.S. CITIES

Figure 6-8 Median required parking for places of worship among large U.S. cities

Offices

Most white-collar workers in the U.S. pass the hours from nine to five in offices or cubicles smaller than the spaces where cars spend their days. Parking requirements affect companies' bottom lines and burden the economy at large. They increase the cost of hiring employees by raising the cost of each square foot of office space. Demand management strategies that encourage employees to carpool, ride transit, walk, or bike to work could allow businesses to save on parking expenses. Instead, the surplus created by overzealous requirements destroys the incentive to pursue such programs. Likewise, campaigns to encourage more sustainable commuting habits are less effective when carbon-intensive car storage continues to be built regardless.

When it comes to office parking requirements, there is huge variation from city to city—ranging from zero to 400 spaces for buildings of the same size. These differences do not seem to follow any logical pattern. Notice the spread between El Paso and Albuquerque or Kansas City and Omaha. Surely these cities are not so different that such significant variations are justified.

Figure 6-10 shows that the majority of large cities exempt downtown offices from parking requirements. While the rest of the city remains in the thrall of sprawl-inducing parking minimums, however, these

Figure 6-9 Parking requirements for offices

Figure 6-10 Required parking for an office building, plus downtown reductions

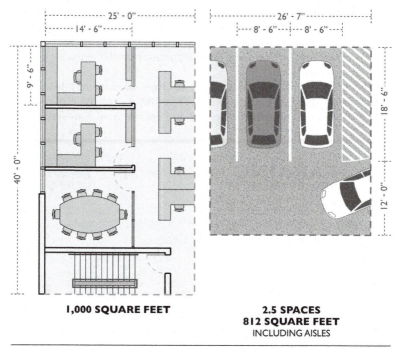

1,000 SQUARE FEET

2.5 SPACES
812 SQUARE FEET
INCLUDING AISLES

MEDIAN REQUIRED PARKING
FOR AN **OFFICE BUILDING**
AMONG LARGE U.S. CITIES

Figure 6-11 Median required parking for an office building among large U.S. cities

localized abatements remain mostly symbolic. Reducing the need for parking—at both ends of a trip—is one of the core benefits of public and active transportation. Cities will struggle to promote transit so long as they allow only a small area to take full advantage of it.

Restaurants

In restaurants, you can choose whether to order a drink with dinner and decide if you want to add dessert, but minimum parking requirements ensure that your meal always comes with a heaping side of parking. This set of graphics illuminates the jarring spatial mismatch between cars and people at restaurants and suggests the obstacle these ordinances present to those who wish to create humane, walkable towns and cities.

Parking minimums deny business owners the freedom to allocate their resources to better serve customers and generate revenue. Concerns that businesses would overcrowd shared street parking can be alleviated by managing occupancy with parking meters. Charging a market price for public street space used to store private vehicles is surely fairer than a blanket mandate for supersized infrastructure that precludes productive uses of urban land. Without parking requirements,

Figure 6-12 Parking requirements for restaurants

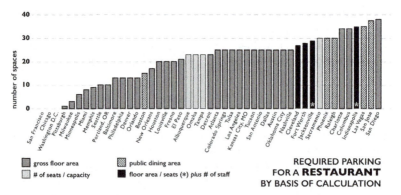

Figure 6-13   Required parking for a restaurant by basis of calculation

restaurateurs might decide that under-occupied spots are not worth the cost of constructing and maintaining. These costs, along with the cost of the real estate parking occupies, are passed along to all restaurant customers in the price of their meal, regardless of whether they arrived in separate vehicles, carpooled, or did not drive at all.

As with the preceding land uses, there is befuddling variation between cities. Why does Nashville require more than 2.5 times the parking of Memphis? Is there really such a vast difference in parking demand from middle to western Tennessee? Why do Cleveland and Columbus require 25+ parking spaces for a medium-size restaurant while Pittsburgh only requires one space for a similar establishment?

Apartments

One of the greatest barriers to creating walkable, affordable communities is the inextricable link between housing and parking. Required parking is often more than half as large as the apartment it accompanies. The enormous cost of constructing parking is regularly hidden from buyers and renters alike because it is bundled into the price of each unit. When the costs of parking are automatically included in the rent, the financial benefit of living car-free is greatly diminished. Even people who cannot afford to buy a car bear the costs of free parking. Some cities, like Dallas and Austin, raise the amount of required parking with each additional bedroom in a unit. These cities place an especially high burden on families with children who may need more bedrooms but not extra cars.

Looking at Figure 6-15, familiar questions arise, such as why would a two-bedroom apartment in Omaha need twice the parking as the same

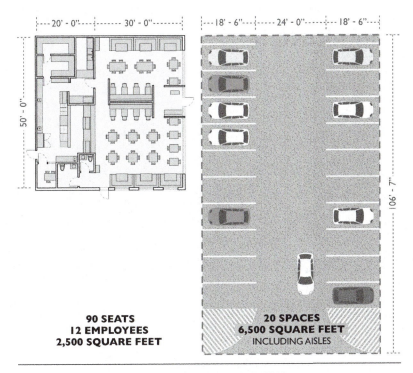

90 SEATS
12 EMPLOYEES
2,500 SQUARE FEET

20 SPACES
6,500 SQUARE FEET
INCLUDING AISLES

MEDIAN REQUIRED PARKING
FOR A **RESTAURANT**
AMONG LARGE U.S. CITIES

Figure 6-14 Median required parking for a restaurant among large U.S. cities

Note: The plan above considers the median requirement only among cities using gross floor area as the basis of calculation.

apartment in Kansas City? Meanwhile, the plan in Figure 6-17 demonstrates just how big all that parking is and hints at the opportunity cost of building it. Could the apartment have been larger or of a higher quality if not for the parking? A balcony overlooking trees and a garden could have replaced the desolate pavement.

REFORM AND REPAIR

This chapter has highlighted the inconsistency of parking requirements for identical buildings between otherwise similar cities, but there is also nonsensical variation *within* many zoning codes between building types. Cities frequently mandate above-average amounts of parking for

Figure 6-15 Parking requirements for apartments

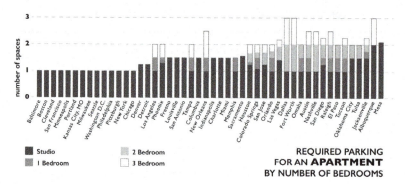

Figure 6-16 Required parking for an apartment by number of bedrooms

some uses and below-average quantities for others. Denver apparently believes that its citizens demand above-average amounts of parking at high schools while needing well below the average at churches. The opposite is true in Columbus and Albuquerque. Elsewhere, Memphis and Miami have heavy parking minimums for offices while both require well below the national median for restaurants. Kansas City and Columbus do the opposite. It is dubious at best that these incongruent requirements reflect actual lifestyle differences between cities. If

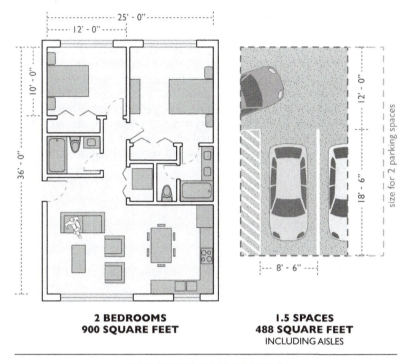

2 BEDROOMS
900 SQUARE FEET

1.5 SPACES
488 SQUARE FEET
INCLUDING AISLES

MEDIAN REQUIRED PARKING
FOR AN **APARTMENT**
AMONG LARGE U.S. CITIES

Figure 6-17 Median required parking for an apartment among large U.S. cities

they were simply accounting for regional preferences for car travel, we would expect to see a consistent deviation within each city regardless of the building type.

The lack of evidence-based justification for parking minimums is significant because of the massive physical, financial, and ecological impact that parking has on U.S. cities. Parking costs thousands—often tens of thousands—of dollars per space to construct, yet regulations specify exorbitant minimum quantities across the U.S. The results have been disastrous, precluding transit- and people-oriented development and shifting the financial burden of car storage from drivers to society at large. Parking requirements effectively deny the viability of alternatives to the car by making walking, biking, and transit inefficient and hazardous. Planners and elected officials who use anemic mass transit as an excuse to keep parking requirements should consider that ample free parking itself stunts the demand for better transit and pedestrian infrastructure.

Minimum parking requirements are not the only obstacle to separating the cost of parking from the cost of everything else. Policies that effectively manage on-street parking are a necessary companion to repealing off-street requirements. City planners and politicians have spent the last decades focused on creating an inexhaustible supply of parking. Until recently, they have done little to manage demand. Now deeply accustomed to accommodating cars, private entities too must be convinced to break habits formed over many years of enforced excess parking. While there is no silver bullet, repealing minimum parking requirements is a foundational step toward sustainable, affordable, and equitable cities.

7

The Fiscal and Travel Consequences of Parking Requirements

By Chris McCahill, Norman Garrick, and Carol Atkinson-Palombo

Throughout the twentieth century, central cities struggled to stay attractive and competitive amid fast-growing suburbs that offered wide streets and convenient, free parking. In central cities, providing wide streets and free parking proved a major challenge. Many city leaders and urban designers tried to compete with the suburbs by demolishing buildings on a grand scale to make room for a mixture of freeways, modernist high-rises on superblocks, and vast expanses of parking. These changes offered a temporary salve for car access in cities, but they left the cities chopped up, hollowed out, and still struggling to compete with the suburbs. At the same time, traffic congestion continued to grow. To make matters worse, many cities continue to add more parking, as though the earlier additions were not enough.

In the 1960s, the Hartford, Connecticut, City Council pushed to add more parking in the city's downtown to compete with free parking in suburban shopping plazas. The land devoted to parking in Hartford grew by roughly 150 percent between 1960 and 2000.

Hartford's story is not unique. For this study, we examined historical aerial photography of Hartford and five additional cities: Lowell, Massachusetts; Berkeley, California; Arlington, Virginia; New Haven, Connecticut; and Cambridge, Massachusetts. Among these cities, the number of off-street parking spaces increased by 50 to 100 percent between 1960 and 1980, and by another 10 to 40 percent in the following two decades. While all these cities saw increases in the amount of land dedicated to parking, their experiences differed in significant ways.

For example, cities with the largest growth in the number of parking spaces per person also experienced the largest increases in auto commuting—adding to local traffic, pollution emissions, and opportunities for crashes. Those cities also added the fewest residents and jobs, and lost larger portions of their potential tax base by replacing buildings with off-street parking. Other cities that reversed the trend of increasing parking supply beginning in the 1980s offer important lessons for managing parking, providing transportation alternatives, and tapping into valuable urban assets that include a dense, diverse mix of activities and people-oriented environments.

TRACKING THE CHANGES IN AMERICAN CITIES OVER 40 YEARS

For our study, we tracked changes in land use, parking supply, buildings, travel behavior, and tax revenues for the six small cities mentioned above. Our primary data sources include the following:

> *Aerial photographs* dating back to the 1950s, from which we estimated the amount of land devoted to buildings, surface parking, and parking garages, and the approximate height of built structures. We estimated the number of parking spaces by dividing the total area of parking by 350 square feet (the average area needed per space).

> *Census data* including the Census Transportation Planning Package, which provides information on the numbers of residents, workers, and private vehicles in cities, as well as commute mode.

> *Municipal parcel data* including tax assessments.

Figure 7-1 shows the percentage change in parking and people in each city over the study period (1960–2000). Generally, cities with the largest parking growth experienced a decrease in residents and employees, while cities with the smallest parking growth added people—particularly employees.

THE FORM, FUNCTION, AND VALUE OF URBAN LAND

The physical transformation of cities and the loss of valuable, active urban land are probably the most visible consequences of urban parking growth. This transformation was planned decades earlier in the

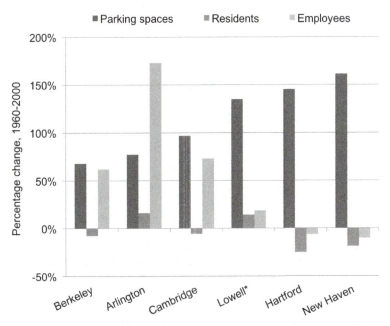

Figure 7-1   Percentage change in parking, residents, and employees, 1960–2000

* Employment data for Lowell available only from 1980–2000.

futuristic forms popularized by Le Corbusier, Norman Bel Geddes, Frank Lloyd Wright, and others. In these designers' collective vision, high-rise towers were surrounded by parks and plazas and connected by giant, free-flowing highways. Missing from most of these early images, however, were the many cars required to move people around in these increasingly disconnected places and the space to store those cars while not in use. Only now can we see and measure those outcomes.

To quantify those changes, we estimated actual parking ratios—the number of parking spaces per 1,000 square feet of building space—for the central business districts of each of the six cities in our study. Between 1960 and 2000, we found that parking ratios increased considerably—between 63 and 122 percent—in Hartford, Lowell, and New Haven's central business districts. This is attributable to both the substantial growth in off-street parking and the slow growth in the amount of useable building space. At the same time, on-street parking was removed to facilitate traffic flow and parking was relocated into off-street lots and garages.

In the central business districts of the other three cities—Arlington, Berkeley, and Cambridge—parking ratios decreased. In each of these

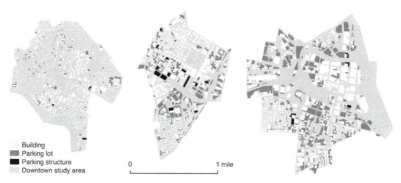

Building
Parking lot
Parking structure
Downtown study area

0   1 mile

Figure 7-2 Distribution of parking and buildings in the central business districts of Cambridge, New Haven, and Hartford

cases, the number of off-street parking spaces grew by less than 40 percent (or decreased, in Berkeley) and on-street parking continued to account for between 60 and 80 percent of the available parking supply. The useable building space in these city centers grew between 16 and 174 percent.

Figure 7-2 shows the parking supplies in the centers of Cambridge, New Haven, and Hartford in 2009. Cambridge has the lowest parking ratio of 0.1 parking spaces per 1,000 square feet of building space. New Haven and Hartford have the highest parking ratios, 0.6 and 0.9 respectively.

Changes in the form and use of urban land affect property values and property-tax revenue. To better understand those changes, we estimated the tax revenue produced by parking lots, garages, and other properties throughout each city center in our study. After accounting for factors like tax exemptions and smaller parking facilities whose value is bundled into the buildings, we estimate that land used for off-street parking produces only 40 percent of the tax revenue that land used for buildings does, on average. This ranges from 17 to 88 percent depending on the city. As a result, cities with the greatest growth in parking experienced a gradual weakening of their property tax base. For the six cities we considered, each parking space added since 1960 reduces potential property tax revenues by between $500 and $1,000 per year. Depending on the number of parking spaces added, the loss attributable to parking spaces represents 20 to 30 percent of the total central business district tax revenues in 2012.

There is some argument to be made that urban land values might already have been in natural decline and that parking is now the best use of that land. Given the role municipal policies have played in driving up public and private parking supplies, however, it is difficult to know for sure. In either case, our work shows that parking is a far less productive use of land than active building space, fiscally speaking, and that reasonable efforts should be made to encourage land uses other than parking.

CHANGING TRAVEL BEHAVIOR

Many urban policies implemented during the mid-twentieth century, including those related to parking, roads, and building design, were in response to rising car use and to expectations of continued increases in use. By making more room for cars, policymakers hoped to avoid traffic congestion. Ironically, as our work suggests, these efforts likely increased vehicle traffic in places that once thrived without it.

To understand the extent to which the physical changes in cities affected travel behavior, we compared the growth of parking in each city to commuting records from the U.S. Census. Parking growth represents only one aspect of the physical changes that occurred, but because it occurred on such a large scale, it is the most useful indicator of the overall changes taking place in a city. Similarly, while commuting reflects only one element of overall trips made in a city, it is the most consistently available travel metric over time and a vital trip for residents. The census shows the commute modes for travel to, from, and within each city by car dating back to 1960. We chose to focus on local commute trips—those that begin and end within a single city—as they are generally the shortest and can more likely be made without a car.

Between 1960 and 2000, we found a strong link between the amount of parking available and the share of residents and employees in each city who commuted by car. The mechanisms governing this relationship are not clear because parking is both a cause and an effect of driving. Yet, the changes in commuting behavior in cities that added the most parking suggest that more parking increases driving.

We found that as parking increased in cities, so did car use for local commute trips. While ample parking improves access for drivers, large parking lots also hinder walking, biking, and transit use by breaking up the built environment. The effect of increased parking supply on commuting behavior was most pronounced between 1960 and 1980, when the supply grew most rapidly. In New Haven and Hartford, where the number of parking spaces per person more than doubled, the car commuter mode share increased by 16 and 30 percent, respectively. After 1980, when a majority of highway construction and road-capacity enhancements had been completed, the growth in parking and the rise in local car use both slowed, but

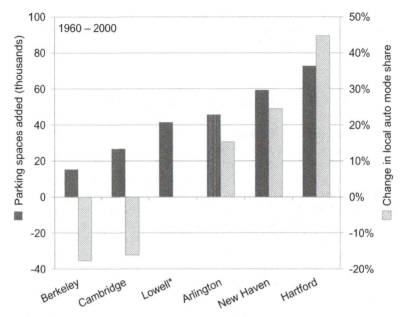

Figure 7-3 Changes in parking and local automobile use between 1960 and 2000
* Employment data for Lowell available only from 1980–2000.

the relationship endured. Over the entire study period (1960 to 2000), changes in the share of local commuters traveling by car are almost directly related to the number of parking spaces added in that city, as shown in Figure 7-3.

LOOKING FORWARD

While parking and car use have increased in a majority of American cities, our work also offers important counter examples. Despite their pronounced differences today, it is important to first recognize that the cities in this study were once very similar both in terms of built form and travel behavior. A century ago, each functioned well without automobiles and only later evolved to accommodate cars, especially by adding parking. Most cities changed drastically toward auto dominance, though in a few cities parking growth slowed or even reversed.

In Cambridge, for example, leaders pushed for more parking throughout the 1960s and 70s, but changed course around 1980. In 1981, policymakers introduced limits on the amount of new parking allowed by the city's zoning code. An ordinance followed in 1998 restricting parking growth even further and requiring developers to reduce parking and discourage excessive driving trips. The city also invested heavily in initiatives to improve bicycling and walking. These actions allowed Cambridge to attract more than 5,000 residents and 30,000 employees between 1980 and 2000, while adding fewer than 5,000 off-street parking spaces.

Arlington and Berkeley, similarly, have emphasized non-car travel in their policies and plans. Since 1980, the combined number of residents and employees in each city has matched or surpassed the growth in parking. Arlington added 37,000 residents and 51,000 employees, but only 11,000 parking spaces.

In contrast to the cities that added the most parking, the share of local commuters traveling by car since 1980 decreased from 61 to 59 percent in Arlington, from 38 to 35 percent in Berkeley, and from 30 to 24 percent in Cambridge. This has not only kept additional vehicles off the roads, it has also redirected many trips to active transportation modes such as walking and biking, which account for 18 percent of local commute trips in Arlington, 47 percent in Berkeley, and 57 percent in Cambridge.

Perhaps most important, the cities that added the least parking have recovered exceptionally well after losing residents and businesses, and are now thriving. While many factors contribute to a city's successes and failures, our work suggests that providing convenient and inexpensive parking does not enhance city life or economic vitality. In fact, it seems to do the opposite. For many decades, officials and urban designers in cities throughout the nation have considered parking as a necessity for ensuring access. However, due to the amount of space needed, direct costs, and other negative impacts of parking, cities with excessive amounts of parking may not be reaching their full potential. Instead, these places should consider policies that attract more residents, employees, and visitors by meeting their access needs in ways that depend less on driving and automobile infrastructure.

REFERENCES AND FURTHER READING

Blanc, Bryan, Michael Gangi, Carol Atkinson-Palombo, Christopher McCahill, and Norman Garrick. 2014. "Effects of Urban Fabric Changes on Real Estate Property Tax Revenue." *Transportation Research Record* 2453: 145–52.

McCahill, Christopher, and Norman Garrick. 2014. "Parking Supply and Urban Impacts." in *Parking: Issues and Policies*, edited by Stephen Ison and Corinne Mulley. Bingley, UK: Emerald Group Publishing Limited, pp. 33–55.

McCahill, Christopher, Jessica Haerter-Ratchford, Norman Garrick, and Carol Atkinson-Palombo. 2014. "Parking in Urban Centers: Policies, Supplies and Implications in Six Cities." *Transportation Research Record* 2469: 49–56.

McCahill, Christopher, and Norman Garrick. 2012. "Automobile Use and Land Consumption: Empirical Evidence from 12 Cities." *Urban Design International* 17, no. 3: 221–27.

McCahill, Christopher, and Norman Garrick. 2010. "Influence of Parking Policy on Built Environment and Travel Behavior in Two New England Cities, 1960 to 2007." *Transportation Research Record* 2187, 2010: 123–30.

8

The Environmental Impacts of Parking Lots

By Emma Kirkpatrick, Amélie Davis, and Bryan Pijanowski

Urbanization tends to occur gradually, and it is easy to overlook both the amount of land devoted to parking lots and their cumulative environmental impacts. In this chapter, we summarize how we: 1) estimated the surface area covered by parking lots in the Upper Great Lakes region, and 2) used this information to estimate two general environmental consequences of these parking lots: degradation of water quality and loss of ecosystem services due to the conversion from natural land to impervious surfaces.

ESTIMATING THE SURFACE AREA OF PARKING LOTS AT COUNTYWIDE AND REGIONAL SCALES

Our pilot study in Tippecanoe County, Indiana, was the first to estimate the amount of land covered by surface parking lots in the U.S. Using GIS and high-resolution orthophotographs (aerial photographs that have been referenced to the earth so that measurements can accurately be taken on them), we digitized all clearly discernible paved surfaces with at least three parking spaces in the county (Figure 8-1). We disaggregated the estimated cover of all parking lots at the ZIP code level.

Using the information gathered from the first study, we repeated the process for the Upper Great Lakes region, expanding the study area beyond Indiana to include Illinois, Michigan, and Wisconsin.

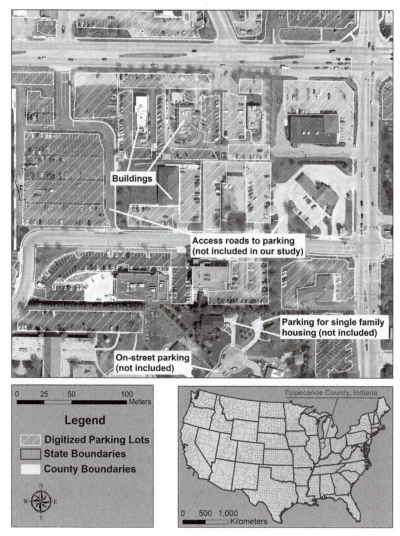

Figure 8-1 Example of digitized parking lots from orthophotographs
Source: Davis et al. (2010)

This study area is comprised of several large cities, including Chicago, Detroit, Milwaukee, and Indianapolis. Across the four states, there are more than 3,800 ZIP codes. These ZIP codes were classified further into the following categories based on their respective level of development: Rural, Suburban, and Highly Urban.

We applied a stratified sampling scheme to estimate the area covered by surface lots in the Upper Great Lakes region. Half of the ZIP codes are classified as "Rural," but the "Highly Urban" category has both the largest percentage of land devoted to parking lots and the greatest median parking-lot cover. Furthermore, the amount of land devoted to parking lots varies greatly in the ZIP codes classified as "Suburban," with one suburban ZIP code devoting 9 percent of its land cover to parking lots! In contrast, one of the ZIP codes classified as "Rural" has no surface lots, while one of our "Highly Urban" ZIP codes (located in downtown Chicago) only has 0.1% of its area devoted to surface lots.

ESTIMATING THE NUMBER OF PARKING SPACES AT COUNTYWIDE AND REGIONAL SCALES

Once we determined the amount of land devoted to surface parking lots, we estimated the number of parking spaces within those lots by randomly selecting 100 parking lots, counting the number of spaces visible on the orthophotographs for those lots, and fitting a linear regression to those data. This approach yielded a conservative estimate of 43 million total parking spaces in the Upper Great Lakes region.

In the Upper Great Lakes region, for example, parking lots account for almost 5 percent of urban land use. In Tippecanoe County, this percentage was even higher, with 6.5 percent of the urban footprint designated as parking lots. However, we know that these are underestimates. Only paved surfaces with clearly designated parking spaces (those where the painted stripes were plainly visible) and parking lots with more than three cars aligned in an organized fashion were digitized and counted as parking surfaces in the previously mentioned studies. Not included in the digitalization efforts were on-street spaces, junkyards, truck-storage spaces, gravel lots, or the space required to provide access to parking lots from the street (although the space required to navigate within the parking lots was included). Parking garages (multi-level structures) were included only if their top floor was exposed. Finally, residential parking spaces, such as wide driveways leading to a garage, were omitted even if they had multiple cars parked in the driveway. Personal garages from private residences were also excluded. Parking lots associated with residential apartment buildings were included if they consisted of a clearly discernible paved surface with at least three parking spaces. We were unable to ascertain how much of an impact these omissions had on the metrics specified in this chapter, but this is a needed future area of research.

ENVIRONMENTAL IMPACTS: RUNOFF AND WATER QUALITY

Parking lots create water runoff that increases flood risks and degrades water quality. Parking surfaces are typically impervious, with the exception of those built with permeable pavement, grass, or gravel lots, all of which are uncommon. During and after rainfall, water is unable to filter through the impenetrable layer of concrete or asphalt, inevitably finding its way into storm drains and ultimately bodies of water. This has numerous consequences for the surrounding environment.

Stormwater runoff carries pollutants that collect on parking lots (for example, oil from cars) and transfers them into nearby water sources. Instead of being absorbed by pervious surfaces, increased runoff enters storm drains. This increases the risk of flooding downstream and ultimately leads to greater sediment and pollutant loads. Additionally, sealants that are used to protect parking lot surfaces from harsh weather conditions may leak into the surrounding environment and pollute nearby waterways.

In our Tippecanoe County study, we combined our figures on parking-lot cover with a hydrologic model called Long-Term Hydrologic Impact Analysis (L-THIA) to estimate the changes in recharge, runoff, and nonpoint source pollution resulting specifically from the land area devoted to surface parking lots (Pandey et al. 2000). The model showed that runoff increased tremendously (by as much as 900 percent) when comparing pre-development hydrology to development with just parking lots (i.e., only considering the hydrological impact of the parking lot cover in Tippecanoe County and not of any other impervious surfaces). Furthermore, pollutants such as nitrogen and phosphorus also increased substantially (by approximately 200 percent) in average annual runoff when development included parking lots (Figure 8-2).

Furthermore, expansive parking lots are generally paved with dark asphalt, which has low albedo (low reflectivity) and thus high heat capacity, making it a prime contributor to the urban heat-island effect (the increase in urban temperature compared to surrounding rural areas). In Northern Hemisphere summers, the temperature of stormwater runoff can also be affected as the water comes into contact with these hot surfaces. As a result, the higher temperature of nearby streams or water bodies has been shown to affect biological communities.

Not only do paved parking lots reduce the green infrastructure (such as trees and bioswales) that could be (or already was) present in urban and suburban environments; they also provide no habitat for species (even humans), no biodiversity (they are considered biologically inert), and no ecosystem services (the benefits we derive from nature for free). Ecologists have shown that urban sprawl, which is exacerbated by large flat parking lots, regularly contributes to habitat fragmentation.

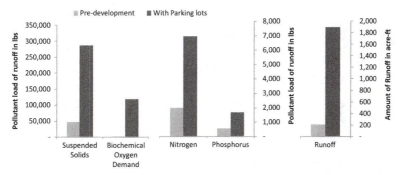

Figure 8-2 Pollutant loads and runoff estimated for pre-development hydrology versus post-development, including only impervious areas devoted to parking lots in Tippecanoe County, Indiana

Source: Davis et al. (2009).

As development projects encroach upon natural areas, the wellbeing of wildlife is compromised both in terms of animals' movement through the landscape and their use of natural resources for habitat and breeding.

Local policy solutions to mitigate these impacts are often ineffective—and can even exacerbate conditions. Many municipalities require building retention ponds near new buildings and their associated parking lots, in order to hold stormwater runoff and slowly release it after a storm. While these retention areas are certainly necessary for lots built with impervious materials, the added space needed for the retention pond effectively increases the existing lots' surface areas, further affecting natural areas.

ECONOMIC IMPACTS IN TERMS OF LOST ECOSYSTEM SERVICES

Converting urban land to parking lots comes at an ecological price rarely calculated. In a process called ecosystem service valuation, Costanza and colleagues (1997) estimated the extent to which a variety of ecosystem services would be lost if natural areas were converted for human use, such as urban or agricultural land cover. They used several ecological economics approaches to estimate the value of natural areas, such as wetlands, and numerous ecologists have used these techniques to estimate the cost of the loss of other ecosystem services (for example, denitrification and water purification). Using data from our Tippecanoe County study on parking lots, we were able to apply these valuations to the area of land taken up by parking lots. We assumed that all

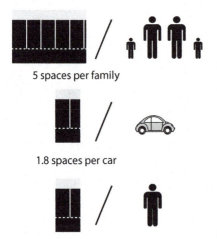

5 spaces per family

1.8 spaces per car

1.7 spaces per adult

Figure 8-3 Parking space footprint metrics

parking-lot coverage was of the same type and proportion of original natural cover (wetlands, grasslands, forest) that exists outside of urban and agricultural land. We were able to show that the ecological-services valuation of parking lots in Tippecanoe County, Indiana, was $22.5 million in 1997 USD. We also determined that if all parking lots were converted to wetlands, then the ecological-services value of all land in the county would increase by more than 38 percent.

HOW MUCH IS TOO MUCH PARKING?

Our study found that approximately 5 percent of the urban area in the Upper Great Lakes region was devoted to paved lots. This is a conservative estimate of total paved parking coverage because our estimate includes neither on-street parking spaces nor off-street residential parking spaces. Nevertheless, the parking lot area we did measure in Illinois, Indiana, Michigan, and Wisconsin accounts for almost half the area of the state of Rhode Island. We estimated that 0.24 percent of the land in those four states was used for paved parking lots. If this were scaled up to the entire conterminous U.S., the paved area (just for parking) would cover 7,092 square miles, nearly the entire state of New Jersey.

To put it in perspective, our conservative estimate of parking lot cover leads us to conclude that, at a minimum, there are almost twice as many parking spaces as adults of driving age in the four states mentioned above. In the same four states, there are at a minimum

Figure 8-4 Representation of the number of parking spaces available as a function of demand

about five spaces available per family (Figure 8-3). If we add all the on-street parking spaces and all the parking spaces at home, these spaces are spread out between common travel destinations, such as schools, workplaces, shopping centers, and recreational locations. Though each adult in a family may have a space at each destination, these spaces are not all occupied at the same time. Drivers cannot be in all of these places at once, and the unused spaces will remain empty. It is important to note that even with our conservative estimate of parking-lot cover, we estimate that the four states combined contain a minimum of 43 million parking spaces. Given the number of cars available in these states, there would be 27.5 million unused parking spaces if all cars were to park somewhere other than their home at the same time (Figure 8-4). One wonders what all this space could be used for instead of empty asphalt.

CONCLUSION

Measuring parking lot footprints on a regional scale is valuable because it can determine how impervious surfaces affect local ecosystems on a broader scale. Even conservative estimates suggest an over-supply of parking in our study area, and the problem stems from how our cities are developed. Zoning regulations often split uses into industrial, commercial, and residential areas, and assign each zone its own distinct parking requirements. Shifting the focus of planning to a broader level, rather than local or building-specific regulations, can moderate the allotment of new, unnecessary parking facilities. We did not estimate the additional footprints of on-street parking, parking garages, and parking at private residences. Counting these additional parking spaces would reveal the total number of underused spaces and highlight the need to plan for parking in a more holistic fashion.

Can cities make parking lots into memorable places, or spaces that provide ecosystem services, or both? We think they can, but it will require a collective effort from planners, developers, local businesses, and community leaders. The result would dramatically improve the environmental, social, and economic fabric of our cities.

REFERENCES AND FURTHER READING

Costanza, R., M. A. Wilson, A. Troy, A. Voinov, S. Liu, and J. D'Agostino. 1997. "The Value of the World's Ecosystem Services and Natural Capital." *Nature* 387: 253–260.

Davis A., B. Pijanowski, K. Robinson, and P. Kidwell. 2010. "Estimating Parking Lot Footprint in the Upper Great Lakes Region of the USA." *Landscape and Urban Planning* 27(2): 255–61.

Davis, A., B. Pijanowski, K. Robinson, and B. Engel. 2009. "The Environmental and Economic Cost of Sprawling Parking Lots in the United States." *Land Use Policy* 96(2): 68–77.

Pandey, S., R. Gunn, K. Lim, B. Engel, and J. Harbor. 2000. "Developing a Web-enabled Tool to Assess Long-term Hydrologic Impact of Land Use Change: Information Technologies Issues and a Case Study." *Urban and Regional Information Systems Journal* 12(4): 5–17.

9

Parking and Affordable Housing in San Francisco

By Bill Chapin, Wenyu Jia, and Martin Wachs

Housing affordability and parking availability are two of the most vexing problems in the nation's largest cities. In San Francisco, most working people find it almost impossible to find a house, condo, or apartment at an affordable price. Finding a parking space is nearly as difficult. Residents say parking problems are the bane of urban life. Many houses are situated on very narrow lots, and numerous curb cuts for driveways reduce on-street parking. Cars trawl for the rare empty space. In many other urban centers—including New York, Chicago, Boston, and Seattle—housing costs and parking availability are twin public-policy problems that become enormous when combined.

Although Americans rarely connect housing affordability and parking availability, the two problems are intimately linked, presenting planners with a conundrum. In an effort to ease parking shortages, cities require that new dwelling units provide off-street parking. But parking spaces add significantly to construction costs, thus raising sales prices or monthly rents. So, inevitably, increasing the supply of parking also increases the cost of housing. If municipalities allowed new housing units to be built without parking spaces, housing prices would be lower but streets might eventually overflow with parked cars.

By providing parking spaces with new housing, developers invite more cars into the city. Planners often encourage "transit-oriented development" to increase public transit use and lessen residents' reliance on automobiles. It would seem logical to reduce the number of parking spaces in neighborhoods that have good transit access, as many in San Francisco do. Neighborhoods with fewer parking spaces and efficient transit service may attract families who avoid or limit car trips. But even neighborhoods with few car owners can suffer parking shortages. The double and triple parking common on Manhattan's residential streets occurs in densely populated communities where car ownership rates are comparatively low.

Should cities require builders to provide more parking—to alleviate parking shortages? Or should they limit parking—to promote cheaper housing and more transit use? Choosing the former may result in higher residential prices, more cars, and less transit use. Choosing the latter may lead to cheaper housing units on streets congested by parked cars. This paper reports on two studies of housing prices and residential parking performed 20 years apart in San Francisco. Together they shed some light on this dilemma.

When the first of these studies was undertaken in 1996, San Francisco required one parking space per new dwelling unit. If the new housing was specifically intended for the elderly, fewer parking spaces were required, presuming older occupants own fewer cars than younger residents. Many other cities require larger numbers of parking spaces per dwelling unit (often one parking space per bedroom). Still, San Francisco's requirement may influence housing affordability. Because many dwelling units were built before current parking requirements were enacted, we studied the relationship between parking and housing by comparing the sale prices of units that included parking spaces with those that did not (Jia and Wachs 1999). We controlled for the effects on sales prices of other variables, including the units' age, size, and amenities.

RESEARCH DESIGN OF THE EARLIER STUDY

We looked at six San Francisco neighborhoods with fairly typical demographics (including income, household size, racial composition): North Beach, Haight-Ashbury, Duboce Triangle, Russian Hill, Noe Valley, and the Castro District. We considered data on the units sold in 1996: address, initial asking price, selling price, number of days until the unit sold, date sold, size in square feet, number of bedrooms and bathrooms, unit's age, architectural style, off-street parking availability, and neighborhood description. The study geographically linked these real estate data with the 1990 census so that real estate and community demographic information could be considered simultaneously. In total, there were data describing 232 dwelling units listed for sale in 1996, distributed among 28 census tracts in the selected neighborhoods.

We used a hedonic model to assess the effects of off-street parking on the sales prices of the housing units, while holding constant effects of other variables. We found that parking dramatically affected housing affordability.

THE EFFECTS OF OFF-STREET PARKING ON HOUSING COSTS IN 1996

Single-family dwelling units with off-street parking sold for an average of $394,779, while units without parking sold for an average of $348,388. This price differential of 12 percent was statistically significant. Similarly, the average selling price of condominiums with garages was $38,804 more than condos without parking, a difference of about 13 percent. Parking availability was the third most influential of many factors that determine selling price. Only unit size and number of bathrooms had a larger effect on prices.

These differences directly affected housing affordability. Most people seeking housing in San Francisco applied for mortgages. Assuming a prevailing rate of 7.5 percent in 1996 for a thirty-year mortgage with a 10 percent down payment, an annual family income of $76,000 was required to qualify for a mortgage on the average single-family home in San Francisco neighborhoods with off-street parking, excluding most lower- and middle-income families from these communities. The average annual household income needed to qualify for a mortgage on a unit without parking was $67,000.

Condominiums at the median sales value in these communities showed similar results. A condominium loan on a median-priced unit with off-street parking required an annual family income of $59,000. A household income of only $51,000 in 1996 would have supported a loan on the average condo without parking. Again, the parking requirement significantly affected housing accessibility in San Francisco.

We estimated that 68,700 San Francisco households could qualify for mortgages on typical single-family units with parking; 16,600 additional households could afford an equivalent home without parking. Thus, 24 percent more households could afford houses if they did not include parking. Similarly, if the parking requirements had not existed, 26,800 additional households could have afforded condominiums. The number of households that could have qualified for loans on condos without parking was 20 percent greater than the number that could qualify for those with off-street parking. Further, condominiums with parking took an average of 41 days longer to sell than those without.

PARKING AND HOUSING IN SAN FRANCISCO TWO DECADES LATER

In the time since the original publication of the research summarized above, urban planners have dramatically shifted their attitudes toward parking. In the last decade, more than 100 cities of varying sizes eliminated minimum requirements in their downtowns. San Francisco was among them. Between 2005 and 2014, the city gradually eliminated minimum requirements for much of its downtown and several surrounding neighborhoods (Chapin 2016).

At the same time, San Francisco's housing crisis did not abate. One in five renters in the city spends more than half their income on housing. The median home price in the region now tops $840,000, which only 23 percent of the population can afford.

Because many of San Francisco's parking reforms were tied to the development of neighborhood plans, the process was slow going. Some plans took more than 10 years to develop. The incremental approach caused some parcels to have different parking standards from their neighbors for years at a time, despite being in close proximity.

A comparison of recent housing development can take advantage of one such situation—analyzing a 2.6-square-mile area straddling Market Street and Van Ness Avenue just east of downtown from early 2008 to late 2014—to explore whether the city's reform efforts achieved their goals, particularly in regard to housing affordability. If evidence shows that elimination of minimum parking requirements did, in fact, reduce the cost of market-rate housing or encourage the development of below-market-rate housing, San Francisco's strategy could prove to be a valuable precedent for other cities.

RESEARCH DESIGN OF THE SECOND STUDY

This second study area was defined as all parcels within 2,000 feet of those segments of Market Street and Van Ness Avenue that fall within one of two official city planning districts: the Market and Octavia Area Plan and the Van Ness Special Use District (SUD). The analysis looked at each parcel marked for development and determined what parking requirements were in place when the project was approved by the San Francisco Planning Commission. The 2,000-foot boundary placed all studied parcels within walking distance of transit stops. This study area included some neighborhoods analyzed in the earlier research, including all of the Duboce Triangle and parts of the Castro District and Russian Hill.

The analysis used a variety of official City and County of San Francisco documents and databases to identify all the residential development projects within this study area and time frame having at least 10 dwelling units, as well as key attributes of each project at the time of its approval. These attributes included measurements used to calculate the following experimental variables:

1. The number of parking spaces per unit.
2. The percentage of units offered at subsidized, affordable rates.
3. The average construction cost per unit, based on estimates listed on building permit applications and the proportion of floor area devoted to noncommercial uses.

This process ultimately identified 30 developments in zoning districts with no minimum parking requirement and 14 developments in districts that required one parking space per dwelling unit. A t-test assessed whether there were any statistically significant differences between these two groups for each of the variables.

THE EFFECTS OF PARKING REFORM ON HOUSING DEVELOPMENT

The analysis found that developments having no minimum parking requirement had an average of 36 spaces for every 100 dwelling units, while those with a requirement had an average of 90 spaces per 100 units. In developments zoned with no minimum requirement, 23 percent of the units met the city's requirements to qualify as affordable, compared to just 6 percent in developments with a minimum requirement. Finally, the estimated construction cost per dwelling unit was $230,208 for buildings with no requirement and $330,666 for buildings with a requirement. These findings were all significant at a confidence level greater than 95 percent.

San Francisco's parking reform efforts allowed for the development of housing with 60 percent less parking. The reduced parking meant developers were able to build dwelling units 30 percent cheaper— enough to allow for market-rate housing that is more in line with the typical San Francisco household's income. In districts without a minimum parking requirement, a developer seeking a 10 percent annual return on investment would have to charge $1,918 in monthly rent to cover construction expenses. The rate in districts with a minimum requirement would be $2,756. A two-person household earning the city's median income of $86,150 would spend 27 percent of their earnings on housing in the district without parking requirements and spend

38 percent of their earnings on housing in the district with parking requirements.

The cost savings from reduced parking did not translate into an increase in inclusionary housing. Regardless of parking requirements, most market-rate developments included the minimum number of affordable units required by the city. However, the study also included five projects consisting entirely of below-market-rate units—all located in zoning districts with no minimum parking requirement. The result was more than three times as much affordable housing in those districts, often serving overlooked segments of the population, such as the chronically homeless and senior citizens.

Interviews with six developers who were active in this area of San Francisco indicated that parking is a major consideration for them. Developers of properties not subject to a minimum requirement were often unsure what they would have done had they been required to build one parking space per unit. In some cases, they said, the development may not have happened at all, exacerbating the city's housing shortage. In other cases, developers would have tried to add more levels of underground parking—expenses that would likely have been borne by residents in the form of higher rents and sales prices.

San Francisco's approach to parking reform also typically involved the creation of new maximum caps on parking. This analysis did not consider how different maximum requirements may have affected development in the study area. One of the interviewees stated that, with market-rate housing, he was looking to include as much parking as zoning and his building footprint would allow. Thus, it may not be enough for cities to simply deregulate off-street parking; they may need to actively impose strict limits.

POLICY IMPLICATIONS

Why is the requirement for a parking space bundled with housing? In Tokyo, families cannot register automobiles until they have off-street spaces for them, but families that do not own cars need not pay for parking spaces attached to their houses. Why should each dwelling unit be required to have a fixed number of parking spaces regardless of the number of cars in the household? Would the public interest be better served if parking and housing were unbundled, creating separate markets for each? Vehicles could be parked off the street in parking garages independent of dwelling units.

Imagine American cities in which housing developers provide dwelling units and parking spaces separately. If there were separate markets for housing and parking, a buyer could opt for a housing unit with zero, one, or two parking spaces depending on need. Long-time neighborhood residents who have cars but no garages in their older dwellings would be able to purchase or lease parking spaces associated with newly constructed housing, while new residents who do not need parking would not be required to pay for a unit that includes parking.

If parking and housing were marketed separately, wouldn't many people choose not to pay for parking and instead park free on local streets? Not necessarily, especially if cities manage their on-street parking properly as described in Chapter 51. Rather than searching endlessly for an on-street space or moving a car frequently to comply with parking time limits, car owners with sufficient income could choose to purchase or lease parking spaces. Others, wishing to save money, would give up cars they rarely use to forego a garage and pay less for housing.

These findings bolster the case for repealing minimum parking requirements as a way to improve housing affordability. Parking reform, on its own, cannot solve San Francisco's housing problems—or those of any other city. A multitude of approaches is needed to tackle such a complex issue. The evidence shows, however, that removing minimum parking requirements can make housing more affordable.

REFERENCES AND FURTHER READING

Chapin, Bill. 2016. "Parking Spaces to Living Spaces: A Comparative Study of the Effects of Parking Reform in Central San Francisco." Thesis submitted for the Master's Degree in Urban Planning, San Jose State University.
Jia, W., and M. Wachs. 1999. "Parking Requirements and Housing Affordability: A Case Study of San Francisco." *Transportation Research Record* 1685 (1999): 156–60.

10

The Unintended Consequences of New York City's Minimum Parking Requirements

By Simon McDonnell and Josiah Madar

Minimum parking requirements are a staple of local land-use controls, despite their potentially harmful effects on housing costs and traffic congestion. In cities new and old, large and small, zoning codes specify a minimum number of spaces developers must provide for each new unit of housing or each square foot of retail or office space. Even Houston, famous for its laissez-faire land-use regulations, imposes parking requirements on new construction.

In a world of free or underpriced on-street parking, the ostensible purpose of parking requirements is to ensure that new construction "pulls its weight" in the ongoing battle for "enough" spaces. As the theory goes, developers who increase the demand for local parking should accommodate this new demand by providing their own off-street parking to prevent parking spillover from any new residents, shoppers, and visitors. Epstein (2002) called the potential threat of spillover parking one of the most intractable and explosive issues in local governance.

The theoretical objections to parking requirements are no doubt familiar to most readers of this book. When zoning specifies the number of off-street parking spaces a developer must provide with each new apartment, office suite, or storefront, it forces the developer to incur a possibly unnecessary cost. If the required parking is more than what the developer would have chosen to provide anyway, the parking requirement adds real costs to construction, and these costs skyrocket when the parking is underground.

The cost of any extra parking space required beyond what the developer would voluntarily provide either gets passed on to consumers or reduces the profitability or even feasibility of development. In addition to raising development costs (and ultimately housing prices), parking requirements also have transportation and environmental consequences. They lock in an oversupply of parking, which lowers the market price of parking and shapes the transportation decisions of visitors, residents, and workers for decades. Ultimately, bundling free or discounted car storage with housing will increase the share of residents who own and use cars.

RESIDENTIAL PARKING REQUIREMENTS IN NEW YORK CITY

At the center of development politics in much of New York City is the conflict between new housing developments and on-street parking for the current residents. Minimum parking requirements have been, and remain, an active part of these politics. Despite the city's uniquely high transit ridership, car ownership is still common, especially outside of Manhattan. According to the 2014 American Community Survey, about 52 percent of New York City households outside of Manhattan have access to at least one car. The age and density of New York's housing stock in many neighborhoods means that many car owners park on the streets. They often vociferously oppose bus lanes, bike lanes, bikeshare parking, and curb cuts for private driveways because they reduce the supply of on-street parking. Residents understandably fear that a new development without enough off-street parking will increase competition for the dwindling supply of free on-street parking.

City policymakers first moved to address "parking shortages" in 1938 when new provisions were added to the zoning code to regulate the construction of off-street lots and garages. By the 1950s, the city began to use its own resources to increase public parking capacity by constructing municipal parking garages and by metering public spaces. By 1954, as in many other cities, New York's zoning code began to require developers of certain types of projects to provide off-street parking. This approach, requiring no direct outlay of city funds, became the bedrock of parking policy and was enforced and strengthened when the new zoning resolution was adopted in 1961. Parking requirements were imposed for all residential, commercial, and manufacturing districts, with the exception of congested areas in Lower Manhattan. In the early 1980s, the exemption was extended to new construction in most of

Manhattan and part of Queens as a result of air-quality concerns. Until recently, parking requirements remained largely unchanged or were even increased in some cases.

In the neighborhoods outside of Manhattan where most New Yorkers live, the zoning that applies to residential development generally requires between 4 and 10 new parking spaces for every 10 new residential units, depending on the particular zoning district (denser district types generally require fewer spaces per unit). As interpreted by city officials, requirements are somewhat lower for certain types of affordable housing. For market-rate development, many zoning districts allow an automatic full or partial waiver of parking requirements for sites below a certain size and projects that would have otherwise required only a few spaces. To avoid the parking requirements, developers then often pay a higher cost to build multiple small buildings on a site rather than one large building.

Since the initial adoption of minimum parking requirements in New York, land has become increasingly expensive. Structured parking costs tens of thousands of dollars per space to construct, and even surface parking is expensive to build. Although parking requirements reduce neighborhood opposition to development, they inhibit affordable development in a city with a significant housing shortage. This might be especially true in transit-rich neighborhoods.

RECENT RESEARCH

In recent research, we pursued two methods to begin to untangle the tension between shielding incumbent residents from competition for on-street parking, and the effects of parking requirements on housing costs and transportation patterns. First, we analyzed the city's zoning regulations to understand how the parking requirements actually intersect with permitted development capacity. Second, we examined recent development patterns to see how much parking developers have been providing in reality.

In our research, we analyzed New York's zoning code and the related zoning maps to estimate how many parking spaces the city's zoning regime would require in each geographic area if all the potential zoning capacity were built out as new housing. By taking existing lot sizes into account within each zoning district (putting aside the fact that lot lines can be redrawn in some cases), we were also able to estimate the effect of "small development" waivers on these requirements.

When we performed this analysis on the city's zoning map as of 2007, we estimated that about 43 parking spaces were required for every 100 units of zoning capacity citywide, if it were developed for market-rate

Table 10-1 Estimated parking requirement per 100 units

	All lots	Within ½ mile of rail transit station	Beyond ½ mile of rail transit station
Bronx	39	34	51
Brooklyn	40	34	61
Manhattan	5	5	3
Queens	66	54	78
Staten Island	122	131	120
All New York City	43	29	72

tenants. That number varied widely across the city's five boroughs, from only five spaces in Manhattan to 122 in Staten Island, the city's lowest-density borough. Despite the lack of any formal mechanism tying parking requirements to transit access, in three of the five boroughs the requirements were far lower within a half-mile walking distance of a subway or commuter-rail station, due to the types of zoning districts used in these neighborhoods (Table 10-1).

These findings suggest that New York requires significant parking for new market-rate housing outside of Manhattan, even when waivers are considered. The implication, of course, is that reducing the parking requirements can reduce development costs and promote future transportation habits less tied to automobile ownership. Our analysis of the requirements, however, was not weighted to focus on the lots where development is most likely to occur, so expression of these requirements into actual new parking spaces could be somewhat different from our rough estimates.

The second part of our analysis was designed to better understand how actual development and parking requirements intersected in New York City. For this step, we identified all market-rate residential construction projects outside of Manhattan with at least five units that were completed between 2000 and 2008, and counted how many off-street parking spaces they included. We then compared this number to the number we estimated were required by zoning.

We concluded from this analysis that the parking requirements were likely binding in most cases where developers did not qualify for a waiver. Waiver availability, however, was an extremely important factor when assessing the zoning code's overall approach to parking.

- Of the approximately 1,000 projects we identified, about two-thirds were small enough to qualify for a waiver, and, of these, fewer than 20 percent provided any parking at all.
- Of the 317 projects that were too large to qualify for a waiver, 65 percent provided the *exact minimum number of required spaces*, or even less than was required.

- Another 12 percent of the projects too large to qualify for a waiver provided a few more spaces than were required (typically one or two extra spaces).
- Only about a quarter of the projects not qualifying for a waiver provided at least 25 percent more spaces than zoning required. This last group made up only 7 percent of the total number of projects we analyzed.

The overall picture is complicated, but we conclude that parking requirements reduce housing development and increase the parking supply as critics argue. The waiver provision for small buildings did remove the nominal parking requirements for many projects. On the other hand, the prevalence of the waiver projects might reflect a "survivor bias" (the logical error of concentrating on the people or things that "survived" some process while inadvertently overlooking those that did not because of their lack of visibility) if parking requirements for larger buildings render potential projects infeasible. Of the larger projects that did not qualify for a parking waiver, a vast majority provided only the required number of parking spaces.

THE PROSPECTS FOR REFORM

Since we began our research on New York's parking requirements in 2009, the salience of regulatory barriers to housing development has only increased. Housing costs in the city have continued to rise faster than incomes, suggesting that the need for more units is greater than ever. The current mayor, Bill de Blasio, assumed office in 2014 after running an election campaign that emphasized housing construction, especially affordable housing. In his first year in office, his administration released an ambitious housing plan to construct 80,000 new units of affordable housing and to increase density in underbuilt, transit-proximate neighborhoods. We suspect that de Blasio's appointment of Vicki Been as commissioner of the Department of Housing, Preservation, and Development also increased the probability of re-examining the city's parking requirements. Vicki Been is a co-author of some of our parking-related work and has a deep understanding of the effects of parking requirements.

Since the Great Recession, larger buildings (those with 50 or more units), which are unlikely to qualify for parking-requirement waivers, have made up a larger share of the development pipeline, which has made the nominal parking requirements more important now than in the years of development we studied.

Even before the de Blasio administration took office, the city showed a new willingness to adjust parking requirements when faced with specific opportunities. In December 2012, the city reduced the parking requirement in booming Downtown Brooklyn from 40 spaces per 100 units to 20 spaces. The neighborhood is among the best served by transit in the city and close to Manhattan's central business district. It had been rezoned in 2004 to permit greater density, but at least one new tower had empty spaces in its parking garage even after the units were fully leased.

The de Blasio administration, however, has demonstrated an appetite for more comprehensive reforms. As part of its broader "Zoning for Quality and Affordability" initiative, in 2015 the city proposed eliminating all parking requirements for new affordable-housing development located within a newly defined "Transit Zone," covering many areas within a half-mile of a subway station. Additionally, through a special permit process, *existing* affordable senior housing and some other affordable housing within the Transit Zone would be able to eliminate parking built to comply with current requirements, freeing up land for new affordable development.

Outside the Transit Zone, the proposal would reduce the parking requirement for new affordable senior housing to only 10 spaces per 100 units, and even this requirement would be newly subject to the automatic waiver provision (which is currently unavailable to affordable senior housing). Through a special permit process, existing affordable senior housing developments outside the Transit Zone would be able to apply for reductions from the current requirements. Requirements for other existing affordable developments in these areas would be unchanged. Formalizing transit proximity as a factor in determining the parking requirements is a promising breakthrough for the city's broader approach to parking and could act as a template for other cities, even if this practice is currently limited to affordable housing.

Unfortunately but not unexpectedly, the zoning initiative, and the changes to parking requirements in particular, drew significant opposition as the city shepherded it through the lengthy land-use approval process. Multiple community review panels recommended that the zoning initiative not be adopted, in part due to concerns over parking. The city council ultimately adopted the zoning initiative in March 2016, but only after reducing the size of the Transit Zone and after making it more difficult for existing parking lots to be redeveloped.

Although largely unsuccessful in this case, the intense community opposition to relaxed parking requirements draws attention to a difficult political choice officials must make in New York and other high-cost cities aiming to ease housing shortages. In many of these cities, officials are seeking to increase zoning density in or near existing neighborhoods, especially near transit. Whether this increased density is politically viable will depend on many neighborhood-specific factors, but parking is sure to be in the mix. There is a danger, then, that in an effort to alleviate housing shortages, city governments capitulate to neighborhood pressure for high parking requirements as a tool to "alleviate" competition for existing spaces. In the short run, this concession may help smooth the way for more housing construction, but in the long run, requiring more off-street parking will increase housing costs, traffic congestion, air pollution, and carbon emissions.

REFERENCE AND FURTHER READING

Epstein, R.A. 2002. "The Allocation of the Commons: Parking on Public Roads." *Journal of Legal Studies* 31, no. 2: 515–44.

11

The Hidden Cost of Bundled Parking

By C.J. Gabbe and Gregory Pierce

Urban renters in the U.S. face fast-rising housing prices, especially in coastal metropolitan areas. Price increases are in part due to restrictive land-use regulations. Minimum off-street parking requirements, a central component of land-use regulation in the U.S., warrant detailed study and potential policy reform. In most cities today, municipal regulation requires developers to provide on-site parking. Renters or buyers then pay for this parking as part of their monthly rent or purchase price; the price of parking is thus "bundled" with the price of the housing unit. While many households might have chosen to pay for on-site parking in a free market, this proportion is surely lower than what has been mandated. Moreover, the historical effect of minimums and bundled parking hides a transportation cost burden in housing prices, leaving households unable to choose. Minimum parking requirements force developers to build costly parking spaces that drive up the price of housing. Urban policymakers have recently taken an interest in reforming parking regulations and allowing unbundled parking based on social equity and environmental sustainability rationales.

In this chapter, we ask what are the effects of parking provision on residential rents in America's cities? We find that the cost of bundled garage parking for renters is approximately $1,700 per year, and the bundling of a garage space adds about 17 percent to a unit's rent. There are about 708,000 households without a car who have a garage parking space. We estimate that these households' payments for parking represent a direct deadweight loss to society (a measure of the large-scale inefficiency associated with minimum parking requirements) of

155

approximately $440 million per year. We argue that this figure represents just the tip of the iceberg when considering the indirect cost of minimum parking requirements. We conclude by suggesting two types of local land-use regulatory changes to reduce the high cost burden of parking: (1) cities should reduce or eliminate minimum parking requirements, and (2) cities should allow or encourage developers and landlords to offer unbundled parking options.

PARKING REGULATION AND HOUSING PRICES

Parking regulations limit housing supply, and increase housing prices, by (1) reducing density, and (2) imposing costly standards on developers. Minimum parking standards reduce density when land that would otherwise be devoted to buildings is instead used for car storage. This makes some infill development physically and/or financially infeasible. Minimum parking requirements can also be very costly to real estate developers. Along with the opportunity cost of devoting space to parking rather than another use, there is a high direct cost of building new parking. Nationally, in 2012, the average cost to build one underground parking space was $34,000 and to build an aboveground parking space was $24,000 (Shoup 2014). These costs are ultimately passed on to the consumer whether they have a car or not.

Several city-specific studies estimate the effect of parking provision on housing costs. In a 1999 study, Jia and Wachs found the average single-family unit in San Francisco with off-street parking sold for 12 percent more and the average condo unit with off-street parking sold for 13 percent more than the price of comparable units without parking. In a 2013 study, Manville analyzed a sample of buildings in downtown Los Angeles that had been converted to housing after the city passed its Adaptive Reuse Ordinance. He found that bundled parking raised the rent for an apartment by about $200 per month and raised the price of a condo by about $43,000. These articles provide preliminary evidence regarding the effect of bundled parking on housing prices, but are limited to select neighborhoods within California cities. Building on these studies, we assess how parking affects housing prices among a national sample of housing units.

USING THE AMERICAN HOUSING SURVEY TO STUDY THE COST OF PARKING

We use data from the 2011 American Housing Survey (AHS), conducted biennially by the U.S. Census Bureau. We concentrate on renters in urban areas because these households are experiencing the worst—and worsening—housing cost burdens. We focus specifically on garage parking because it is the most expensive type of parking to construct and the most prevalent form of parking in central, transit-oriented neighborhoods. Our modelling approach—called hedonic regression—is based on the idea that the price of a house or apartment is a function of its attributes, including building, neighborhood, and locational characteristics. The availability of on-site garage parking is one factor in a household's housing purchase or rental decision, and is the focus on our study.

BUNDLED PARKING AND RENTERS WITHOUT VEHICLES

A large majority (83 percent) of rental housing units in American metropolitan areas included some kind of parking on site. About 38 percent of rental units had garage parking, while 45 percent had surface or other non-garage parking spaces. About 17 percent did not have a parking space, but this varied dramatically by metropolitan area. The New York City area had the highest prevalence of units without parking (73 percent), contrasting sharply with Orange County, California at the other extreme (1 percent). Across metros, approximately 3.5 million rental units did not include parking. These units tended to be smaller, older, and with fewer in-unit amenities than units with bundled parking.

Most American households have at least one automobile; census data show that nationwide only about 7 percent of rental households do not

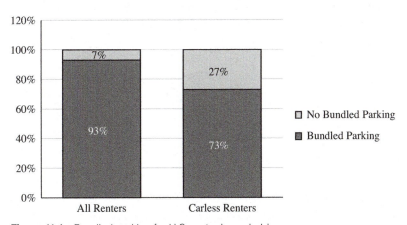

Figure 11-1 Bundled parking for U.S. renter households

have a car. As with bundled parking, there is considerable variation in the share of households without a vehicle across metros, from 26 percent in metropolitan New York City to 1.5 percent in the St. George, Utah, metropolitan area. Across the entire 2011 AHS sample—which includes renter and owner-occupied units—more than 71 percent of carless households live in a housing unit with a bundled parking space, as opposed to more than 96 percent of households with a vehicle. Within our sample of renter-occupied units, these percentages are 73 percent and 93 percent, respectively. Quantifying the relationship between vehicle ownership and parking is important because carless households are paying for something that they most likely do not need or want.

ISOLATING THE PRICE OF A PARKING SPACE

We use the hedonic regression modelling approach to find that a bundled parking garage spot costs about $1,700 per year, or $142 per month. Thought of another way, including garage parking increases the rent of a housing unit by around 17 percent. While these figures were averages for all rental households, we hypothesized that carless renters might place a lower value on parking availability. The data support this hypothesis. For carless renters, bundled garage parking costs an average of $621 a year—a 13 percent premium on their rental price. We calculate the deadweight loss to society stemming from garage parking provided by landlords to residents of 708,000 housing units who do not own a car. At a national level, this deadweight loss amounts to $440 million paid for garage parking spaces unused by residents for parking annually. This amount represents only the direct cost of parking requirements on low-income renters and does not account for the many indirect costs of parking provision (Shoup 2011).

■ Cost of garage parking   □ Cost of other attributes

Figure 11-2   Garage parking as a component of the average household's monthly rent ($913)

DISCUSSION

Our results support the economic logic that an apartment with garage parking, with other conditions remaining the same, will be more expensive than one with surface parking or no parking. On the demand side, garage parking spaces are an important amenity for many urban renters. Garage parking is particularly valuable in higher-density urban neighborhoods where on-street parking is metered or difficult to procure. Carless households and households who do not use their garage for automobile parking may still gain some utility from a garage by using it for storage or even additional living space. This would be more likely for households with a private one- or two-car garage, rather than a household with a designated space in a shared parking structure or underground parking garage.

On the supply side, the direct and indirect costs of parking provision are high, and these costs are passed on to renters. Garage parking is expensive to build and its provision often represents a substantial opportunity cost for a real estate developer, particularly when land area is devoted to parking rather than leasable residential or commercial space. We show that these direct and indirect costs are passed on to consumers in the form of higher rents.

The provision of parking supply without associated demand can only be characterized as wasteful. Minimum parking requirements create a major equity problem for carless households, illustrated by the large deadweight loss ($440 million per year) associated with renters paying for garage parking that they do not use for car storage. Given that the carless population in the U.S. is generally made up of lower-income households, many of the households involuntarily paying for garage parking are the ones that can least afford to do so. In fact, we find the average income of households with a garage space but no car ($24,000) is only slightly more than half the income of other households ($44,000). In the absence of paying for an unused parking space, these rent outlays could be applied to renting a larger or better-located unit, other consumer spending, or saving for a home purchase.

We recommend that cities should reduce or eliminate minimum parking requirements in urban areas. Even if cities reduce parking requirements, as some have recently done, the housing supply takes years to adjust. It would likely be a decade or two before consumers could choose from many housing options with unbundled parking. Reducing or eliminating minimum parking requirements would have the biggest benefits to renters in higher-density, centrally located neighborhoods where garage parking is prevalent.

We also recommend that cities allow or encourage real estate developers to unbundle parking from new housing. This recommendation depends on reform of minimum parking standards. If minimum parking standards are not reduced or eliminated, a developer would have little or no incentive to unbundle parking because there would be an oversupply of parking that could not be rented, and a developer would essentially pay for this. A combination of these policies will allow developers to build housing with less parking and then to use pricing to allocate the parking spaces they construct as they see fit.

CONCLUSION

In this chapter, we examine the effects of bundled parking provision on metropolitan residential rents. Our findings provide the first nationally representative evidence that urban garage parking provision is costly to renters. We provide further evidence that minimum parking requirements are burdensome to renters and lead to societal waste. Carless households, many of whom have low incomes, are disproportionately affected in neighborhoods and cities where garage parking is the norm. Eliminating minimum parking requirements in these locations will allow the market to gradually meet the latent demand for housing options with unbundled parking. Additionally, it will reduce the annual $440 million deadweight loss directly experienced by urban renters without cars. In short, the elimination of minimum parking requirements will help remedy the perverse incentive for driving and discourage the sprawling urban form that these requirements have encouraged over the past 75 years.

REFERENCES AND FURTHER READING

W. Jia, W., and M. Wachs. 1999. "Parking Requirements and Housing Affordability: A Case Study of San Francisco." *Transportation Research Record* 1685: 156–60.
Shoup, Donald. 2014. "The High Cost of Minimum Parking Requirements," in *Parking Issues and Policies*, edited by Stephen Ison and Corinne Mulley. Bingley, UK: Emerald Group Publishing, 87–113.
Shoup, Donald. 2011. *The High Cost of Free Parking*. Revised edition. Chicago: Planners Press.

12

Parking Policies in Asian Cities: Conventional but Instructive

By Paul Barter

The problems caused by parking requirements are chronic (long term and relatively intangible), not acute (painful here and now). They are not obvious to most people, and they are hard to explain. The resulting inefficiencies don't wave big signs saying parking requirements caused me! It takes some analysis and explaining to see them. How many people know that parking requirements make it difficult to restore and re-use inner-city buildings? How many people know that parking requirements make housing less affordable?

Unfortunately, minimum parking requirements are spreading to cities all around the world. To document how parking requirements have spread through Asia, and how they vary among cities, this chapter analyzes the parking policies in 14 large metropolitan areas: Ahmedabad, Bangkok, Beijing, Dhaka, Guangzhou, Hanoi, Hong Kong, Kuala Lumpur, Jakarta, Manila, Singapore, Seoul, Taipei, and Tokyo.

Two main surprises emerge. First, all the cities have minimum parking requirements, and most apply them in rather rigid ways. This is surprising because rigidly applied parking minimums are usually associated with car-dependent cities and seem ill suited to Asia's dense and mixed-use urban fabrics where car use is relatively low. Second, although Tokyo's parking policies include minimum parking requirements, a closer look reveals a uniquely Japanese market-responsive set of parking policies.

The comparisons in this chapter use a new typology of parking policy approaches, which I explain in the next section. Then the following section illustrates the typology as it applies to common approaches in the western world. This sets the scene for three sections that examine how Asian cities compare by looking at their policies towards: a) off-street on-site parking, b) on-street parking, and c) public parking. The chapter ends by taking stock of the findings.

A TYPOLOGY OF LOCAL PARKING POLICY APPROACHES

Figure 12-1 portrays a new typology of municipal parking policy approaches. This typology informs the analysis throughout this chapter. It is based on three dimensions in parking policy thinking.

- The dimension on the z-axis (How much parking supply?) is based on attitudes about the quantity of parking spaces, such as "seeking plentiful parking" or "limiting parking."
- The dimension on the horizontal axis of Figure 12-1 contrasts two different mindsets. The right side of the figure insists that every site be served by on-site parking (justifying minimum parking requirements). The left side of the figure, on the other hand,

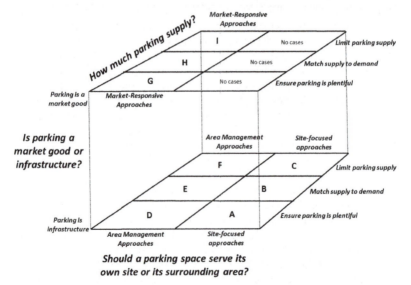

Figure 12-1   A three-criterion typology of approaches to parking policies

Source: Adapted from Barter (2015)

embraces "park-once-and-walk districts," in which parking facilities tend to be open to the public and to serve the surrounding area.

- The vertical dimension in Figure 12-1 is split into two layers. This is based on whether parking is understood to be a type of infrastructure and planned as such (lower layer) or as a market good and therefore enabled to respond to market processes (upper layer). The upper-layer "market responsive" approaches all fall along the left side because market processes in parking are better suited to parking open to the public.

PARKING POLICY APPROACHES IN THE WESTERN WORLD

We can now map onto this typology the parking policy approaches widely found in Europe, the U.S., Canada, Australia, and New Zealand. This also serves to further explain the typology. Below, we will see where the Asian cities fit.

- The squares labelled A, B and C on the lower layer of Figure 12-1 represent site-focused parking approaches that try to meet parking demand within development sites.
  - o Square A represents the version promoting supply with high minimum parking requirements, as in suburbia.
  - o The approach at B involves "right-sized" parking minimums that better match demand and avoid excess.
  - o C represents an on-site approach that restricts supply. This is unlikely as a municipal approach. Large isolated sites, however, such as campuses, may decide to limit their own parking.
- The squares labeled D, E, and F on the lower level of Figure 12-1 are varieties of "area management" parking policy, as found in older areas where requiring on-site parking is infeasible and causes various problems. Many such places emphasize public parking and better management of on-street parking rather than requiring on-site parking.
  - o D, E, and F differ in their attitudes to parking supply. For example, approach D seeks plentiful public parking, as is common in small downtowns in North America. The approach at square F limits parking and is often found in large transit-rich central business districts (CBDs).
  - o Unlike the upper level of the figure, these area management approaches lack strong efforts to promote market responsiveness in parking.

- The squares labeled G, H, and I on the upper level of Figure 12-1 represent market-responsive approaches. These involve policies that encourage local parking demand, supply, and prices to adapt to each other via market processes rather than regulation. These approaches have only recently attracted attention.
  - o The best-known example is Shoup's package of abolishing parking minimums, pricing on-street parking to achieve 85 percent occupancy, and returning revenue to neighborhoods (square H).
  - o In practice, many CBDs have market-responsive parking systems, with widespread commercial parking, no parking minimums, and unregulated market prices. Promoting competition among parking operators and via demand-responsive on-street prices, as in Calgary and Seattle, for example, sometimes enhances this market responsiveness.
  - o Square G in the upper left of the figure is the market-responsive square that represents the possibility of promoting parking supply using market-oriented approaches, such as incentives, rather than regulations or government supply.

What about Asia's cities? Asian cities tend to share key features with older areas of large cities in the Western world, such as high density, relatively low car ownership, and substantial public transport use. Areas in Western cities with these characteristics tend to avoid site-focused parking approaches and to refrain from promoting parking supply. Very few Western cities are experimenting with market-responsive parking policy. By analogy, we might expect Asian cities to do the same.

PARKING STANDARDS, ATTITUDES TO SUPPLY AND ON-SITE PARKING IN ASIA

In this section, I focus on parking standards (maximum or minimum requirements) for commercial buildings and look for insight on two of the dimensions in Figure 12-1: a) attitudes about supply and b) whether policy promotes on-site parking or park-once districts. A deeper understanding of the second dimension will also require a look at public parking in a section below.

Figure 12-2 shows commercial parking requirements compared with car ownership rates. It was a surprise to find that all of the Asian cities in the study have minimum parking requirements throughout, even in their CBDs. And only Seoul, Singapore, and Hong Kong have CBD minimums set lower than in other parts of the city.

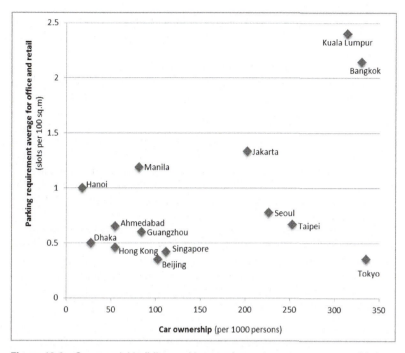

Figure 12-2 Commercial building parking requirements versus car ownership in 2008

Source: Barter (2011)

Note to Figure 12-2: The requirements refer to the averages of three hypothetical buildings, each with 25,000 square meter gross floor area: a CBD office building; a non-central office building; and a non-central shopping center.

The highest commercial parking minimums are in middle-income Southeast Asian cities, especially Kuala Lumpur and Bangkok. This suggests an embrace of suburban-style site-focused approaches along with a stance that promotes supply. This is surprising for cities with relatively high urban densities and widespread mixing of land uses.

By contrast, the richest Asian cities in the study have low minimums. Tokyo's low parking requirements also exempt small buildings and phase in only gradually. In Hong Kong, low maximums in the 1970s gave way in 1981 to parking minimums set at low levels. In 2002, Singapore took a similar stance by reducing its minimums.

The presence of parking minimums at all is surprising because Hong Kong, Seoul, Singapore, Taipei, and Tokyo are "transit metropolises"; that is, in these cities, transit, transport policies, urban planning, and real estate have coevolved or been coordinated to foster public transport. Nevertheless, low parking minimums suggest parking supply is not being strongly promoted. Past efforts in Tokyo and Taipei to increase parking supply via other means, such as public-sector investments and incentives for private-sector investments, have largely ended. Low minimums may also suggest a mindset in which parking spaces serve the local area rather than individual sites.

Parking minimums are at moderate levels in the remaining Asian cities (Ahmedabad, Beijing, Dhaka, Guangzhou, and Hanoi) where vehicle ownership levels have escalated only since 2000 or so. Because car ownership is low among this group of cities, however, these parking minimums do not tell us much about the extent of site-focused attitudes to parking supply. The analysis featured in sections below may lead to a better understanding of such attitudes.

Surprisingly, Seoul is the only Asian city to provide an example of a recent policy that places deliberate limits on parking supply. Seoul applies low parking maximums to buildings in its major transit-oriented business districts. Hong Kong no longer explicitly limits parking supply, but the low maximums applied in the 1970s have left a legacy of high parking prices.

ON-STREET PARKING MANAGEMENT IN THE ASIAN CITIES

How on-street parking is managed provides clues regarding parking policy approaches. Site-focused approaches and an attitude promoting supply tend to arise out of a lack of faith in on-street parking management. Strongly effective on-street parking management is not yet in place across most areas of Ahmedabad, Bangkok, Beijing, Dhaka (Figure 12-3), Hanoi, Jakarta, Kuala Lumpur, and Manila.

On-street parking management is more effective generally in Guangzhou, Hong Kong, Singapore, Taipei, the Makati CBD in Manila, and Seoul. In Seoul's major business districts, parking demand is a factor in on-street price setting. Taipei has a similar policy. Strong on-street parking management can potentially embolden shifts away from site-focused approaches (towards the left on Figure 12-1) and away from approaches that promote plentiful parking (towards the back on Figure 12-1).

Japan has an unusual and effective approach. On-street parking has been almost completely banned since the 1960s. Small numbers of parking meters allow daytime parking only in certain places. A long-running war against illegal short-term on-street parking in Tokyo was won in 2006. Overnight parking is totally banned, backed by a program of late-night towing. This ban is complemented by Japan's proof-of-parking

Figure 12-3   On-street parking in Dhaka's CBD (2009)

law under which registering a car requires proof of long-term access to off-street parking near one's home.

PUBLIC PARKING IN ASIAN CITIES

Despite having parking minimums, several Asian cities nevertheless fall on the left side of Figure 12-1, with parking seen as serving its surrounding area, not just its specific site. Such a mindset is a feature of both the area-management approaches (lower-left on Figure 12-1) and the market-responsive approaches (upper-left on Figure 12-1).

Tokyo seems to have a market-responsive parking approach. A large proportion of parking, even in outer areas, is open to the public although it may be privately owned and operated. Low on-site minimums, the absence of on-street parking, and the proof-of-parking rule have stimulated the supply of commercial parking in most areas, for both residential and other parking. Tiny coin-operated surface parking facilities are ubiquitous (Figure 12-4). Parking prices vary in rough proportion to real estate values, with high prices in the transit-rich core.

Taipei, Hong Kong, Beijing, Guangzhou, and Seoul's five main business districts also have significant roles for priced public parking

Figure 12-4 Coin-operated parking in central Tokyo

(provided by both commercial and government entities). Parking in shopping centers and office buildings in busy localities tends to be priced and open to the public. Many older residential compounds in Beijing and Guangzhou offer public parking during the day, and both have plans for numerous public-sector parking facilities. These cities therefore seem to have shifted away from a site-focused mindset into the area-management approaches, as represented in the lower left squares of Figure 12-1.

Other cities may follow Tokyo's example in adopting a market-responsive approach (moving from lower left to upper left on Figure 12-1). Seoul's major business districts seem closest to realizing this. Prospects for market-responsive parking in Beijing and Guangzhou were improved by the recent abolition of government controls over private-sector parking prices.

Singapore and the rest of Seoul, however, seem to be less decisively on the left side of Figure 12-1 and have a stronger tendency to keep parking on-site than in the cases above.

Bangkok and Jakarta have an especially limited role for public parking. This is not only consistent with their reliance on parking minimums, but also confirms that they have been decisively site-focused in their approaches (on the right side of Figure 12-1).

In Ahmedabad, Hanoi, Kuala Lumpur, and Manila, surveys revealed surprisingly significant roles for off-street public parking, despite their emphasis on parking minimums. This suggests at least some potential for a shift towards seeing parking spaces as serving areas, not individual sites (that is, towards the left side of Figure 12-1).

Public-sector public parking can also provide clues about attitudes about supply. Strong efforts by city governments to build public parking suggest an attitude that promotes supply, and this is indeed what we find in Ahmedabad, Beijing, Dhaka, Guangzhou, and Hanoi.

CONCLUSION

Let us take stock and make some policy suggestions. Figure 12-5 shows my assessment of where each Asian city fits in the new parking policy typology.

Recall that, by analogy with dense and car-lite parts of Western cities, we expected Asia's dense and relatively less auto-dependent cities to avoid promoting supply and site-focused parking approaches. Thus, it was a surprise to find so many Asian cities in square A of the diagram with a site-focused and a parking approach promoting supply; such policies promote car dependence and are poorly suited to these cities' urban and mobility characteristics.

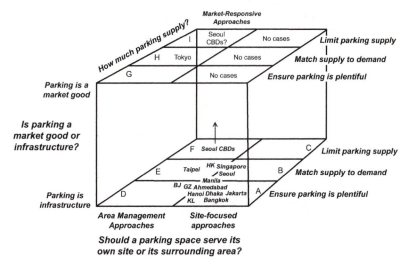

Figure 12-5 Asian cities' parking approaches located on the new parking policy typology

Nevertheless, parking policies in other Asian cities are not as inappropriate as they first seemed based on the presence of parking minimums. For example, Taipei and Hong Kong fit within square E, which represents a supply-neutral area management policy and aligns with expectations by analogy with dense Western cities. Singapore and Seoul (outside its main business districts) are more site-focused than we would expect but do not promote excessive parking supply.

It was surprising to find cases of market-responsive parking approaches in Asia because this is a relatively new topic in the West. Tokyo has a unique market-responsive approach (in square H on the upper level). Seoul's main business districts may also have the beginnings of a supply-restricting, market-responsive approach (square I on the upper level).

What policy suggestions arise for Asian cities? Dense cities with low car usage (most Asian cities) are well suited to supply-neutral or supply-limiting area-management parking policy approaches (squares E or F in Figure 12-1) and should avoid site-focused approaches and excessively promoting the parking supply (squares A, B, and D). Tokyo's example suggests that cities with an area-management approach could benefit from aiming towards market-responsive parking (squares H or I).

The Asian cities that currently sit in squares A, B, or D need better on-street parking management, along with more effective and up-to-date enforcement and pricing practices, to increase their confidence that shifts away from site-focused and/or supply-promoting policies need not cause serious on-street parking problems.

Finally, to varying extents, all Asian cities would benefit from less emphasis on parking minimums and from more explicit efforts to promote park-once-and-walk districts with priced public parking as well as from efforts to make parking more market-responsive.

REFERENCES AND FURTHER READING

Barter, P.A. 2015. A parking policy typology for clearer thinking on parking reform, *International Journal of Urban Sciences*, 19:2, 136–156, DOI:10.1080/12265934.2014. 927740.

Barter, P.A. 2011. "Off-Street Parking Policy Surprises in Asian Cities." *Cities* 29, no. 1: 23–31. http://dx.doi.org/10.1016/j.cities.2011.06.007.

Barter, P.A. 2011. *Parking Policy in Asian Cities*. Asian Development Bank (ADB), Manila. ISBN: 978-92-9092-241-4 (print), 978-92-9092-352-7 (web).

13

Parking and the Environment

By Mikhail Chester, Arpad Horvath, and Samer Madanat

We know surprisingly little about how parking infrastructure affects energy demand, the environment, and the social cost of vehicle travel. Passenger and freight movements are often the focus of energy and environmental assessments, but vehicles spend most of their lives parked. Because abundant free parking encourages solo driving and thus discourages walking, biking, and the use of public transit, it greatly contributes to urban congestion. The environmental impacts of parking and the driving it promotes are often borne by local populations and not the trip-takers themselves.

The transportation life-cycle assessment (LCA) framework allows us to understand the full costs of travel, including energy use and environmental effects. Past LCAs, however, have focused on evaluating the resources directly used for travel and have not considered the extensive parking infrastructure, including the costs of its construction, operation, maintenance, and raw material extraction and processing. This narrow focus is understandable given the diversity of parking spaces and the lack of available data on parking infrastructure. For example, consider the great differences in energy use and emissions associated with curb parking spaces, multistory garages, and private home garages. Furthermore, it is difficult to assign the energy use and environmental effects of parking to individual actors. Should we assign the cost of parking to an automobile driver, or to the builder of the strip mall where the driver shops, or to the shop where the driver parks?

To determine the full social cost of parking, we develop a range of estimates of the U.S. parking space inventory and determine the energy use and environmental effects of constructing and maintaining this parking. We find that for many vehicle trips the environmental cost of the parking infrastructure sometimes equals or exceeds the environmental cost of the vehicles themselves. Evaluating life-cycle effects, including health care and environmental damage costs, we determine that emissions from parking infrastructure cost the U.S. between $4 and $20 billion annually, or between $6 and $23 per space per year.

A U.S. PARKING SPACE INVENTORY

To estimate the number of parking spaces in the U.S., we have developed multiple scenarios that include survey data and new estimates for different types of parking spaces. We evaluate on-street, surface, and structured spaces.

There are roughly 240 million passenger vehicles and 10 million on-road freight vehicles in the U.S. All passenger vehicles require a home base, and commuting vehicles also require a work space. In addition, using data from a nationwide inventory, we reach a figure of 105 million metered spaces. We add to this running total several different estimates of the number of additional spaces of different types, and Table 13-1 summarizes the estimates and their resulting land-use characteristics in four possible scenarios.

Scenario A includes the number of parking spaces at commercial sites, derived from national estimates of commercial floor area and the minimum parking requirements for each land use. This is added to the home spaces, work spaces, and the metered space inventory, taking into account the overlap between commercial square-foot estimates and workspaces. Scenario A, with 722 million spaces, can be considered a conservative inventory before taking into account the high uncertainty about the number of on-street non-metered spaces.

Table 13-1   Parking spaces in the U.S. (in millions)

| | Off-Street | Off-Street | | Total | Parking Area as % of US Land Area |
		Surface	Structure		
Scenario A	92	520	110	722	0.64
Scenario B	180	520	110	810	0.66
Scenario C	150	610	84	844	0.68
Scenario D	1,100	790	120	2,010	0.90

In Scenario B, we evaluate roadway design guidelines and distances of urban and rural roadways to estimate nationwide on-street parking. This estimate takes the mileage of non-bridge and non-tunnel urban arterial, collector, and local roadway shoulders and assumes that one-half of their potential area is designated as on-street parking with either one or both shoulders used. Adding this to Scenario A's estimate produces 810 million spaces. While Scenario B includes on-street parking, the estimate conservatively assumes that only a small fraction of curbside urban roadway area is designated as parking.

Scenario C is based on observed ratios of four spaces per vehicle for cities and 2.2 spaces per vehicle for rural areas. Scenario C weights these ratios by urban and rural vehicle travel to produce a nationwide average of 3.4 spaces per vehicle, or 844 million spaces.

Finally, Scenario D is based on an unverified estimate of 8 spaces per vehicle that is often mentioned in planning literature; it produces an estimate of 2 billion spaces, which is the high end of our range. We include this ratio as an upper-bound assessment that could capture spaces missed in previous scenarios.

EMBEDDED ENERGY AND EMISSIONS IN PARKING INFRASTRUCTURE

Valuing and allocating the total cost of parking infrastructure is not simple because not all externalities can be priced, costs are borne by many people, and parking spaces are spread throughout the built environment. LCA, however, is a framework to estimate the magnitude of these effects. LCA's basic tenet is that an activity like parking cannot function without support from other services. Energy use, environmental degradation, and greenhouse gas emissions (GHG) result from parking construction and maintenance activities. Parking's physical infrastructure requires processed materials, energy, labor, and other inputs, which in turn depend upon their own supply chains. For example, asphalt requires aggregate, which is mined and then must be transported. Each of these activities consumes energy and produces emissions.

We evaluate the life-cycle effects of each parking space type and quantify the materials, energy use, GHG emissions, and conventional air pollutant emissions associated with it. After performing this analysis, we then normalize the results to a passenger-kilometer-traveled basis, taking into account the varying lifetimes of parking spaces and structures. Our methodology measures only air emissions. Other major impacts from parking infrastructure include heat island effects and alterations to water flows (such as more frequent and higher peak

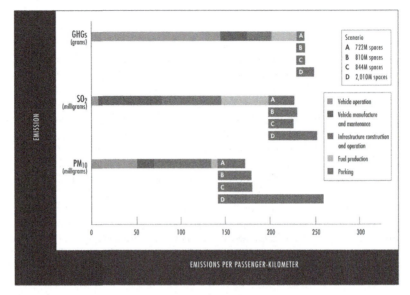

Figure 13-1 Emissions per passenger-kilometer

flows, lower water tables, and increased chemical contamination). Thus our LCA costs are lower bound estimates.

Not all energy use and emissions generated by parking can be allocated to the automobile. The availability of parking encourages people to drive, but at the same time high automobile use encourages businesses, developers, and government agencies to provide parking. Accurately allocating all the environmental effects of parking between drivers and other actors is not possible because causality is unclear. It is important, however, to illustrate the potential total costs of personal vehicle use. Figure 13-1 shows total emissions caused directly and indirectly by automobiles if all the LCA emissions from parking are attributed to automobiles.

In some cases, larger reductions in environmental impacts may be achieved by focusing on parking infrastructure (and other life-cycle components) instead of the vehicle's tailpipe, where significant strides towards reducing pollution have already been made. For certain pollutants, parking infrastructure contributes a significant share—and sometimes even the largest share—of life-cycle effects. For example, parking's contribution to the production of SO2, which causes respiratory damage and acid deposition, largely results from electricity generation in the supply chain. SO2 emissions from parking exceed the SO2 emissions from driving. The majority of parking-related PM10 emissions, which cause cardiovascular harm, stem from hot-mix asphalt plants as well as the mixing and placing of asphalt. PM10 emissions from parking are about the same as those from driving.

VALUING THE IMPACTS OF PARKING INFRASTRUCTURE EMISSIONS

Estimating the monetized health and environmental costs of parking infrastructure represents an important step in developing total transportation cost assessments to inform policy decisions. We evaluate these costs using an approach developed by the National Research Council's Hidden Costs of Energy study. This allows an assessment of the total impact of parking construction and maintenance by assigning damage costs to each pollutant. We can then evaluate the effects of parking in typical high-impact urban and low-impact rural counties. Using these estimates, LCA enables us to attach dollar amounts to the external costs of parking infrastructure.

The parking infrastructure estimated in Scenarios A through C costs the U.S. between $4 billion and $20 billion per year. Per space, this amounts to between $6 and $23 per year. The low end of this range represents a parking space constructed in a low-density rural area, whereas the high end typifies a space in a high-density urban environment. Everyone bears this cost in the form of adverse health impacts, building damage, and reduced agricultural production, to name a few.

Underpriced parking not only increases automobile dependence, but is also environmentally damaging to construct and maintain. We hope that our life-cycle assessment will help planners and public officials understand the full cost of parking.

REFERENCES AND FURTHER READING

Chester, Mikhail, Arpad Horvath, and Samer Madanat. 2010. "Parking Infrastructure: Energy, Emissions, and Automobile Life-Cycle Environmental Accounting," *Environmental Research Letters* 5, no. 3.
Chester, Mikhail, Andrew Fraser, Juan Matute, Carolyn Flower, and Ram Pendyala. 2015. "Parking Infrastructure: A Constraint on or Opportunity for Urban Redevelopment? A Study of Los Angeles County Parking Supply and Growth." *Journal of the American Planning Association* 81, no. 4: 268–86.
Chester, Mikhail, and Arpad Horvath. 2009. "Environmental Assessment of Passenger Transportation Should Include Infrastructure and Supply Chains." *Environmental Research Letters* 4, no. 2.

National Research Council's Committee on Health, Environmental, and Other External Costs and Benefits of Energy Production and Consumption. 2010. *Hidden Costs of Energy: Unpriced Consequences of Energy Production and Use.* Atlanta, Ga.: National Academies Press.

14

The Parking Glut in Los Angeles

By Andrew Fraser, Mikhail Chester, and Juan Matute

Minimum parking requirements create more parking than is needed. This in turn encourages more driving at a time when cities seek to reduce congestion and increase transit use, biking, and walking. After nearly a century of development under these requirements, parking now dominates our cities.

To counter the problem of excessive minimum parking requirements, academics and practitioners have advocated a new suite of parking policies, including reduced parking requirements and demand-based prices for on-street parking. These policies aim to better manage parking and reduce driving, but too much parking works against these goals by spreading the destinations and making the cost of driving artificially low. To more effectively address the issues caused by minimum parking requirements, planners and policymakers should focus not only on future development, but also on the existing parking oversupply.

Relatively little information exists, however, on the amount and location of parking in cities, limiting our understanding of how that parking contributes to land- and automobile-use patterns. To address this knowledge gap, we developed a case study to estimate where parking infrastructure exists in Los Angeles and how it has evolved over time.

PARKING IN LOS ANGELES COUNTY

Like most cities in the U.S., Los Angeles has included minimum parking requirements in its zoning and building codes for nearly a century.

They require developments to provide specified amounts of off-street parking based on land use and project size. What makes Los Angeles unique and well suited for our case study is that 1) a majority of the buildings were erected following the adoption of minimum parking requirements, 2) the pace of construction has slowed dramatically in recent decades, largely due to spatial constraints, and 3) the region is unlikely to see extensive new development.

With a building stock and parking supply that are largely "locked-in," even drastic changes to parking requirements are likely to have little impact on the total number of spaces in the region. To understand how this parking may affect policies intended to curb the use of automobiles, city planners need information on where current parking exists and how much of it there is.

Los Angeles is widely recognized for its automobile dependence and associated issues with traffic congestion. Covering 4,700 square miles, Los Angeles County includes 88 incorporated cities. To evaluate the impact of minimum parking requirements in the county, we estimated the number, location, and year of construction for off-street residential, off-street non-residential, and on-street parking over the past century.

To develop these estimates at a scale that will be useful for policy decisions, we combined models of building and roadway growth, land use and building types, and historical parking requirements covering 55 types of zones. Because there was significant consistency from one city's parking ordinances to another's, we used the median parking requirements from a sample of 19 incorporated cities. Estimates of the on-street parking supply excluded portions of the roadway that would not have on-street parking, such as driveways, bus stops, fire hydrants, and intersections.

PARKING QUANTITY

As of 2010, Los Angeles County had 18.6 million parking spaces, including 5.5 million residential off-street, 9.6 million non-residential off-street, and 3.6 million on-street spaces. This amounts to more than 200 square miles of parking spaces, equivalent to 14 percent of the county's incorporated land area (Figures 14-1 and 14-2). Even though Los Angeles has one of the densest road networks in the U.S. and is recognized worldwide for its expansive freeway system, the total area dedicated to on- and off-street parking is 1.4 times larger than the 140 square miles dedicated to road and highways.

While perceived parking shortages are often used to defend minimum parking requirements in metropolitan areas, there are 3.3 spaces

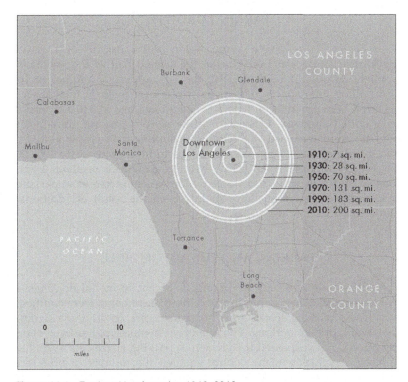

Figure 14-1 Total parking footprint, 1910–2010

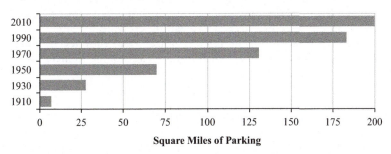

Figure 14-2 Los Angeles County's parking supply, 1910–2010

for each of the 5.6 million vehicles in the county (1.0 residential off-street, 1.9 nonresidential off-street, and 0.6 on-street spaces per vehicle). Although certain areas of Los Angeles do struggle with an imbalance between parking supply and demand, these results show that the indiscriminate application of uniform parking requirements has led to a large oversupply of parking in many areas.

PARKING GROWTH

Los Angeles is a relatively young region, and a majority of its parking infrastructure was built during the second half of the twentieth century. Between 1950 and 2010, the city added 12 million of its 18.6 million total spaces. The greatest rate of growth in total spaces occurred between 1950 and 1980, when an average of 310,000 spaces were added annually. During this time period, parking grew faster than the number of road lane miles, contributing to increased auto use and resulting congestion. Average space additions slowed to 190,000 per year from 1980 to 2010. By 1990, the growth of residential and roadway infrastructure also slowed. More recent increases in parking spaces across the county have mainly been the result of additional non-residential parking spaces.

PARKING AND THE AUTOMOBILE

The automobile was only beginning its ascent to modal dominance in Los Angeles when minimum parking requirements were codified. As a result, parking spaces grew faster than cars, leading to a significant oversupply of parking. The rate of car ownership, however, soon caught up, and surpassed the growth of parking spaces. By 1975, the number of vehicles in the county equaled the number of off-street residential spaces. Since then, this ratio of vehicles to off-street spaces has remained consistent, approaching one to one in 73 percent of the census tracts in Los Angeles County. Residential off-street space requirements may be effective at preventing cruising for street parking in neighborhoods, but the results indicate that they incentivized vehicle adoption, ultimately contributing to additional vehicle miles traveled and congestion.

PARKING DENSITY

The growth of parking has varied across the county. Since 1950, much of the growth in parking occurred outside the urban core in low-density residential and commercial developments. Neighborhoods *within* the urban core, however, have the greatest parking space densities (Figure 14-3). In fact, the central business district has the highest density of parking spaces, most of which are associated with non-residential development. This abundance of parking in areas with high-quality transit and dense mixed-use development limits transit use, cycling, and walking. While we did not directly assess how the parking supply

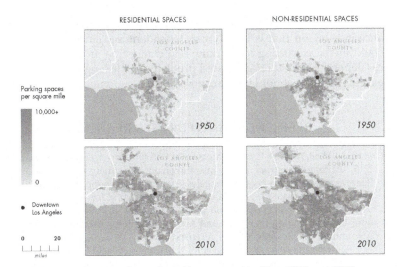

Figure 14-3 Los Angeles County's parking space densities, 1950 and 2010

affects congestion, we suspect that high parking density contributes to congestion on nearby roads. Reforming existing parking requirements may limit parking additions in the future but is unlikely to address existing congestion issues.

REDUCING THE PARKING SUPPLY

Our findings suggest that cities should reduce the existing oversupply of parking that encourages automobile travel and works against other policies that are intended to limit driving or to promote alternative transportation modes. It may be necessary to reduce the number of existing parking spaces to fully realize the positive impacts of these policies.

There is also a substantial opportunity to redevelop our cities by transitioning existing parking to alternative land uses. Space for development is limited in urban areas, but our findings show that a significant portion of developable land in Los Angeles is dedicated to parking. While repurposing parking lots or structures may offer the greatest opportunity for large redevelopment projects, planners should also consider the benefits of transitioning residential parking, especially home garages, toward other uses. Converting residential parking spaces to additional dwelling units, for example, could help alleviate the housing shortage in Los Angeles.

Reducing the existing parking supply will likely meet strong resistance in a region that is largely car dependent and, in the short term, could increase cruising for parking and congestion. In order to reduce car dependency and its associated problems in the long term, however, existing parking should be repurposed.

REFERENCES AND FURTHER READING

Chester, Mikhail, Andrew Fraser, Juan Matute, Carolyn Flower, and Ram Pendyala. 2015. "Parking Infrastructure: A Constraint on or Opportunity for Urban Redevelopment? A Study of Los Angeles County Parking Supply and Growth." *Journal of the American Planning Association* 81, no. 4 (2015): 268–86.

Chester, Mikhail, Arpad Horvath, and Samer Madanat. 2010. "Parking Infrastructure: Energy, Emissions, and Automobile Life-cycle Environmental Accounting." *Environmental Research Letters* 5, no. 1.

Fraser, Andrew, and Mikhail Chester. 2016. "Environmental and Economic Consequences of Permanent Roadway Infrastructure Commitment: City Road Network Life-Cycle Assessment and Los Angeles County." *ASCE Journal of Infrastructure Systems* 22, no. 1.

Reyna, Janet and Mikhail Chester. 2015. "The Growth of Urban Building Stock: Unintended Lock-in and Embedded Environmental Effects." *Journal of Industrial Ecology* 19, no. 4: 524–37.

This chapter previously appeared in ACCESS, *Fall 2016, where it was adapted from "Parking Infrastructure: A Constraint on or Opportunity for Urban Redevelopment? A Study of Los Angeles County Parking Supply and Growth,"* Journal of the American Planning Association *81, no. 4 (2015).*

15

Less Off-Street Parking, More Mexico City

By Rodrigo García Reséndiz and Andrés Sañudo Gavaldón

There is a popular saying in Mexico, *"mientras más, mejor,"* which translates to "the more the merrier." Chilangos, the informal name for Mexico City's inhabitants, commonly use this phrase when referring to things like money, food, or the number of guests coming to a gathering. Unfortunately, "the more the merrier" was until recently also the attitude of planners and decision makers toward the city's off-street parking. But when it comes to parking, less can be better.

Mexico City's previous off-street parking regulations were created following the not-so-rigorous process of copying other cities' parking requirements. This pseudoscience led to parking policy that required enough spaces to satisfy the peak demand for free parking, which made Mexico City more friendly to cars than to people. Everyone who lives or works in the city faces the consequences of these poor policy choices: unbearable traffic congestion, expensive housing, and bad air quality.

The good news is that Mexico City has changed this parking paradigm. City officials and organizations like the Institute for Transportation and Development Policy (ITDP), which published a research document this chapter builds on, worked hard to repeal unwise policies that shaped the contemporary, auto-centric city. The parking revolution started in 2012 with the regulation and management of on-street parking (Chapter 49). In 2017, Mexico City eliminated all its off-street parking minimums, and adopted parking maximums in their place.

PREVIOUS REGULATION

For years, Mexico City's policy makers assumed that cheap and ample parking would reduce or eliminate traffic congestion, when in fact more parking encourages more driving and sprawling, automobile-oriented development. Several city policies regulated the location, operation, and characteristics of off-street parking. Almost all these codes, rules, and norms produced the free parking that drivers want.

Mexico City first regulated off-street parking more than 50 years ago, but it was not until 1973 that it required developers to provide parking for every land use in proportion to building characteristics, such as floor area, number of rooms, and number of dwelling units. In the late 1980s, the city enacted a building code that required parking only in proportion to floor space, repealing the option to consider other building characteristics when providing off-street parking. This code permitted adaptive reuse of historic buildings without providing new parking spaces and reduced parking requirements according to population density, public transit access, and parking demand. While historic buildings are exempt from providing new parking spaces, Figure 15-1 shows that some buildings were required to dedicate more than half of their space to off-street parking.

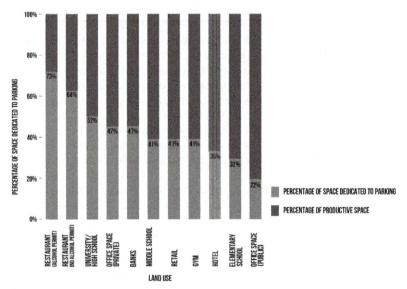

Figure 15-1 Percentage of space dedicated to parking for an 8,000-square-foot building

Source: ITDP, 2014

AN ASSESSMENT OF PREVIOUS REGULATIONS

While a reform to the building code in the 1990s produced some benefits, a 2014 analysis conducted by ITDP of 251 real estate projects shows that the area of land dedicated to off-street parking grew faster than any other land use in Mexico City from 2009 to 2013 (Figure 15-2). Parking requirements help to explain this fast growth in the parking supply. Developers could not provide fewer off-street parking spaces than required even if they demonstrated that the demand for parking is lower than the minimum requirement. Figure 15-3 shows that almost half of the total square meters built in Mexico City between 2009 and 2013 were for off-street parking, which translates into more than 250,000 new parking spaces.

Data from the 251 developments suggest that parking requirements dictated project's size. Most developers provided only the minimum required parking. This was likely because more parking reduces the leasable residential and commercial space, and therefore project revenues. On average, the developments provided 10 percent more spaces than required. Why might some developers provide more spaces than required? The answer is marginal cost. For example, if the number of required spaces in a parking structure is more than can be provided on two levels, a developer is forced to build a third level. Because the marginal cost of each additional space on the third level may be low, and the developer will provide a full third level of parking resulting

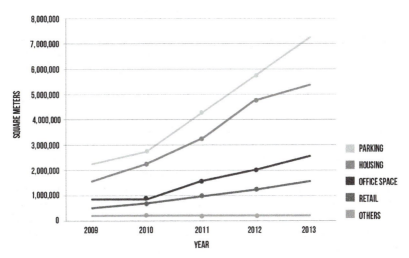

Figure 15-2 Number of square meters built, by land use, 2009–2013
Source: ITDP, 2014

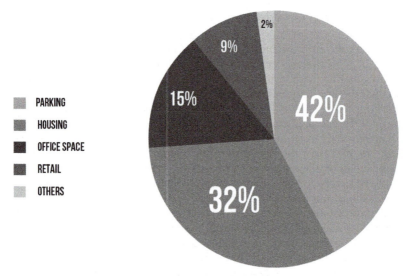

Figure 15-3   Percentage of total of square meters built, by land use, 2009–2013
Source: ITDP, 2014

in more spaces than the city requires. Less than a third of the developments provided 10 percent or more spaces than required.

RETAIL USES

Housing and office developers rarely provided significantly more parking than required. Mixed-use developments supplied about 7 percent above the minimum if the development included housing, and only 6 percent more when there was no housing. Big-box retail developers, however, usually built many more parking spaces than required. On average, retail projects provided 22 percent more parking than required, while all other uses provided 10 percent more.

It is not surprising that big-box retailers provided more parking than required. These projects are characterized by their automobile-oriented designs with ample parking that nears capacity only around Christmas and a few other holidays. But the convenience of finding a parking space during the holidays was not the only incentive to provide more parking for retailers. In Mexico City, parking lots also generate revenue for retailers, since most malls charge for parking.

Previous regulations put a cap on off-street parking fees, and most on-street parking is free. So, while city officials claimed to promote smart growth, in practice they created and promoted an oversupply of free or cheap parking.

THE IMPACTS OF MINIMUM PARKING REQUIREMENTS

Minimum parking requirements distorted transportation choices and urban design, and damaged the economy and the environment. These impacts can be divided in three main areas: economic, urban, and traffic.

Economic Impacts

In Mexico City, constructing off-street parking costs on average $10,000 per space, without considering the land value. In a large development, parking costs typically amount to between 30 and 40 percent of the total cost of the project. Needless to say, developers transfer the cost to residents and shoppers by charging higher prices for housing, goods, and services. Because only 30 percent of trips in Mexico City are made by automobile, the non-driving majority subsidizes parking for the driving minority.

Urban Impacts

Because minimum parking requirements increase development costs, some developers chose to build where land is cheaper, usually at the city's periphery. In addition to urban sprawl, parking minimums resulted in underutilized land, as shown above in Figure 15-1. This underuse not only reduced the amount of productive land, but also degraded the quality of urban design.

Traffic Impacts

Minimum parking requirements encourage car ownership, resulting in more traffic congestion and increased external costs (e.g., pollution). It was therefore important to find new, smarter ways to manage transportation. For example, for the cost of 2,000 new parking spaces (about $20 million), the city could add more than 7,300 shared bicycles, two miles of bus rapid transit, or roughly two miles of complete streets that are designed, operated, and maintained to enable safe, convenient, and comfortable travel and access for users of all ages and abilities (regardless of their mode of transportation).

OFF-STREET PARKING REFORMS

Mexico City's new off-street parking policies published in July 2017 include three elements:

1. **No minimum parking requirements**
   Mexico City no longer requires developer to provide off-street parking based on the building area or the land use. Existing parking spaces can also be converted to other uses.
2. **New maximum parking limits**
   Mexico City established *maximum* parking limits to prevent developers from building excessively large parking lots. While most of the new maximum parking limits are identical to the previous minimum parking requirements, some land uses experienced increases or decreases in the new maximums compared to the previous minimums. Table 15-1 shows these three different scenarios, where some land uses have new maximums that are the same as the previous minimums, some have new maximums higher than the previous minimums, and some have new maximums that are lower than the previous minimums.

Table 15-1   Previous parking requirements and new parking limits in Mexico City

Zoning	Land Use	Size	Previous Requirement (minimum)	New Limit (maximum)
		(Square meters/unit)	(Parking spaces per unit or square meter)	
Housing	Single Unit Home	Up to 120	1 per unit	
		Up to 250	2 per unit	
		More than 250	3 per unit	
	Multi-family housing (no elevator)	Up to 65	1 per unit	
		Up to 120	1.25 per unit	
		Up to 250	2 per unit	3 per unit
		More than 250	3 per unit	
	Multi-family housing (elevator)	Up to 65	1 per unit	
		Up to 120	1.5 per unit	
		Up to 250	2.5 per unit	
		More than 250	3.5 per unit	
Commercial	Gas Station	Gross Floor Area	1 per 150 m^2	1 per 150 m^2
	Supermarket	Building Floor Area	1 per 40 m^2	1 per 25 m^2
	Mall	Building Floor Area	1 per 40 m^2	1 per 25 m^2
	Hospital	Building Floor Area	1 per 50 m^2	1 per 50 m^2
Services	Elementary School	Building Floor Area	1 per 60 m^2	1 per 100 m^2
	University	Building Floor Area	1 per 40 m^2	1 per 40 m^2

3. **Incentives to reduce off-street parking in areas well served by public transit**
Previous transportation policy viewed more off-street parking as a way to mitigate traffic. The new policy not only discourages the construction of off-street parking spaces by establishing maximums but also by charging a fee to developers who want to provide off-street parking within the central city. The developer fee guidelines are still pending for completion, but essentially these new rules will require developers to pay a fee if they build somewhere between 50 and 100 percent of the maximum parking allowed within the central city and areas well served by public transit. The parking fees paid by developers will be collected in a trust and used exclusively to finance improvements to public transit. These transit improvements will help to justify and maintain the new parking maximums. The guidelines for the new fees and the trust management are still pending for approval but the first step towards a more livable city has been taken.

NEXT STEPS

Converting minimum parking requirements into maximum parking limits will gradually but profoundly improve Mexico City's transportation and land use. To conclude, we also suggest three more reforms to consider.

1. **Regulate the location and design of new and existing public parking lots in the city**
Because parking lots create external costs, a comprehensive parking policy should regulate the construction of new parking lots and encourage enhanced technology in existing lots. Enhanced technology would better manage current off-street parking spaces and reduce the need to build new ones.
2. **Strengthen on-street parking regulations**
Eliminating off-street parking requirements is incomplete if it is not supported by regulating on-street parking. Mexico City's Parking Benefit Districts, ecoParq, have proven to be a successful on-street parking management program, and they can be extended to more areas within the city (Chapter 49). In addition, ecoParq's rules need to be flexible and in accordance to the specific characteristics of each neighborhood, such as demographics and off-street parking supply.

3. **Evaluate the new off-street parking policy**
   The new off-street parking policy should be regularly evaluated to revise the maximums based on market demand. The policy should also be evaluated to confirm that it is incentivizing more compact and dense developments that require less car infrastructure and helping to provide more housing options to the people who do not want, or cannot afford, to have a car.

CONCLUSION

For years, parking policy has been based on the fallacy that there is not enough space to park, while what is really lacking is effective parking management. Requiring all buildings to provide ample off-street parking was a policy that needed to be repealed because ample free parking comes at the expense of the city's future. Now, when it comes to parking, less is merrier.

REFERENCES AND FURTHER READING

Medina, Salvador, and Jimena Veloz Rosas. 2012. "Planes Integrales de Movilidad: Lineamientos para una movilidad urbana sustentable. Instituto de Políticas para el Transporte y Desarrollo México." New York: ITDP. http://mexico.itdp.org/archivo/documentos/manuales/?tdo_tag=reduccion-del-uso-del-automovil

Sañudo, Andrés. 2014. "Menos Cajones, Más Ciudad: El Estacionamiento en la Ciudad de México. Instituto de Políticas para el Transporte y Desarrollo México." New York: ITDP. https://www.itdp.org/wp-content/uploads/2014/09/Menos-cajones-m%C3%A1s-ciudad.pdf

Gaceta Oficial de la Ciudad de México. 2017. "Acuerdo por el que se Modifica el Numeral 1.2 Estacionamientos de la Norma Técnica Complementaria para el Proyecto Arquitectónico." http://data.consejeria.cdmx.gob.mx/portal_old/uploads/gacetas/b1a0211fbbff641ca1907a9a3ff4bdb5.pdf

Schmitt, Angie. 2017. "It's Official: Mexico City Eliminates Mandatory Parking Minimums." Streetsblog USA. http://usa.streetsblog.org/2017/07/19/its-official-mexico-city-eliminates-mandatory-parking-minimums/

16

From Parking Minimums to Parking Maximums in London

By Zhan Guo

Minimum parking requirements create too much parking, reduce the supply of housing, and increase traffic congestion. Without parking requirements, the market would provide fewer parking spaces, resulting in fewer cars and more housing units. Evidence to support this argument is inconclusive, however, in part because few local governments have removed their parking requirements. Even when they do adjust parking requirements, the changes are usually quite minor, often targeting small areas (for example, near a rail station) and including only a few development types.

One exception is London. In 2004, London reversed its parking requirements, eliminating the previous minimums and putting new maximums on parking supply for all developments in the metropolitan area (Figure 16-1). No other major city has reformed its parking requirements on such a radical, comprehensive scale. Examining the effects of this reform provides much-needed empirical evidence of how parking reforms can affect cities.

LONDON PARKING REFORM

The London parking reform was part of a national agenda to transform transportation policy in the UK that began years earlier. In

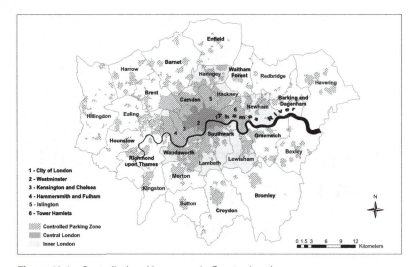

Figure 16-1   Controlled parking zones in Greater London

Source: Transport for London and London Burroughs (Controlled Parking Zones were mapped by author)

March 2000, the UK government published *Planning Policy Guidance 3-Housing* which explicitly stated that "developers should not be required to provide more parking than they or potential occupiers might want," and that local parking standards should not result in developments with more than an average of 1.5 off-street parking spaces per dwelling.

In 2001, the government then published *Planning Policy Guidance 13-Transport*, which stated, "There should be no minimum standards for development, other than parking for disabled people," and that "maximum standards should be designed to be used as part of a package of measures to promote sustainable transport choices."

Following these national policies, the Greater London Authority (GLA), the regional government for the metropolitan area, passed the London Plan in February 2004, requiring local authorities to shift from parking minimums to maximums. As a result of the national and regional policy changes, 30 of London's 33 boroughs updated their local plans to replace parking minimums with maximums and used these standards in the review process for planning applications.

DATA

In our research, we focused on residential developments because residential parking accounts for 71 percent of all off-street parking spaces in London. We used two sources of data. First, we used the application decision reports from residential developments built between 1997 and 2000. This dataset includes 216 residential developments with 2,666 housing units in 30 boroughs. Second, we used the London Development Database (LDD), containing records of all new development permits in London between 2004 and 2010.

Because information on the previous minimum standards was available for only 22 boroughs, we used a smaller subsample of only these boroughs, which included 8,257 developments with 204,181 units. This filtering ensured our study included only boroughs with information on the previous minimum and new maximum parking standards.

Large developments supplied the majority of new housing stock in our sample. Although developments with more than 30 housing units only accounted for 10 percent of new projects, they accounted for 81 percent of all new units.

With our new subset, we compared the number of parking spaces supplied under the new maximums to the number of spaces that would have been supplied under the previous minimums.

PARKING SUPPLY CHANGES

Our sample of the pre-reform developments provided 2,994 parking spaces, or 1.1 spaces per unit (Table 16-1). Because some planning exceptions were allowed, the sample provided only 94 percent of the minimum 3,197 spaces required (Table 16-2).

Our sample of the post-reform developments provided 128,350 parking spaces (0.63 spaces per unit), much lower than both the previous minimum of 248,628 spaces and the post-reform maximum of 188,592 spaces. Therefore, the overall supply is only 52 percent of the previous minimum requirement and only 68 percent of the currently allowed maximum (Table 16-2). In other words, after the reform, the parking

Table 16-1 Spaces per unit, pre- and post-reform

	Developments	Housing Units	Parking Spaces	Spaces per Unit
Pre-Reform	216	2,666	2,994	1.1
Post-Reform	8,257	204,181	128,350	0.63

Table 16-2 Total parking spaces supplied versus minimum and maximum required

	Parking Spaces	Required Spaces Based on Old Minimum Standard	Percent of Spaces Provided Based on Old Minimum Standard	Allowed Spaces Based on New Maximum Standard	Percent of Spaces Provided Based on New Maximum Standard
Pre-Reform	2,994	3,197	94%	N/A	N/A
Post-Reform	128,350	248,628	52%	188,592	68%

supply fell from 94 percent to 52 percent of the previous minimum requirements.

Before the 2004 parking reform, roughly half of the 216 developments provided parking at exactly the minimum required level, and only 26 percent provided parking above that level. After 2004, only 17 percent provided parking at the previous minimum required level, and 67 percent provided parking below the previous minimum level. With the minimum but no maximum, most developments did not provide more than the minimum required, whereas with the maximum but no minimum, most developments provided less than the maximum allowed.

After the switch to parking maximums, one-quarter of all the developments provided no parking at all. Under the previous minimums, these developments would have been required to provide at least 30,154 parking spaces. Twenty-two percent of developments provided parking at the maximum cap level, but these developments account for only 4.2 percent of the housing units. In other words, the new maximum was not preventing many parking spaces from being built, but the previous minimum would have required many parking spaces that ultimately did not get built.

EFFECTS OF DENSITY AND TRANSIT ACCESSIBILITY

Because density and transit accessibility are integral to parking policy, we examined how the parking requirements and actual supply vary in relation to these factors using the post-reform dataset. We calculated the average actual supply, the maximum allowed supply, and the minimum required supply of parking spaces per unit for nine density levels (Figure 16-2) and eight transit-accessibility levels (Figure 16-3). Some developments exceed the maximum parking standards because each application is approved case by case.

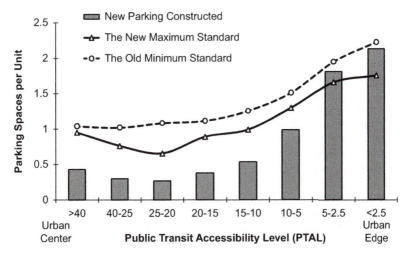

Figure 16-2 Post-reform parking supply compared to population density

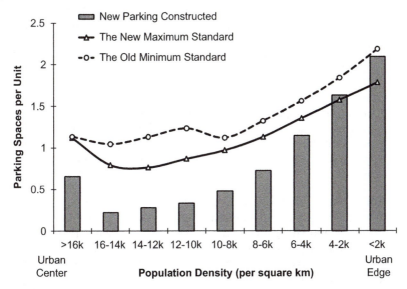

Figure 16-3 Post-reform parking supply compared to transit accessibility

Note: PTAL is an index used by Transport for London to measure the accessibility level of public transit. The higher the value, the better access to transit.

Both figures reveal considerable differences among the parking minimums and maximums applied to the 8,257 developments built between 2004 and 2010. The new maximums allowed per unit are consistently *below* the previously required minimums. The differences between the two are greatest in the areas surrounding Central London—the densest and most transit-accessible in the region. Although the required minimums increased as density and transit accessibility decline, the allowed maximums exhibit an unexpected "U-shaped" curve, declining as developments move inward from Outer London but increasing again in the city center. Areas with the highest levels of density and transit accessibility actually have *higher* parking caps compared to the immediately surrounding areas.

There are two possible explanations for this finding. The first is that housing units tend to be larger in Central London than in adjacent areas, which might necessitate more parking. Indeed, the average unit size in the densest area is 2.4 bedrooms, which is 30 percent larger than the unit size in the second-densest area. Similarly, the average unit size in areas with the highest levels of transit accessibility is 2.3 bedrooms, which is approximately 13 percent greater than the next-most-transit-accessible area.

A second possible explanation is that local boroughs are reluctant to reduce the parking maximums in central areas because they are concerned about parking spillover on already crowded local streets. One planning officer in Westminster, the only Central London borough with significant residential development, expressed this concern in our interview:

> [Borough council] members, in respect of new private residential developments, will normally be seeking car-parking provision as close to the maximum standards. [They] do not accept car-free developments. In general, given the high levels of car ownership in the Borough and the pressure that existing on-street spaces experience, new developments should incorporate parking.

This attitude contrasts starkly with the Inner London boroughs immediately adjacent to Central London, such as Camden, that actively advocate for parking-free housing developments. Parking-free developments accounted for only 44 percent of developments in the highest-density areas but approximately 69 percent in the second-highest-density areas.

PARKING SUPPLY

The actual parking supply exhibits a U-shaped curve similar to the maximum standard curve and—apart from Outer London—is consistently below the maximum allowed levels. The highest-density areas consistently outpace the second-highest-density areas when it comes to parking. The highest-density areas provide three times as many parking spaces per dwelling unit as the second-highest-density areas (0.66 spaces versus 0.22 spaces). More developments in the highest-density areas provide parking than in the second-densest areas (56 percent compared to 31 percent). Developments that do provide parking also provide more spaces per unit (1.17 spaces compared to 0.71 spaces).

Similar differences are found for transit accessibility. The most transit-accessible areas provide 0.43 spaces per unit. This amount is 43 percent more than the second-most-accessible areas (Figure 16-3). Although 36 percent of developments in both areas provide parking, developments in areas with the highest level of transit accessibility provide more parking per unit (1.19 spaces compared to 0.82 spaces).

Differences in housing size might explain some, but not all, of these differences. Another possible explanation for the differences may be purely market based. The benefits of providing parking might exceed construction and opportunity costs in areas with the highest levels of density and transit service. Developers might actually obtain a higher premium by allocating some floor space to parking instead of to living space. This possibility is plausible for Central London because households in this area have the highest median income in the metropolitan area. In addition, the cost of one off-street parking space in Central London could equal the cost of a single-family home in other regions. This type of market does not exist in the areas outside Central London.

CONCLUSION

The number of parking spaces supplied after the 2004 parking reform fell by approximately 40 percent when compared to the number of parking spaces that would have been supplied with the previous minimum parking requirements. This means that from 2004 to 2010, the new parking requirements led to a total of 143,893 fewer spaces. No other alternative explanations (car ownership saturation, development constraints, congestion charging, oil price spike, etc.) account for such a dramatic decline. Furthermore, almost all the reduction in parking supply was caused by eliminating the minimum standards, with only 2.2 percent of the decline due to the adoption of maximum standards.

We also found that the market actually provided more parking in areas with the highest density and best transit service than in the immediately adjacent areas with lower density and poorer transit service. Therefore, parking caps may still be necessary for an efficient parking market because the deregulated market appears to provide more parking in the densest and transit-richest areas, and does not take into account the high social cost of driving in these areas, which are often congested.

Elected officials may oppose parking caps because of concerns about parking spillover in dense areas. But solving on-street parking congestion doesn't require higher off-street parking requirements. Instead, parking congestion requires effective regulation of on-street parking, such as residential parking permits and properly priced parking meters. Minimum parking requirements only cause a maximum amount of problems.

This chapter previously appeared in ACCESS, Fall 2016, where it was adapted from "From Minimum to Maximum: The Impact of Parking Standard Reform on Residential Parking Supply in London from 2004–2010," published in Urban Studies 50, no. 6 (2013): 1191–98.

17

Putting a Cap on Parking Requirements

By Donald Shoup

Off-street parking requirements increase the cost and reduce the supply of affordable housing. Most cities do not intend to exclude low-income residents when they require off-street parking, but even good intentions can produce bad results. Thoughtless planning for parking can be as harmful as a perverse and deliberate scheme.

Perhaps because of growing doubts about parking requirements, cities have begun to reduce or remove them, at least in their downtowns. Planners and elected officials are beginning to recognize that parking requirements increase the cost of housing, prevent infill development on small lots where it is difficult to build all the required parking, and prohibit new uses for older buildings that lack the required parking spaces.

According to recent newspaper articles, some of the reasons cities have reduced or removed their parking requirements include "to promote the creation of downtown apartments" (Greenfield, Massachusetts), "to see more affordable housing" (Miami), "to meet the needs of smaller businesses" (Muskegon, Michigan), "to give business owners more flexibility while creating a vibrant downtown" (Sandpoint, Idaho), and "to prevent ugly, auto-oriented townhouses" (Seattle).

Given this policy momentum, I thought the time to reform parking requirements had arrived when the California legislature considered Assembly Bill 904 (the Sustainable Minimum Parking Requirements Act of 2012). AB 904 would set an upper limit on how much parking cities can require in transit-rich districts: no more than one space per dwelling unit or two spaces per 1,000 square feet of commercial space.

The bill defined these districts as areas within a quarter mile of transit lines that run every 15 minutes or better. If passed it would have been a huge boon for both housing and transit.

There are good reasons to adopt this policy. Federal and state governments give cities billions of dollars every year to build and operate mass transit systems, yet most cities require ample parking everywhere on the assumption that nearly everyone will drive for almost every trip. Minimum parking requirements counteract the transit investments.

For example, Los Angeles is building its Subway to the Sea under Wilshire Boulevard, which already boasts the city's most frequent bus service. Nevertheless, along parts of Wilshire the city requires at least 2.5 parking spaces for each dwelling unit, regardless of the number of rooms. Similarly, 20 public transit lines serve the UCLA campus near Wilshire Boulevard in Westwood, with 119 buses per hour arriving during the morning peak. Nevertheless, across the street from campus, Los Angeles requires 3.5 parking spaces for every apartment that contains more than four rooms. We have expensive housing for people but we want free parking for cars.

Also on Wilshire Boulevard, Beverly Hills requires 22 parking spaces per 1,000 square feet for restaurants, which means the parking lot is seven times larger than the restaurant it serves. Public transit in this over-parked environment resembles a rowboat in the desert.

Cities seem willing to pay any price and bear any burden to assure the survival of free parking. But do people really want free parking more than affordable housing, clean air, walkable neighborhoods, good urban design, and many other public goals? A city where everyone happily pays for everyone else's free parking is a fool's paradise.

If cities want more cars and less housing, minimum parking requirements are the right policy. We build parking for cars the way Egyptians built pyramids for the afterlife. The Egyptians diverted an ungodly amount of resources from housing for people to housing for corpses, just as we divert an ungodly amount of money from housing for people to housing for cars. The Egyptians built Pharonic mausoleums, we build Pharonic garages. And, in the end, the Egyptians have more to show for all their misguided burial plans 4,000 years ago than we will ever have to show for all our misguided parking plans now.

WHY CAP PARKING REQUIREMENTS?

Do city planners know how many cars each family needs? If not, how do they know how many parking spaces each residence needs? If you have a car you need a parking space, but not every car is "needed," and therefore not every parking space is needed. Because the number of available parking spaces affects the number of cars a family will buy, the number of cars a family owns cannot predict the number of parking spaces planners should require.

The supply of parking creates its own demand, and planners estimate the demand for free parking as the guide to require the supply. It is as if planners required storage space in every residence based on their estimates of all the stuff they think people will need to store. If drivers paid prices for parking that covered the cost of constructing and maintaining the parking spaces, we would own fewer cars and use them more sparingly.

Minimum parking requirements create an asphalt wasteland that blights the environment. A powerful force field of free parking encourages everyone to drive everywhere. A cap on parking requirements in transit-rich neighborhoods can reduce this parking blight by making parking-light development feasible.

How will reducing off-street parking requirements affect development? Zhan Guo and Shuai Ren at New York University studied the results when London shifted from minimum parking requirements with no maximum, to maximum parking limits with no minimum (Chapter 16). Comparing developments completed before and after the reform in 2004, they found that the parking supplied after the reform was only 52 percent of the previous minimum required and only 68 percent of the new maximum allowed. This result implies that the previous minimum was almost double the number of parking spaces that developers would have voluntarily provided. Guo and Ren concluded that removing the parking minimum caused 98 percent of the reduction in parking spaces, while imposing the maximum caused only 2 percent of the reduction. Removing the minimum had a far greater effect than imposing a maximum.

Cities usually require or restrict parking without considering the middle ground of neither a minimum nor a maximum. This behavior recalls a Soviet maxim: "What is not required must be prohibited." AB 904, however, was something new. It would not have restricted parking but instead would have imposed a cap on minimum parking requirements, a far milder reform. A cap on how much parking cities can require will not limit the parking supply because if developers think market demand justifies the cost they can always provide more parking than the zoning requires. Cities that require two parking spaces per dwelling unit forbid any dwelling units with less than two parking spaces, which is a strong intervention in the housing market.

There are good precedents for limits on parking requirements. Oregon's Transportation Systems Plan requires local governments to amend their land-use and subdivision regulations to achieve a 10 percent reduction in the number of parking spaces per capita. The United Kingdom's transport policy guidelines for local planning specify that "plans should state maximum levels of parking for broad classes of development ... There should be no minimum standards for development, other than parking for disabled people."

FAILURE AND SUCCESS IN THE LEGISLATURE

To my dismay, the California Chapter of the American Planning Association (APA) lobbied against AB 904, arguing that it "would restrict local agencies' ability to require parking in excess of statewide ratios for transit intensive areas unless the local agency makes certain findings and adopts an ordinance to opt out of the requirement."

City planners must, of course, take direction from elected officials, but the APA represents the planning profession, not cities. AB 904 gave the planning profession an opportunity to support a reform that would coordinate parking requirements with public transportation, but instead the California APA insisted that cities should retain full control over parking requirements, despite their poor stewardship. Cities now require bicycle parking spaces to encourage cycling, but planners and elected officials don't seem to understand that the car parking spaces they require will encourage driving.

AB 904 failed to pass in 2012 but was resurrected in a weaker form as AB 744 and was successful in 2015. AB 744 addresses the parking requirements for low-income housing within half a mile of a major transit stop. If a development is entirely composed of low-income rental housing units, California now caps the parking requirement at 0.5 spaces per dwelling unit. It also caps the parking requirement for a development that includes at least 20 percent low-income or 10 percent very low-income housing at 0.5 spaces per bedroom. Developers can of course provide more parking if they want to, but cities cannot require more parking unless they conduct a study that demonstrates a need.

Affordable housing advocates initially opposed AB 744 because it would have capped the parking requirements for all housing in transit-rich areas. Another California law (SB 1818) already reduces the parking requirements for developments that include some affordable units. Reducing the parking requirements for all housing would therefore dilute the existing incentive to include affordable units in market-rate developments. Affordable housing advocates opposed any statewide cap on parking requirements because it would weaken their power to extract concessions in return for reduced parking requirements. But the harm caused by the parking requirements themselves vastly outweigh the small concessions made by the few developers who provide the affordable housing needed for permission to provide less than the required parking.

Confining AB 744's parking reduction only to affordable housing was therefore necessary to gain political support from the affordable housing advocates, even though a cap on parking requirements for all housing would increase the supply and reduce the price of housing without any subsidy.

Statewide caps on parking requirements may be difficult to impose in the face of the demand for local control in all land use decisions. Nevertheless, the California experience shows that a statewide cap can be feasible if it is linked to affordable housing. This link attracted political support from affordable housing advocates who know that parking requirements are a severe burden on housing development. The easiest way to deflect low-income housing from a neighborhood is to make it provide plenty of parking. Reducing the parking requirements for affordable housing will increase its supply.

Without the support from affordable housing advocates, California's cap on parking requirements near transit would probably not have been enacted. Until more people recognize that parking requirements cause widespread damage, one way to increase political support for a cap on parking requirements is to use it as an incentive for building affordable housing. This approach, however, may then lead affordable housing advocates to oppose any general reduction in parking requirements even if it makes all housing more affordable.

AN ARRANGED MARRIAGE

Many people believe that Americans freely chose their love affair with the car, but it was an arranged marriage. By recommending parking requirements in zoning ordinances, the planning profession was both a matchmaker and a leading member of the wedding party. But no one provided a good prenuptial agreement. Planners should now become marriage counselors or divorce lawyers where the relationship between people and cars no longer works well.

Like the automobile itself, parking is a good servant but a bad master. Parking should be friendly—easy to find, easy to use, and easy to pay for—but cities should not require or subsidize parking. Cities will look and work much better when markets rather than planners and politicians govern decisions about the number of parking spaces. Putting a cap on parking requirements is a good place to start.

REFERENCES AND FURTHER READING

California Assembly Bill 744. 2015. "AB-744 Planning and Zoning: Density Bonuses."

Guo, Zhan, and Shuai Ren. 2013. "From Minimum to Maximum: Impact of the London Parking Reform on Residential Parking Supply from 2004 to 2010." *Urban Studies* 50, no. 6: 1183–1200.

Letters about AB 904 from mayors, planning academics, planning practitioners, and the California Chapter of APA are available here: shoup.bol.ucla.edu/ LettersAboutAssemblyBill904.pdf

Shoup, Donald. 2015. "Putting a Cap on Parking Requirements." *Planning*, May, pp. 28–30.

18

Parking Requirements and Housing Development in Los Angeles

By Michael Manville

When cities require off-street parking with all new residential construction, they shift what should be a cost of driving—the cost of parking a car—into the cost of housing. The price drivers should pay at the end of their trips becomes a cost developers must bear at the start of their projects. Faced with these minimum parking requirements, developers may build less housing, and the housing they do build may be more likely to include parking. Parking requirements could therefore reduce both the amount and variety of housing in a city.

Will parking requirements always have this impact? No. In low-density areas where parking is cheap, developers might build lots of parking even if it isn't required. In downtowns and inner cities, however, parking requirements could profoundly alter the housing stock. Downtown land is expensive, its parcels are often small and irregular, and its buildings frequently cover their entire lots. In these situations, any on-site parking must be subterranean or structured, which is always expensive and sometimes physically impossible.

When parking is difficult to provide, laws that require it on site with housing are laws that constrain the housing market. Minimum parking requirements can make it difficult to build housing for certain people, on certain parcels, in certain buildings, or in certain neighborhoods. When cities require on-site parking with every unit, developers cannot build housing explicitly for people without cars (who are often low income residents) or for people who own cars but are willing to park off site. The law also makes it difficult to construct housing on small parcels and to convert old buildings into housing.

The latter issue is a particular problem. Central cities have many architecturally and historically significant buildings that predate widespread vehicle ownership, and thus don't have parking or the space to add it. These old buildings should be a competitive advantage for cities; they are a pleasing amenity most suburbs lack. If parking requirements keep these buildings vacant, however, they become albatrosses rather than assets. And if old buildings and small parcels dominate a neighborhood, as they do in many inner cities, then parking requirements can stifle an entire neighborhood's growth. Parking requirements could, in sum, obstruct infill development, affordable development, and neighborhood redevelopment.

The logic above suggests that if cities remove parking requirements, they will encourage more and more varied housing. In 1999, Los Angeles put this idea to the test by enacting an Adaptive Reuse Ordinance (ARO) for its downtown. The ARO was designed to convert vacant commercial buildings into housing. The law had three components. First, it allowed these buildings to use an alternative fire and earthquake code. Second, it allowed developers to change the buildings' use (from commercial or industrial to residential) without variances, thereby avoiding lengthy appeals and delays. Last and most important, the law exempted the buildings from minimum parking requirements. Although developers couldn't remove any existing parking, they also didn't have to add any. If developers chose to provide parking, it didn't have to be on site or reserved for residents. And unlike developers of conventional buildings, ARO developers could lease spaces to commuters, businesses, or visitors.

The ARO thus provided an opportunity to answer two questions. First, would removing parking requirements help convert these empty buildings, many of them vacant for decades, into housing? Second, and perhaps more interesting, were downtown's parking requirements influencing the type of housing produced there? Because new ground-up housing was still subject to parking requirements, the ARO turned downtown into a laboratory for parking regulation. The law created a set of downtown buildings that faced the same market conditions as other properties—the same amenities, crime levels, and transit access—but that did not have minimum parking requirements. The ARO therefore lets us compare what unregulated developers *did* with what they *would have had to do* if they were regulated. The law also lets us compare unregulated developers to those who faced parking regulations. Did the unregulated developers provide less parking than zoning would have called for, and less parking than their regulated counterparts? If so, how did this affect the quantity and type of type of housing built?

To answer these questions, I surveyed 56 ARO developments and gathered information about how they provided parking. I also examined more than 1,500 downtown housing units using real estate transaction records and interviewed planners, developers, and architects involved in converting ARO buildings into housing. What I found suggests that when cities remove parking requirements, developers build more housing with less parking, often in buildings and neighborhoods they had long ignored.

HOUSING, HISTORIC BUILDINGS, AND THE ADAPTIVE REUSE ORDINANCE

The exact number of downtown housing units the ARO created is hard to determine, partly because the city doesn't keep precise records and partly because the boundaries of downtown LA aren't clearly defined. Almost everyone agrees, however, that the law generated a lot of housing. By my own conservative count, between 1999 and 2008 developers used the ARO to create about 6,900 units in downtown LA. By way of comparison, between 2000 and 2010, downtown LA added a total of 9,200 housing units, meaning the ARO accounted for more than 75 percent of that decade's housing construction. Between 1970 and 2000, downtown LA added 4,300 housing units. The ARO created more housing in less than 10 years than had been created in the previous 30 (Figure 18-1).

The ARO buildings were disproportionately old—their median year of construction was 1922—and many were near each other. Thousands of ARO units are clustered in a single census tract. This neighborhood, once known as the "Wall Street of the West," was home to Bank of America's headquarters, the Los Angeles Stock Exchange, and other financial institutions. It has the nation's largest collection of intact office buildings constructed between 1900 and 1930, many of them exemplars of West Coast Beaux Arts and Art Deco architecture, and is listed on the National Register of Historic Places. In the 1960s, however, this elegant district began to decline, and in 1982 the *Los Angeles Times* described it as "a neighborhood of hoodlums, derelicts and winos ... echoing buildings full of absolutely nothing above the ground floor." In 1980, the census tract had just slightly more than 3,100 housing units and 1,700 residents. Subsequent housing growth was tepid; by 2000, the tract had a little more than 3,600 housing units. From 2000 to 2010, however, the area came to life. Both the housing stock and population more than doubled, with ARO buildings accounting

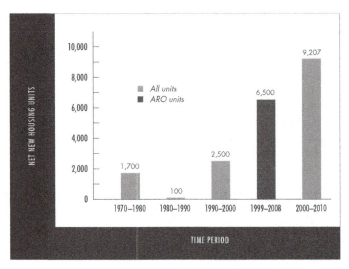

Figure 18-1   Housing growth in downtown Los Angeles

for most of the increase. A dozen large ARO conversions alone created more than 2,200 housing units.

Housing booms are easier to document than explain. What caused the downtown turnaround? More specifically, we know that the ARO played a role, but can we say that the ARO's parking deregulation in particular was responsible for all this development? My interviews suggest that parking reform was a necessary but not sufficient condition for the ARO's—and neighborhood's—success. Simply removing parking requirements would not have let developers convert these buildings to housing because the buildings didn't conform to many aspects of the zoning code. At the same time, however, most respondents said that if the parking requirements had not been removed, converting these buildings into housing would have been impossible.

If parking requirements prevented adaptive reuse, we should see ARO developers provide less parking than conventional zoning would mandate. The conventional zoning says that apartment developers must provide one covered, on-site parking space for each rental unit of up to three "habitable rooms" (kitchen, common area, or bedroom). In larger buildings with larger units, the city requires 1.25 covered, on-site spaces per unit.

Condo parking requirements are at the discretion of a special planning advisory agency, which until 2005 usually required 2.25 to 2.5 covered, on-site spaces per unit. After 2005, however, the agency

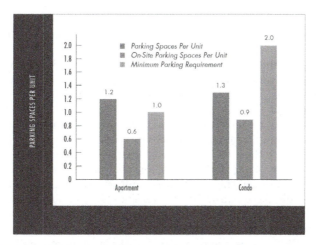

Figure 18-2   Parking spaces provided in ARO housing

began requiring fewer spaces, often two spaces per unit and sometimes as few as 1.5.

Figure 18-2 compares these requirements to the amount of parking ARO developers actually provided. I conservatively assume that, without deregulation, the city would have required one space per unit for all ARO apartments, and two spaces per unit for condos.

At first blush, the results are surprising. Deregulated apartment developers actually provided *more* parking than zoning required. The downtown requirement calls for one space per unit, and ARO developers provided an average of 1.2 spaces. But these averages don't tell the whole story, for four reasons.

First, the baseline is conservative; many apartments would actually have required 1.25 spaces each. Second, the averages mask substantial variation. Some upscale apartment buildings provided two spaces per unit, while others provided less than one, and one building provided none at all. With parking requirements, any variation below the minimum would have been illegal, meaning the variety in housing options would be smaller. Third, some of these buildings had large amounts of pre-existing parking (one building sat atop a parking structure), and these spaces bias the count upward. Fourth and most important, the average ignores the parking's location. Stricter parking requirements exert more influence on housing development, and stringency is determined not just by how many spaces the city requires, but where the city requires them.

LA requires all parking on site, and this requirement can rapidly increase construction costs. On a tight parcel, the first four surface spaces might cost $4,000 apiece, but a fifth space could require building a parking structure or digging a garage. In that case, the fifth space can cost tens of thousands of dollars—far more than any value it adds to a housing unit. Letting developers provide some or all parking off site lets them control the cost of that next space. Rather than dig costly garage spaces, developers can rent existing, and often underused, spaces nearby.

ARO developers took full advantage of the law's locational flexibility. ARO apartment buildings provided an average of 1.2 spaces per unit, but only half of those spaces were on site. The rest were usually leased from nearby parking structures or lots that had excess capacity. Had ARO buildings been subject to the downtown parking requirement, all spaces would have had to be on site. The ARO let developers devote more of their land and capital to housing, and helped make better use of the surplus parking the neighborhood already had.

With ARO condos, the disparity between zoning requirements and developer behavior is even larger. The 19 condo buildings in the sample account for about 2,100 housing units, and on average, each condo unit has 1.3 parking spaces, much less than zoning would require. Yet as was the case with rental units, the difference is magnified when we take the parking's location into account. ARO condos provided less than 1 space per unit on site.

Sixteen of the 56 ARO buildings provided all their parking off site, while an additional nine buildings offered tenants some combination of on- and off-site parking. Twelve more buildings provided at least some parking in an uncovered surface lot, which would also be illegal under LA's parking requirements.

MORE DIVERSE AND LESS EXPENSIVE HOUSING

Since most housing includes parking, new housing without parking diversifies the housing stock. And because this new housing lacks parking, it might also be less expensive. According to the Census Bureau's American Housing Survey, 90 percent of LA's housing units include a parking space in their rent or purchase price. In contrast, more than one-third of the ARO buildings did not include parking in the price of their units. This probably isn't a coincidence. Developers often bundle parking with housing because parking requirements force them to oversupply spaces, at costs well above what those spaces could sell for on their own. Developers thus have little choice but to bundle the parking's cost into the rent or purchase price. In addition, LA requires developers to reserve parking spaces for residents. This rule, which virtually guarantees bundled parking, helps no one. Developers can't sell extra spaces to nonresidents who want to buy them, and residents without cars are forced to pay for parking they don't want.

Freed from these rules, ARO developers unbundled their parking. I analyzed statistics for 1,559 downtown lofts for sale or rent in downtown LA. These units were in 45 different buildings, 29 of which were converted to housing using the ARO. ARO apartments were three times more likely to be offered without parking as non-ARO apartments (13 percent to 4 percent), and ARO condos twice as likely (31 percent to 14 percent). My results also suggest that units without parking are less expensive than units with parking. Controlling for many other differences, bundled parking was associated with about $200 a month in additional rent for apartments, and over $40,000 in additional selling prices for condos. Unregulated developers supplied a different, less expensive product than regulated developers.

NO PARKING REQUIREMENT ≠ NO PARKING

Residents often worry that without parking requirements, developers won't build parking at all, leading new residents to park on and congest the street. The ARO shows that such fears needn't come to pass. Many housing buyers and lenders want parking, so most developers provide it. The ARO's parking exemption was valuable not because it let developers forgo parking completely, but because it let them supply parking creatively. If developers thought they could sell some units without parking or with parking off site, they were free to try. And they were not forced to construct individual spaces that were wildly expensive (for example, spaces that forced them to dig a second garage level).

Minimum parking requirements address a real problem (the demand for parking) but also tell developers how to solve that problem (provide a set number of covered spaces on site with every unit). Removing parking requirements doesn't remove the problem (buyers might still want parking), but it does remove the one-size-fits-all solution. Developers can provide parking in the way they think is best, the same way they already provide pools, fitness centers, and other amenities their customers might want.

This suggests some important lessons. First, removing a parking requirement is not the same as prohibiting parking; ending a mandate is not the same as enacting a ban. Second, because developers remain free to provide parking, cities can remove parking requirements even if most people drive. The end of parking requirements doesn't assume the end of driving. Plenty of people drive in downtown LA (it's LA, after all). And when most people drive, most developers supply parking.

But what if some developers do construct buildings without parking and residents do bring cars? That situation arose in Portland, Oregon, in early 2013 and caused both street parking congestion and a zoning controversy. Yet nothing of the sort occurred in LA, for a simple reason: LA regulates its downtown streets. There is no destructive competition for free street parking in downtown LA because there is no free street parking. Downtown streets are metered from 8 a.m. to 8 p.m., and on most streets overnight parking is prohibited. This is perhaps the most important lesson of the ARO: deregulated off-street parking needs regulated on-street parking. When cities don't give on-street spaces away for free, developers will provide—and drivers will pay for—spaces off-street.

CONCLUSION

Minimum parking requirements force a marriage between housing and vehicle ownership, and make it hard to build housing for people without cars. Because parking can consume so much space and money, parking requirements needlessly reduce variety in the type and location of housing available: they render some parcels, buildings, and neighborhoods unprofitable for residential development. This result is unfortunate. Housing consumers, like consumers in all markets, have myriad tastes. Of course many people want parking attached to their unit. But "many people" is not "everyone." Some people will live in buildings with little parking. Maybe these people don't drive or don't mind parking a small distance from where they live. Perhaps they could not afford housing if it automatically included a parking space. Parking requirements deprive these people of options and threaten the vitality of cities. Cities thrive when they offer more rather than fewer choices; cities that remove parking requirements will create more diverse and inclusive housing markets, and become more diverse and inclusive places.

REFERENCES AND FURTHER READING

Manville, Michael. 2013. "Parking Requirements and Housing Development." *Journal of the American Planning Association* 79, no. 1: 49–66.
Manville, Michael, Alex Beata, and Donald Shoup. 2013. "Turning Housing into Driving." *Housing Policy Debate* 23, no. 2: 350–75.
Shoup, Donald. 2011. *The High Cost of Free Parking.* Revised edition. Chicago: Planner's Press.

19

Parking Reform Made Easy

By Richard Willson

Parking requirements in zoning ordinances create one of the most wasteful elements of transportation and land-use systems: unoccupied parking spaces. Each space requires more than 300 square feet of valuable land or building area, yet many sit empty. Minimum parking requirements at shopping malls, for example, often lead to sprawling developments surrounded by large, underused parking lots. Spaces for workplaces may be well used during the day but remain unoccupied in the evening because they are not shared with other land uses. Sometimes, the parking required is greater than the amount of parking ever used.

Parking is overbuilt and underused for two reasons: 1) zoning requires an excessive parking supply, and 2) it prevents efficient sharing of parking among different land uses. Both reasons reflect a legacy of single-use zoning and an automobile-first approach to planning. Minimum parking requirements prevent private developers from responding to market conditions and lessen developers' interest in sharing parking or developing sites that are accessible without driving. Planners sometimes claim that developers would build the same amount of parking regardless of regulations, but if that's true, then why impose minimum parking requirements in the first place?

Parking requirements should be framed as a means of providing access, not an end. Parking requirements are only one of several ways to ensure storage for private automobiles. Private auto transportation, in turn, is only one of several ways to provide access. To carry out parking reform, we must counteract the decades-old practice of thinking about access in terms of roadways and parking. In my recent book, *Parking Reform Made Easy*, I examine the origins of parking requirements, the impediments to change, and how we can reform these antiquated laws.

WHY PARKING REQUIREMENTS?

Early zoning ordinances did not have parking requirements. Zoning sought to manage the external impacts of properties, such as when a new building represented a fire hazard to the structure next door. In the mid-twentieth century, parking requirements were added to address surface street congestion caused by patrons driving in search of parking. Planners didn't foresee that minimum parking requirements would favor private vehicle travel, lower overall density, and increase traffic.

In 1995 and again in 2013, I led studies that surveyed Southern California local planners about parking requirements and found a tautological justification for minimum parking requirements: planners wished to "ensure an adequate number of parking spaces." This response reflects a lack of critical thinking about fundamental public objectives, such as accessibility, economic development, and sustainability. The response also reflects an outdated vision of separated land uses, unrestricted auto mobility, and plentiful free parking. Thus, many parking requirements are relics that undermine current land-use and transportation goals.

WHY CHANGE IS DIFFICULT

Some regional and state policymakers recognize that existing parking requirements are excessive, but most have neglected the issue because parking is a responsibility of local governments. Yet parking requirement reforms are crucial to accomplishing federal, state, and regional objectives in transportation, land use, and the environment. There are recent indications that if local governments do not carry out reforms, states may do it for them. In 2012, a proposal in the California legislature (AB 904) sought to override local parking requirements in transit-rich areas (see Chapter 17). Legislators subsequently tabled the proposal, however, showing the power of local governments to resist state interference in parking policies.

Many local planners know the parking requirement status quo is wrong. They have observed wasted land, turned away restaurant proposals in historic districts, and seen affordable housing not pencil out. Despite these undesirable outcomes, planners have not made changes. Why? Some may feel powerless to change ossified regulations, sensing weak political support and lacking technical expertise to justify changes. Others may want the negotiating leverage that excessive parking requirements provide to extract public benefits from developers. Furthermore, planners know that parking is a key point in NIMBY resistance to development, so avoiding parking controversy can help ensure economic development. In effect, cities are addicted to parking requirements. The addiction is analogous to smoking, where immediate gratification overwhelms future costs.

Change means freeing ourselves of parking dogma, habits, and golden rules. The old reality dictated fixed parking requirement ratios and exhibited an unwillingness to deviate from standard practice, even when it made sense to do so. This approach emphasized apparent precision and uniformity. It undervalues important considerations of local variability, policy relationships, environmental capacity, and human behavior. All the land-use plans, design reviews, and streetscape renderings in the world will not produce desired outcomes if we do not reform parking requirements.

WHY NOT ELIMINATE PARKING REQUIREMENTS?

Deregulating off-street parking would allow markets to determine parking supply levels and provoke a fresh debate about justifications for public regulations and subsidies for all transportation modes. Currently, minimum requirements compel the provision of access for driving and parking, whereas zoning codes seldom impose equivalent requirements for bus, bicycle, or pedestrian facilities. When they do, those requirements have been added more recently and are at a lower investment level.

Under minimum requirements, even those who do not drive share in paying the cost of parking. Parking costs are embedded in higher retail prices, lower workplace salaries, higher rents, and the like. In these ways, most minimum requirements tend to prioritize private vehicles. Eliminating minimum requirements would begin to level the playing field for all travel modes.

Cities such as Philadelphia, Portland, and Seattle have recently reformed their parking requirements and adopted limited deregulation. Deregulation shifts the approach from automatically requiring parking to not supplying it until it is economically justified. It is a big change from standard practice and should be coupled with programs for shared parking and parking management. Still, the idea of eliminating minimum parking requirements hasn't gained traction in many places. Local officials are often buffeted by demands from residents, storeowners, and employees for more parking, not less.

Approaches to parking reform will vary from community to community. Accordingly, Table 19-1 shows the range of reform options, including the traditional approach in which the minimum requirements exceed expected use. At the other end of the spectrum is deregulation, with no minimum or maximum parking requirements. In many cities and towns, the best approach is somewhere in between, with deregulation in central business districts and transit-oriented developments, and reduced minimum requirements in other areas.

MOVING TOWARD REASON AND ACTION: 12 STEPS

In my book, I explain how planners can use a 12-step toolkit to inform reasoned decisions about minimum parking requirements. The process begins by measuring parking use rates and moves through a series of adjustments that consider local context and policy goals.

Step 1

Measure existing parking use, which varies from place to place. This use is expressed as a rate, such as spaces occupied per 1,000 square feet of occupied building area or per residential unit. Planners assemble a sample of these measurements to provide an accurate assessment for a land use. The current use rates *do not* directly suggest future

Table 19-1 Developer response to parking requirements

Approach	Minimum Requirement	Maximum Requirement	Developer Response
Traditional	> Utilization	None	Rarely builds more than the requirement
Moderate reform	= Utilization	None	Assess market for project, may exceed minimum
Big city approach	< Utilization	A fixed or percentage of minimums	Makes market decision whether to supply the minimum or build to the maximum
Partial deregulation	None	A fixed ratio	Makes market decision whether to supply any parking or build to the maximum
Deregulation	None	None	Makes the market decision whether/how much to build

requirements, however, since perpetuating the existing levels can preserve undesirable conditions: underpriced and oversupplied parking, separated and low-density land uses, and automobile-first design.

Step 2

Consider future parking use. Despite regional transportation plans that must account for development 20 years into the future, parking requirements are often stuck in the past. For example, planners commonly use the Institute of Transportation Engineers Parking Generation handbook, which includes parking use measurements from decades ago. Since buildings last decades, or even centuries, parking requirements should consider how trends (for example, the growth of shared mobility services) will affect future parking use levels. Most trends suggest a decrease in parking use per unit of development; the Step 1 rate is adjusted to account for expected increases or decreases in the parking use rate over the selected time period.

Step 3

Begin moving from use rates to prospective parking requirements. There is a policy choice about whether parking requirements should be based on the expected average use or other values such as 33rd or 85th percentile use levels, as drawn from sample data. Choosing an 85th percentile level means requiring every development build as much parking as sites with close to the highest observed use, while the 33rd percentile means requiring less than the average observed use, allowing developers to decide whether to build any more than that. Decisions about this "basis for the rate" depend on community goals and shared parking opportunities. The appropriate Step 2 use rate (average or percentile) is employed as a prospective parking requirement based on this policy decision.

Step 4

Adjust the prospective parking requirement to account for particular characteristics of the project or land-use category, as well as area land-use and transportation conditions. For example, cities should require less parking near transit stops than near freeway off ramps. These project and context adjustments are applied as an adjustment to the Step 3 prospective parking requirement.

Step 5

Account for market conditions and policies regarding parking pricing, unbundling of parking costs from rents, or parking cash-out programs. These pricing policies generally reduce parking demand, so cities should reduce the Step 4 prospective requirement for developments with these policies.

Step 6

Consider plans for facilities and programs to increase transit and shuttle services, bicycling, and walking. Planned improvements to these travel modes may reduce parking-use levels and justify a downward adjustment to the Step 5 prospective parking requirement.

Step 7

Assess the impact of local practices and policies that affect how efficiently spaces are used. For example, if spaces are designated for specific individuals in a development, an upward adjustment to the Step 6 prospective parking requirement may be made because efficient internal sharing of parking spaces cannot occur. Similarly, designating a vacancy goal such as 5 to 10 percent to ease the process of finding a space would also suggest an upward adjustment to the Step 6 prospective parking requirement.

Step 8

Recognize that community parking resources, either on street or in other off-street facilities, may justify a reduction in the parking requirement for new development. It involves measuring excess parking supply in the area and assessing its availability. If community parking resources are credited toward new development, the portion credited is subtracted from the Step 7 prospective parking requirement.

Step 9

Conduct a shared-parking analysis, which applies when parking requirements are being developed for mixed-use zoning categories or blended requirements (requirements that apply to a broader range of land uses in a district). The Step 8 prospective parking requirements for each land use being considered are entered into a shared-parking model that considers peak demand times for each use, the opportunity for multiple land uses to share parking spaces, and calculates an overall parking requirement for the land use mix.

Step 10

Evaluate the prospective parking requirement, as adjusted through Step 9, and consider whether it supports community goals and plans. These goals are found in comprehensive plans and vary among communities. They often address transportation, design, urban form, economic development, environmental sustainability, and social equity. For example, a community with aggressive goals for transit and non-motorized transportation may decide to adopt lower parking requirements, or to eliminate them. A community with strong economic goals may embrace parking deregulation because it can reduce development cost. An iteration of Steps 3 through 9 may be considered to align parking requirements with community goals.

Step 11

Address regulations about the minimum size of parking spaces to allow an efficient yield of spaces per square foot of parking area. Jurisdictions may choose to adopt smaller dimensional requirements to more efficiently use land and building area. This decision considers the effects of use type, vehicle mix, self-parking technology, and parking space turnover on desired dimensions.

Step 12

Consider regulations allowing tandem parking (one car behind another), valet parking, and automated parking. Each measure can increase the yield of parking spaces per square foot of parking area. Policies allowing these measures are differentiated by land use category and local conditions.

This twelve-step process is an alternative to setting a parking requirement based on a neighboring city's requirement or a national average. It can be used to establish (or eliminate) parking requirements for a land-use category, for a district, or for a particular project. Ideally, local governments will reform requirements based on a clear sense of the benefits. If they don't, regional or state agencies can use this process to recommend or mandate parking ratios for local governments. Regional agencies, for example, could develop suggested parking requirements that vary by context features, such as transit accessibility, mixed uses, and density. They can also integrate parking reform with regional planning and modeling activities. For example, in King County, Washington, the Metro Transit's web-based GIS tool provides data on parking use for multifamily housing and tests alternative parking ratios in terms of costs and impacts.

IN PRAISE OF INCREMENTALISM

In the past decade, many cities initiated comprehensive zoning code reform, and others are planning such efforts. Comprehensive reform efforts allow planners to rethink parking requirements while they consider the basic organization and functioning of the zoning code. These efforts also allow planners to bypass the complexity of older codes that have undergone countless revisions. Ideally, planners will amass enough political clout and financial resources in order to undertake the daunting task of a comprehensive zoning code revision.

There are many situations, however, where financial resources and political capital are not sufficient for comprehensive parking reform. In these cases, an incremental approach can produce good results. It makes sense to start where there is support, either from elected officials or from community or district stakeholders. Code reformers can work with these stakeholders to produce parking requirement reforms, parking overlay zones, or a partial deregulation without creating the opposition that might emerge in a citywide effort. These early successes often build support for larger, more comprehensive efforts. Rather than viewing pilot projects or experiments as somehow inferior to comprehensive parking reform, we should see them as effective ways of producing valuable information, testing innovative ideas, and ultimately generating change.

Small victories enable learning and create momentum. Let the reform begin!

FURTHER READING

Institute of Transportation Engineers. 2010. *Parking Generation*. 4th Edition. Washington D.C.: Institute of Transportation Engineers.
King County Metro. 2013. "Right Size Parking." http://metro.kingcounty.gov/programs-projects/right-size-parking/
Shoup, Donald. 2011. *The High Cost of Free Parking*. Revised edition. Chicago: Planners Press.
Willson, Richard. 2013. *Parking Reform Made Easy*. Washington, D.C.: Island Press.

Willson, Richard. 2000. "Reading between the Regulations: Parking Requirements, Planners' Perspectives and Transit." *Journal of Public Transportation* 3: 111–28.

This chapter is adapted from Parking Reform Made Easy, *Washington, D.C.: Island Press, 2013.*

20

Parking Management for Smart Growth

By Richard Willson

Parking is the sacred cow of land uses. It claims privileged status in zoning codes, and there is simply too much of it in cities. All the chapters in this book reveal problems with minimum parking requirements; show how excess parking harms livability, sustainability, and equity; and explain how pricing can manage its use. This chapter demonstrates that progress requires more than code reforms and better pricing; it requires coordinated, comprehensive parking management. We need to shift from building parking to managing it.

Figure 20-1 shows the result of parking's privileged status: vast heat islands seldom used for their intended purpose. Future social trends and technological advances will disrupt the private vehicle ownership model, making these empty spaces even *less* justified. The question is how do we transition from too much parking to efficient use of a smaller parking supply? The answer is parking management.

Parking management uses a wide range of tools—parking sensors, pricing, regulations, and information systems—in an effort to use parking efficiently. Efficiency occurs, for example, where the most convenient spaces serve many different parkers per day and different land uses share all spaces. Said another way, parking management prevents spaces from seldom or never being used.

Every community that has a two-hour time limit for downtown curb parking is engaged in parking management. The problem is that parking management is ad hoc, infrequently adjusted, and uncoordinated. In most communities, parking management is a "set it and forget it" enterprise. Figure 20-2 shows a locale where this set-it-and-forget-it

Figure 20-1   Ontario Mills mall parking lot, Ontario, California

Figure 20-2   No parking

mentality has been in place so long that a tree grew around the parking sign. Even in America's largest cities, a baffling, arbitrary, and non-optimal set of practices often manage on- and off-street parking spaces located in both private and public facilities.

As with any critique, the skeptic rightly asks how could this be? There are three reasons for America's lack of proper parking management. First, our cultural ideals embed the notion that parking should be a free and available right in front of any destination. The introduction of parking management can signify broader, highly charged social changes as communities become denser and traffic increases.

Second, the responsibility for parking is extremely fragmented. Cities, transit agencies, property owners, employers, commercial facilities, and parking operators all play important roles. Even *within* governments, parking responsibility is divided between the departments of public works, planning, economic development, finance, and the police. Few cities think about the big picture in a comprehensive way.

Finally, the oversupply of parking means that we have not had to manage it well. When there is too much parking everywhere, there is no need to efficiently direct parkers to a space that suits the length of their stay. Most zoning codes have forced up the parking supply, which creates artificially low prices that do not create an incentive for better management.

Parking management shifts thinking about parking spaces from objects to services. While two parking spaces may have identical dimensions, one may seldom be used while the other serves many users and many trips per day. The first space is practically useless; the second effectively supports automobile access to a district.

The best way to measure parking use is by measuring the share of total hours a space is occupied (during a day, week, or year). Better parking use means we need fewer parking spaces to provide enough parking to satisfy actual need. Thus, as communities grow, the parking supply can grow more slowly or even shrink.

Figure 20-3 shows how parking perceptions differ from reality. The first, largest circle represents the number of parking spaces that stakeholders *think* they need when there is no management. Transportation demand management (TDM) allows a district to function successfully with fewer parking spaces. The second, smaller circle represents the number of parking spaces needed after conventional TDM. This reduction in spaces occurs, for example, when cities charge for parking and some drivers shift to carpooling, walking, biking, or transit. The third, smallest circle represents the number of spaces needed when better parking management more efficiently uses the spaces we already have.

Fortunately, there has been an explosion of techniques and technologies that facilitate parking management. Sensors can determine parking

Strategies to Reduce the Number of Parking Spaces Needed at a Site

Figure 20-3   Strategies to reduce the number of parking spaces needed at a site

occupancy. This real-time information can reduce search times, allow sophisticated pricing schemes, and support efficient enforcement. Parking meters can vary price by time of day and parking duration to encourage space turnover. Meters that accept credit cards or smartphone payments eliminate the hassle of finding quarters to pay for parking.

The other piece of good news is that cities are increasingly adopting parking pricing for on- and off-street spaces. This aligns the drivers' costs with the broader social costs of accommodating cars. Parking pricing encourages the use of alternative travel modes and can achieve space occupancy goals by dynamically varying prices to achieve space availability on every block. Dynamic pricing projects in Los Angeles and San Francisco use time-of-day pricing and frequent price adjustments to achieve space occupancy goals.

Combining parking pricing with new technologies will help resolve the parking management issue. Unfortunately, these tools alone are not enough. We need collective action when markets don't function properly, such as when landowners don't respond to price signals because they are unaware of profit opportunities from sharing their parking. Planners may need to persuade property owners about the benefits of parking management or to give assistance in managing their parking.

The best solution is comprehensive and coordinated parking management. Improved management maximizes shared parking, uses parking prices to allocate spaces to parkers, and provides choices, predictability, and reduced search time for parkers.

Parking management requires a strategic plan that goes beyond traditional planning for parking. Plans must call for policy makers to engage with multiple organizations, not just one. These organizations must collaborate, design operating protocols, and perform assessments. Strategic plans should also include elements that are programmatic, which means that they can start as pilot projects and be adjusted in response to conditions. Changing meter prices or "loading zone" dedications is much easier than building or tearing down a parking structure.

Figure 20-4 Parking management strategies

Stakeholders often think of parking management options in ways that align with their background or expertise. Someone trained in economics is likely to think of pricing strategies. Someone trained in education and marketing may think about information systems. In Figure 20-4, box 1 provides examples of strategies that an engineer might envisage, such as advanced parking equipment. Box 2 presents the pricing techniques used by an economist. Box 3 displays parking rules that reflect a regulatory approach. Finally, box 4 contains education and marketing strategies.

Parking managers should consider all four approaches. They may not all apply, but a multipronged approach in which strategies are coordinated will be more successful than any one strategy. There may also be connections (and trade-offs) between approaches. For example, dynamic pricing requires advanced parking equipment to support the pricing algorithm (box 1). This equipment works best if parkers have apps that guide them to the location and price they want (boxes 2 and 4). Rules about who gets to park in what space are likely still required for special parking uses, such as locations where curb parking is permitted (box 3). Education is also essential to avoid the negative perception that this is just a money grab by the city (box 4).

Portland-based parking consultant Rick Williams argues that an integrated management entity can best coordinate parking strategies. Some cities create a parking authority and achieve a high level of coordination between private and public parking. Other cities form joint authorities with transit agencies to cooperatively manage parking resources as well. Williams outlines the following steps for creating a managed, integrated, and financially sustainable parking district.

1. Establish management principles
2. Create organizational structure

3. Define roles for on- and off-street parking
4. Establish rate-setting protocols
5. Measure performance
6. Communicate how the integrated parking system works
7. Evaluate new technologies
8. Conduct financial analysis for ongoing management

As cities consider a future economy that emphasizes use rather than ownership and services rather than facilities, many are innovating parking management. In addition to Los Angeles and San Francisco, cities representing a full spectrum of sizes and locations are following suit: Redwood City and Pasadena, California; Boulder, Colorado; Washington, D.C.; Portland, Oregon; and Seattle and Tacoma, Washington.

Meanwhile, several emerging trends suggest that parking use rates will decrease in the future. This shift is due to new services (such as shared-ride mobility), alternative arrangements to owning a car, and improved transit, walking, and bicycling options. Land-use changes, such as mixed-use developments, will have a similar effect, while preferences for an auto-free lifestyle may reduce parking use rates as well. Furthermore, technology can reduce driving (such as online shopping), and self-parking cars reduce the space needed per parked vehicle.

The best strategy for creating a managed, integrated, and financially sustainable parking district is to start with an appeal to broader community goals. Show how parking management supports revitalization. Educate stakeholders, especially by showing them how parking management works in communities that are similar to theirs. Appeal to people's self-interest, such as when parking pricing produces revenue for street improvements or public amenities. Finally, find allies, like multimodal transportation advocates, infill and affordable housing developers, small businesses, and historic preservationists. All of them can help strengthen the case for parking management.

Parking management is the key to smart growth. As we shift toward providing parking as a service rather than as an object, so must we shift from building parking to managing it. We can manage parking more efficiently by ensuring that its price aligns with the value it provides. Parking management is right on time for this new era.

This article was previously published in ACCESS, *Fall 2016, where it was adapted from the book,* Parking Management for Smart Growth, *Island Press, 2015.*

21

On-Street Parking Management Versus Off-Street Parking Requirements

By Donald Shoup

Why do cities require so much off-street parking for new apartment buildings? Because many people seem to think that parking spaces in an apartment building are as essential as lifeboats on a cruise ship. They argue that residents who own cars will park on the streets if a building doesn't have enough off-street spaces. Others counter that parking requirements increase housing costs to subsidize cars. A third group says that banks will not finance new apartment buildings without parking, developers will not build them, and tenants will not rent them.

Portland, Oregon, tested these claims by removing the parking requirements for apartment buildings located within 500 feet of frequent transit service—38 percent of all parcels in the city. What happened next? Banks are lending, developers are building, and tenants are renting new apartments without parking. The market for these apartments is large because almost a quarter of Portland's renter households do not own a car.

Between 2006 and 2012, developers built 122 apartment buildings on lots exempt from parking requirements. Fifty-five of these buildings have no off-street parking, and the other 67 have an average of 0.9 parking spaces per apartment. Altogether, the 122 buildings have an average of 0.6 parking spaces per apartment.

As predicted, however, many tenants in apartments without off-street parking do own cars and park them on the nearby streets. Residents of the surrounding neighborhoods understandably complain about parking spillover. They want to keep parking easy for themselves and fear their home values will fall if the curb parking is crowded. As a result, they want the city to require off-street parking for all new apartments.

If parking requirements merely ensured enough parking spaces to prevent spillover, they wouldn't create problems. But they also increase housing costs, subsidize cars, and degrade urban design. Are off-street parking requirements worth these costs? No, because there are cheaper and better ways to prevent parking spillover from apartment buildings. Instead of requiring off-street parking, cities can better manage on-street parking.

In Parking Permit Districts, one simple way to prevent parking spillover from an apartment building with fewer than the required number of parking spaces is to apply an *if-then* condition to the development. If the developer agrees to the condition that residents of the building will be ineligible for on-street parking permits, the developer is exempt from the minimum parking requirement. This no-permits-for-on-street-parking condition will give developers an incentive to build as much off-street parking as tenants demand. The city can also require that the building owner must inform potential buyers or renters that they will be ineligible for on-street parking permits. Because the residents who buy or rent an apartment will know they are ineligible for on-street parking, they will not move in and expect to park on the street. The municipality issues both the building permits and the parking permits, so linking the two should be manageable. Chicago and Washington, D.C., have used this policy to approve apartment buildings with less than the required parking.

Another simple strategy to prevent curb parking spillover from apartment buildings near single-family neighborhoods is to allow the residents of any block to adopt an Overnight Parking Permit District. These districts prohibit overnight parking on the street except by residents and thus prevent nonresidents from storing their cars in front of residents' homes. Los Angeles, for example, charges residents $15 per year (less than half a cent per day) for an overnight permit. Residents can also buy guest permits for $1 per night. Enforcement is easy because officers need to make only one visit during a night to cite all cars parked without permits. If nearby residents don't want an overnight permit district on their block, the spillover from apartments without parking can't be that bad.

Some cities, like Boulder, Colorado, sell a few permits to nonresidents on blocks that regularly have a vacancy rate greater than 25 percent. Nonresidents pay market prices for the permits, each permit is valid only for a specific block, and the city sells no more than four nonresident permits on any block.

To encourage residents to accept a few nonresident permits on their block, the city can dedicate the resulting revenue to pay for added public services on the block. For example, a block that allows overnight parking by four nonresidents at $50 a month will raise $2,400 a year for public services such as cleaning and repairing the sidewalks. Residents can keep all the on-street parking on their block for themselves, but blocks that allow a few nonresident permits will receive new public investment.

When the tenant of an apartment without parking buys an overnight permit in a nearby neighborhood, the money saved by not building off-street parking will indirectly finance public investment in the nearby neighborhood. And because an apartment without parking will have a lower market rent than an otherwise identical apartment with parking, tenants who do not own cars will no longer subsidize parking for tenants who do.

To attract tenants without cars to apartments without parking, cities can require landlords to include a free transit pass in the lease for each unit without an off-street parking space. This requirement will not burden development because providing a transit pass costs far less than building a parking space. The combination of apartments without parking, overnight permit districts, and free transit passes will encourage residents to ride public transit, cycle, and walk.

Overnight permits will not solve all problems that removing off-street parking requirements can create. Drivers who visit or work in buildings without off-street parking may park in nearby neighborhoods during the day. In this case, the city can add daytime permit districts on blocks that request one. If the residents agree, the city can also allow nonresidents to pay for parking on blocks that have daytime vacancies, and the revenue will pay for better public services. Chapter 51 proposes a more comprehensive way to manage on-street parking in residential neighborhoods.

If everyone can easily park free on the street, developers have little incentive to build off-street parking and little ability to charge for the parking spaces they do build. Therefore, cities should manage the on-street parking supply when they remove their off-street parking requirements. Parking permit districts are a politically feasible way to begin managing on-street parking. Favoring insiders over outsiders for parking on public streets may seem unfair, but political reforms must start from the status quo, and progress is often merely a small step in the right direction. As Supreme Court Justice Benjamin Cardozo wrote, "Justice is not to be taken by storm. She is to be wooed by slow advances."

This chapter was originally published in ACCESS, *Number 42, Spring 2013.*

22

Abolishing Minimum Parking Requirements: A Guide for Practitioners

By Patrick Siegman

For more than 20 years, I have encouraged communities to adopt three reforms:

1. Charge the right prices for curb parking.
2. Return the parking revenue to the blocks where it is generated, to pay for public services.
3. Remove minimum parking requirements.

The first two can be seen as a means for adopting the third (and most important) reform: removing minimum parking requirements. This chapter shares lessons I have learned as a transportation consultant about how to help U.S. communities adopt these policies, and why these reforms advance prosperity, environmental protection, and a fairer society.

ENACTING LOCAL PARKING REFORMS: A STEP-BY-STEP APPROACH

Cities frequently ask my firm, Nelson\Nygaard, to help craft citywide, neighborhood, and corridor-level plans. Success often comes by removing or sharply reducing minimum parking requirements. For these projects, my colleagues and I have developed a 10-step approach that can easily be tailored to fit local circumstances.

1. Start by Listening

Consider two typical plans in Hayward, California, the South Hayward BART/Mission Boulevard Form-based Code and its parking strategy, and the Mission Boulevard Corridor Specific Plan and its parking strategy. The plans arose from a community's desire to renew several aging, auto-oriented neighborhoods in Hayward by transforming them into compact, walkable districts, like the one shown in Figure 22-1. But Hayward's zoning code included strict parking requirements, such as requiring four parking spaces for every 1,000 square feet of retail space, a ratio which often leads to a landscape of one-story buildings

Figure 22-1 A typical walkable district (Downtown Palo Alto, CA)

Photo credit: Patrick Siegman

Figure 22-2 A typical landscape of one-story buildings surrounded by fields of parking (Dana Point, California)

Photo credit: Patrick Siegman

Agenda

1. **Introduction (5 minutes)**
2. **Commission & Public Input (20 minutes)**
   - Did you participate in previous Town Center planning efforts?
   - What **problems** should this plan address?
   - What **opportunities** exist for improvement?
   - What does success look like?

3. **Presentation (35 minutes)**
   - Existing Conditions data
   - A "Toolkit" of Parking Strategies

4. **Commission & Public Input (25 minutes)**
5. **Timeline & next steps (5 minutes)**

Figure 22-3 Public meeting agenda for the South Hayward BART/ Mission Boulevard Form-based Code

surrounded by fields of parking, with more than half of each parcel carpeted in asphalt (Figure 22-2).

Figure 22-3 presents the agenda for the South Hayward BART project's first public meeting on transportation issues. After a brief introduction to set expectations (e.g., defining study area boundaries), I began by listening. Once people had a chance to be heard, they became more willing to listen. I could then also tailor my remarks to respond to their fears and aspirations.

Next, I delivered a presentation where I began by suggesting goals (drawn from the larger community goals set forth in the city's General Plan) for further discussion, then summarized existing conditions, and concluded with a toolkit of potential strategies for achieving the community's goals. I left ample time for feedback.

2. Point Out that Parking is Not an End in Itself, but Rather a Means of Achieving Larger Community Goals. Discuss the Community's Overall Goals Early and Often

Properly framing the problem to be solved is crucial. If you choose to describe your work as a single-issue exercise in improving parking, the likely outcome will be a community that is optimal for storing automobiles and suboptimal for everything else.

You should extract and summarize stated aspirations from the community's policy documents, such as the General Plan. In Hayward, I suggested that the goal of our parking study should be to implement the overall vision of the South Hayward BART/Mission Boulevard Corridor as a series of walkable neighborhoods.

When the community agreed to make that the overarching goal, it led to supportive reforms. These plans and the city's follow-up actions comprehensively reformed the city's approach to parking by:

- removing minimum parking requirements in several neighborhoods;
- charging BART rail commuters to park on nearby streets, with rates set to keep curb parking well-used but readily available;
- returning all parking revenues to the neighborhoods to help fund security, lighting, trash pickup, and graffiti cleanup; and
- protecting existing residents from curb parking shortages with residential permit districts.

The reforms helped make it possible for a development team to invest $121.5 million to transform former BART parking lots into 357 new affordable and market-rate homes.

3. Check Your Ego at the Door, but Not Your Values

When offering advice, remember that you are just a guest in someone else's hometown. Nobody voted for you, and you are not in charge; however, the community has hired you to offer ideas, technical expertise, and a point of view. Don't hesitate to offer policies and recommendations that arise from your personal values. But emphasize that the ideas you are sharing may or may not be right for their town.

4. Whenever Possible, Tie Parking Plans to a Larger Place-Making Vision

Parking reforms are most easily adopted when they are part of a larger vision. This approach is exemplified in our work on the *Ventura Downtown Mobility & Parking Plan*. All of its reforms (described below) were motivated by the city's newly crafted *Downtown Specific Plan*, which called for making a place with the highest standards of urban design, where people prefer to walk or bike rather than drive.

5. Describe the Two Key Parts of Every Parking System: (1) Quantity (The Number of Spaces) and (2) Management (The Policies, Regulations and Prices Governing Them)

It is important to raise the question: Are your current policies, for both the quantity and the management of parking, helping you achieve your big-picture community goals? Then, help people separate reality from fiction, by mapping and photographing existing conditions.

Take a lesson from the hotel industry. Managers of even the cheapest fleabag motels know that they must keep track of how many rooms they have, and how many people stay in them each night. Hoteliers also don't build additional rooms, unless the ones they already own are generating enough revenue to cover their costs. Yet, surprisingly often, city planners set parking policies without knowing how many parking spaces they already have, how full they are, and what it would cost to build more.

Document the parking supply and occupancy rates in the study area, including both public and private supplies. Explain current conditions using both photographs and maps of peak hour parking occupancy.

In downtown Ventura, for example, the data revealed that the overall parking supply greatly exceeded demand. At least 45 percent of spaces were empty at even the busiest hour of the week, even though virtually all parking was given away for free. Many local merchants perceived (incorrectly) that the city had an overall parking shortage. All the visible curb parking on Main Street was often full (Figure 22-4), but parking lots and garages just a block away sat half-empty (Figure 22-5).

We asked the community: Since you have underused off-street garages, can you solve the curb parking problem by building still more garages? Mapping and photographing Ventura's existing conditions helped the community realize that they had a parking management problem, not a parking supply problem. Parking quantities were ample, but parking management was lacking.

Such "spot shortage" problems can often be quickly resolved by instituting performance-based pricing for the prime parking spots. In Ventura, free curb parking was replaced with performance-based parking pricing (aimed at achieving an 85 percent occupancy goal on each block), which generated revenue for local neighborhoods. Minimum parking requirements were also decreased sharply, allowing buildings to be constructed with no on-site parking.

The first "Class A" office building erected in downtown Ventura since the 1920s (Figure 22-6), was then built without any on-site parking. As City Manager Rick Cole pointed out, the building was made possible by the new parking code. Without this change, the new building, located on a small infill site, would have been physically and financially infeasible.

Bill Fulton, then mayor of Ventura, described what happened on the day that Ventura's performance-based parking pricing program went into effect:

> At about 10:30 this morning, I step out of my office. ... Almost immediately, I notice something different. ... The paid parking portion of our downtown

Figure 22-4 Parking on Ventura's Main Street was underpriced and overcrowded
Photo credit: Patrick Siegman

Figure 22-5 Ventura's downtown public parking garage often sat half-empty

Photo credit: Patrick Siegman

parking management program had gone into effect at 10 a.m., and it was already showing results. People who park all day downtown have moved into the lots and the upper levels of the parking garage. Spaces on the street are now available for shoppers, diners, and others who were running short-term errands. In other words, only 30 minutes after we instituted the parking management program, it is working.

6. Explain the History, Purpose, Origin, and Unintended Harmful Consequences of the City's Existing Parking Requirements

Summarizing the data on existing parking conditions usually reveals that the community has excessive quantities of asphalt, but insufficient management to solve common complaints.

This sets the stage for explaining why minimum parking requirements were first adopted, what purpose they were originally intended to serve, where they came from, what their unintended negative consequences have been, and how and why they often undermine progress towards communities' larger goals. The history and unfortunate consequences of this failed attempt to alleviate traffic congestion may be found in reports, such as the *Pasadena Traffic Reduction Strategies Study,* and are summarized in presentation slides, such as those I delivered in public meetings for the San Marcos University District Specific

Figure 22-6 Ventura's first "Class A" office building since the 1920s

Photo credit: David Sargent

Plan. In presentations, I typically: quote the local zoning code's stated purpose for parking requirements (see Figure 22-7); note that code requirements often exceed peak occupancy rates, even at isolated locations where transit is nonexistent and parking is given away for free; illustrate the remarkable physical space requirements (Figure 22-8) and high cost (in downtown Ventura, $40,000 to $60,000 per parking space) of complying with minimum parking requirements; and note the unintended side effect of skewing travel choices toward solo driving.

This stage in a presentation is a good time to point out that while we can hide the cost of parking, we cannot make it go away. Initially, building developers may pay the cost of complying with parking requirements, but they pass the cost along to building occupants in the form of pricier leases. Eventually, we all pay in the form of higher prices for everything except parking.

Minimum Parking Requirements

Purpose

Palo Alto: "to alleviate traffic congestion"?

San Diego: "to reduce traffic congestion and improve air quality"

Hayward: "to relieve congestion on streets" …to prevent spill-over parking problems

Figure 22-7 Zoning codes' stated purposes for minimum parking requirements

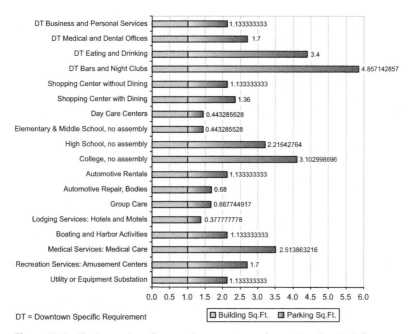

DT = Downtown Specific Requirement

☐ Building Sq.Ft.   ■ Parking Sq.Ft.

Figure 22-8 Zoning codes often require more space for parking than buildings

Source: Nelson\Nygaard Consulting

7. Illustrate Better Alternatives to Minimum Parking Requirements by Offering a "Toolkit" of Parking Strategies

Offering a toolkit—and emphasizing that certain tools in the kit may not be right for their community—allows you to introduce reform ideas and to share success stories in a way that is interesting, unthreatening, and invites exploration.

In presentations for the Hayward and San Marcos plans, for example, I offered 12 strategies for consideration:

1. Charge the right prices for curb parking.
2. Return meter revenue to the neighborhoods.
3. Invest parking revenues in demand management programs.
4. Provide residents and employees with Universal Transit Passes (i.e., deeply discounted group transit passes).
5. "Unbundle" parking costs from the cost of other goods and services.
6. Cash out employer-paid parking.
7. Strengthen transportation demand management requirements.
8. Remove minimum parking requirements.
9. Set maximum parking requirements.
10. Improve transit.
11. Improve bicycle and pedestrian facilities and programs.
12. Institute congestion pricing for roadways.

We illustrated each strategy with a story describing the successful use of that approach elsewhere in the U.S. As described earlier, many of the strategies were embraced and eventually implemented by each community.

This is also a good moment to address equity issues directly. Point out how minimum parking requirements harm low-income families and describe how the alternative strategies can improve social equity. In Hayward, for example, removing minimum parking requirements made it financially feasible to convert underused parking lots into below-market-rate housing for struggling families and seniors. Moreover, a portion of the savings on parking construction were reinvested in providing each new resident with free transit passes—a benefit usable by all, not just those able to afford an automobile.

8. Gain the Backing of Key Interest Groups by Spending Parking Revenue on the Public Services that they Most Desire

When introducing the idea of parking pricing, sit down with the key organized interest groups, such as local business and residents' associations, and make a list of how they would want to see any new parking revenues spent. Unless these politically influential interest groups support parking pricing, the concept may not gain a solid council majority in support, and then there won't be any parking revenue to spend.

After downtown Ventura installed its 318 new meters, for example, city staff initially considered spending the resulting $530,000 per year in new parking revenue on a downtown shuttle. But when merchants made it clear that improving security was a higher priority to them, the city devoted most revenues to new foot patrols instead. The new patrols, explains Ventura Police Sergeant John Snowling, have "had a tremendous impact in the amount of street-level crime during the daytime hours." In the first year after the meters' installation, downtown crime decreased by 29 percent, a benefit that helped maintain the support of the downtown merchants during the controversial initial months of the parking pricing program.

9. Protect Existing Residents from Excessive Spillover Parking

As is typical in cities across the country, in Hayward, San Marcos, and Ventura, there were spillover parking problems despite ample overall parking supply. Essentially, motorists heading for nonresidential destinations nearby frequently filled up all the curb parking on some residential blocks. To resolve this, I typically recommend instituting parking benefit districts that charge visitors to park and providing permits to residents to park for free. You will gain immense support from residents by spending new parking revenues from fees levied on nonresidents who park in the neighborhood on whatever public services the residents most want.

Remember these fundamentals of neighborhood parking politics. Residents are often highly organized, have a concentrated interest in parking on their blocks, and they vote. By contrast, the nonresident motorists filling a neighborhood's streets are less organized, garner less sympathy, and to the extent that they are from out of town, can't vote locally. Limiting parking privileges or reducing parking subsidy programs for these nonresidents is often politically feasible. Similarly, eliminating parking subsidy programs and privileges for future residents (who aren't yet present and therefore can't vote) is also highly feasible.

10. Distill Strategies into a Practical, Financially Feasible, and Implementable Plan

Through public meetings, follow-up meetings with city staff, and one-on-one meetings with councilmembers (within the limits prescribed by open meeting laws), you should be able to discern which reforms can gain majority support. Distill these into a coherent, workable plan, and provide sample ordinances and code language from cities that have implemented similar reforms.

CONCLUSIONS: A BIPARTISAN WAVE OF REFORM

Minimum parking requirements have long been obscure and unexamined. They are a regulatory approach promoted mostly by unelected technocrats and largely unknown to the average citizen. Once cities learn how to (1) prevent curb-parking shortages by pricing curb parking, and (2) make priced parking politically popular by returning parking revenues to the priced neighborhoods, they can solve common parking complaints without resorting to minimum parking requirements.

Modern technologies, ranging from pay-by-cell-phone parking payments to license plate recognition systems, are making it cheaper, faster, and easier to implement parking pricing. Communities are also increasingly realizing that many cities have turned away from minimum parking requirements entirely, adopted better strategies, and have seen neighborhoods thrive as a result.

As shown by the examples cited in this article and the larger wave of reform sweeping across the U.S., cities are increasingly embracing performance-based parking pricing and either removing or sharply reducing minimum parking requirements. From liberal Berkeley, where registered Democrats outnumber Republicans by 15 to 1, to conservative San Marcos, California, where Republicans dominate the political arena, Americans are turning away from minimum parking regulations.

REFERENCES AND FURTHER READING

Siegman, Patrick, Brian Canepa, and Kara Vuicich. 2011. "Downtown Berkeley Parking and Transportation Demand Management Report." Report Prepared for City of Berkeley, California. www.cityofberkeley.info/uploadedFiles/Public_Works/Level_3_-_Transportation/BERKELEY%20PTDM%20DRAFT%20FINAL%20-%20NEW.pdf

Siegman, Patrick, and Brian Canepa. 2009. "San Marcos University District Parking & Transportation Demand Management Plan," Report Prepared for City of San Marcos, California. www.san-marcos.net/Home/ShowDocument?id=2010

Siegman, Patrick. 2008. "Traffic Reduction: A Toolkit of Strategies." Presentation prepared for City of San Marcos, California, University District Specific Plan. http://www.san-marcos.net/Home/ShowDocument?id=989

Siegman, Patrick, Brian Canepa, and Jessica Alba. 2006. "Traffic Reduction
Strategies Study." Report Prepared for City of Pasadena, California. http://ww2.
cityofpasadena.net/councilagendas/2007%20agendas/Feb_26_07/Pasadena%20
Traffic%20Reduction%20Strategies%2011-20-06%20DRAFT.pdf
Siegman, Patrick, and Jeremy Nelson. 2006. "Downtown Ventura Mobility &
Parking Plan." Report Prepared for City of San Buenaventura, California.
www.cityofventura.net/files/community_development/planning/planning_
communities/resources/downtown/Ventura_FinalMobility+PkngMngmntPl
an.04.06_Accepted.pdf

23

Buffalo Abandons Parking Requirements

By Daniel Baldwin Hess

Reforms involve not only adopting good policies,
but also repealing bad policies.

DONALD SHOUP

Municipal zoning codes remain the foundation for establishing and maintaining urban built environments in the U.S., dictating land use as well as building height, scale, mass, and other characteristics. Parking accommodation is typically required by local zoning codes, which means a minimum number of off-street parking spaces for new developments must be provided. Usually the number of parking spaces for every land use is based on the building's square footage or unit of development. Minimum parking requirements exist to prevent new parking demand generated by a given property from overwhelming on-street parking (known as "spillover").

Minimum parking requirements proliferated in zoning codes during the Eisenhower-era expansion of automobile infrastructure to accommodate demands for driving and growth in suburbs. Eventually, parking minima became standard in every U.S. zoning code, creating an oversupply of free or underpriced parking. Minimum parking requirements encourage automobile dependence and distort land use. Parking mandates encourage driving and automobile ownership, produce sprawl and low-density development, create social inequity, destroy dense urban environments, increase development costs, and complicate building reuse. Land devoted to parking diminishes street life, disrupts urban vibrancy, interrupts building flow, and reduces the convenience of walking, cycling, and riding public transit. By subsidizing the cost of using vehicles and encouraging driving, minimum parking requirements deepen automobile dependence.

Urban planners, city officials, and the general public in various locales have grown concerned with these consequences and have begun to broadly question minimum parking requirements. There is now greater recognition that minimum parking requirements produce a wasteful oversupply of parking, which is a poor use of resources that is detrimental to city fabric. In response, planners can adopt parking reforms to prevent an oversupply of parking and improve transportation, environmental, and social outcomes. Minimum parking requirements persist, however, and reform efforts are progressing slowly.

NEW APPROACHES FOR REGULATING PARKING SUPPLIES

Parking requirements are an integral part of zoning codes and can be restructured in ways that activate streetscapes and spur revitalization. By reforming the parking requirements, planners can address: (a) underused land in central cores; (b) downtown development pressure; and (c) ineffective one-size-fits-all mandates.

In recent years, parking requirements have been abolished in cities in Australia, Brazil, France, Germany, and New Zealand, and nationwide in England. Since 2005, more than 120 U.S. cities have removed parking requirements in city centers or specific districts. In transit-rich neighborhoods, where rates of driving may be lower, local reductions in minimum parking requirements align supply and demand for parking. For example, parking requirements have been reduced in plans for transit-oriented and transit-adjacent residential developments in Brooklyn, New York; Calgary and Vancouver, Canada; Philadelphia, Pennsylvania; and Boulder, Colorado. Minimum parking requirements have also been eliminated in downtown and mixed-use districts in Cincinnati, Ohio; Eugene and Portland, Oregon; San Francisco, California; and Seattle, Spokane, and Tacoma, Washington.

REFORMING OFF-STREET PARKING REQUIREMENTS IN BUFFALO, NEW YORK

Buffalo eliminated all parking requirements in the city's new zoning ordinance, adopted in January 2017. This chapter examines the process used to repeal parking requirements during a wholesale zoning reform and discusses outcomes for development and multimodal transport planning.

Urban Decline in Buffalo

A historic industrial city at the eastern end of Lake Erie, Buffalo declined throughout the twentieth century following the demise of its manufacturing industry. Buffalo's population exceeded 580,000 during the 1950s, but the city has since lost more than half its residents. In 2015, the city population was 259,000 and the metropolitan area population was 899,000 (down from 1.13 million in 1950).

With a declining metropolitan population, growth (and sprawl) in Buffalo's suburbs meant the central city suffered. Development aspirations in 1950s Buffalo were typical of many U.S. cities coping with a fast-paced post-World War II exodus to the suburbs. To make downtown attractive for business, city leaders were eager to provide cheap or free parking. During this period of urban renewal, which began in the 1950s and lasted several decades, the city expanded parking capacity by demolishing buildings as a means of solving "parking problems." Figure 23-1, for example, shows the view looking to the northwest from downtown in the 1970s, depicting a large

Figure 23-1 Downtown Buffalo, 2016. Surface parking lots can be found throughout the CBD

Source: Western New York Heritage Press

■ Surface Lots ■ Parking Ramps

Figure 23-2 Parking supply in downtown Buffalo in 2003

Source: New Millenium Group

surface supply of parking in the CBD. In the figure, the surface parking lot to the east of the Seneca One Tower (known then as the Marine Midland Building) is now the site of a baseball stadium, Coca Cola Field.

With great support and little opposition, parking requirements were added to the Buffalo zoning code by the late 1950s. A study from The New Millennium Group (Figure 23-2) demonstrates an over-abundance of parking in Downtown Buffalo in 2003. Today, approximately 28 percent of the land area in Downtown Buffalo is used for off-street parking.

A New Zoning Code Promotes New (And Old) Urbanism

In what is the first comprehensive zoning reform in Buffalo since 1953, a new Unified Development Ordinance (UDO), called the Green Code, is reaching the end of a five-year development process. The 1950s zoning

Figure 23-3   Schematic of mixed-use edges in the Buffalo Green Code
Source: City of Buffalo, Mayor's Office of Strategic Planning

manual emphasized separation of uses following Euclidean principles, typical of American zoning codes of its era.

In contrast, the Green Code emphasizes zoning regulations tailored to contextual settings, following a new movement in zoning that prioritizes form above use. Walkable, sustainable, and mixed-use neighborhoods popular in Buffalo in the first half of the twentieth century, are once again the preferred development style. An image from the heavily illustrated Green Code suggests the outcome of form requirements in mixed-use centers in N-2C districts (Figure 23-3).

Repealing Minimum Parking Requirements

The Green Code completely removes minimum parking requirements citywide, exchanging the regulatory-based parking requirement in the previous zoning code for a market-based approach. Off-street parking is not required for any land use in Buffalo in the new zoning code. Parking requirements are repealed with a single sentence: "There are no provisions that establish a minimum number of off-street parking spaces for development." With the repeal of parking requirements, developers and property owners avoid legal obligations to provide off-street parking; furthermore, existing parking spaces can be sold, leased, or converted to other uses. The Green Code gives property owners autonomy in determining how many parking spaces make sense for a property and deciding whether to provide off-street parking at all.

While the new zoning code in Buffalo no longer requires off-street parking, parking remains subject to regulation. The ordinance continues with a second and final sentence: "where provided, off-street vehicle parking must comply with the standards of this section." This approach reinforces design requirements (including walkways, drop-off areas, surface materials, etc.) for surface parking lots and structured parking.

The Vision for a Development Process Unfettered by Required Off-Street Parking

As the process of zoning reform began in Buffalo, the Western New York Environmental Alliance and two preservation groups (the Campaign for Greater Buffalo History, Architecture, and Culture, and Preservation Buffalo Niagara) expressed their opposition to minimum parking requirements, which prevented preservation and reuse of the city's ample historic buildings.

Soon after, city planners presented the public with a vision for zoning changes at the Buffalo Green Code: the New Directions in Zoning Public Forum in April 2012. During the event, the city planning team—buoyed by support from the environmental and preservation groups—tested the idea of removing minimum parking requirements. The results were astonishing: 74 percent of attendees (from a total of 300) expressed strong support for repealing minimum parking requirements (Figure 23-4).

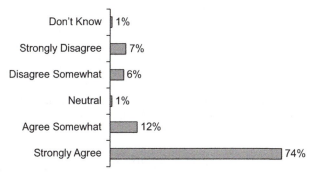

Figure 23-4 Acceptability of removing minimum parking requirements

Note: Responses to the prompt, "Minimum parking requirements should NOT be included in the UDO, allowing the market to decide how much parking is needed."

n = 300

Source: City of Buffalo, Mayor's Office of Strategic Planning

In proposing to remove minimum parking requirements in the Green Code, the energetic planning team knew they took an unorthodox step. They were prepared to make compromises, such as reducing but not eliminating minimum parking requirements. Surprisingly, developers, downtown business representatives, and even the public approved of the radical change. The consultant team retained to assist in developing the new zoning code, hesitant to disrupt the status quo and provoke controversy, proved more conservative than city planners in their recommendations.

Opposition Fails to Emerge

Various local organizations publicly endorsed the draft version of the Green Code, in particular the removal of minimum parking requirements. Developers and downtown business representatives attended outreach events and reported that minimum parking requirements were a hindrance that drove development costs. With a glut of off-street parking spaces and underutilized on-street parking, developers estimated that the existing supply of parking space could satisfy demand.

Predicted Consequences and Opportunities

Absent parking requirements, developers can build apartment or office buildings without having to supply off-street parking. Repealing minimum parking requirements reduces the supply of off-street parking and requires better management of on-street parking. When drivers cannot locate off-street parking, they demand more on-street (curbside) parking. Performance- or demand-based pricing strategies could be used to manage supply and demand. In parking benefit districts, for example, revenue from parking fees is used to fund neighborhood improvements. In this scenario, free parking is converted to metered spaces and priced so as to achieve 85 percent occupancy. Residential parking permits, exempt from meter fees, could be distributed to residents in the immediate vicinity of parking meters.

DISCUSSION

In repealing minimum parking requirements, city planners in Buffalo rejected a regulatory approach that viewed off-street parking spaces as necessary for land development. Minimum parking regulations are one of a number of outmoded regulations discarded in the city's Green Code due to a new focus on smart growth and sustainability.

The Relationship between Development, Parking, and Transport Amid Urban Decline

In cities with declining populations, resources are strained and development is scarce. Mandated parking minimums add burdensome development costs and complications, creating unnecessary challenges for improving cities. This condition can be overcome with parking reform, as seen in Buffalo. The repeal of minimum parking requirements makes sense for cities like Buffalo that are highly walkable, bicycle friendly, and transit-rich. It is also a logical response to parking oversupply.

Throughout Buffalo, the parking supply is likely to be consistent with (or exceed) demand, with ample opportunity for both free and paid off-street and on-street parking. Population decline and slow economic development (until recently) have tempered overall demand for parking in the city. These conditions, coupled with a lack of development pressure, ultimately made it reasonable to propose the repeal of minimum parking requirements during a zoning reform. Parking availability is adequate (or better), and there was little resistance to the idea of erasing parking requirements in outreach proceedings.

Development and Parking: Meeting Minimum Parking Requirements

With the removal of minimum parking requirements, the future may bring substantial variation in the provision of off-street parking, especially for residential sites. Developers of high-end housing will likely provide the same number of parking spaces as required in the previous zoning code, but different housing types may emerge to satisfy other markets, including smaller housing for low-income families who do not own cars or need parking spaces. Preferences for walking, bicycling, and riding public transit over driving may also be reflected in new residential site selection and development. As development costs become unbundled from the cost of providing parking, more diverse and cheaper housing in Buffalo will likely increase.

Without minimum parking requirements, developers will have fewer problems situating buildings and parking spaces on lots, or funding the construction of expensive parking infrastructure. The freedom gained by eliminating parking requirements may encourage creative uses for vacant land, potentially enhancing opportunity for entrepreneurship since developers can forego providing parking and instead maximize leasable or revenue-producing space. The Green Code enhances the preservation-readiness of many sites, since developers are not hamstrung by a requirement to provide on-site parking and thus may find it easier to realize the potential of historic buildings and sites. (Many historic buildings, which predate parking minimums, abut parcel boundaries on all sides and are limited in their uses because they thus cannot accommodate off-street parking on the same property; to meet parking requirements, developers of historic buildings must seek variances or acquire adjacent properties with space for parking lots.) Underused land can be developed, as the market allows, without the burden of providing off-street parking.

The repeal of minimum parking requirements in Buffalo does not signal the end of off-street parking. Banks, for example, require developers and property owners to provide parking for residents, tenants, and guests as a way to make properties more attractive to renters. Marketability is critical for residential and commercial development projects, and conservative financiers prefer sufficient parking to attract renters and thereby ensure profitability and guarantee loan repayment.

FINDINGS

Two key findings emerged from the repeal of parking requirements in Buffalo's new Green Code:

1. **Removing minimum parking requirements is easiest where off-street parking demand is low.** Support from special interest groups and support from the general public in an early phase of zoning reform—followed by little disagreement—gave the planning team confidence about making a dramatic change to parking requirements in Buffalo.

   In active development markets with economic and population growth, minimum parking requirements are seen as vital for ensuring parking access at all land uses. Securing on-site parking is critical for developers and property owners in order to protect income streams. However, in no-growth or slow-growth settings like Buffalo, minimum parking requirements hinder development. In Buffalo's core, only 63 percent of parking downtown is occupied on a typical weekday, and parking fees ($76 per month in a municipal parking structure) are inexpensive.

   The removal of minimum parking requirements in Buffalo is a sweeping change, but it surprisingly created minimal conflict. Expected opposition did not materialize and a high level of public support emerged after the introduction of the idea. Events in Buffalo suggest that removing minimum parking requirements may be easier than suspected, especially in places of prolonged decline. Community support for repealing Buffalo's parking requirements may stem from a realization that parking minima do not help (and may even hurt) development prospects, especially in Buffalo's slow-development atmosphere; conversely, a lack of required parking may make it more feasible to renovate and to redevelop abandoned and historic buildings.

2. **Public support can make changing parking policy easier for planners.** Planners and city officials with land-use and zoning responsibilities have long assumed that lessening or removing minimum parking requirements would be a difficult and lengthy process because many people would oppose removing minimum parking requirements where they thought it could negatively affect their own personal interests. Donald Shoup succinctly captures this sentiment: "parking requirements cannot be eliminated all at once ... instead cities can dismantle their parking requirements gradually." Buffalo's repeal occurred more swiftly than Shoup predicted. Buffalo erased the entire history of its city parking requirements, which were virtually unchanged since they were amended in the late 1950s (as addenda to the 1953 code).

Public reaction during the early events related to zoning reform suggests that the public was not supportive of a status quo approach to parking control. The planning team in Buffalo introduced the revolutionary idea of repealing minimum parking requirements and gained confidence to pursue this dramatic parking reform after receiving positive public reception. If the public had expressed strong support for maintaining minimum parking requirements, repealing them would have proven far more difficult or impossible.

CONCLUSION

Most city leaders, developers, and urban planners have long assumed that cities could not function without parking requirements. The removal of parking requirements in the zoning ordinance of a mid-sized American city such as Buffalo represents a paradigm shift and may, over time, have far-reaching effects on land development, sustainable transportation, the economy, and the environment. This zoning change is a simple innovation that addresses an oversupply of undervalued parking by repealing an unproductive mandate rather than adding new regulations. It is possible that a repeal of minimum parking requirements could be replicated in other small, medium, and large Great Lakes or Rust Belt cities, but the process will be a greater challenge in cities with greater parking constraints.

Decisions made today will affect cities for generations to come, and parking requirements are poorly aligned with progressive concerns for sustainability, equity, and social responsibility. Donald Shoup has argued that no urban planning action has had a greater effect on "distorting" land use and built environments in U.S. cities than minimum parking requirements. Planners in Buffalo have rescinded an ineffective regulation and overcome the institutional inertia related to parking control.

Hess, Daniel Baldwin. 2017. "Repealing Minimum Parking Requirements in the Green Code in Buffalo: New Directions for Land Use and Development." *Journal of Urbanism: International Research on Placemaking and Urban Sustainability.* Vol. 10. no. 4. pp. 442–467.

24

Solar Parking Requirements

By Donald Shoup

Solar panels have found a new place in the sun—on parking lots surrounding commercial and industrial buildings, mounted on canopies providing shade for the parked cars. Parking lots in asphalt-rich cities have great solar potential because the panels can be oriented to maximize power production during summer afternoons when electricity is most valuable. Solar-powered parking lots can mitigate the substantial increase in peak-hour energy demand that major developments create, but few developers now install solar canopies over their parking lots. Nevertheless, although the demand for electricity peaks on days when the sun shines brightest, solar power accounts for less than 1 percent of our total electricity supply.

How can cities increase power production from parking lots? Cities could specify that a share of the surface parking spaces at any new development must be covered with solar panels to meet the increased peak-hour power demand created by new buildings. New buildings increase the demand for electricity during peak hours, and a solar requirement for the parking spaces will help to meet this demand. Because the air conditioners for new buildings increase the risk of neighborhood power failure on hot summer days, it seems reasonable to require developers to offset this risk.

Cities can amend their zoning codes to require solar power in the parking lots of new buildings. Requiring a specific electric generating capacity, such as 1 kilowatt per parking space, will give developers the freedom to meet the requirement in the most cost-effective way. (Covering one parking space with solar panels will produce about

2 kilowatts of generating capacity, so covering half the spaces in a parking lot will produce about 1 kilowatt per space.) Because the solar potential of a parking lot depends on many factors, such as climate and topography, solar power requirements would differ among locations and land uses, just as parking requirements do. Cities should not adopt solar requirements in all locations and for all land uses, but sunny areas with large parking lots are a good place to start. Cities can also offer developers who prefer not to install solar panels on their parking lots the option to pay for equivalent renewable energy or conservation measures elsewhere, perhaps at a school or other public building.

Solar arrays will not mar the appearance of parking lots because most parking lots are already ugly. Solar canopies, which resemble hi-tech trellises, can improve the appearance of most parking lots and become an important architectural feature of a building. They can also help to reduce the visual blight and NIMBY problems associated with building power plants and transmission lines.

If each solar canopy has an electric-vehicle charging station at its base, the solar parking requirement will help to distribute charging stations throughout the city. In California, one solar-covered parking space can generate about 5 kilowatt-hours of electricity a day, which is enough to drive an electric vehicle for about 20 miles. Solar canopies at work can therefore fuel the trips to and from work for many commuters' electric cars. California requires that, by 2025, 15 percent of all cars sold in the state must have zero tailpipe emissions, and other states are adopting similar requirements. Solar canopies over parking lots can provide some of the electricity needed for these cars without straining the grid's generation and distribution systems.

The intermittent nature of solar power output makes it well suited to charging electric cars. If the solar energy is being stored in batteries rather than fed into the electric grid, the power fluctuations caused by clouds will not cause stability problems for the grid. The solar power output can also directly charge batteries without the power loss caused by conversion to alternating current for the grid.

Solar parking lots are highly visible evidence of a company's commitment to the environment. If the parking lots at new buildings come with solar canopies, vast parking lots without solar panels could begin to look antisocial. The owners of some older buildings might update their parking lots with solar arrays to keep up with the green look of the new competition. Even drivers who don't own electric cars can feel green when they park in the shade of solar panels.

The federal government and many state governments subsidize solar panels, so developers will not have to pay the full cost of complying with a city's solar parking requirement. Because parking lots are usually bigger than the buildings they serve, and usually have unobstructed

Figure 24-1 A solar parking lot
Photo credit: Donald Shoup

solar access, the solar panels can take advantage of economies of scale in construction and can capture more of the available sunlight. In contrast, few houses have properly oriented roofs, unobstructed solar access, and the structural capacity to support solar panels. Therefore, parking lots will generate more electricity per dollar of government subsidy than houses can.

Solar canopies not only produce power but also reduce the demand for it. Shading parked cars will reduce the use of air conditioning by motorists when they leave the shade on sunny days, resulting in better fuel efficiency and reduced tailpipe emissions. The canopies can also reduce the heat island effects of parking lots around buildings, and thus reduce air conditioning demand in the buildings.

Beyond their economic advantages, solar-powered parking lots will be a decentralized source of back-up electricity in an emergency, such as a natural disaster or terrorist attack. Reducing the demand for energy from the electric grid will also reduce power plant emissions that contribute to air pollution and climate change. Some states require electric utilities to obtain a specific share of their energy from renewable sources, and solar parking lots can help satisfy these requirements.

Solar panels in parking lots will start producing power far sooner than conventional power plants, which take years to construct. Solar parking lots distributed throughout the city will also generate electricity right where it is used, reducing transmission losses on the power grid and helping to prevent power outages caused by overloaded transmission lines. Because solar panels produce the most electricity on sunny days when the demand for air conditioning peaks, they reduce the load on conventional power plants at the most critical time. With only a slight change to the parking requirements in their zoning ordinances, cities can lead the way toward a future powered by renewable energy. We shouldn't wait until the next heat wave to think about getting solar power from our parking lots.

This chapter was originally published in ACCESS, *No. 40, Spring 2010.*

Part II

Charge the Right Prices for On-Street Parking

As he turned from Oberlin Avenue round the corner into Third Street, N.E., he peered ahead for a space in the line of parked cars. He angrily just missed a space as a rival driver slid into it. Ahead another car was leaving the curb, and Babbitt slowed up, holding out his hand to the cars pressing on him from behind, agitatedly motioning an old woman to go ahead, avoiding a truck which bore down on him from one side. With front wheels nicking the wrought-steel bumper of the car in front, he stopped, feverishly cramped his steering-wheel, slid back into the vacant space and, with eighteen inches of room, maneuvered to bring the car level with the curb. It was a virile adventure masterfully executed.

—SINCLAIR LEWIS, BABBITT

25

Cruising for Parking

By Donald Shoup

A surprising amount of traffic isn't caused by people who are on their way somewhere. Our streets are congested, in part, by people who have gotten where they want to be but are hunting for a place to park.

DRIVING IN CIRCLES

Cruising for parking appeared early in travel writing. In *Touring New England on the Trail of the Yankee*, Clara Whiteside (1926, 124) described the problems she encountered while on an automobile tour in Connecticut in the 1920s:

> We started out to view the town. ... Round and round the blocks we drove trying to find a place to park. ... Every curb was black with backed-in cars. ... There's a place! Alas! It was the wrong side of the street. So on we would go to the next corner hoping to be able to turn but invariably the traffic officer would firmly signal us, till time after time, we would find ourselves ... in the very center of things, entangled in the traffic.

Apart from the disappearance of traffic officers at every corner, cruising for parking has changed little since this experience in the 1920s.

Cruising for parking also pops up in fiction. The first 29 pages of Tom Wolfe's *Back to Blood* recounts what is surely the most spectacular case of cruising, all in the parking lot of a Miami restaurant. Calvin Trillin's parking novel, *Tepper Isn't Going Out*, explains the exhilaration

261

of successful cruising in New York (*The High Cost of Free Parking*, pages 285–86).

Perhaps because cruising is a disguised source of congestion, most transportation planners and engineers have ignored it. Cruising creates a mobile queue of cars waiting for curb vacancies, but cruisers are mixed with traffic that is going somewhere, so no one can see how many cars are in the queue. Nevertheless, a few researchers have analyzed cruising by videotaping traffic flows, driving test cars to search for a curb space, and interviewing drivers who park at the curb or are stopped at traffic lights. Twenty-one studies of cruising behavior were conducted between 1927 and 2011 in the central business districts of thirteen cities on four continents (Table 25-1). The average time it took to find a curb space was 7.5 minutes, and on average 34 percent of the cars in the traffic flow were cruising for parking.

For example, when researchers interviewed drivers who were stopped at traffic signals in New York City in 2007, they found that 28 percent of the drivers on one street in Manhattan and 45 percent on a street in Brooklyn were cruising for curb parking. These estimates

Table 25-1   Cruising for parking

Year	City	Share of traffic cruising	Average search time
		(percent)	(minutes)
1927	Detroit (1)	19%	
1927	Detroit (2)	34%	
1933	Washington		8.0
1960	New Haven	17%	
1965	London (1)		6.1
1965	London (2)		3.5
1965	London (3)		3.6
1977	Freiburg	74%	6.0
1984	Jerusalem		9.0
1985	Cambridge	30%	11.5
1993	Cape Town		12.2
1993	New York (1)	8%	7.9
1993	New York (2)		10.2
1993	New York (3)		13.9
1997	San Francisco		6.5
2001	Sydney		6.5
2005	Los Angeles	68%	3.3
2007	New York	28%	
2007	New York	45%	
2008	New York		3.8
2011	Barcelona	18%	
Average		**34%**	**7.5**

Source: *Shoup, The High Cost of Free Parking*, 2011

cannot, of course, be extrapolated to suggest that 28 percent of all traffic in Manhattan is cruising for parking or that 45 percent of all traffic in Brooklyn is cruising for parking.

The results in Table 25-1 do not suggest that 34 percent of all city traffic is cruising. On a street where some curb spaces are vacant or where curb parking is not permitted, no cars will be cruising. No cars on freeways are cruising for parking. On a congested street where no curb spaces are open, however, many of the cars in the traffic flow may be cruising.

Even if a high share of traffic is cruising, the number of cruisers will be low if the traffic flow is low. For example, at 3 a.m. on a street where all the curb spaces are occupied and only two cars travel along it during the hour, only two cars will be cruising even if they are 100 percent of the traffic flow. But at 3 p.m. where all the curb spaces are occupied and traffic is congested, many cars can be cruising even if they are only 10 percent of the traffic flow.

The share of traffic that is cruising can change from one minute to the next because cruising is a variable, not a constant, but cruising can vary regularly by location and time of day, just as the volume of traffic does. There can be an average share over the day, but that average doesn't predict the share of traffic that is cruising at any particular time or location. Chapter 11 in *The High Cost of Free Parking* explains the details of the studies in Table 25-1.

Cities have changed since these observations were made, and the data in Table 25-1 are selective because researchers study cruising only when and where they expect to find it—where curb parking is underpriced and overcrowded. Nevertheless, cruising itself has not changed since the 1920s when old photographs and postcards showed cars parked bumper to bumper along both sides of downtown streets. Cruising for parking has wasted time and fuel for many decades. The sun never sets on cruising.

On a congested street where all the curb spaces are occupied, one simple way to estimate how much of the traffic is cruising is to observe whether the first car that approaches a newly vacated space parks in it. If, for example, the first or second driver who approaches a newly vacated curb space always parks in it, this suggests that most of the traffic is cruising for parking.

An even simpler and quicker (though perhaps less humane) way to sample the traffic flow is to approach the driver-side door of a car parked at the curb with a key in your hand, as if to open the door. If the first driver to see you with a key apparently poised to unlock the door always stops to wait for the space, most of the traffic is probably cruising. The stopped car blocks a lane of traffic just like a double-parked car. Unfortunately, you must then use body language to suggest that you have changed your plans and have decided not to leave, regrettably disappointing the driver who expected to park in the space. If you do this several times, and the first or second driver to see you with a key in your hand always stops to wait for a space, what share of the cars in traffic would you think are cruising? I tried this key-in-the-door test on Pike Place in Seattle, about five minutes after I thought of it. The first driver who saw me with a key in my hand always stopped traffic to wait for the space.

Even a small search time per car can create a surprising amount of traffic. Consider a congested downtown where it takes three minutes to find a curb space and the parking turnover is 10 cars per space per day. For each curb space, cruising thus results in 30 extra minutes of vehicle travel per day (3 minutes × 10 cars). If the average cruising speed is 10 miles an hour, cruising creates five vehicle miles traveled (VMT) per space per day (10 mph × 0.5 hour). Over a year, this driving in circles amounts to 1,825 VMT for each curb space (5 miles × 365 days), greater than half the distance across the U.S. If cruisers drive 10 miles an hour, that amounts to 182 hours of cruising a year for each curb space.

For each additional hour that a car is parked on a crowded street, other drivers have more difficulty finding an open space and will spend more time cruising for parking. Inci, Ommeren, and Kobus (2017) estimate that for each hour that a car parks at a crowded curb, the total extra time that other drivers waste while cruising for parking is worth about 15 percent of what an average worker earns in an hour. For example, if the average wage rate is $10 an hour, the external cost of parking at a crowded curb for an hour is about $1.50. This external cost is only for the additional time spent by drivers who are cruising for parking, and cruising does far more than waste the cruisers' time. Most queues waste only the time of people in the queue and don't harm anyone else, but drivers who spend time cruising for parking also congest traffic, pollute the air, endanger pedestrians and cyclists, and create CO_2 emissions. In addition to wasting the cruisers' time, cruising therefore harms almost everyone else. All these extra costs show that underpriced parking costs a lot more than properly priced parking.

CHOOSING TO CRUISE

Suppose curb parking is free but all the spaces are occupied, so you have to cruise until you find a space being vacated by a departing car. Off-street parking is available, but you have to pay the market price for it. How do you decide whether to cruise or to pay? If off-street parking is expensive, many drivers will hunt for curb parking, an entirely rational response to prices. Thus, by underpricing their curb parking, cities tell drivers to cruise. To study this incentive, I collected data on the price of curb and off-street parking for an hour at noon at the same location—city hall—in 20 cities throughout the U.S. In 2004, the average price of curb parking was only 20 percent of the price of parking in a garage *(The High Cost of Free Parking,* 328). Cruising saved drivers the most money in New York, where the price of off-street parking was $14.38 for the first hour, but curb parking was only $1.50.

Consider the high price of off-street parking in downtown Boston, which stems in part from the city's cap on the number of off-street parking spaces. This supply cap drives up the market price of off-street parking and produces an unintended outcome: the combination of low prices for curb parking and high prices for off-street parking increases the incentive to cruise. Boston limits the private off-street parking supply but fails to charge the market price for its own public curb parking. In 2016, the price of off-street parking closest to Boston City Hall was $25 for the first hour, but Boston charged $1.25 an hour at all parking meters in the city. If you want to park for an hour, the possibility of saving $23.75 is a strong incentive to cruise.

Everyone would criticize off-street parking operators if long lines of cars regularly spilled into the streets and snarled traffic because the lots and garages were always full. Cities create the same result with underpriced curb parking, but the cruising cars hide in the general traffic flow.

CRUISING IN LOS ANGELES

To learn more about cruising, my students and I made 240 observations of how long it takes to find a curb parking space at four sites in Westwood Village, a commercial district next to the UCLA campus. Curb parking in metered spaces was only 50 cents an hour during the day and free in the evening, while the cheapest off-street parking was $1 an hour. For each observation we drove to the site and circled the block until we found a curb space. Because the curb spaces were occupied almost all the time, we rarely found a vacant space when we arrived. Instead, we usually searched until we found a parked car about to vacate a space, and then waited for it to leave.

Most drivers who are cruising for parking try to avoid following directly behind another car that appears to be cruising, so as to maximize the chance of being the first to see a vacant spot. Driving a car to measure cruising times may therefore influence the behavior being studied. To avoid this potential pitfall and to get some exercise, we decided to make most of the observations by bicycle. The average cruising speed by car in Westwood was only 8 to 10 miles an hour because every intersection has a stop sign or traffic light, so a cyclist can easily keep up with vehicle traffic. For the tests, we equipped each bicycle with a cyclometer to measure elapsed travel time, distance traveled, and average speed.

Drivers cruised an average of 3.3 minutes to find a parking space, and they cruised for about half a mile (about 2.5 times around the block). The small distances cruised by individual drivers add up quickly because the turnover rate for curb parking was 17 cars per space per day. With 470 metered parking spaces in the Village, almost 8,000 cars parked at the curb each day (17 × 470). Because so many cars parked at the curb, a short cruising time for each driver created an astonishing amount of traffic. Although the average driver cruised only half a mile before parking, cruising around the 15 blocks in the Village created almost 4,000 VMT every weekday (8,000 × 0.5).

Over a year, cruising in Westwood Village created 950,000 excess VMT—equivalent to 38 trips around the earth or four trips to the moon. The obvious waste of time and fuel is even more appalling when we consider the low speed and fuel efficiency of cruising cars. Because drivers averaged about ten miles an hour in the Village, cruising 950,000 miles a year wasted about 95,000 hours (11 *years*) of drivers' time in a year. And here's another inconvenient truth about underpriced curb parking: cruising 950,000 miles wasted 47,000 gallons of gasoline and produced 730 tons of CO_2 emissions in a small business district. Beyond that, there are additional pollution and greenhouse gas emissions from all the other cars idling in traffic congestion caused by the cruising. Chapter 14 in *The High Cost of Free Parking* presents this case study of cruising for parking in Westwood Village.

THE RIGHT PRICE FOR CURB PARKING

When drivers compare the prices of parking at the curb or in a garage, they usually decide the price of garage parking is too high. Instead, the reverse is true—the price of curb parking is too low. Underpriced curb spaces are like rent-controlled apartments: they are hard to find, and once you find a space, you'd be crazy to give it up. This makes curb spaces even harder to find and increases the time cost (and therefore the congestion and pollution costs) of searching for them. Like rent-controlled apartments, curb spaces go to the lucky more than to the deserving. One person might find a curb space and park there for days while others are left to circle the block.

The top panel of Figure 25-1 shows a typical commercial block in Westwood where curb parking is underpriced and all the spaces are

CURB PARKING PRICES AND CRUISING

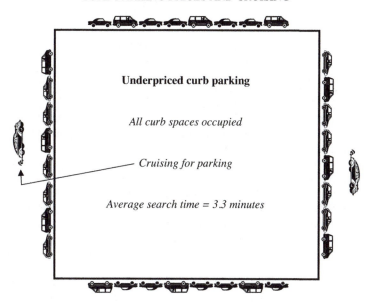

Figure 25-1   Curb parking prices and cruising

occupied. The block has eight curb spaces on each side, the average cruising time to find a curb space is 3.3 minutes, and two cruisers are circling the block. In contrast, the bottom panel shows what happens if a city charges the lowest price that will produce a few vacant spaces. Drivers have no reason to cruise because they can always find a vacant curb space near their destination, search time is zero, and cruising cars do not add to traffic congestion.

Because the right price for curb parking responds to the demand for parking, the prices will shift up and down as demand shifts up and down. For this reason, the prices are sometimes called demand-based, variable, performance, or dynamic prices. Cities do not need complex models to set prices; they only need to pay attention to the results. After shifting to an outcome goal for the parking system and choosing the occupancy rate to indicate the desired outcome, the city council will no longer have to vote on parking prices. If too many curb spaces are vacant, the price will go down, and if no curb spaces are vacant, the price will go up. Wanting more money will no longer justify raising prices. Relying on the power of an impersonal rule to set prices makes an end run around the politics of parking.

Pricing curb parking to ensure a few vacancies does not mean that travel will become unaffordable. Drivers can use several strategies to economize on curb parking without reducing their travel. They can (1) drive at off-peak hours when curb parking is cheaper, (2) park where prices are lower and walk farther to their destinations, (3) park for a shorter time, (4) park off street, (5) carpool and split the cost of parking, or (6) take public transit, ride a bike, or walk to their destinations. Diverting some trips to carpools, public transit, cycling, and walking will reduce vehicle travel without reducing human travel, and all real travel is by people, not cars.

How will market-priced curb parking affect the total amount of driving? Where a lot of the traffic is now cruising it would quickly reduce VMT. Like good and bad cholesterol, perhaps we should distinguish between good and bad VMT. Underpriced curb parking encourages bad VMT because people are driving around but not going anywhere. Market-priced curb parking enables good VMT because people are driving to where they want to go without having to drive around after they get there.

Demand-based prices are much better than time limits to manage curb parking. Using time limits to create turnover encourages drivers to cruise around hoping to see a car leaving so they can take the space. Using market prices to create an open space on every block eliminates the incentive to cruise. Cruising is especially harmful in crowded areas where many pedestrians are breathing the exhaust of drivers who are hunting for a parking space. Consider how awful traffic would be if off-street garages and lots used time limits and turnover rather than prices to manage occupancy.

GET THE PRICES RIGHT

Market prices can reduce conflict over scarce resources. Where curb parking is underpriced, drivers spend time cruising for a curb space, but when drivers pay market prices for curb parking, cities receive money to pay for public services. Cruising for parking transforms wasted time and gasoline into stress and CO_2 emissions. Charging the right price for curb parking can eliminate this cruising and all its harmful side effects. Because city governments set the prices for curb parking, they choose whether drivers will cruise.

If cities want to reduce congestion, clean the air, save energy, reduce greenhouse gas emissions, improve neighborhoods, and do all this quickly, they should charge the right price for curb parking and spend the resulting revenue to improve local public services. Getting the price of curb parking right will do a world of good.

REFERENCES AND FURTHER READING

Inci, Eren, Jos van Ommeren, and Martijn Kobus. 2017. "The External Cruising Costs of Parking," *Journal of Economic Geography*. doi: 10.1093/jeg/lbx004.

Schaller Consulting. 2006. "Curbing Cars: Shopping, Parking and Pedestrian Space in SoHo," Report prepared for Transportation Alternatives, New York City.

Shoup, Donald. 2011. *The High Cost of Free Parking*. Revised edition. Chicago: Planners Press.

Trillin, Calvin. 2001. *Tepper Isn't Going Out*, New York: Random House.

Whiteside, Clara. 1926. *Touring New England on the Trail of the Yankee*. Philadelphia: The Penn Publishing Company.

Wolfe, Tom. 2012. *Back to Blood*. New York: Little, Brown and Company.

26

Free Parking or Free Markets

By Donald Shoup

Cities should charge the right prices for curb parking because the wrong prices produce such bad results. Where curb parking is underpriced and overcrowded, a surprising share of cars on congested streets can be searching for a place to park. Twenty-one studies conducted between 1927 and 2011 found that, on average, 34 percent of the cars in congested downtown traffic were cruising for parking. When researchers interviewed drivers stopped at traffic signals in New York City in 2006 and 2007, they found that 28 percent of the drivers on a street in Manhattan and 45 percent on a street in Brooklyn were cruising for curb parking.

In another study in 2008, the average time it took to find a curb space in a 15-block area of the Upper West Side of Manhattan was 3.1 minutes, and the average cruising distance was 0.37 miles. For each individual driver, 3.1 minutes is not a long time, and 0.37 miles is not a long distance, but because there are so many drivers, the cumulative consequences are staggering. In a year, cruising for underpriced parking on these 15 blocks alone creates about 366,000 excess vehicle miles of travel (equal to 14 trips around the earth) and 325 tons of CO_2.

PERFORMANCE PARKING PRICES

Free curb parking in a congested city gives a small, temporary benefit to a few drivers who happen to be lucky on a particular day, but it imposes large social costs on everyone else every day. To manage curb parking and avoid cruising, some cities have begun to adjust their curb parking prices by location and time of day. These cities do not have a complicated pricing model, and they do not aim to raise a certain amount of revenue. Instead, they have established a target occupancy: they aim to produce about an 85 percent occupancy rate for curb parking, which on a typical block with eight curb spaces corresponds to one open spot. The price is too high if many spaces are vacant and too low if no spaces are vacant. But if one or two spaces are vacant on a block and drivers can reliably find open curb spaces at their destinations, the price is just right. We can call this the Goldilocks principle of parking prices.

Some cities refer to the policy of setting prices to produce one or two open curb spaces on every block as performance pricing. It can improve performance in three ways. First, curb parking will perform better. If all but one or two curb spaces are occupied on every block, parking will be well used but also readily available. Second, the transportation system will perform better because cruising for curb parking will not congest traffic, waste fuel, pollute the air, and waste drivers' time. Third, the local economy will perform better. In business districts, drivers will park, buy something, and leave promptly, allowing other customers to use the spaces.

SFPARK

San Francisco has embarked on an ambitious program, called SF*park*, to get the prices of curb parking right. The city has installed meters that charge variable prices and sensors that report the occupancy of each space in real time. The city thus has information on curb occupancy rates and the ability to adjust prices in response to the occupancy rates. The city adjusts prices once a month, never by more than 50¢ an hour. By nudging prices up or down in a trial-and-error process, the city seeks a structure of prices that vary by time and location throughout the city, yielding one or two open spaces on every block.

SF*park* embodies two important ideas. The first is that you cannot set the right price for curb parking without observing the occupancy. The goal is to set the price that will yield one or two open spaces on every block; this is the lowest price the city can charge without creating a parking shortage. The second is that small changes in parking prices and location choices can lead to big improvements in transportation efficiency. Nudging up the price on a crowded block by enough to shift only one car to a less crowded block can significantly improve the performance of the transportation system. This shift will eliminate cruising on the crowded block and take advantage of the empty spaces on the less crowded block. Even if all the curb spaces on all blocks are occupied, shifting only one car per block from a curb space to nearby off-street parking can also eliminate cruising.

Beyond managing the curb parking supply, SF*park* can help depoliticize parking by stating a clear principle for setting the prices for curb spaces: the demand for parking will set the prices. After shifting from a revenue goal to an outcome goal for the parking system and choosing the occupancy rate for the desired outcome, the city council will no longer have to vote on parking prices. If too many curb spaces are vacant, the price will go down, and if no curb spaces are vacant, the price will go up. Wanting more revenue will no longer justify raising prices. Relying on the power of an impersonal market test to set prices makes an end run around the politics of parking.

Some critics argue that charging market prices for curb parking will hurt poor people. Most really poor people don't own cars, and, if they do own cars, they drive them far less than rich people do. Instead, many poor people ride buses, bicycle, or walk. The buses they ride are often mired in traffic caused by richer people who are cruising for curb parking. When they bike or walk, they have to contend with cars circling each block driven by richer people who are cruising for cheap curb parking. Those who really want to help the poor should appreciate that San Francisco charges the lowest price it can without creating a shortage of curb parking and spends all the parking revenue to subsidize public transit. The buses will run faster, and the subsidy will pay for more bus services. Walking and biking will be safer. It is deeply misguided to argue that free curb parking will help the poor in San Francisco.

IF THE PRICE IS RIGHT, CUSTOMERS WILL COME

Proposals to increase parking prices or run the meters later in the evening usually provoke vehement complaints like, "If this city operates the parking meters in the evening, I will never drive downtown to eat in a restaurant again." This threat to boycott downtown restaurants would be a convincing argument if many curb spaces remained empty after the meters began operating in the evening. But this threat ignores the key argument for performance prices: If the meters are priced right, cars will fill most of the curb spaces, leaving only one or two vacant spaces on each block. If most curb spaces are filled, parking meters can't be chasing all the customers away.

Meters will chase away some drivers, but the curb spaces these drivers would have occupied will become available to customers who will pay for parking if they can easily find a convenient curb space. Because the curb spaces will remain almost fully occupied, merchants shouldn't worry that performance prices will harm their businesses.

Another advantage of performance prices is that they will decline when demand declines during a recession. The price of curb parking will automatically fall to keep the customers coming. The cheaper curb parking will help businesses survive and prevent job losses. But if curb parking prices remain unchanged during a recession, curb spaces will be underoccupied, stores will lose customers, and more people will lose jobs.

If cities eliminate cruising by charging performance prices for curb parking, where will the cruising cars go? Because drivers will no longer have to arrive at their destinations 5 to 10 minutes early to search for a curb space, their vehicle trips will be 5 to 10 minutes shorter. The reduction in traffic will come not from fewer vehicle trips but from shorter vehicle trips.

The price of parking will vary just like other prices in the economy. The price of gasoline varies by location, for example, and it goes up and down over time. There are different prices for different octane ratings, and for self service or full service, and these prices don't seem to confuse motorists or make it difficult to pay for gasoline. The price of gasoline adjusts to balance supply and demand, and the price of parking can too. Off-street parking operators also charge different prices at different locations and at times of day and for lengths of stay. Some off-street parking operators also charge different prices for self parking or valet parking, and this doesn't confuse most drivers. Paying market prices for curb parking may take time to get used to, but anyone who can't figure out how to pay a parking meter probably shouldn't be driving a car. Perhaps the test for a driver's license should include not only the ability to parallel park but also the ability to pay at a meter.

Everybody wants something for nothing, but we shouldn't promote free parking as a principle for transportation pricing and public finance. Using performance prices to manage curb parking can produce a host of benefits for businesses, neighborhoods, cities, transportation, and the environment. Cities get the traffic they plan for and the travel behavior they subsidize. Parking wants to be paid for.

REMOVING MINIMUM PARKING REQUIREMENTS

Reforms involve not only adopting good policies but also repealing bad policies. Requiring all buildings to provide ample parking is one such bad policy that cities should repeal. Some cities have begun to remove minimum parking requirements, at least in their downtowns, for two reasons. First, parking requirements prevent infill redevelopment on small lots where fitting both a new building and the required parking is difficult and expensive. Second, parking requirements prevent new uses for many older buildings that lack the parking spaces required for the new uses. Because governmental arm-twisting has created ubiquitous free parking, the resulting transportation and land-use patterns do not represent free-market choices.

A search of newspaper articles found 129 reports of cities that have removed off-street parking requirements in their downtowns since 2005. Although newspaper articles don't represent what all cities are doing, they do include many comments on why cities are changing their policies. At least in downtown business districts, some elected officials think that parking requirements put the brakes on what they want to happen and accelerate what they want to prevent.

Removing a parking requirement is not the same, however, as restricting parking or putting the city on parking diet. Rather, parking requirements force-feed the city with parking spaces, and removing a parking requirement simply stops this force-feeding. Ceasing to require off-street parking gives businesses the freedom to provide as much or as little parking as they like. Cities can remove minimum requirements without imposing maximum limits, and opposing minimum parking requirements should not be confused with supporting maximum parking limits.

A QUIET REVOLUTION IN PARKING POLICIES

Requiring Peter to pay for Paul's parking, and Paul to pay for Peter's parking is a bad idea. People should pay for their own parking, just as they pay for their own cars and gasoline. Parking requirements hide the cost of parking but they cannot make it go away, and free parking often means fully subsidized parking. At the very least, parking requirements should carry strong warning labels about the dangerous side effects.

Despite institutional inertia in the practice of planning for parking, reforms are sprouting. Paradigm shifts in urban planning are often barely noticeable while they are happening, and afterward it is often hard to tell if anything has changed. But shifts happen. Planners simply begin to understand cities in a new way and can scarcely remember a time when they understood cities differently. The incremental reforms now under way suggest that off-street parking requirements will not quickly disappear but will gradually erode. Cities may slowly shift from minimum parking requirements to performance parking prices without explicitly acknowledging that planning for parking had ever gone wrong. Eventually, however, planners may realize that minimum parking requirements were a poisoned chalice, providing ample free parking while hiding the many costs. They may then marvel at how their predecessors could have been so wrong for so long.

REFERENCES AND FURTHER READING

Schaller, Bruce. 2006. "Curbing Cars: Shopping, Parking and Pedestrian Space in SoHo." New York: Transportation Alternatives.

Transportation Alternatives. 2008. "Driven to Excess: What Under-Priced Curbside Parking Costs the Upper West Side." New York: Transportation Alternatives.

Transportation Alternatives. 2007. "No Vacancy: Park Slope's Parking Problem and How to Fix It." New York: Transportation Alternatives.

This chapter is condensed from an article in ACCESS, *Number 38, Spring 2011.*

27

Informal Parking: Turning Problems into Solutions

By Donald Shoup

If you want to make enemies,
try to change something.

WOODROW WILSON

Cities regulate almost every aspect of both on- and off-street parking, and they employ legions of parking enforcement officers to ensure that drivers obey the regulations. If so much parking is formal, regulated, and policed, what is informal parking?

INFORMAL MARKETS FOR OFF-STREET PARKING

Informal parking markets operating outside the regulated system fill a market niche that is hard to serve by formal means. They often appear near sites that generate short, sharp, infrequent increases in parking demand. Near the Los Angeles Coliseum, for example, residents charge for parking in their driveways on game days. Drivers may have to walk a few blocks to the stadium, but after the game they can leave from residential driveways much faster than from a crowded stadium lot where everyone is trying to exit at the same time. These dispersed informal lots also reduce the congestion caused by peak entry and exit queues.

The demand for game-day parking is so strong that some cities have legalized the informal markets. For example, Michigan Stadium in Ann

Arbor is the largest sports arena in the U.S., drawing crowds of more than 100,000 for every home game since 1975. The large stadium crowds have created an informal market for off-street parking. Ann Arbor prohibits parking on lawns, except on football game days. Residents park their own cars on the streets before the games to create off-street spaces on their lawns, driveways, and back yards. Many drivers think that paying for parking is un-American, but residents who receive the revenue know that paying for what you use is a traditional American value.

INFORMAL MARKETS FOR ON-STREET PARKING

In neighborhoods where curb parking is scarce but free, informal markets can be quite profitable. Apartment building doormen in expensive neighborhoods in New York and San Francisco, for example, have become successful parking entrepreneurs, using their buildings' taxi zones to park cars for visitors and earning tips for their service. When a curb space opens up near the building, the doorman moves the visitor's car into it. If a resident who parks on the street then comes home and cannot find a curb space, the doorman moves the visitor's car back to the taxi zone to create a curb vacancy, the resident parks in it, and the doorman receives another tip.

Alternate-side parking regulations in New York City create another informal market. To allow for street cleaning, New York prohibits parking for a 90-minute period on one side of the street on Mondays, Wednesdays, and Fridays, and on the other side on Tuesdays, Thursdays, and Saturdays. During the 90 minutes when parking is prohibited on the side being cleaned, many residents double park their cars on the other side of the street. This alternate-side regulation creates an informal market controlled by doormen. Residents who park on the street give their car keys to their doormen, who charge a monthly fee to move the cars from one side of the street to the other. When drivers want to use their cars, they ask the doorman where their car is. Some doormen leave gaps of curb space in front of and behind each vehicle they park, but not enough of a gap for someone to park in it. Then, a doorman who needs to park another car simply moves the first car forward to create a second parking space.

Informal markets can also have a work requirement for the parkers. Residents of Boston and Chicago who have shoveled out a parking space after a snowstorm traditionally use lawn chairs or trash cans to claim it until they return. A Boston City Council member explained, "It's a cultural thing. When people work hard to clean a spot, you want people to respect that. It's part of living in a dense community."

INFORMAL PARKING ON SIDEWALKS

Parking on sidewalks has evolved as an informal custom in some older neighborhoods in response to a shortage of free parking on the streets. I began to study this informal parking market when teaching a course on Urban Transportation Economics at UCLA. Many students live in North Westwood Village, a 15-block neighborhood next to campus. Drivers often park on the aprons of driveways (the paved area between the sidewalk and the street), with the front of the car extending over the sidewalk. Others park in the driveway with the back of the car extending over the sidewalk (and no part of the car on the apron). No matter how far the cars extend over the sidewalk from either the apron or the driveway, drivers call it apron parking. Landlords charge their tenants for the right to park in the aprons, usually about $50 a month. This informal market for parking on sidewalks lets landlords charge for parking spaces they don't own and shows that parked cars are more important than pedestrians.

Parking on a sidewalk violates both California and Los Angeles laws, but parking enforcement officers ignore this violation in the North Village because it is a student area and its city councilmember requested "relaxed enforcement." The result is a good example of what George Kelling and James Wilson referred to as the "broken windows" theory of urban disorder:

> Social psychologists and police officers tend to agree that if a window in a building is broken and is left unrepaired, all the rest of the windows will soon be broken ... one unrepaired broken window is a signal that no one cares, and so breaking more windows costs nothing.

If we substitute cars parked on sidewalks for broken windows, North Westwood Village illustrates this theory. Where enforcement officers do not ticket the first cars parked on the sidewalk, more drivers will park on the sidewalk. Eventually, drivers will park on sidewalks throughout the neighborhood. Because the city has relaxed enforcement in North Westwood Village, an informal parking market has taken over the sidewalks.

My students began to study informal parking in the North Village, counting curb spaces and parked cars, analyzing census data, interviewing residents and property owners, and taking photographs. The students counted 205 cars parked on the driveway aprons on a typical day. This might seem like a small number compared to the neighborhood's 11,000 residents, but these 205 cars were enough to block the sidewalks on every street.

Curb parking provides a valuable buffer between cars in traffic and pedestrians on the sidewalks. Parked cars also protect pedestrians on the sidewalk from getting sprayed from cars driving over puddles, or slush if you live in the northeast. But parking on the sidewalk provides only a temporary advantage for a few people and makes life worse for everyone else every day. A tiny minority inconveniences life for the vast majority.

THE AMERICANS WITH DISABILITIES ACT

Informal parking on sidewalks may seem to be only a local issue, but the U.S. Supreme Court ruled in 2003 that the Americans with Disabilities Act (ADA) applies to sidewalks. The decision in *Barden v. Sacramento* requires cities to make public sidewalks accessible to people with disabilities. Because of this ruling, cities must remove barriers that block access to sidewalks. This decision has created a serious liability for cities like Los Angeles that have informally allowed drivers to park their cars on sidewalks.

Two ADA lawsuits against Los Angeles have spurred reform. Both lawsuits address broken sidewalks and cars parked on the sidewalks. After years of neglect, these lawsuits have forced the city to reconsider

Figure 27-1 Informal parking on sidewalks

Photo credit: Donald Shoup

the informal policy of relaxed enforcement and to decide exactly what should be legal and what should not. Given the threat of ADA lawsuits over inaccessible sidewalks, all cities that informally allow illegal parking on sidewalks will need to find ways to mitigate the withdrawal pains caused by enforcing the law.

EASING THE PATH TO FORMALITY

The loss of apron parking will increase the already high demand for curb parking, but overnight parking permits can help solve the problem. Like many other cities, Los Angeles allows neighborhoods to adopt an overnight parking permit district that prohibits overnight on-street parking except by permit holders. Enforcement officers need to make only one visit during a night to cite all cars parked without permits. Los Angeles charges residents $15 per year (less than half a cent per day) for each permit in the districts. Residents can also buy guest permits for $1 per night.

Given the high residential demand for on-street parking in North Westwood Village, the demand for overnight permits will greatly exceed the supply of on-street spaces. The city could keep the permit price low and limit the number of permits in some way, such as by a lottery. Alternatively, the city can charge a fair market price for the permits, so the number of permits demanded will equal the supply of on-street parking spaces.

Suppose the city charges the same price for parking permits in the North Village that UCLA charges for parking permits in the nearby campus residence halls ($96 a month). If the city charges $96 a month (about $3 a day) for 857 overnight permits (equal to the number of on-street parking spaces in the North Village), the new revenue to pay for public services will amount to about $987,000 a year ($96 × 12 × 857), or about $66,000 a year for each of the 15 blocks in the North Village.

Paying for curb parking will never be politically popular, but it will make finding a curb space much easier. To increase the acceptability of this market-based solution, the city can spend the new parking revenue to improve public services in the North Village: to repair broken sidewalks, plant street trees, and fill potholes—all of which the North Village needs. Public safety is another issue. In 2012, North Westwood Village experienced three rapes, 15 robberies, 20 aggravated assaults, 58 burglaries, and 89 larceny thefts. Using some of the parking revenue to improve public safety can be far more valuable than providing free parking for a few cars.

Dedicating parking revenue to the neighborhood that generates it has built political support for priced parking in other cities (see

Chapters 44–51 below). The public improvements financed by fair market prices for 857 curb spaces will improve life for the North Village's 11,000 residents and can help to satisfy the city's obligation to make the sidewalks accessible.

THE SOUND OF CHANGE

Solving the problems created by parking on the sidewalks will create long-term economic and environmental benefits, but also short-term political conflict. As Niccolò Machiavelli wrote in *The Prince* in 1532:

> There is nothing more difficult to take in hand, or more uncertain in its success than to take the lead in the introduction of a new order of things. Because the innovator has for enemies all those who have done well under the old order of things, and lukewarm defenders in those who may do well under the new.

Or as Woodrow Wilson said almost 400 years later, "If you want to make enemies, try to change something."

Most people want sustainable cities, good public transportation, walkable neighborhoods, public safety, and less traffic. But they also want free parking, which undermines these other goals. Fortunately, few people will have to give up their car if the city enforces the law against parking on the sidewalks and creates a formal market for parking on the streets. Instead, a few car owners will decide that a neighborhood without free parking is not the best place for them to buy or rent an apartment. People who cannot afford or choose not to own a car will take their place. During the transition, all the whining will be the sound of change.

TURNING PROBLEMS INTO OPPORTUNITIES

Informal parking markets often respond to the failure of cities to create formal markets for on-street parking. Even on some of the most valuable land on Earth, cities offer free curb parking on a first-come, first-served basis. In dense neighborhoods, how could informal markets for this free parking not emerge?

If curb parking is free, entrepreneurs will find ways to create informal markets that serve drivers who are willing to pay for convenience. These informal markets respond to the problems caused almost entirely by free curb parking. The shortage of free curb parking is not merely a problem, however. It is also an opportunity to create a formal market with fair prices that efficiently allocate land for parking. A formal market for on-street parking will reduce traffic congestion, air pollution, and greenhouse gas emissions, and will generate ample revenue to pay for neighborhood public services.

Fair market prices can end the Hundred Years' War over free curb parking, and the revenue will provide a peace dividend to rebuild our neglected public infrastructure. Livable, walkable cities are worth far more than free parking on the streets and sidewalks.

This chapter was condensed from a chapter in The Informal American City: Between Taco Trucks and Day Labor, *edited by Vinit Mukhija and Anastasia Loukaitou-Sideris. Cambridge, Mass.: MIT Press, 2014, pp. 277–294. It was also published in* ACCESS, *Number 46, Spring 2015.*

CHAPTER

28

Progressive Parking Prices

By Michael Klein

Albany, New York, has increased parking revenue, reduced parking violations, and increased parkers' choices—all without raising the price of curb parking. Albany previously charged $1.25 per hour at meters in the Central Business District (CBD) and lower prices farther from the city center, with a two-hour time limit and a prohibition on meter feeding. The change was simple: a progressive price structure related to the length of parking duration. The city kept the meter price of $1.25 per hour for the first two hours, removed the time limit, allowed re-feeding the meters, and increased the price for each successive hour after the first two hours by 25¢. Figure 28-1 and Table 28-1 show the new price schedule in the CBD.

Several other cities (including Aspen, Colorado, and Sacramento and Santa Cruz, California) have also introduced progressive parking prices similar to those in Albany. During the summer tourist season, Aspen

Figure 28-1 Progressive parking prices in Albany, New York

Photo credit: Michael Klein

283

Table 28-1   Progressive parking prices

Parking Time	Price per Hour	Total Price
First hour	$1.25	$1.25
Second hour	$1.25	$2.50
Third hour	$1.50	$4.00
Fourth hour	$1.75	$5.75
Fifth hour	$2.00	$7.75
Sixth hour	$2.25	$10.00
Seventh hour	$2.50	$12.50
Eighth hour	$2.75	$15.25
Ninth hour	$3.00	$18.25
Tenth hour	$3.25	$21.50

Source: Michael Klein

has steeply progressive prices: $1.00 for 30 minutes, $3.00 for the 1st hour, $7.50 for the 2nd hour, $13.50 for the 3rd hour, and $21.00 for the 4th hour.

New meter technology that allows different prices for different parking durations enables these new progressive price structures. Payment by credit or debit cards rather than coins removes the difficulty of paying the higher fees for longer durations. About 75 percent of Albany's meter revenue now comes via credit and debit cards, and the trend is toward even more non-cash payments over time.

This progressive pricing avoided raising the previous price of $1.25 an hour with a two-hour time limit. Customers can maintain their previous payments for parking, and they have the option to pay more to stay longer. The choice is theirs, and the new options allow for improved customer satisfaction. Albany's Mayor Gerald Jennings said, "Progressive parking prices in Albany have reduced parkers' anxiety by providing customers with a simple solution to the on-street parking challenge. Customers no longer worry about the old two-hour time limits, parking generates more revenue, and curb space is better managed with market forces.

Table 28-1 shows that all-day parking costs $21.50 if paid once, but drivers can also feed the meter to buy shorter durations every two hours. If a driver pays $7.75 each for two five-hour segments, the cost of all day parking is only $15.50. In the extreme case of re-feeding the meter every two hours, it would cost only $12.50. Some people will pay extra for convenience, and few people need more than two hours to conduct their business. After the price change, the average parking duration near the State Capitol was 115 minutes, turnover was 3.5 cars per space per day, and the paid occupancy rate was 63 percent.

Only 22 percent of the customers parked for more than the previous two-hour limit, but they contributed 59 percent of the total meter revenue. While they paid disproportionately more than other drivers, they were able to park as long as they needed, without fear of receiving a ticket. We learned that customers like the progressive pricing system much more than the previous time limit. Since the long-stay customers are so few and the revenue is so large, both customers and the city benefit.

Back-office payment data can over- or under-state actual parking occupancy. Therefore, in addition to analyzing payment data, we performed field audits. These audits identified the relationship between the length of time purchased, the actual time in the parking space, and the likelihood of being ticketed for illegal parking. We found that people typically overpay for about an extra 15 minutes of time, which equates to approximately 13 percent overpayment for the average parking duration. Also, we found that approximately 10 percent of drivers left their cars parked illegally, either by not paying the meter or not paying for all the time they used. The probability of receiving a ticket for those parked at expired meters was below 20 percent. When we took all these factors into account, the net impact of overpayment (by drivers who paid for more time than they occupied) and underpayment (by drivers who paid for less than the time they occupied) was almost zero.

The issues of parking compliance and parking enforcement influence people's perceptions of parking in dense cities; these are big quality-of-life issues, and they also have substantial budget impacts. When a person's impression of a city is based on a negative parking experience, that person will think twice before returning for dinner and a show, or some other outing in the city. A city should set up a system that serves people's needs in a flexible and economically sustainable method, with payment for services perceived as reasonable, and with tickets for non-payment a smaller proportion of the total budget.

Progressive parking prices provide a customer-centric environment with a readily understandable variety of choices. They give drivers new options and avoid penalties for overstaying time at the meter. With new parking meter technology and a new philosophy of pricing, cities can enhance their economic vitality and be friendly to both people and cars.

29

Progressive Parking Fines

By Donald Shoup

Good games depend on good rules more than they depend on good players.
JAMES BUCHANAN

Cities often increase parking fines when they need more money. When Los Angeles faced a major budget crisis in 2009, for example, it increased the fines for all parking tickets by $5, regardless of the violation. This across-the-board hike suggests that the higher fines are more about raising money than about enforcing the law. But a few cities have discovered how to enforce the law and raise money without costing most drivers anything: progressive parking fines.

Fines are necessary to enforce parking regulations, and enforcement is important because violations have victims. If a driver stays over the time limit, others have a harder time finding a space and businesses suffer from low turnover. Double parking can block a whole lane of traffic. Illegal parking in a disabled space makes life even more difficult for people with disabilities.

Setting the right fine for each parking violation is complicated because a few repeat violators often account for a large share of all violations. In Los Angeles, 8 percent of all the license plates that received tickets in 2009 accounted for 29 percent of all the tickets in that year. In Beverly Hills, 5 percent of license plates accounted for 24 percent of all tickets. Californians are not the only serial offenders. In Manchester, New Hampshire, 5 percent of the plates accounted for 22 percent of all tickets and in Winnipeg, Canada, 14 percent of the plates accounted for 47 percent of all tickets.

Most drivers rarely or never receive a parking ticket, and for these drivers modest fines are a sufficient deterrent. But some drivers routinely break the law and pay the penalties. The many tickets for a few repeat offenders suggest that modest fines do not deter drivers who view parking tickets as an acceptable gamble or just another cost of doing business. If cities raise parking fines high enough to deter the few chronic violators, they unfairly penalize many more drivers for occasional (and often inadvertent) violations.

Most drivers rarely or never receive a parking ticket, and for these drivers modest fines are a sufficient deterrent. But some drivers routinely break the law and pay the penalties. Progressive parking fines are a way to deter the chronic violators without unfairly punishing anyone else. Progressive fines are lenient for the many cars with only a few tickets but punitive for the few cars with many tickets. In Claremont, California, for example, the first ticket for overtime parking in a calendar year is $35, the second $70, and the third $105. For illegally using a disabled parking space, the first ticket is $325, the second $650, and the third $975.

For minor violations like overtime parking, some cities issue a warning for the first offense and progressive fines for subsequent offenses. The warnings show citizens that the city aims to encourage compliance rather than to raise revenue. Because parking tickets create hostility toward both the enforcement officers and city hall, a warnings-first policy for minor offenses can reduce political opposition to enforcement. Repeat offenders will pay more but everyone else will pay less. A warnings-first policy and subsequent progressive fines will show most citizens that the city is at their side, not on their backs.

Progressive parking fines were impossible until recently because enforcement officers had no way to know how many previous tickets a car had received. Now, however, officers carry handheld ticket-writing devices that wirelessly connect to the city's ticket database. These devices can automatically assign the proper fine for each violation according to the number of previous tickets for the license plate.

A driver who receives many tickets for the same offense is probably either careless, unlucky, or a scofflaw. Risking a ticket may thus be a rational choice. A study by the Boston Transportation Department, for example, found that the price of a ticket multiplied by the probability of citation for illegal curb parking was often less than the price of off-street parking for three or more hours, so the temptation to risk a ticket is strong. Scofflaws can do a simple cost-benefit calculation; they may get a ticket for one in 10 violations, but the conventional fines never increase. Higher fines for serial violators can reduce the total number of violations without harshly penalizing occasional violators. Progressive fines are therefore fairer and more effective than flat-rate fines.

Most cities will no doubt continue to rely on parking fines to help balance the budget, but the next time they need more money from this source, cities should increase the fines for chronic offenders without unfairly penalizing everyone else.

This chapter is updated from the earlier version published in ACCESS, *No. 37, Fall 2010.*

30

Disabled Placard Abuse

By Michael Manville and Jonathan Williams

Anyone walking through downtown Los Angeles might notice many cars parked at expired meters without a ticket. On some streets, every space is occupied, the meters are unfed, and enforcement officers walk by without issuing citations. What gives? The drivers have credentials—often disabled placards—that let them park free.

LA isn't alone. In 2010, a reporter for the *Oakland North* newspaper surveyed vehicles parked in downtown Oakland on a weekday and found that 44 percent were displaying disabled placards. Chicago famously leased its parking meters to a private consortium in 2008; the consortium soon said that placards were costing it millions of dollars in lost revenue (a claim that triggered both arbitration and a change in Illinois law). News reports from Seattle to Washington, D.C., tell stories of widespread placard use. In the country's densest, most congested cities, it seems many people park without paying.

Policymakers should worry about this nonpayment, and not just because it costs cities money. Transportation scholars generally agree that cities could greatly reduce congestion and pollution if they priced driving more accurately. Charging people to drive, of course, is politically, legally, and logistically difficult. Charging people to park, while hardly easy, is at least easier. People are accustomed to paying for parking, and cities already have the authority to charge for it. Many cities are therefore interested in market prices (sometimes called "performance prices") for street parking. Both San Francisco and Los Angeles have run ambitious pilot tests of performance-priced parking.

The San Francisco project, SF*park*, cost $24.7 million. In Los Angeles, LA Express Park cost $18.5 million.

If nonpayment is sufficiently pervasive, experiments like these could fail, and so too could future efforts to price parking accurately. Indeed, some evidence already suggests that nonpayment has been rampant in both the LA and San Francisco programs, and that it undermined their effectiveness. A price system works only when people who don't pay don't get the service. Every day we rely almost unthinkingly on prices to allocate toasters, televisions, and gasoline, but this entire edifice would crumble if 20 percent of the population could take as much gasoline as they liked, whenever they liked, regardless of price.

The government isn't going to hand out free gasoline anytime soon, but at least 15 states (including some of the nation's most populous) and many local governments do distribute free parking passes in the form of disabled placards. These placards not only grant access to spaces reserved for people with disabilities, but also let their holders park free, often for unlimited time, at any metered space. Nor are placards difficult to get. In California, for example, doctors, nurses, nurse practitioners, optometrists, and chiropractors can all certify people for placards, for everything from serious permanent impairments to temporary conditions like a sprained ankle.

We recommend that cities and states limit or eliminate free parking for disabled placards. We believe the payment exemption has high costs and few benefits. It harms both the transportation system and the environment, and offers little help to most people with disabilities.

THE LOGIC OF PRICED PARKING AND THE PROBLEM OF NONPAYMENT

Street parking is a source of endless frustration for many city residents, and this frustration has a surprisingly simple source. Cities take parking spaces that have very different values and offer them to drivers for the same price, usually zero. This mispricing has predictable results. Underpriced goods lead to shortages, so most cities suffer shortages of curb parking at busy times. Rather than accurately pricing on-street parking, however, cities force developers to supply off-street parking. This costly and counterproductive solution makes driving less expensive and housing more so.

Suppose instead that a city allows meter rates to vary by place and time of day. On any given block, the city charges the lowest price that generates a constant 85 percent occupancy rate, leaving one or two spaces always open. The parking shortage disappears, and so too does the need to provide expensive parking with every building. And because only one or two spaces are open, no one need worry that spaces are underused, or that prices have chased away customers. The city has established a market in curb parking.

Markets only work, however, when participants have to pay. Figure 30-1 shows data taken from sensors under parking spaces on Hollywood Boulevard in 2009. Occupancy is consistently high—never below 80 percent—but payment is consistently low. At 1 p.m., for example, about 85 percent of parking spaces are occupied, but fewer than half the vehicles have paid. At 10 a.m. and noon, almost no spaces are vacant, suggesting prices should be higher. But at both times fewer than half of drivers have paid, suggesting that higher prices might create little vacancy.

Not all nonpayment comes from disabled placards, of course. Some drivers have government credentials that let them park free. In other instances, meters are broken. Many people just cheat, and park without paying. How can we be certain placards are the primary culprit?

Los Angeles has about 38,000 curb parking meters, spread across 80 zones that match the city's neighborhoods. In the spring of 2010, we chose 13 of the largest zones and sent researchers to record whether spaces in those zones were occupied, whether occupied spaces were paid for, and—if unpaid—the reason for

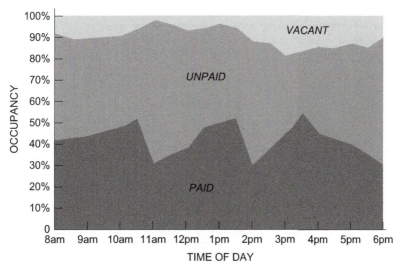

Figure 30-1 Parking occupancy and payment, Hollywood Boulevard, Los Angeles, 2009 ($1/Hour)

Source: ACCESS, Spring 2013

nonpayment. The areas we selected had parking rates ranging from $1 an hour (usually on the west side of Los Angeles) to $4 an hour (in parts of downtown). We surveyed just under 5,000 meters, about 13 percent of the city's total. Because we examined each meter at different times of day, we ended up with more than 11,300 observations.

Across all surveyed neighborhoods, 61 percent of the meters were occupied, which suggests prices were too high. But fewer than half of the vehicles in these occupied spaces had paid, and 27 percent of them were displaying disabled placards (Figure 30-2). (The percentages sum to more than 100 because a few vehicles fell into more than one category, such as a vehicle with a disabled placard at a failed meter.) If we look only at vehicles that didn't pay (Figure 30-3), we see that government credentials were a minor issue, accounting for 6 percent of nonpayments. Meter failure was a substantial problem, accounting for 19 percent. This problem, however, is solvable. Newer, computerized meters rarely break down, and failure drops sharply as the share of computerized meters rises. Since we completed our surveys, LA has upgraded all its meters.

This leaves two reasons for nonpayment: disabled placards and scofflaws who simply park without paying. As Figure 30-3 shows, placards account for 50 percent of all nonpayment, twice the share accounted for by scofflaws. There is ample room to address the scofflaw problem because 94 percent of the illegally parked cars were not cited. But placards, not scofflaws, appear responsible for most of LA's unpaid parking.

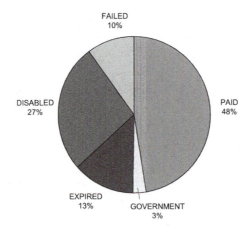

Figure 30-2 Occupied parking spaces

Source: ACCESS, Spring 2013

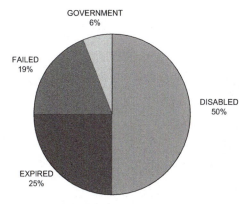

Figure 30-3   Occupied but unpaid parking spaces

Source: ACCESS, Spring 2013

The extent of placard use became even more apparent when we conducted a second set of surveys. Figures 30-2 and 30-3 showed how much space placard-displaying vehicles consumed. But parking also involves time. To measure how much time vehicles consumed, we sent researchers to five separate locations to watch one side of a city block for an entire metering period—usually eight or ten hours. The researchers recorded the start and end of every parking session, the time and length of payment, and any visible reason for nonpayment.

Disabled placards consumed not just the most unpaid time of any vehicle category, but also the most occupied time. Vehicles with placards swallowed almost 40 percent of all meter-hours, easily exceeding the time consumed by paying drivers and dwarfing the 8 percent of time consumed by scofflaws.

Figure 30-4 shows a minute-by-minute representation of parking on one block of Flower Street in LA's Financial District on March 8, 2010. At 8 a.m., when the meters started operating, vehicles with disabled placards already occupied 70 percent of the spaces. The placard share increased until noon, when placards occupied all spaces and no vehicles were paying. This universal nonpayment lasted almost four hours, and then gradually fell as the workday ended. Placards consumed an astonishing 80 percent of the block's total meter time. Parking on Flower Street was $4 an hour, but despite being occupied 95 percent of the time, the meters collected only 28 cents an hour.

This massive consumption of time—and massive loss of revenue—occurred not because many drivers used disabled placards. Rather, drivers with placards parked much longer. Disabled placards

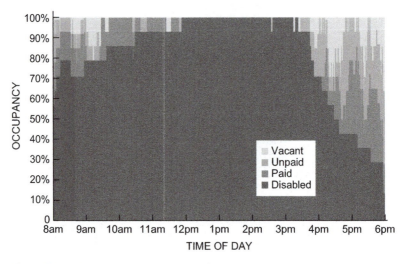

Figure 30-4 Occupancy rates on Flower Street, Los Angeles

accounted for only 12 percent of all parking sessions on Flower Street, and never exceeded 25 percent in any surveyed location. But where the average vehicle without a placard parked 32 minutes, the average placard-displaying vehicle parked almost four hours. Placard holders stay longer than paying drivers because they aren't paying. They park longer than scofflaws who also aren't paying because they are parking legally. A scofflaw parked a long time is asking to be caught. A placard holder operates with no such fear, and as a result, even a relatively small number of placards can badly undermine a system of priced parking.

ENDING FREE PARKING FOR PLACARDS

If placards account for most nonpayment, and this nonpayment both costs the city money and hurts efforts to reduce pollution and congestion, then perhaps placards shouldn't entitle their holders to free parking.

The natural objection to such a proposal is that it would harm people with disabilities. But would it? To answer this question, we must distinguish between two types of benefits that placards currently offer. First, placards provide access, by setting aside some spaces for people with disabilities. Access is an important public goal, and placards are an effective way to accomplish it. Placards also redistribute income, by making parking at meters free for some people. Redistribution is also important, but disabled placards are a lousy a way to achieve it.

A good income redistribution program will be both generous and efficient. It will help those who need help, provide enough help to be useful, and not extend help to those who don't require it. Redistributing income through placards makes sense if: most people with disabilities have low incomes; low-income people with disabilities regularly use parking meters; and most people with disabled placards are disabled. There is good reason to doubt all of these statements.

Most people with disabilities aren't poor. People with disabilities are more likely to be poor than the able-bodied, but both the Census and the federal Survey on Income and Program Participation show that only about a fifth of people with disabilities live below the poverty line. Poverty is more common (27 percent) among those with severe disabilities, but people with severe disabilities are also less likely to drive, either because of their age (severe disability is more common in the elderly), because they are homebound or unable to operate a vehicle, or because poverty makes vehicle ownership unaffordable.

Is the placard payment exemption useful? Free street parking is worth little to people who don't use vehicles. For vehicle users, the value of the placard is the price of parking, which means a placard's value depends on location. A credential worth $4 an hour in a large city might be worth nothing in a low-density suburb where all parking is unpriced. Disabled placards make metered parking free, but not everyone—and certainly not everyone with a disability—uses metered parking. Thus while many poor people with disabilities need income support, guaranteed free parking is not the best way to help them. By contrast, for affluent people with disabilities who live where parking is expensive, the payment exemption is useful but not necessary: it's just a subsidy for driving.

For the sake of argument, however, assume most people with disabilities are poor and do live in places with expensive parking. Even this wouldn't justify the placard exemption because the population of people with disabilities is very different from the population of people with placards. The vast majority of people with placards aren't poor, and many aren't disabled by any conventional definition. When a wealthy investment banker breaks his leg kitesurfing and winds up on crutches, it makes sense to let him park in a convenient spot. It doesn't make sense to let him park everywhere for free.

The second reason the population with placards differs from the population with disabilities is fraud. Precisely because placards offer free parking, many people in perfect health use them illegally. Note that the incentive to misuse placards is greatest in places where parking is most expensive—which are also places where congestion is worst and performance parking prices can do the most good. Placard abuse will thus be most common where it does the most harm.

And placard abuse is common. Police stakeouts in Alexandria, Virginia, in 2010 found that 90 percent of disabled credentials were being used illegally. In 2012, a disability rights advocate called Illinois's placard exemption "wide open and eligible for abuse." In 2013, a local CBS station used hidden cameras to film members of a high-end LA gym hanging placards in vehicles and then vigorously working out. Our own surveyors repeatedly witnessed what appeared to be fraud. In a particularly galling example, a man hung a placard in a van, loaded a dolly with heavy boxes, and then bounced the dolly down a flight of stairs into a subterranean food court. He remained parked for more than 10 hours.

Able-bodied people who abuse placards deny curb parking spaces to others, including people with legitimate disabilities. They deprive cities of revenue, breed cynicism about social policy, and place people whose disabilities aren't outwardly apparent under an unfair cloud of suspicion. This fraud is almost entirely driven by the placard's payment exemption.

States could end placard payment exemptions and dedicate some or all of the increased meter revenue to programs for people with disabilities, such as providing paratransit services and repairing sidewalks. Such programs will benefit all people with disabilities, not just those who park free at meters. Indeed, better sidewalks improve mobility for everyone, including the able-bodied. This reform will transfer income from able-bodied frauds to people with disabilities.

CONCLUSION

Good laws are hard to write, and many well-intentioned statutes go awry. Laws granting free parking to people with disabled placards confuse an undeniable need for more access with a less obvious—and often nonexistent—need for more income. Most people with disabilities aren't poor, and most poor people don't have disabilities. Perhaps more importantly, many people with disabled placards suffer from neither poverty nor disability: they are affluent and able-bodied. Thus placard exemption ordinances give income to many people who don't need it, don't give income to many people who do, deprive cities of revenue, and obstruct efforts to price driving more accurately. These laws have also created a jungle of duplicity and fraud. Ending these misguided subsidies will make cities more efficient, more equitable, and more sustainable.

REFERENCES AND FURTHER READING

Brault, Matthew. 2008. "Americans With Disabilities, 2005." Current
Population Reports. Washington, D.C.: U.S. Census Bureau.

Manville, Michael, and Jonathan Williams. 2012. "The Price Doesn't Matter if
You Don't Have to Pay: Legal Exemption and Market-Priced Parking." *Journal
of Planning Education and Research* 32, no. 3: 289–304.

Shoup, Donald. 2011. *The High Cost of Free Parking*. Revised edition. Chicago:
Planners Press.

Shoup, Donald. 2011. "Ending the Abuse of Disabled Parking Placards." *ACCESS*
39 (Fall): 38–40.

This chapter was previously published in ACCESS, *Spring 2013. It is adapted
from "The Price Doesn't Matter if You Don't Have to Pay: Legal Exemption
and Market-Priced Parking," originally published in the* Journal of Planning
Education and Research *32, no. 3: 289–304.*

31

Ending the Abuse of Disabled Parking Placards

By Donald Shoup

Disabled placard abuse seems to be everywhere, and sometimes pops up in fiction. In *Lucky You*, the Miami novelist Carl Hiaasen wrote:

> Pure good fortune and a round of free beers led to a friendship with an amateur forger, who entrusted Chub with his printing equipment while he went off to state prison. In no time, Chub was cranking out fake handicapped stickers and selling them for cash to local motorists. His favoring hangout was Miami's federal courthouse, infamous for its dearth of parking spaces. Among Chub's satisfied customers were stenographers, bondsmen, drug lawyers, and even a U.S. magistrate or two. Soon his reputation grew, and he became known throughout the county as a reliable supplier of bootleg wheelchair emblems. ... Some of Chub's acquaintances, especially the war veterans, disapproved of his handicapped-parking racket. Not Bode. "Think about it," he'd said to Chub. "How many wheelchair people you actually see? And look how many thousands of parkin' spaces they got. It don't add up."

Anecdotes and fictional accounts are not hard evidence, but if placard abuse were rare, one would expect to find some studies that report little abuse. I have never seen one. Instead, I have seen several careful studies that show widespread abuse. A survey in downtown Los Angeles showed how extensive the abuse can be (see Chapter 30). A research team from UCLA observed a block with 14 parking meters for a full day, and most of the curb spaces were occupied most of the time by cars with disabled placards. For five hours of the day, cars with placards occupied all 14 spaces. The meter rate was $4 an hour, but the meters earned an average of only 28¢ an hour. Cars parked free with placards consumed $477 worth of meter time during the day, or 81 percent of the potential meter revenue on this block. Several drivers with disabled placards were observed carrying heavy loads between their cars and the adjacent businesses.

Placard abusers steal revenue from cities, and drivers with real physical disabilities have a harder time finding curb spaces, which are usually the most convenient spots for people with disabilities to park. When all the curb spaces near their destinations are occupied, drivers who have difficulty walking may have to park much farther away or even abandon their trips.

If a state exempts all cars with placards from paying at meters, how can cities prevent placard abuse and preserve disabled access? Virginia has a sensible policy. It exempts drivers with disabled placards from paying at meters, but it also allows cities to set aside this exemption if they give reasonable notice that payment is required. In 1998, Arlington removed the exemption for placards and posted "All May Park, All Must Pay" on every meter pole. Because it is easier to pull into and out of the end space on a block, Arlington puts meters reserved for drivers with disabilities at many of these end spaces. The purpose is to provide parking in convenient locations for people with disabilities, not to offer a subsidy that invites gross abuse. Cities can reserve the most accessible metered spaces for placard holders, accessible but not free.

A neighboring city, Alexandria, has considered a similar opt-out policy as part of a broader strategy to reduce placard abuse. To gauge the seriousness of abuse, the Alexandria Police Department interviewed drivers who were returning to cars displaying disabled placards and found that 90 percent of the placards checked were being used illegally.

Because parking with placards seems to be an almost ethics-free zone, cities should aim to avoid creating financial incentives to abuse any placard policy. Raleigh, North Carolina, for example, allows drivers with disabled placards to park for an unlimited time at meters but requires them to pay for all the time they use. Placard users push a button on the meter allowing them to pay for time beyond the normal limit for other drivers, and enforcement officers can then check to see whether the cars using this privilege display a placard.

If people with disabilities must pay at meters, their difficulty in getting to and from the meters may be a barrier, especially at pay-and-display meters. If it is raining or snowing, the barrier will be even greater. To solve this problem, some cities offer placard holders the option to pay with in-vehicle meters or by cell phone. Offering these options can forestall objections that the payment method is itself an obstacle to people with disabilities.

Ending free parking for placard users will bring in new revenue that can pay for services benefiting all people with disabilities, not just drivers with placards. If a city proposes to end free parking for cars with placards, it can estimate the meter revenue currently lost because of placard use and commit all the new meter revenue to pay for specialized transportation services for everyone with disabilities.

The data from Alexandria illustrate how an all-must-pay policy can benefit the disabled community. The police survey found that placard abuse accounts for 90 percent of the revenue lost from the placard exemption. Alexandria also estimated that an all-must-pay policy would yield $133,000 a year in new meter revenue currently lost to the placard exemption. If placard abusers account for 90 percent of this lost revenue, they misappropriate $120,000 of the subsidy intended for people with disabilities, while people with disabilities receive only $13,000. Spending the full subsidy to provide paratransit services or taxi vouchers for everyone with disabilities seems much fairer than wasting 90 percent of it to provide free parking for able-bodied placard abusers. The transportation subsidy for the disabled community would increase by 10 times, at no additional cost to the city government. Because almost all the additional spending would come at the expense of disabled placard abusers, it is easy to see why Arlington is not considering a return to the all-placards-park-free policy.

Beyond raising revenue to finance new transportation services for everyone with disabilities, the all-must-pay policy can also eliminate the culture of corruption that has grown up around using disabled parking placards as free parking passes. Cities and states encourage this corruption by making it so easy, so profitable, and so rarely punished. Because enforcement is difficult, the chance of getting a ticket for placard abuse is so low that even high fines do not prevent violations.

Charging all drivers for parking at meters and spending the new revenue to provide transportation for the entire disabled community can improve life for almost everyone—except the drivers who now abuse disabled parking placards.

REFERENCES AND FURTHER READING

Williams, Jonathan. 2010. "Meter Payment Exemption for Disabled Placard Holders as a Barrier to Managing Curb Parking." Thesis submitted for the degree of Master of Arts in Urban Planning, University of California, Los Angeles.

This chapter is adapted from an article in ACCESS, *Number 39, Fall 2011.*

32

Ending Disabled Placard Abuse at Parking Meters: The Two-Tier Solution

By Donald Shoup and Fernando Torres-Gil

Almost everyone can tell an anecdote about disabled placard abuse. One of mine stems from a visit to the California capitol building in Sacramento. After noticing that cars with disabled placards occupied almost all the metered curb spaces surrounding the Capitol, I talked to one of the state troopers guarding a driveway entrance. He watched all the arrivals and departures at the nearby metered spaces every day. When I asked the trooper to estimate how many of the placards he thought were being used illegally, he responded, "All of them."

Newspapers often report placard abuse, such as the scandal that occurred when 22 UCLA football players were found to be using disabled placards to park on campus; the athletes got their placards by forging doctors' signatures for such conditions as asthma and palsy. UCLA seems to be unusual only in the large number of athletes who were caught misusing disabled placards, because similar scandals have erupted on other campuses. Placard abuse is common enough to have its own website, handicappedfraud.org.

Quite aside from all the fraud, many drivers who have disabilities that do not impair mobility use the placards simply to park free at meters. Equal access under the Americans with Disabilities Act (ADA) should mean convenient parking for every person with impaired mobility, not free parking for every car with a disabled placard. Because of widespread abuse, we cannot assume every driver with a placard has a serious physical disability. Some placard users park free at a meter and walk several blocks rather than pay for off-street parking at their destinations.

Making curb parking accessible to people with disabilities is an essential goal, but treating disabled placards as free parking passes has encouraged widespread abuse by able-bodied drivers who park wherever they want, whenever they want, without paying anything. Because of widespread abuse, disabled placards do not guarantee a physical disability. Instead, they often signal a desire to park free and a willingness to cheat the system. Placard abusers learn to live without their scruples, but not without their cars.

Frequent and flagrant placard abuse makes it harder for drivers with seriously impaired mobility to find convenient parking. If curb spaces near their destinations are occupied by placard abusers, drivers with serious disabilities must park farther away or even abandon their trips. Reducing placard abuse will therefore increase accessibility for drivers with serious disabilities. The goal should be to give convenient access to mobility-impaired drivers, not to subsidize every car with a disabled placard.

State governments encourage placard abuse by mandating that any driver with a disabled placard can park free for an unlimited time at any municipal on-street meter. Drivers in Los Angeles and San Francisco can save up to $40 a day by using a disabled placard at a parking meter. The high cash value of a placard and its ease of abuse help explain why 2.1 million people in California have disabled placards.

Placard abusers not only harm the disabled community but also damage businesses and kill jobs. A UCLA study in downtown Los Angeles found that cars with disabled placards park an average of seven times longer than other cars (see Chapter 30). One placard abuser thus takes up a space that would otherwise be used by seven paying parkers. By reducing turnover, placard abusers steal parking spaces from customers of nearby businesses.

Placard abusers also steal public revenue. The UCLA study found that 44 percent of the cars parked at meters in downtown Los Angeles displayed disabled placards. Meters on one block charged $4 an hour but earned only 28¢ an hour because cars with placards occupied most of the spaces for most of the day. The meter exemption is an invitation to obtain and abuse placards for personal gain.

Because California requires free parking at meters for placard users without compensating cities for the lost revenue, the meter exemption is an unfunded mandate. How big is this unfunded mandate? If, for example, cities lose meter revenue of only $100 a year per placard, the total statewide loss is $210 million each year lost to placards. Little of that subsidy benefits drivers with seriously impaired mobility. An audit in San Francisco found that the city lost $23 million in 2013 because cars with disabled placards accounted for 20 percent of all the occupied time at on-street meters.

Placard abuse is not a victimless crime. If all Americans knew the extent of this uncontrolled abuse, most would be outraged and the rest might try to get their hands on a placard if they don't already have one.

Requiring all placard holders to pay at meters would eliminate the financial incentive for fraud. Nevertheless, some drivers have disabilities that severely limit mobility, and free parking at meters increases their access. Rather than require all placard holders to pay at meters, states can adopt a two-tier reform that allows free parking at meters for everyone with a disability that seriously limits their mobility.

THE TWO-TIER SOLUTION

Michigan and Illinois have adopted a two-tier system that takes into account different levels of disability. Drivers with disabilities that seriously limit mobility continue to park free at meters. Drivers with less serious disabilities must pay at meters. Enforcement is simple: able-bodied drivers who use the special serious-disability placard that allows free parking at meters are obviously breaking the law as soon as they hop out of a car and stride away.

Giving free parking only to drivers who have serious physical disabilities can eliminate the scourge of placard abuse and thus ensure convenient parking for truly disabled drivers. This new policy can be based on the models in Michigan and Illinois. In 1995, Michigan adopted a two-tier placard system that takes into account different levels of disability. Drivers with severe disabilities receive special placards allowing free parking at meters. Drivers with less severe disabilities receive ordinary placards and must pay at meters. Before this reform, Michigan had issued 500,000 disabled parking placards allowing all users to park free at meters. After the two-tier reform, only 10,000 people (2 percent of the previous placard holders) applied for the special placards that allow free parking at meters for drivers with severe disabilities.

To explain the two-tier reform, here is the key provision in the Illinois law:

> The Secretary of State ... shall issue a meter-exempt decal or device to a person with disabilities who ... is unable to ... approach a parking meter due to his or her use of a wheelchair or other device for mobility or walk more than 20 feet due to an orthopedic, neurological, cardiovascular, or lung condition in which the degree of debilitation is so severe that it almost completely impedes the ability to walk.

In addition to exempting drivers with impaired mobility, the Illinois law also exempts persons who can walk but are unable to operate a parking meter. Many of those who cannot operate a parking meter, however, are chauffeured by someone who can operate a parking meter. To accommodate the few who do drive but cannot operate a parking meter, cities can waive the usual transaction surcharges for paying by cell phones or other in-vehicle devices.

States can also mandate additional measures to ensure that convenient meter spaces are available to drivers with limited mobility. For example, the state can require cities to dedicate a specific share of convenient curb spaces only for cars with a limited-mobility disabled placard, and these spaces would not need meters.

When Illinois adopted the two-tier reform, Chicago Mayor Rahm Emanuel said, "This law is about preserving free on-street parking for motorists with disabilities that prevent them from being able to pay a meter." The Commissioner of the Mayor's Office for People with Disabilities said, "The availability of accessible parking has long been an issue that needed to be addressed on behalf of the disability community. The high level of abuse prevents people with disabilities from carrying out day-to-day activities and also limits their full participation in the community."

The two-tier reform will greatly reduce the financial incentives to cheat and will improve life for everyone except drivers who now abuse disabled placards. If a state does remove its mandate for free parking at meters for all cars with placards, however, any city can continue to offer free parking at its own meters for all cars with placards.

USING THE NEW REVENUE

The two-tier reform will reduce placard abuse and increase accessibility for drivers with impaired mobility, but it will also require meter payments from legitimate placard holders with less severe disabilities. Although the goal of reform is to curb placard abuse, the increased meter payments can give the impression that cities want reform mainly because they want the meter revenue. To encourage the disabled community to support the two-tier reform, states can require cities to dedicate the new meter revenue to pay for services that can benefit people with disabilities, such as safer sidewalks, curb ramps, and audible devices at pedestrian crosswalks to assist the visually impaired across intersections.

Much of the new meter revenue will come not from drivers with disabilities but from the profligate and unmonitored parking subsidies now being stolen by placard abusers. A study in Alexandria, Virginia, illustrates how placard reform can greatly benefit the entire disabled community. Police officers who interviewed drivers returning to cars displaying disabled placards found that 90 percent of the placards checked were being used illegally. These placard abusers therefore stole 90 percent of the meter subsidy intended for people with disabilities. Spending the full meter subsidy to provide public services that benefit all people with disabilities seems much fairer and more efficient than wasting 90 percent of the subsidy to provide free parking for placard abusers.

Because California has issued 2.1 million disabled placards for its 24 million licensed drivers, about 9 percent of all drivers have placards. The current policy for issuing disabled placards seems to be, "Ask and it shall be given unto you." To improve life for the disabled community after placard reform, the state could require cities to dedicate 10 percent of their total meter revenue to increase mobility services for all people with disabilities. In 2012, cities and counties reported $410 million in parking revenues. A 10 percent dedication for placard reform could therefore provide about $41 million a year for disabled mobility services.

REDUCED PLACARD ABUSE AND INCREASED DISABLED ACCESSIBILITY

Beyond improving access for drivers with severe disabilities and providing funds to finance new mobility services, the two-tier solution will counter the culture of corruption that has developed around disabled parking placards. States encourage this licensed fraud by making placard abuse easy, profitable, and rarely punished. Because enforcement is so difficult and the chance of getting a ticket is so low, even high fines do not prevent abuse.

This simple two-tier solution will reduce placard abuse, increase accessibility for drivers with severe disabilities, and finance added services for all people with disabilities.

REFERENCES AND FURTHER READING

Bergal, Jenni. 2014. "Parking Abuses Hamper Disabled Drivers." *Stateline.* November 13. www.pewtrusts.org/en/research-and-analysis/blogs/ stateline/2014/11/13/parking-abuses-hamper-disabled-drivers

Chicago Office of the Mayor, "New Illinois State Law Limiting Disabled Placard Use Goes into Effect, December 31, 2013." www.cityofchicago.org/city/en/depts/

mayor/press_room/press_releases/2013/december_2013/new-illinois-state-law-limiting-disabled-placard-use-goes-into-e.html

Illinois Public Act 097-0845. www.ilga.gov/legislation/publicacts/fulltext. asp?Name=097-0845

Lopez, Steven. 2012. "Cracking Down on Parking Meter Cheaters." *Los Angeles Times*, February 15. www.articles.latimes.com/2012/feb/15/local/la-me-0215-lopez-placardsting-20120213

Manville, Michael, and Jonathan Williams. 2013. "Parking without Paying." *ACCESS* 42 Spring, 10–16. www.uctc.net/access/42/access42_parkingwoutpaying.shtml

Michigan Disabled Parking Placard Application. www.michigan.gov/documents/bfs-108_16249_7.pdf

Portland Bureau of Transportation. 2014. "Disabled Parking in Portland." July 1. www.portlandoregon.gov/transportation/64922

San Francisco Office of the Controller. 2014. "Parking Meter Collections." www.sfcontroller.org/Modules/ShowDocument.aspx?documentid=5985

Shoup, Donald. 2011. "Ending the Abuse of Disabled Parking Placards." *ACCESS* 39 Fall, 38–40. http://www.uctc.net/access/39/access39_almanac.pdf

This chapter is adapted from an article in Parking Professional, *January 2015, pp. 20–23.*

33

Parking Charity

By Donald Shoup

'Tis pleasant to be deemed magnanimous,
the more so while obtaining our own ends.

LORD BYRON, *DON JUAN*

In December 2010, the City Council of Berkeley, California, voted to give what they thought was a generous Christmas gift to the city's merchants: free parking at all parking meters in the city. "There are a couple of messages going out here," said councilmember Laurie Capitelli. "One is that we are inviting customers to our commercial districts. Two, we're sending a message to our small businesses, saying 'we are hearing your concerns, and we do want to respond to them.'"

The Downtown Berkeley Association cheerfully informed its members, "There will be no pay and no time limits! And, remember that this is a gift to our customers. Please tell your employees to leave this space available for customers." Berkeley's city manager estimated the city would lose between $20,000 and $50,000 in meter and ticket revenue for each day of the meter holiday.

Merchants may thank elected officials for free parking at the time of peak demand, but open spaces will become even harder to find. Drivers will congest traffic and pollute the air while searching for curb spaces, and the lucky ones who find a space will occupy it longer than if they were paying to park. Parking holidays are well intended, but the gift is more like a lump of coal for businesses that depend on parking turnover.

CREATING A COMMONS PROBLEM AT CHRISTMAS

Free curb parking creates a classic commons problem—no one owns it, and everyone can use it. In his famous essay, "The Tragedy of the Commons," Garrett Hardin used free curb parking at Christmas to illustrate the problem:

> During the Christmas shopping season the parking meters downtown were covered with plastic bags that bore tags reading: "Do not open until after Christmas. Free parking courtesy of the mayor and city council." In other words, facing the prospect of an increased demand for already scarce space, the city fathers reinstituted the system of the commons.

Hardin also used parking meters as an example of social arrangements that encourage responsible behavior:

> To keep downtown shoppers temperate in their use of parking space we introduce parking meters for short periods, and traffic fines for longer ones. We need not actually forbid a citizen to park as long as he wants to; we need merely make it increasingly expensive for him to do so. Not prohibition, but carefully biased options are what we offer him.

Despite the need to manage parking demand during the peak shopping season, many cities continue to wrap their parking meters in December, giving motorists a commons problem for Christmas. Consider the program in Bellingham, Washington:

> This year, for the two weeks before Christmas the city will offer all-day free parking. ... To help shoppers park close to businesses and keep spaces available, the city is asking that people still observe the time limits at meters. Shoppers planning to be downtown for more than a couple of hours are encouraged to park on the ground floor of the Parkade.

HARNESSING THE SEASONAL URGE TO HELP MANKIND

Rather than provide free parking, cities could instead post signs during the Christmas season saying, "The city will donate all parking meter revenue in December to pay for food and shelter for the city's homeless population." Shoppers might like this more than a parking holiday that makes it harder to find a curb space. They might also feel better about paying to park downtown if they know their money is going to help the homeless. Parking charity rather than meter holidays will help those in greatest need, prevent parking shortages, and aid businesses that depend on curb parking. Wanting free parking for Christmas will begin to look quite greedy.

Parking charity can extend beyond the Christmas season. Many stores and malls reserve the most convenient parking spaces for disabled access, but able-bodied drivers sometimes park in them. To deal with this problem, and to provide spaces for all drivers who want quick access, a store can install parking meters in a few spaces adjacent to the disabled spaces, while keeping all other spaces in the lot free. To justify this policy, the store can place a sign on every meter saying that all the revenue will be donated to charity.

The prices for the charity meters can be set at a level that will keep one or two spaces open, allowing able-bodied drivers to park in convenient spots without harming disabled shoppers. Able-bodied drivers who do park in disabled spaces will look even more contemptible if they can instead donate to charity at a nearby meter.

Some drivers may be happy to pay for convenient parking when they really want it. Suppose the charity meters charge $1 an hour. A driver who is in a hurry to make a quick purchase and who parks for only 15 minutes might not mind donating 25 cents to charity to park near the front door, while a driver who parks for four hours can park farther away and save $4. A higher turnover of cars in the charity spaces will also benefit the store because customers who park in them will probably spend more per minute while they are in the store. And customers who walk past the charity meters might applaud the store's altruistic parking policy.

If cities donate their meter money to charity during the Christmas season, and if stores place a few charity meters in their most convenient spots, drivers will begin to see that charging for parking can do some good for the world. Only a Grinch would demand free parking for Christmas.

REFERENCES AND FURTHER READING

Bayshore Town Center Change for Charity Foundation. www.bayshoretowncenter. com/communityfoundaton.aspx

Easton Town Center Change for Charity Meter Foundation. www.eastontowncenter. com/community-foundation.aspx

Hardin, Garrett. 1968. "The Tragedy of the Commons." *Science* 162: 1243–48.

Klein, Eric. 2010. "Parking Holiday Approved for Christmas Shopping." Berkeleyside. December 8.

Mathis, Brandon. 2013. "Free Parking Downtown Not Loved by All: One Merchant Says He Sees a Frantic Frenzy Just to Find a Spot." *Durango Herald*, December 23.

Paben, Jared. 2010. "Bellingham to Offer Free Downtown Parking for Two Weeks before Christmas." *Bellingham Herald*. December 13.

Zona Rosa Change for Charity Foundation. www.zonarosa.com/communityfoundaton.aspx

This chapter is adapted from an article in ACCESS *44, Spring 2013.*

34

Popular Parking Meters

By Donald Shoup

Most people view parking meters as a necessary evil, or perhaps just evil. Meters can manage curb parking efficiently and provide public revenue, but they are a tough sell to voters. To change the politics of parking, cities can give price discounts at parking meters for their own residents.

PARKING DISCOUNTS FOR RESIDENTS

In Miami Beach, residents pay $1 an hour at meters, while nonresidents pay $4 an hour. Some British cities give the first half hour at meters free to residents. Annapolis and Monterey give residents the first two hours free in municipal parking lots and garages.

Pay-by-license-plate technology enables the resident discounts. Drivers pay either by cell phone or by entering their license plate number at a parking kiosk and paying with cash or credit card. Both the cell phones and the meters can automatically give discounts to all cars with license plates registered in a city. Cities link payment information to license plate numbers to show enforcement officers which cars have paid. Pay-by-plate is common in Europe, and several U.S. cities, including Pittsburgh, now use it.

Like hotel taxes, parking meters with resident discounts can generate substantial local revenue without unduly burdening local voters. The price break for city plates should also please merchants because it will give residents a new incentive to shop locally. More shopping closer to home can then reduce total vehicle travel in the region.

Resident parking discounts are justified because residents already pay taxes to maintain the streets and municipal garages in their city. The discounts are also justified because they can increase voter support for the meters needed to manage the parking supply. Parking meters with resident discounts come close to the ideal way to raise public revenue: Monty Python's proposal to tax foreigners living abroad.

Taking a cue from behavioral economics, cities can also offer prizes for paying at parking meters. If a city makes its residents eligible for cash prizes in a monthly drawing, every dollar paid for curb parking can equal an entry in the monthly drawing. When Walmart tried this approach to encourage its customers to save money in its MoneyCard Vault, the number of Vault users more than doubled (Walker 2017, 74).

PARKING DISCOUNTS FOR SMALLER AND CLEANER-RUNNING CARS

Cities can also use parking discounts to achieve economic and environmental goals. If a city classifies license plates by car length, it can give discounts for smaller cars that take up less curb space. Parking meters in Calgary, for example, give a 25 percent discount for cars that are 3.8 meters (12.5 feet) or less in length. Because smaller cars tend to be more fuel efficient, discounts for smaller cars will also reduce fuel consumption and CO_2 emissions. Parking discounts based on car size will therefore produce local economic benefits and reduce global environmental costs.

Table 34-1 illustrates parking discounts based on car lengths. Column 1 shows a selection of cars, and Column 2 shows their lengths, ranging from 20 feet for a Rolls Royce down to 8.8 feet for a Smart car. The typical length of a marked on-street parking space is 20 feet, but pay-by-plate systems do not require marked spaces, so more small cars can fit on a block with unmarked curb parking. Column 3 illustrates the discount for each car based on its length. Because the Rolls Royce is 20 feet long, it pays the full price. The 17.2 foot Lincoln is 14 percent shorter, so it receives a 14 per cent discount, while the 10-foot Scion is 50 percent shorter so it receives a 50 percent discount. Two Scions pay the same as one Rolls, so the payment per foot of curb space is the same for both cars.

Parking discounts for shorter cars also favor higher fuel efficiency and lower CO_2 emissions. Column 4 shows each car's fuel efficiency, ranging from 14 miles per gallon for the Rolls up to 37 miles per gallon for the Scion. Finally, Column 5 shows each car's CO_2 emissions per

Table 34-1 Parking discounts based on car length

Make and Model (in 2014)	Length (feet)	Discount (percent)	Fuel Efficiency (miles/gallon)	CO_2 Emissions (grams/mile)
(1)	(2)	(3)	(4)	(5)
Rolls Royce Phantom	20.0	0%	14	637
Lincoln MKS	17.2	14%	22	400
Buick Regal	15.8	21%	24	371
Ford Fiesta	14.5	28%	29	301
Chevrolet Spark	12.1	40%	34	258
Scion iQ	10.0	50%	37	238
Smart	8.8	56%	36	243

Data on length are from theautochannel.com.
Data on fuel economy and carbon emissions are from fueleconomy.gov.

mile. For example, the Ford emits less than half as much CO_2 as the Rolls. If cities want to reduce CO_2 emissions, they don't have to wait for state or federal action before offering discounts for small cars. Each city can choose its own parking discounts according to its own priorities.

Are parking discounts for small cars fair? The manufacturer's suggested retail price starts at $474,990 for a 20-foot Rolls Royce Phantom and $13,270 for an 8.8-foot Smart car. In this case, it seems unfair not to offer parking discounts for small cars. Most people who can afford to buy a longer car can probably afford to pay more to park it.

Cities with serious air pollution can also give parking discounts for cars with low hydrocarbon or nitrogen oxide emissions. Parking meters in Madrid, for example, charge 20 percent less for low-pollution cars and 20 percent more for high-pollution cars. Cities can give these discounts by linking license plate records to emissions data from car manufacturers or smog tests. According to the head of Madrid's sustainability division, "We thought it would be fair if the cars that pollute more pay more, and compensate those who use more efficient vehicles."

Cities may have to raise their pre-discount meter prices to prevent overcrowding the curb, but only nonresidents with the biggest and dirtiest cars will pay the pre-discount prices. To manage curb parking efficiently, cities should charge the lowest meter price that will leave one or two open spaces on every block. Residents will then gain two great advantages. First, they will easily find an open curb space wherever they want to park, and second, they will pay a discounted price when they do park.

Parking discounts may seem complicated, but few residents will be confused by or object to discounts automatically given at meters. The meters can even print the discounts on parking receipts to reinforce the rewards of shopping close to home and driving small, clean cars

Figure 34-1 Discounts at parking meters

(Figure 34-1). The resident discounts will appeal to local voters, and the other discounts will achieve public goals.

Prices are the most reliable way for cities to send signals about the behavior they want to encourage, and parking discounts can easily send these price signals. If meters give discounts for smaller and cleaner cars, more people will drive them.

USING THE METER MONEY

Cities can also increase political support for parking meters by using the meter revenue to improve local public services. Pasadena, for example, offers neighborhoods a package that includes both parking meters and additional public services financed by the meters. The meters not only manage curb parking, but also provide a steady stream of revenue to pay for cleaning and repairing the sidewalks. The parking meters in Ventura, California, provide free public Wi-Fi on the metered streets (Chapter 46). People who live, work, shop, and own property in the metered neighborhoods can then see their meter money at work. With discounts for residents, locals will see that parking meters are working for them rather than against them.

Some cities increase meter rates when special events sharply increase the demand for curb parking. For example, San Francisco can increase the meter price up to $18 per hour at special occasions like the Pride Parade, when more than a million visitors assemble to revel in the streets. If a city dedicates some of the extra meter revenue to a charity associated with the special event that increases parking demand, the city can raise prices with a good conscience, and the drivers who pay the higher prices can feel better about helping a cause they support.

A WORLD OF GOOD

In the past, we have adapted our cities to our cars, rather than adapt our cars to our cities. As a result, many cities suffer from congested curb parking, polluted air, and poor public services. To solve these problems cities can charge fair market prices for curb parking, spend the revenue to improve public services on the metered streets, and give price discounts for residents, small cars, and clean cars. By changing the politics of parking, cities can meter more of their valuable curb space and produce more money to pay for public services, with less traffic, cleaner air, and a cooler planet. Parking meters can then do a world of good.

REFERENCES AND FURTHER READING

Annapolis Resident Discounts. www.parkannapolis.com/cityresidents.shtml
Kolozsvari, Douglas, and Donald Shoup. 2003. "Turning Small Change into Big Changes." ACCESS 23: 2–7.
Miami Resident Discounts. www.miamiparking.com/en/discount-program.aspx
Miami Beach Resident Discounts. http://web.miamibeachfl.gov/parking/default.aspx?id=79498
Monterey Resident Discounts. www.monterey.org/en-us/departments/parking/residentparkingprograms.aspx
Pittsburgh Pay-by-Plate Meters. www.pittsburghparking.com/meter-policies
Walker, Rob. 2017. "How to Trick People into Saving Money," *The Atlantic*, Vol. 319, No. 4, May.
Data on fuel economy and carbon emissions are from fueleconomy.gov/
Data on length are from theautochannel.com/

This chapter is adapted from an article in ACCESS 45, Fall 2014.

35

Parking Limits: Lean Demand Management in Berkeley

By Elizabeth Deakin

The City of Berkeley and the University of California, Berkeley, implemented two new parking initiatives in 2012. The initiatives were intended to simultaneously increase parking revenue and reduce vehicle travel.

The city's parking management project, goBerkeley, aims to better use the available parking supply. Staff use meter data and field studies to monitor parking occupancy rates and to periodically adjust parking rates and regulations. Parking prices are raised in high-demand areas and reduced in low-demand areas. In addition, time limits are adjusted based on local demand patterns to allow parkers adequate time to complete their activities without risking a ticket. The goBerkeley project is a less expensive and lower-tech version of SF*park*; this "lean" demand management may be especially suitable for small cities.

The price in "premium" zones of high demand initially increased from $1.50 per hour to $2.25 per hour with a two-hour time limit. In "value" zones with low demand, the price was set at $1.50 per hour with a time limit of eight hours. Garage rates were raised to a daily maximum of $20, with a half-price "early bird" rate for cars arriving before 9 a.m. After the first year, rates were increased to $2.75 per hour for the premium zones.

In parallel, the university raised fees for monthly parking from about $85 per month to about $100 per month, and also used information and incentives to encourage commute alternatives.

RESEARCH DESIGN AND PRELIMINARY FINDINGS

The research design for the city and university projects included examining revenues, parking availability, and occupancy rates prior to implementation through 2014. We monitored parking data from other districts of the city to provide "with-and-without" comparison, and reviewed sales tax data to track trends in the local economy. In addition, both the city and the university evaluated the impacts of efforts to encourage alternative modes of travel.

The effects on revenues and occupancies were roughly consistent with expectations. Accounting for price increases in high-demand premium zones and price decreases in low-demand value zones, the city's revenues increased by about 12 percent in the first year and 4 percent in the second year when price increases were smaller.

Occupancy data showed mixed results. In downtown Berkeley, parking availability increased in the premium zone, and the percentage of block faces that were over 85 percent full dropped from 37 percent to 25 percent; 10 fewer block faces were overcrowded. Occupancy in the off-street parking facilities increased modestly, but the value-priced spaces remained underused. In the Southside area, however, an identical price increase had little effect on the use of prime parking spaces, which remained fully occupied much of the day. In addition, the city garage in the district was more heavily used than other parking facilities, and occupancy of value-priced spaces increased relative to the premium-priced spaces.

Keeping a few spaces open on each block can reduce the time and the vehicle miles traveled (VMT) associated with searching for parking. Cruising decreased in downtown even though the busiest blocks remain parked up. Cruising has largely disappeared as a problem for employees with parking permits. It is less clear that there was any reduction in cruising for parking in the Southside or among campus affiliates and visitors without a parking permit.

The university's initiatives had similar results. Revenues increased about 10 percent, reflecting increases in parking permit prices offset by a small decline in the number of permits sold. Discount transit pass sales to employees continued at about the same rate as previously. A special effort to promote commute alternatives through marketing to individuals received a modestly favorable reception, with about 5 percent of the target market agreeing to try transit, biking, or walking.

City parking revenues outside the project areas increased by only 3 percent, suggesting that most but not all of the parking revenue increases in the city's project areas were due to the goBerkeley program. Sales tax revenues proved inconclusive as a measure of background trends, showing substantial quarter-to-quarter and district-to-district variations without any clear pattern or relationship to parking use. Many other changes were occurring at the same time, and the evaluation designs were not sufficiently complex to control for them. Among the changes were an increase in downtown housing, an increase in student enrollment at the university, a decrease in downtown vacancies, an increase of downtown businesses catering to nightlife activities, a relocation of campus and downtown accounting staff to a facility two miles away, and changes in the level of service offered by the Alameda-Contra Costa Transit District. In all likelihood, these changes affected parking demand but were not accounted for.

DIGGING DEEPER INTO PARKING BEHAVIOR

Observed changes in parking and transit use show what happened, but not why. To sort out the factors behind the observed changes, we developed a model of mode choice among university employees. We also analyzed the impacts of resident permit parking (RPP) on nonresidents' parking choices and investigated parkers' responses to metered parking price and regulations. About 150 parkers participated in the focus groups, about 350 nonresidents who parked in the RPP zones responded to surveys, and nearly 200 meter users participated in the intercept surveys for the two areas. In addition, we interviewed 24 merchants, business leaders, university officials, and neighborhood group leaders.

The modeling found that the price elasticity of demand for parking varied between -0.1 to -0.6 across most trip purposes and market segments. The higher elasticities occur when parking in another location is an option. Thus, price increases only slightly deterred auto trips.

Focus groups and surveys found that middle-income travelers are most likely to change travel modes; neither high-income nor low-income drivers were deterred by the increased parking prices. For wealthier parkers, price increases were shrugged off. As one put it, "I am going to spend fifty bucks on lunch. A few dollars for parking is not an issue." For lower-income parkers, a lack of competitive alternatives was the main reason for driving, and relatively few felt they could reconsider their mode of travel. Instead, higher prices led them to look for cheaper parking.

In the focus groups and surveys, many drivers indicated that they value the community and environmental benefits of transit and are willing to spend an extra 10 or 15 minutes to use it. But an extra half-hour or more each way is more than they are willing to endure. Simply offering free or deep discount transit passes does not overcome the time barrier or make up for sparse midday and evening transit service. "Bus service needs to be more frequent and more reliable if I am ever going to use it to run downtown. I can't wait around half an hour or more for the next bus to arrive," as one driver put it.

While saving time is a key reason for driving, saving money is the principal motivation for nonresident parking in the RPP areas. Field studies and university surveys indicate that there are hundreds of non-resident RPP parkers who remain in the RPP zones for three to eight or nine hours at a stretch, in addition to the visitors and shoppers who stay only an hour or two. Most who overstay the time limit park in the RPP zones to save the expense of a monthly parking permit. However, there also is a libertarian streak among the violators of RPP rules: a sizeable group said they enjoyed getting some exercise by parking a few blocks away in free parking spots and moving their cars around several times a day to outwit the enforcers and avoid getting a ticket. They park in the RPP zones closest to their destinations, with the result that RPP streets within a half-dozen blocks of the commercial districts or university remain parked up while those more than six blocks away are mostly empty.

Most of the meter parkers who participated in the focus groups or surveys visited the study area several times a month and reported that they knew their way around fairly well. They used meters for trips of short duration (two hours or less) and would go to a garage or off-street lot (or search for a space in an RPP zone) if they expected to stay more than two hours.

While most merchants and business leaders were concerned that Berkeley's parking supply is too tight and that higher parking prices would deter customers, those who actually were parking downtown and in Southside were not particularly concerned about these issues. The vast majority of parkers stated that finding a parking space was fairly easy, and there were few complaints about the price. Most had noticed the longer time limits and appreciated them. Nevertheless, parkers remained highly aware of time limits and the risk of a ticket, and nearly all knew how much parking time they had purchased. In contrast, as a group they were far less certain about what their parking space had cost them, especially if they paid by credit card. ("I just put my card in and pushed for the maximum time.") The majority did not know what the hourly rate was, ranging from 71 percent in Southside to 65 percent downtown. These findings indicate that time limits and fear of tickets are a bigger issue with current parking users than the price of parking, at least at the current prices of up to $2.75/hour.

Regular visitors and employees reported shorter search times for parking than new or infrequent visitors. Those who frequented the area knew where to look for parking and reported that they usually were able to quickly find a parking space within a block or two of their destination (often by taking an available space before reaching their destination.) As one focus group member stated, "When I get within two or three blocks, if it is a busy time of day I just park where I find a space and walk the rest of the way." Those who were less familiar with the area were more likely to have searched longer for parking (partly because they circled the block hoping for an opening) and also were more likely to have parked four or more blocks away after giving up on cruising the immediate area and deciding to search farther away from their destination. These findings suggest that cruising for parking is inversely related to familiarity with the area as well as with actual parking supply.

CONCLUSION

The Berkeley case shows that parking management can increase revenues, open up parking spaces, reduce cruising for parking, and encourage drivers to consider alternative travel modes. Interviews with merchants, city and university officials, and environmentalists found that almost all were favorably impressed by the program's results. "It seems to have helped—there haven't been as many complaints from customers as we had earlier, when parking was tighter," said one merchant. Added another, "I was surprised, but people who are coming downtown don't seem too concerned about having to pay a few dollars an hour to park." City officials were pleased that revenues were up and that the city had been able to manage its parking supply without having to invest millions in new equipment and sensors, as had been done in San Francisco. University staff noted that the parking price increases were important as a cost recovery measure and also helped reduce demand. "Complaints are down even though prices are up— the faculty and staff who drive to campus are clearly more concerned about finding a space quickly than about a moderate price increase, and the price increase encouraged a few more people to try other ways of getting to work." Overall, responses to the parking pricing programs have been positive, and both programs have been continued. In the city, monitoring and adjustments are ongoing: the price for premium parking in downtown and Southside increased to $3.25/hour and value parking increased to $2/hour in June 2016. At the university, annual price increases intended to cover full costs of the transportation and parking program have been announced.

Still, there are limits to parking management's efficacy as a travel demand management measure. The price elasticity of demand for parking is low, so it takes substantial price increases to make big changes in parking behavior. While parking prices and restrictions can induce travelers to consider other modes, the other modes must offer robust alternatives well matched to traveler needs to induce modal change. Bus pass programs did not change travel choices significantly because for many drivers the time cost greatly exceeded the dollar cost savings. For commuters in this situation, driving is likely to remain the preferred mode unless the other means of transportation can be improved. As one environmental leader noted, "Getting the parking price right is a step forward for demand management, but it is no magic bullet. We need to find a way to improve transit services, and make biking and walking safer if we want to reduce the number of cars moving around in the city."

Overall, Berkeley has shown that it is possible to manage parking using readily available data from parking meters with occasional field reviews and outreach to stakeholders. Multimillion dollar investments in sensors and other elaborate equipment need not be part of an effective parking management strategy—what's really needed is a commitment to make the most effective possible use of the available parking supply and a staff with the time and skills to carry the program forward.

REFERENCES AND FURTHER READING

Deakin, E., Aldo Tudela Rivadeneyra, Manish Shirgaokar, William Riggs, with contributions from Alex Jonlin, Jessica Kuo, Eleanor Leshner, Qinbo Lu, Warren Logan, Ruth Miller, Emily Moylan, Wei-Shiuen Ng, Matthew Schabas, and Kelan Stoy. "Parking Innovations in the City of Berkeley: Evaluation of the goBerkeley Program." Institute of Urban and Regional Development, University of California, Berkeley, December 2014.

Moylan, E., M. Schabas, and E. Deakin. 2014. "Residential Permit Parking." *Transportation Research Record: Journal of the Transportation Research Board* 2469 (December): 23–31. http://docs.trb.org/prp/14-4129.pdf

Ng, W. S. 2014. *Assessing the Impact of Parking Pricing on Transportation Mode Choice and Behavior.* (Doctoral dissertation, University of California, Berkeley). http://escholarship.org/uc/item/56f3v4wg

Proulx, F., B. Cavagnolo, and M. Torres-Montoya, M. 2014. "Impact of Parking Prices and Transit Fares on Mode Choice at the University of California, Berkeley. "*Transportation Research Record: Journal of the Transportation Research Board* 2469: 41-48. http://trrjournalonline.trb.org/doi/pdf/10.3141/2469-05

Riggs, W., and J. Kuo. 2015. "The Impact of Targeted Outreach for Parking Mitigation on the UC Berkeley Campus." Case Studies on Transport Policy 3, no. 22: 151–58. http://www.sciencedirect.com/science/article/pii/S2213624X15000061

36

SF*park*

By Jay Primus

With SF*park* San Francisco demonstrated a new approach to managing parking, in particular using demand-responsive pricing to manage parking. The project is an example of how cities can use pricing to ensure that drivers can easily find available parking near their destinations. Readily available parking has benefits that go far beyond simple driver convenience. When parking is difficult to find, many people double-park or circle to find a space. Circling wastes time and fuel, generates needless greenhouse gas emissions, and endangers other roadway users (see Chapter 25). Circling drivers are distracted drivers who are more likely to hit someone crossing the street, a cyclist, or another car.

Mismanaged parking also has other less obvious consequences. Public transit must often maneuver around double-parked cars or circling cars waiting to turn, making transit not as fast or reliable as it could be. Slower buses encourage people to drive more often, further increasing congestion and making it still harder to find a space. Parking availability also affects economic competitiveness—if drivers cannot quickly find a parking space in a particular commercial area, they are less likely to return.

By increasing parking availability and improving the overall parking experience, the SF*park* approach benefits drivers while also delivering broad social benefits such as improving transit speed and reducing greenhouse gas emissions.

PROJECT FOUNDATIONS

The SF*park* project was facilitated by a number of factors. The first is the sensible organizational structure of the San Francisco Municipal Transportation Agency (SFMTA), which plans, manages, and operates the city's transportation network, including local public transit, roads, sidewalks, on-street parking, parking enforcement, and much of the city's off-street parking supply. Because San Francisco has a unified transportation agency with all aspects of parking management under one roof, implementing SF*park* did not depend on interdepartmental coordination, which was an advantage.

The project also benefited from legislative changes that gave the SFMTA's director the power to set parking prices at meters and municipal garages in SF*park* pilot areas. Thus, rather than subjecting every price change to political debate and negotiation, SFMTA staff could adjust parking prices in SF*park* pilot areas within the framework of a transparent, data-driven, and outcomes-based approach approved by its board. This depoliticized parking pricing changes, allowing them to be treated as a powerful tool to achieve transportation goals rather than simply as a way to raise revenue.

Another foundation for SF*park* was a singular focus on managing parking demand to achieve parking availability. Focusing on parking availability avoided vague and sometimes nonsensical notions related to parking turnover (the number of different cars that park in a space during an hour or day), a commonly cited but ill-defined and hard-to-measure goal for parking management. What is the right amount of turnover in general or on a particular block? How does the right amount of turnover change on a block that's empty in the morning but crowded in the late afternoon? There are no clear answers to these questions, and they illustrate the trouble with using turnover either as a goal or a measure. Availability is the ultimate goal of turnover, and SF*park*'s focus on availability provided a clearly defined, easy to measure, and meaningful metric.

Other decisive factors for successfully implementing SF*park* included engaging technology and communications experts from the start. In many ways, implementing SF*park* was a complex IT project requiring significant expertise in managing and analyzing data. Anticipating that fact was essential.

Similarly, SF*park* benefited from anticipating the challenges and opportunities related to communications and dedicating significant attention and resources to marketing, design, and outreach was decisive. SF*park* asked San Franciscans to understand and accept a new approach to managing parking – at heart, it asked people to have a new relationship with parking. This required the SFMTA to talk more skillfully about parking, and creating the new SF*park* brand made it easier to form a new relationship with our customers. Strong planning and execution with communications, including involvement of community leaders from the start, as well as an emphasis on sound visual design and user experience, greatly reduced pushback to the SF*park* approach.

WHAT IS SF*PARK*?

Prior to SF*park*, paid parking in San Francisco was managed much like it is in most North American cities. Management emphasized time limits as a way to achieve vague turnover goals. Parking meters, prices, and citations were mainly viewed as a way to balance budgets. Meter and garage prices were not tied to transportation policy goals, and prices were the same all day, every day, regardless of demand. Worse, prices at on-street parking meters were set lower than the prices at municipal garages, giving drivers a financial incentive to circle to find on-street parking.

The pricing at SFMTA's parking garages was particularly counterproductive. The SFMTA offered steep discounts to "early bird," daily, and monthly parkers, giving people even more incentive to commute by car, and making San Francisco's already bad congestion even worse. These early bird policies aggravated congestion because their typical requirement for drivers to be in by 10 a.m. and out by 6 p.m. encourages drivers to be on the streets during rush hour.

As a result of SFMTA's pricing in garages, commuters occupied most of the spaces, and in some garages few spaces were available for short-term parkers, such as shoppers and people stopping for appointments. The municipal garages were built to support local economic vitality, not to increase solo driving to work.

SF*park* used the following strategies to make it easier to find a parking space and improve the parking experience:

- **Demand-responsive pricing**. SF*park* was obligated to find the lowest price that achieved a minimum level of parking availability on the street and ensured that garages were rarely full so that when people chose to drive, it would be easy to quickly find a parking space.
- **Making it easier to pay at meters and avoid citations**. Part of providing a better experience for drivers was introducing new parking meters that accept credit cards as well as pay-by-phone to make it easy to pay. Increasing payment options reduced anxiety and citations.

- **Peak-period discounts at garages**. SF*park* offered a $2 discount for entering or exiting a municipal garage at off-peak times (for a total discount of up to $4) as a strategy to reduce congestion for cars and transit. This innovative and simple strategy avoids the technological complexity, cost, surveillance, and political challenge of congestion pricing schemes as in London and Stockholm. Off-peak garage discounts are tantamount to congestion pricing but are framed as a favorable bonus rather than as a distasteful peak-period penalty.
- **Longer time limits at metered spaces**. Time limits were extended from one or two hours to four hours, and in some areas time limits were eliminated altogether. SF*park* emphasized demand-responsive pricing rather than inconvenient time limits as the tool to achieve a minimum level of parking availability. Longer time limits also made it easy for drivers to compare prices at on- and off-street parking, creating a more efficient overall market for parking, helping prices to be more effective.
- **Improved information for drivers**. Smarter pricing was complemented by better information about where parking was available so drivers could find a parking space and get off the street as quickly as possible—saving drivers time and reducing congestion for everyone else. The new information technology included directional way-finding signs to garages as well as real-time data on parking availability from garage gate systems and wireless sensors at on-street spaces.
- **Improved user interface and product design**. Careful attention was paid to the user experience at every point a customer interacted with SF*park*. The goal was to create a parking experience that is simple, clear, and respectful rather than confusing, governmental, or Kafkaesque.

The SFMTA implemented SF*park* in seven pilot areas that contain more than 6,000 metered spaces, about a quarter of the city's total metered parking spaces, and 12,250 spaces in 14 of the SFMTA's 19 garages. Altogether, SF*park* managed the majority of publicly available parking in most pilot areas. These areas are shown on the map in Figure 36-1.

Implementing SF*park* also required SFMTA to devise a powerful data management system that represents a quantum leap forward in how it uses data to make informed decisions. This tool enabled SFMTA to: store the tremendous amounts of data generated by new and existing data sources (e.g., parking sensors, meters, citations, transit vehicles, etc.); make data-driven decisions (e.g., to adjust

SF*park* pilot and control areas

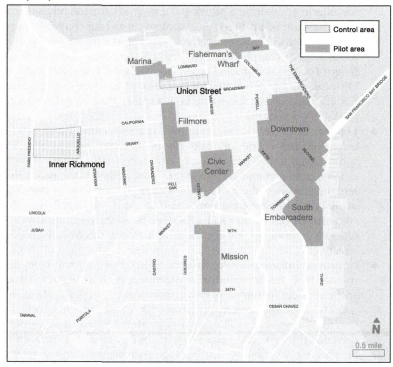

Figure 36-1 SF*park* pilot and control areas

parking prices); provide real-time data feeds; improve day-to-day operations; do performance-based contract management; support a rigorous evaluation of SF*park*'s effects; and perform sophisticated analysis for other SFMTA operations, such as transit. While SF*park* was an important demonstration of a new approach to managing parking, it also exemplified what is often implied by the term "smart cities."

DEMAND-RESPONSIVE PRICING

At the heart of the SF*park* approach is demand-responsive pricing, gradually and periodically adjusting prices up or down at meters and in garages to ensure that parking is both readily available and well used. The goal is to make it easy for drivers to find a parking space on every block and in every garage.

On-Street Parking

For on-street parking, we set a target occupancy rate of 60–80 percent. To achieve this target, we used occupancy data from the in-ground parking sensors in each space to adjust prices at meters up or down about every eight weeks. Rates varied by block, time of day, and day of week, with weekday prices differing from weekends. Each data-driven price adjustment used the following rules. When average occupancy was:

- 80–100 percent, the hourly price was raised by $0.25
- 60–80 percent, the hourly price was not changed
- 30–60 percent, the hourly price was lowered by $0.25
- Less than 30 percent, the hourly price was lowered by $0.50

Hourly prices were not allowed to exceed $6.00 per hour or go below $0.25 per hour, as agreed upon by the SFMTA Board. Over the course of the two-year pilot evaluation period (i.e., from July 2011 through June 2013), SFMTA made 10 on-street price adjustments and has since continued to adjust prices periodically in SF*park* areas.

We used an occupancy target of 60 to 80 percent rather than the commonly cited 85 percent threshold for several reasons. First, we didn't want to over-manage parking prices. We wanted to change prices as little as possible in order to achieve our goals. Defining success as a range rather than as a single number allowed prices to stabilize in an equilibrium rather than constantly teetering between two sides of an extremely narrowly defined goal.

Using a single percentage target can make sense when limited occupancy data is available—say, just a few snapshots in time from manually collected occupancy data. But the rich occupancy data from parking sensors both allowed and required redefining occupancy targets or thresholds. Among hundreds or thousands of data points over the course of a day, which occupancy figure should one use when determining how to adjust prices? For SF*park*, we used minute-by-minute occupancy data from each minute in each three-hour time period (from 9 a.m. to 12 p.m., 12 p.m. to 3 p.m., and 3 p.m. to 6 p.m.) to calculate an average occupancy for the time period. When developing the occupancy target range of 60 to 80 percent, we compared this average occupancy range to our experience as drivers in the field and found this range roughly delivered the experience we were looking for: ensuring that most drivers, most of the time, could quickly find a space. An average occupancy of 90 percent implied an experience and perception that it was difficult and time consuming to find a space.

Off-Street Parking

As SFMTA-managed parking garages were converted to the SF*park* approach, the agency simplified price structures, reduced discounts that previously encouraged peak-hour commuting (e.g., early bird, daily, monthly), and moved to the same time-of-day pricing (as opposed to the typical length-of-stay pricing) used at parking meters to make sure it was easy for drivers to compare prices between meters and garages. Another goal at garages was to make it easier for customers to understand what they would be charged, further increasing the effectiveness of price changes as well as improving the overall customer experience.

At SF*park* garages, the SFMTA changed the hourly price schedules every three months according to the following rules. When average occupancy was:

- 80–100 percent, the hourly price was raised by $0.50
- 40–80 percent, the hourly price was not changed
- Less than 40 percent, the hourly price was lowered by $0.50

In addition to demand-responsive pricing, SF*park*'s garage pricing policies aimed to minimize garage entries and exits during peak traffic times. Time-of-day pricing made parking more expensive at peak times and cheaper at off-peak times. Off-peak discounts provided a discount for drivers who entered the garage before the morning rush hour or left after the evening rush hour. SF*park* provided financial incentives for drivers to be off the streets during peak times by requiring early bird parkers to enter by 8 a.m. rather than the previous 10 a.m., as well as eliminating the requirement to leave before 6 p.m.).

EVALUATING SF*PARK* – THE RESULTS

SF*park* gathered an unprecedented amount of data to support a rigorous evaluation of its effects. To isolate and measure how well it delivered the expected benefits, SFMTA gathered before, mid-point, and after data citywide, in pilot areas, and in two additional control areas that had the same level of data collection but no changes to parking management or technology. The data collection plan and methodologies were as rigorous as possible, developed in collaboration with consultants and a team of experts put together by the federal funders. The variety, quality, and completeness of the data are without parallel in the field, with every data point linked to a specific time and place, making it easy to discover and to analyze relationships and trends.

While the SF*park* pilot project had many goals, its primary focus was to make it easier to find a parking space. More precisely, the goal was to increase the amount of time that there was a minimum level of parking available on every block and in garages. Besides helping drivers, making it easier to park was expected to deliver other benefits, such as reducing circling, double parking, and greenhouse gas emissions. A summary of results follows.

Parking Prices Dropped

Overall, as a result of demand-responsive price adjustments, SF*park* decreased prices on half of all blocks and increased prices on the other half, with average hourly meter prices falling 4 percent from $2.69 to $2.58 during the pilot. At garages, the average hourly price fell 12 percent from $3.45 to $3.03. Figure 36-2 summarizes these changes.

These results are surprising because from 2011 and 2013, the SF*park* demonstration coincided with a boom in San Francisco's economy. So even as car ownership, population, economic activity, and overall parking demand increased over this period, SF*park* ended up lowering parking prices. This helped to address fears in some communities that the ulterior motive of SF*park* was to raise rates. Mistrust of government runs high, but strictly following a transparent data-driven approach helped SFMTA build trust among stakeholders.

The way on-street parking prices evolved over the course of the pilot evaluation period was interesting and instructive. As summarized in Figure 36-3, from their starting point in summer 2011, prices quickly spread between $0.25 and $6.00 per hour, the upper and lower limits approved by the SFMTA Board. By the end of the first 14 rate changes,

Figure 36-2   Hourly parking rates in SF*park* areas

Rate	Initial meter rates	Meter rate adjustment #1	Meter rate adjustment #2	Meter rate adjustment #3	Meter rate adjustment #4	Meter rate adjustment #5	Meter rate adjustment #6	Meter rate adjustment #7	Meter rate adjustment #8	Meter rate adjustment #9	Meter rate adjustment #10	Meter rate adjustment #11*	Meter rate adjustment #12	Meter rate adjustment #13*	Meter rate adjustment #14	Rate
$0.25					0.0%	0.4%	1.9%	4.7%	6.1%	7.5%	16.4%	16.7%	16.9%	16.1%	16.5%	$0.25
$0.50					0.4%	0.9%	2.7%	1.6%	2.5%	3.2%	4.3%	4.9%	4.0%	4.1%	5.5%	$0.50
$0.75				0.2%	0.3%	2.7%	2.5%	3.1%	4.0%	5.2%	2.7%	3.1%	4.4%	4.3%	3.7%	$0.75
$1.00				0.3%	3.4%	3.3%	3.2%	4.0%	4.1%	2.7%	3.8%	4.0%	4.5%	4.5%	4.7%	$1.00
$1.25				3.8%	2.8%	3.3%	3.9%	4.6%	3.5%	4.2%	3.2%	3.3%	3.4%	3.2%	4.0%	$1.25
$1.50			0.2%	4.0%	4.0%	4.6%	6.4%	5.1%	6.1%	4.0%	4.5%	4.9%	4.0%	4.3%	4.2%	$1.50
$1.75		0.0%	4.7%	5.6%	7.0%	8.9%	5.9%	6.7%	4.1%	5.6%	5.4%	4.1%	4.2%	3.2%	3.5%	$1.75
$2.00	40.5%	5.6%	6.1%	14.5%	16.2%	11.4%	13.2%	10.8%	9.8%	8.9%	6.7%	6.4%	5.8%	6.3%	5.0%	$2.00
$2.25		20.1%	14.5%	13.1%	9.0%	9.8%	5.8%	5.6%	5.4%	4.9%	4.0%	5.0%	4.6%	4.9%	5.1%	$2.25
$2.50		14.8%	8.6%	8.5%	10.1%	7.8%	5.6%	5.8%	5.9%	5.5%	5.1%	3.4%	3.8%	4.0%	4.3%	$2.50
$2.75		2.2%	21.3%	18.1%	6.6%	5.6%	7.0%	4.6%	4.4%	4.2%	3.1%	3.7%	3.1%	3.1%	3.6%	$2.75
$3.00	29.3%	12.8%	6.7%	6.3%	14.2%	8.7%	7.2%	7.3%	6.0%	4.9%	4.5%	4.3%	5.0%	4.2%	4.3%	$3.00
$3.25		11.9%	11.0%	5.0%	4.7%	11.1%	5.2%	5.1%	5.9%	4.7%	4.7%	4.2%	4.1%	4.3%	4.9%	$3.25
$3.50		13.9%	6.6%	10.1%	9.4%	7.1%	14.1%	10.1%	8.7%	9.0%	6.0%	5.7%	5.5%	5.8%	4.0%	$3.50
$3.75	30.2%	13.1%	13.4%	5.0%	4.0%	4.0%	3.8%	8.4%	5.3%	4.6%	5.2%	4.0%	2.9%	3.2%	3.9%	$3.75
$4.00		5.7%	2.8%	5.0%	3.9%	3.5%	2.7%	2.7%	7.7%	5.2%	4.8%	5.3%	5.1%	4.5%	3.8%	$4.00
$4.25			4.1%	2.2%	1.4%	3.6%	2.8%	2.1%	2.2%	6.8%	4.3%	4.4%	5.0%	5.3%	4.9%	$4.25
$4.50				3.3%	2.6%	1.0%	3.3%	2.3%	1.6%	1.6%	4.7%	3.6%	3.4%	3.8%	3.1%	$4.50
$4.75						2.4%	0.9%	3.0%	2.1%	1.4%	1.3%	3.4%	3.2%	2.9%	2.6%	$4.75
$5.00							2.1%	0.7%	2.6%	2.2%	1.4%	1.2%	2.7%	2.5%	2.0%	$5.00
$5.25								1.8%	0.7%	2.0%	1.1%	1.2%	0.8%	2.6%	2.2%	$5.25
$5.50									1.5%	0.8%	1.7%	1.2%	1.1%	0.5%	1.3%	$5.50
$5.75										1.0%	0.5%	1.1%	1.0%	0.9%	1.8%	$5.75
$6.00											0.6%	0.9%	1.6%	1.6%	1.2%	$6.00
Total	100%	100%	100%	100%	100%	100%	100%	100%	100%	100%	100%	100%	100%	100%	100%	Total

*Rate adjustments 11 through 14 occurred after the official pilot period and are not included in this analysis.

Figure 36-3 Meter rate change table: Percent of total meter operating hours

more than 30 percent of metered hours in SF*park* areas were $1 per hour or less (with 16.5 percent at $0.25 per hour, possibly the cheapest metered parking in California). Just 6.5 percent were more than $5 per hour, contrary to many people's fears and expectations.

The geographic distribution of prices was also unexpected, with some $0.25 per hour parking spaces literally around the corner from much more expensive parking. This reinforces the lesson that it is likely impossible to predict the "right" price for parking for any given time and place. Empirically adjusting prices in response to observed demand is a better approach, yielding superior outcomes.

SF*park* Improved Parking Availability Significantly

The primary goal of the SF*park* approach was to improve the availability of parking, and so the primary measure of success. Over the course of the SF*park* evaluation period, parking availability at meters improved by 16 percent in pilot areas while falling 50 percent in control areas (Figure 36-4). In other words, SF*park* made it much easier to find a parking space quickly.

A related goal was to improve the use of parking, or in other words to reduce the amount of time that blocks would sit largely empty. Figure 36-5 shows that SF*park* improved parking use significantly; the program achieved a 31 percent increase in the number of metered hours in which the target occupancy was met. Fewer blocks were sitting empty less of the time.

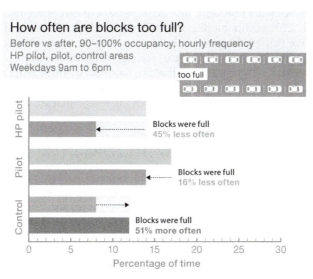

Figure 36-4   Change in parking availability

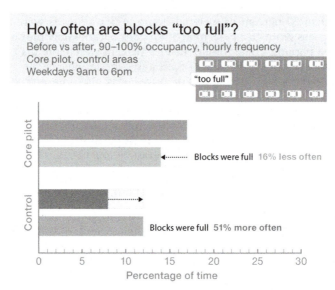

Figure 36-5   Change in parking utilization

As shown in Figures 36-4 and 36-5, parking availability and use improved even more in the pilot area's High Payment (HP) blocks, which are blocks that had high payment compliance (i.e., on blocks where most people paid for parking). On HP blocks, parking availability increased 45 percent, and achievement of target occupancy rate doubled. This result more accurately reflects the effects of demand-responsive pricing for parking because prices are more effective when most people pay them. Cities can strongly influence compliance (i.e., the percentage of hours parked that are paid for) by improving enforcement and reducing or eliminating permits that exempt some drivers (e.g., government workers, cars with disabled placards, etc.) from paying at meters or observing time limits.

SF*park* Parking Garages were Better Used

SF*park* improved parking availability for both on- and off-street parking while at the same time increasing the use of SF*park* garages. Overall, use at SF*park* garages grew by 11 percent, far exceeding non-SF*park* garages. The greatest increase (14 percent) occurred during off-peak periods. This improved use of city assets helped to reduce on-street parking demand, supporting the goal of improving parking availability.

Perhaps more important than improving garage use, especially from the perspective of improving San Francisco's economic vitality

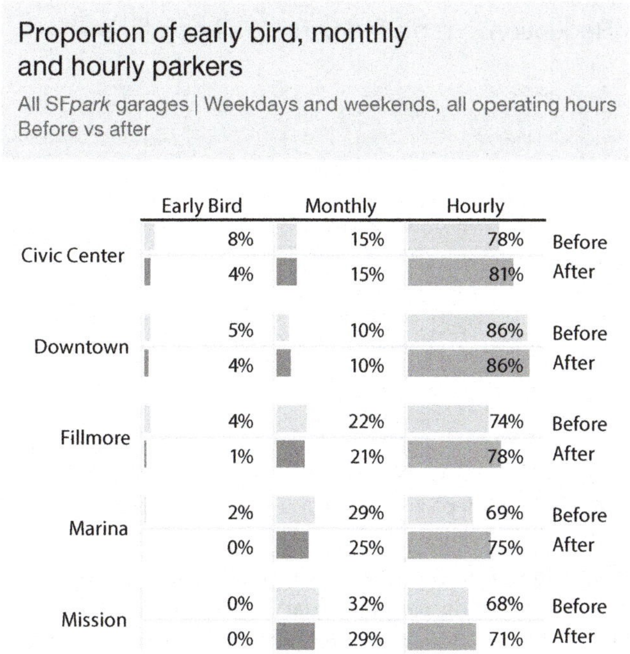

Proportion of early bird, monthly and hourly parkers

All SFpark garages | Weekdays and weekends, all operating hours
Before vs after

	Early Bird	Monthly	Hourly	
Civic Center	8%	15%	78%	Before
	4%	15%	81%	After
Downtown	5%	10%	86%	Before
	4%	10%	86%	After
Fillmore	4%	22%	74%	Before
	1%	21%	78%	After
Marina	2%	29%	69%	Before
	0%	25%	75%	After
Mission	0%	32%	68%	Before
	0%	29%	71%	After

Figure 36-6   Proportion of early bird, monthly, and hourly parkers

and competitiveness, SF*park* reduced the number of daily commuters parking in SFMTA garages and increased the number of short-term hourly parkers. As summarized in Figure 36-6, subtle changes to the pricing structure and significant reductions to parking discounts reduced the numbers of early bird and monthly parkers while reductions in hourly parking rates increased the number of short-term parkers. This supported the goals of reducing commuting by car and improving economic vitality. While these improvements were modest, more aggressively reducing discounts for early bird and monthly parking—or eliminating those discounts altogether—would provide a bigger benefit, as well as significantly reduce commuting by car.

It Became Easier for Drivers to Find a Parking Space

We also gathered data to determine how much improving parking availability would reduce the time people spend searching for a parking space. As summarized in Figure 36-7, in SF*park* pilot areas, the average amount of reported time it took to find a space decreased by

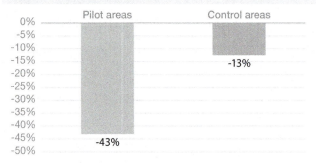

Figure 36-7 Changes in parking search time (minutes)

43 percent, compared to a 13 percent decrease in control areas. This is a dramatic shift, saving people valuable time in their day, and greatly improving their experience parking in San Francisco.

Vehicle Miles Traveled and Greenhouse Gas Emissions Decreased

As a result of less circling, vehicle miles traveled (VMT) in pilot areas fell 30 percent from 8,134 miles per day in 2011 to 5,721 miles per day by 2013, while VMT decreased by only 6 percent in control areas.

Reduced VMT while looking for parking reduced greenhouse gas emissions. Because drivers circle for parking at very low speeds with stop-and-go behavior, they slow traffic and emit more greenhouse emissions per mile (see Chapter 25). SF*park* reduced greenhouse emissions from circling by the same 30 percent in VMT—or possibly more—given these other factors. As summarized in Figure 36-8, on a per-parking-meter basis, the 30 percent decrease in VMT translates into reducing VMT per parking meter from 3.7 to 2.6 miles (compared to a negligible change in control areas).

Peak Period Congestion Decreased

SF*park* reduced congestion by reducing circling for parking and encouraging people to drive at off-peak times. On-street parking availability improved by 22 percent during peak periods and by 12 percent during

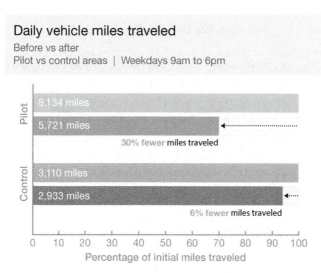

Figure 36-8   Daily vehicle miles traveled

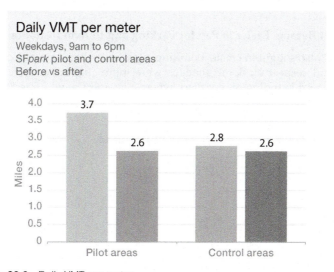

Figure 36-9   Daily VMT per meter

off-peak. Figure 36-9 shows that morning peak entries in SF*park* garages rose 1 percent while off-peak entries rose 14 percent, and evening peak exits rose 3 percent while off-peak exits rose 15 percent. This suggests that SF*park* helped to reduce peak-period congestion, which makes the roads flow more smoothly for drivers and transit.

Double Parking Decreased

Double parking increases dramatically as parking occupancy exceeds 80 percent. Double parking decreased by 22 percent versus a 5 percent decrease in control areas (Figure 36-10).

Transit Speed Improved Where Double Parking Decreased

To evaluate how SF*park* affected transit speed, 30 percent of buses had transponders installed and were dispatched from bus yards at random. In evaluating the transit travel times collected from these buses, we asked how changes in double parking affected transit speed. Transit speed increased 2.3 percent from 6.4 to 6.6 mph along corridors where we observed reduced double parking, and speeds decreased 5.3 percent from 7.1 to 6.7 mph along corridors with increased double parking (Figure 36-11). This improvement can appear small but is quite significant for transit operations, and benefits many riders. Besides increasing transit speed, fewer unpredictable delays help transit operate more reliably, which is even more important for riders and transit operators.

It Became Easier to Pay for Parking and to Avoid Citations

SF*park* also sought to create a parking experience that is simple, consistent, and respectful. Some changes were more subjective, such as the design and branding of any place where customers would interact with

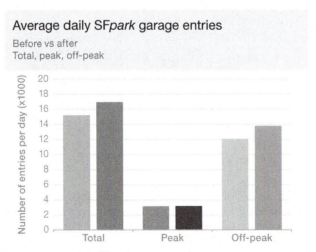

Figure 36-10   Average daily SF*park* garage entries

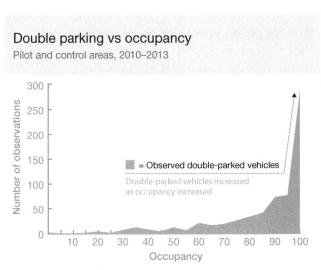

Double parking vs occupancy
Pilot and control areas, 2010–2013

= Observed double-parked vehicles

Double-parked vehicles increased
as occupancy increased

Figure 36-11   Double parking vs. occupancy

Transit speed and double parking
Transit speed on corridors with increased vs.
decreased double parking (DP)
Weekdays, 9am to 6pm
Before vs after

	Before	After	Net change	% change
Corridors w/decrease in DP	6.4	6.6	0.2	2.3%
Corridors w/increase in DP	7.1	6.7	(0.4)	-5.3%

Figure 36-12   Transit speed and double parking

the parking system. More concrete improvements included lengthening time limits and making it much easier to pay. Drivers surveyed before and after implementing SF*park* were asked to rate their parking experience; after SF*park*, the likelihood of reporting that it was somewhat or very easy to pay for parking increased in pilot areas by 75 percent, or twice as much as in control areas that did not receive new meters or longer time limits.

Parking tickets are another indicator of the parking experience. Simplifying the parking payment process in SF*park* areas made it easier for drivers to avoid tickets. SFMTA gave 23 percent fewer parking-meter-related citations per meter than before the pilot, with compliance increasing as well (Figures 36-12 and 36-13). This is a great success of

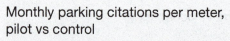

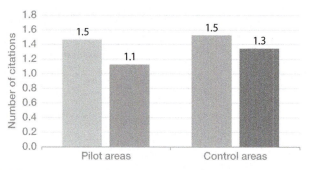

Figure 36-13   Average monthly parking citations per meter

the program; no one likes getting tickets, and SFMTA would prefer that everyone pay, which would make pricing parking that much more effective. Reducing the number of tickets issued also produced subtle secondary benefits, such as allowing parking control officers to focus on other duties like enforcing double parking, and reducing SFMTA's costs associated with adjudicating citations (i.e., processing people's complaints that they didn't deserve a ticket).

Net Parking Revenue Increased Slightly

Though the purpose of SF*park* was to deliver transportation, social, and environmental benefits, it also appears to have increased SFMTA net parking revenues by approximately $1.9 million per year. In comparing the pilot areas to citywide trends, the installation of credit-card-enabled parking meters and the longer time limits in SF*park* areas increased net annual revenues from meters by approximately $3.3 million from FY2011 to FY2013. Figure 36-14 summarizes the average monthly revenue per meter changes as a result of different SF*park* policies and technologies.

In the same period, annual citation revenues decreased by approximately $0.5 million in SF*park* pilot areas. SF*park* appears to have slightly slowed the growth of revenue for garages, accounting for about $0.9 million in lost annual revenue that may have been earned had SF*park* garage revenue grown at the same pace as non-SF*park* garage

Payment compliance rates by area

Pilot areas^
Weekdays, 9am to 6pm
Before vs after

	Before	After	Net change	% change
Civic Center	37%	50%	13%	35%
Downtown	32%	39%	7%	22%
Fillmore	48%	55%	7%	15%
Fisherman's Wharf	38%	54%	16%	42%
Marina	68%	66%	-2%	-4%
Mission	49%	57%	8%	16%
South Embarcadero	41%	59%	18%	45%

^ Data unavailable for control areas

Figure 36-14   Payment compliance rates by area

revenue, though revenue from SF*park* garages has increased at a faster rate since FY2012. While the annual parking tax collected in pilot areas increased by $6.5 million, or 43 percent, during the same period, compared to a 3 percent increase in the rest of the city, it is unclear what portion of that is attributable to SF*park*.

Improved Availability Supports Economic Vitality

Improved parking availability improves access to commercial districts and supports economic vitality. Figure 36-15 compares sales tax revenue collected in SF*park* pilot areas with sales tax revenue collected from the rest of the city. Sales tax revenues increased significantly faster in SF*park* areas during the pilot period. This suggests that SF*park* helped make these areas more economically competitive.

To evaluate how SF*park* influenced the number of visitors to an area, the SFMTA administered an intercept survey in the Downtown and Marina pilot areas as well as in control areas. The share of people visiting pilot or control areas for shopping, dining, or entertainment did not change over the course of the pilot project. Of those who drove to the pilot areas, however, there was a 30 percent increase in people who visited to shop or dine compared to people who drove for other reasons, such as work or school. In other words, more people who drove to pilot areas after SF*park* were visiting to shop, eat, or for entertainment. Control areas showed no change. This trend suggests that

SF*park* made it more attractive for drivers to shop, dine, and participate in other entertainment activities – exactly the outcome we wanted to see.

Safer Streets

Reduced circling by distracted drivers looking for parking helps to reduce collisions with pedestrians, cyclists, and other cars. This was not yet evaluated, however, because historical data were unavailable at the time of the SF*park* pilot evaluation.

WHAT'S NEXT?

Parking is a universal urban issue, and San Francisco's experience with SF*park* is relevant for other cities because this approach to parking management can be replicated—it's a readily scalable solution.

In 2014, after seeing the benefits of SF*park*, the SFMTA Board decided to expand SF*park* to all paid parking in San Francisco. Other cities, such as Los Angeles, New York, Seattle, and Washington, D.C., have also started to implement the same kind of approach. SF*park* was explicitly designed as a demonstration project, and its ultimate purpose was to measure the benefits to managing parking in this manner, and to make it easy for other cities to adapt or improve on the SF*park* approach. This is important because the more cities that replicate and improve upon this approach, the more significant the net social and environmental benefits. If 1,000 cities around the world were to manage parking more effectively, the benefits, including reduced greenhouse gas emissions, would be far greater.

In one sense, SF*park* was a demonstration not of parking pricing but of a parking-based approach to congestion management. Parking availability and price are two of the most important factors when people choose whether to make a trip by car. The combination of demand-responsive pricing and off-peak discounts at garages reduces circling and double parking, and influences when and how people choose to travel. Managing demand for publicly available parking can be even more effective when paired with other parking-based strategies, such as managing supply—the ultimate determinant of how many car trips will be made—and other transportation demand management strategies.

Parking management strategies complement other congestion management strategies, such as congestion pricing, but have several advantages: they are low cost (or actually generate income); do not present privacy issues; require only local approval (rather than state approval,

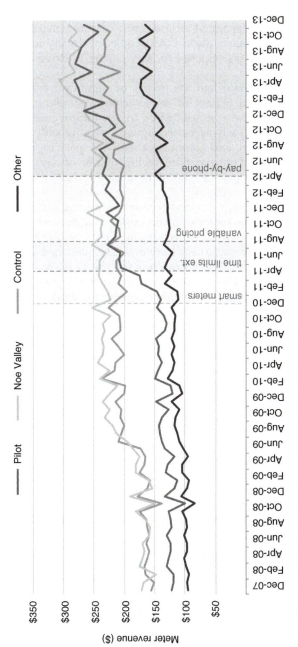

Average meter payment revenue by month, per meter
Pilot, control and other areas
Weekdays and weekends, all operating hours
January 2008 to July 2013

——— Pilot ——— Noe Valley ——— Control ——— Other

Meter revenue ($)

$350
$300
$250
$200
$150
$100
$50

Dec-07 Feb-08 Apr-08 Jun-08 Aug-08 Oct-08 Dec-08 Feb-09 Apr-09 Jun-09 Aug-09 Oct-09 Dec-09 Feb-10 Apr-10 Jun-10 Aug-10 Oct-10 Dec-10 Feb-11 Apr-11 Jun-11 Aug-11 Oct-11 Dec-11 Feb-12 Apr-12 Jun-12 Aug-12 Oct-12 Dec-12 Feb-13 Apr-13 Jun-13 Aug-13 Oct-13 Dec-13

smart meters
time limits ext.
variable pricing
pay-by-phone

Figure 36-15 Average meter payment revenue by month, per meter

which some congestion management strategies require); use existing parking management infrastructure (parking meters and garages); and take advantage of the fact that people are already accustomed to paying for parking (as opposed to, say, paying to drive on a road that was formerly free).

San Francisco had the luxury of significant federal funding when implementing SF*park*, but implementing a similar parking management approach does not need to be costly. Improvements to the customer experience, such as better signage, require only strong leadership, better design, and communication. Any parking meter can be easily programmed to have more intelligent time-of-day, block-by-block, and day-of-week pricing, and modern meters make it easy to update rates wirelessly.

To implement demand-responsive pricing a city needs occupancy data. Parking sensors remain costly, but manual data collection is a simple, low-cost, and effective alternative. Seattle and other cities have found that this approach enables less frequent or granular rate changes. Another promising approach is the use of license-plate-reading technology (typically mounted in parking enforcement vehicles) to gather occupancy data. Yet another approach—used in SF*park* areas since January 2014 after parking sensors were deactivated—is to use historical meter payment data combined with data about non-compliance (i.e., the percentage of time parked that isn't paid for) to impute occupancy on a block-by-block, time-of-day, and weekday-vs.-weekend basis. That is a cost-effective way to obtain rich data without the expense and complexity of parking sensors. Going forward, other solutions will emerge and costs will fall.

There are more subtle and perhaps more important benefits to better parking management, especially when it comes to shaping cities for the better. The availability and cost of parking are two of the biggest factors when people choose whether to drive, and the parking supply—how much parking is built, or not, and where—has a profound influence on the shape, life, and vitality of a city. Regardless of how much parking is added or taken away, that supply is ultimately finite, and demand for that supply can and should be managed intelligently. Managing public parking more effectively enables more informed conversations and more intelligent decisions about how much parking to build or eliminate in light of more clearly defined trade-offs. People will know that how much parking there is will determine how many car trips there are and the resulting level of congestion. In other words, the SF*park* approach can shape cities for the better by enabling them to grow more gracefully.

REFERENCES AND FURTHER READING

SFMTA's overview of the SF*park* pilot project "SF*park*: Putting Theory into Practice."
http://sfpark.org/wp-content/uploads/2014/06/SFpark_Pilot_Overview.pdf
SFMTA's summary of its in-depth evaluation of the SF*park* pilot project. http://
sfpark.org/wp-content/uploads/2014/06/SFpark_Eval_Summary_2014.pdf
SFMTA's in-depth evaluation of the SF*park* pilot project. http://direct.sfpark.org/
wp-content/uploads/eval/SFpark_Pilot_Project_Evaluation.pdf
SFMTA's technical manual for the SF*park* pilot project. http://sfpark.org/wp-
content/uploads/2014/07/SFpark_Tech_Manual_web1.pdf
FHWA's evaluation of the SF*park* pilot project. http://ntl.bts.gov/
lib/54000/54900/54928/032515_rev_san_fran_508_final_FHWA-JPO-14-128.pdf

CHAPTER

37

SF*park:* Pricing Parking by Demand

By Gregory Pierce and Donald Shoup

In 2011, San Francisco adopted the biggest price reform for on-street parking since the invention of the parking meter in 1935. Most cities' parking meters charge the same price all day, and some cities charge the same price everywhere. San Francisco's meters, however, now vary the price of curb parking by location and time of day.

SF*park*, San Francisco's new pricing program, aims to solve the problems created by charging too much or too little for curb parking. If the price is too high and many curb spaces remain open, nearby stores lose customers, employees lose jobs, and governments lose tax revenue. If the price is too low and no curb spaces are open, drivers who cruise to find an open space waste time and fuel, congest traffic, and pollute the air.

In seven pilot zones, San Francisco installed sensors that report the occupancy of each curb space on every block, and parking meters that charge variable prices according to the time of day. In response to the observed occupancy rates, the city adjusts parking prices about every two months.

Consider the prices on a weekday at Fisherman's Wharf, a tourist and retail destination (Figure 37-1). Before SF*park* began in August 2011, the price was $3 an hour at all times. Now each block has different prices during three periods of the day—before noon, from noon to 3 p.m., and after 3 p.m. By May 2012, prices on almost every block had decreased for the period before noon and increased between noon and 3 p.m. Most prices after 3 p.m. were lower than during midday.

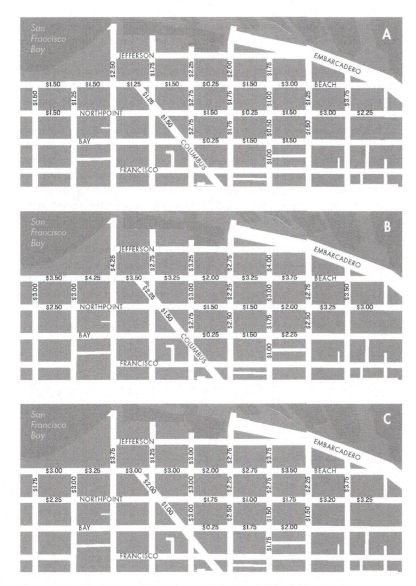

Figure 37-1 Weekday parking prices at Fisherman's Wharf, May 2012
(A) Before noon
(B) Noon to 3 p.m.
(C) After 3 p.m.

SF*park* bases these price adjustments purely on observed occupancy. Planners cannot reliably predict the right price for parking on every block at every time of day, but they can use a simple trial-and-error process to adjust prices in response to occupancy rates. Figure 37-2 illustrates how nudging prices up on crowded Block A and down on under-occupied Block B can shift a single car to improve the performance of both blocks.

Most cities use time limits to promote parking turnover, but turnover isn't the right goal. Occupancy is a better policy target, and it is unambiguous. Open spaces are either available or not. Turnover is ambiguous not only because no one knows what the right turnover is, but also because the turnover is influenced by the activities that people do once they park. High turnover may be desirable outside a coffee shop but not a theater. High turnover also congests traffic as people slow, stop, park, and leave a park space.

Beyond managing the on-street supply, SF*park* helps to depoliticize parking by setting a clear pricing policy. San Francisco charges the lowest prices possible without creating a parking shortage. Transparent, data-based pricing rules can bypass the usual politics of parking. Because demand dictates the prices, politicians cannot simply raise prices to gain more revenue.

Before SF*park*

Block A – Central Business District Location   No Open Spots

Block B – Nearby Location   3 Open Spots

After SF*park*

Block A – Central Business District Location   1 Open Spot

Block B – Nearby Location   2 Open Spots

Figure 37-2 Performance prices balance occupancy on every block

DID SF*PARK* MOVE PARKING OCCUPANCY IN THE RIGHT DIRECTION?

After several years of planning, the San Francisco Municipal Transportation Authority (SFMTA) launched SF*park* in April 2011 by installing new parking meters and extending or removing the time limits on curb spaces. The pilot program covers seven zones that contain 7,000 metered curb spaces. The initial prices in each zone were simply carried over from the previous, uniform pricing scheme. Under the new SF*park* program, most meters operate daily from 9 a.m. to 6 p.m., with prices that vary by the time of day and between weekdays and weekends. SFMTA established the desired target occupancy rate at between 60 and 80 percent for each block. If the average occupancy on a block for a given period falls in this range, the price will not change in the following period. San Francisco's pricing policy is thus data-driven and transparent, while most other cities' pricing policies are political and opaque.

In setting a target occupancy rate, SF*park* has two goals: to make curb parking readily available and to ensure that curb parking accommodates as many customers as possible for the adjacent businesses. These two goals conflict because when meter rates increase to encourage one or two open spots per block, the higher prices also reduce average occupancy.

For example, large groups gathering at a restaurant may generate exceptionally high parking demand on a block on some days, so cities cannot aim for a consistently high occupancy rate of 80 to 90 percent without often reaching 100 percent occupancy, which produces unwanted cruising. A lower average occupancy, however, means fewer customers. San Francisco set the target occupancy rate at between 60 and 80 percent to cope with the random variation in parking demand and to balance the competing goals of reliable availability and high occupancy. If SF*park* works as intended, prices will move occupancy rates toward this target range.

During its first two years, SF*park* adjusted prices 11 times on each block for three different periods during the day. Prices increased in 31 percent of the cases, declined in 30 percent, and remained the same in 39 percent. On average, prices declined in the morning and increased in the midday and afternoon. The average price fell 4 percent, which means SF*park* adjusted prices up and down according to demand without increasing prices overall.

Because occupancy rates have moved toward the target goals, the share of blocks needing no price adjustment has slowly increased since the program began. By August 2013, after the program had been operating for two years, 62 percent of blocks were in the target range. Altogether, a third of all the blocks that had been over- or under-occupied at the beginning of SF*park* had shifted into the target occupancy range.

We can use an example of parking prices and occupancy rates on Chestnut and Lombard Streets in the Marina District to show the effects of SF*park*. In July 2011, these parallel streets had the same meter rate ($2 an hour) but very different occupancy rates. All five blocks of Chestnut were over-occupied (above 80 percent); of the five blocks on Lombard, two were under-occupied (below 60 percent), and three were in the target range (60 to 80 percent). What would it take to shift a few cars from the over-occupied blocks on Chestnut to the under-occupied blocks on Lombard?

Figure 37-3 shows the path of average prices and occupancy on the five blocks of Chestnut and Lombard Streets from 3 p.m. until 6 p.m. In response to the over- and under-occupancy, SF*park* began to increase the prices on Chestnut and reduce them on Lombard. After 10 price changes in two years, the average price on Chestnut had climbed by 75 percent to $3.50 an hour, and on Lombard it had fallen by 50 percent to $1.00 an hour. As prices on the two blocks diverged, occupancy rates converged within the target range.

Figure 37-4 shows the parking prices on each block in April 2013. Between Pierce and Scott Streets, for example, the price on Chestnut was $3.50 an hour, and just a block away the price on Lombard was only 50 cents an hour, yet both blocks were in the target occupancy range. Parking spaces so close together seem close substitutes

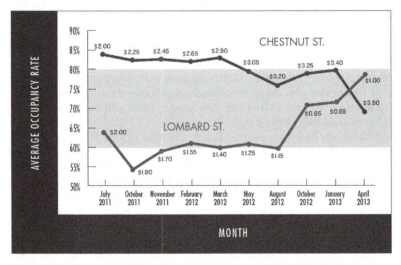

Figure 37-3 Average parking prices and occupancy rates on Chestnut and Lombard streets, 3 p.m. to 6 p.m.

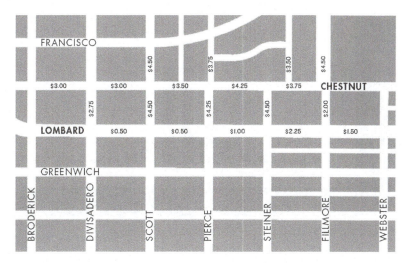

Figure 37-4   Parking prices on Chestnut and Lombard streets, April 2013, 3 p.m. to 6 p.m.

for each other, but the huge price differences reflect either very different local demand patterns or drivers' lack of information about the prices. One way to increase information would be to encourage shops and restaurants to post maps of the parking prices on their premises, to show their customers the opportunities to save money on parking.

PRICE ELASTICITY OF DEMAND

Before each price change, SF*park* publishes data on the occupancy and prices for all curb spaces in the pilot zones. The price elasticity of demand measures how these price changes affected occupancy rates. Economists define price elasticity as the percent change in the occupancy rate (the quantity of parking demanded) divided by the percent change in the meter price. For example, if a 10 percent price increase leads to a 5 percent fall in occupancy, the price elasticity of demand is -0.5 ($-5\% \div 10\%$).

We calculated the elasticity of demand revealed by all the price changes during SF*park*'s first year. For each price change, we compared the old price and average occupancy to the new price and average occupancy during the following period. We thus have 5,294 elasticity measurements, one for each price change during the year at each time of day at each location.

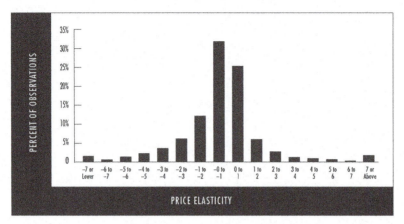

Figure 37-5 Distribution of elasticities for 5,294 price changes

The *average* price elasticity of demand was −0.4, but when we plot the elasticity for individual price changes at the block level, we find astonishing variety. Figure 37-5 shows the distribution of the price elasticities calculated for 5,294 individual price and occupancy changes on 1,492 city blocks.

The wide range of price elasticities suggests that many variables other than price affect parking demand. Higher prices should reduce occupancy, and lower prices should increase occupancy. In many cases, however, occupancy either rose after prices rose or fell after prices fell. Higher prices do not cause higher occupancy, and lower prices do not cause lower occupancy, so random variation or other factors must have overwhelmed the effects of prices on occupancy in the cases of positive price elasticity.

The wide range of elasticity at the block level also suggests that the circumstances on individual blocks vary so greatly that planners will never be able to estimate an accurate elasticity to predict the prices needed to achieve the target occupancy for every block. Instead, the best way to achieve target occupancy is to do what SF*park* does: adjust prices in response to the observed occupancy. This trial-and-error method mirrors how other markets establish prices, so it should work in the market for on-street parking.

EQUITY IN PERFORMANCE PRICING

While it is clear that performance parking prices can improve transportation efficiency, are they fair? In San Francisco, 30 percent of households do not own a car, so they don't pay anything for curb parking. How the city spends its parking revenue also affects the equity implications of charging for parking. San Francisco uses all its parking meter revenue to subsidize public transit, so automobile owners subsidize transit riders. SF*park* further aids bus riders by reducing traffic caused by drivers cruising for underpriced curb parking.

Performance pricing is not price discrimination because all drivers who park on the same block at the same time pay the same price. Performance pricing is also not the same as maximizing revenue. Because demand was, on average, inelastic, the city could increase revenue by charging higher prices. SF*park*'s goal, however, is to optimize occupancy, not to maximize revenue, and the average price of parking fell by 4 percent during SF*park*'s first two years.

THREE SUGGESTED IMPROVEMENTS

Our findings suggest three ways to improve SF*park*: (1) refine the periods of operation, (2) shift from reaction to prediction in setting prices, and (3) end the abuse of disabled placards.

Refine the Time Periods

Most meters stop operating at 6 p.m., so anyone who arrives at 5 p.m. and pays for one hour can park all night. Drivers who park during the evening thus have an incentive to arrive during the last hour of meter operation while a few open spaces are still available. Since SF*park* sets the price to achieve an average target occupancy for the period from 3 p.m. to 6 p.m., a price can be too high at 4 p.m. (and occupancy too low) but too low at 5 p.m. (and occupancy too high).

One way to solve this problem is to operate the meters in the evening for as long as they are needed to achieve the optimal occupancy. Free parking after 6 p.m. is a holdover from the days when meters had one- or two-hour time limits to increase turnover during the daytime. Most businesses closed by 6 p.m., so parking turnover was not needed in the evening. Today many businesses remain open after 6 p.m., so the old rationale for free parking in the evening no longer applies. The purpose of metering in the evening is to prevent shortages, not to create turnover.

Because the occupancy sensors and parking meters are already in place for the pilot program, it seems unwise to cease operating at 6 p.m. simply because the old meters did. If, during the day, SF*park* reduces cruising, congestion, traffic accidents, energy waste, air pollution, and greenhouse gases, San Francisco can incrementally extend metering to additional evening hours when it will provide similar benefits. SF*park* has not increased curb parking prices overall, so the major benefit is better parking management, not more revenue from the existing meters. Nevertheless, more revenue can come from installing more meters and extending meter hours.

Taking this process to its logical end, SF*park* can refine its pricing strategy to fit the demand on specific blocks at different times of the day across different days of the week. Narrowing the pricing windows to meet varying demand will increase the program's efficiency.

Shift from Reaction to Prediction

The wide range of occupancy changes after each price change shows that many factors other than prices affect parking demand. Therefore, basing the next period's parking prices only on the previous period's occupancy rates will not reliably achieve occupancy goals. For example, SF*park* should not increase prices in January because occupancy rates were high during the Christmas shopping season. Seasonal adjustments based on occupancy rates in previous years may greatly improve the program's performance.

By shifting from reaction to prediction when adjusting prices, SF*park* may be able to get closer to target parking occupancy rates. Like hockey players who skate to where the puck will be, SF*park* can price parking based on future demand, not simply on past occupancy.

End the Abuse of Disabled Placards

Abuse of disabled parking placards helps explain why occupancy does not reliably respond to price changes. Because California allows all cars with disabled placards to park free for an unlimited time at parking meters, higher prices for curb parking increase the temptation to misuse disabled placards to save money. Higher prices at meters may therefore drive out paying parkers and make more spaces available for placard abusers. If so, disabled placard abuse will reduce the price elasticity of demand for curb parking.

Placard abuse is already rampant in California. A survey of several blocks in downtown Los Angeles in 2010, for example, found that cars with disabled placards occupied most of the curb spaces most of the time. Drivers using disabled placards were often seen carrying heavy loads between their cars and the adjacent businesses. Chapter 32 explains a two-tier placard reform that can greatly reduce placard abuse.

How will ending placard abuse affect SF*park*? If reform reduces placard abuse at meters, more spaces will open up for paying parkers. SF*park* will then reduce prices to increase occupancy, but all the new parkers will pay for the spaces they occupy, so parking revenue will probably increase. The lower prices, higher revenue, and greater availability of curb spaces will benefit almost everyone except placard abusers.

CONCLUSION: A PROMISING PILOT PROGRAM

SF*park* is a pilot program to examine the feasibility of adjusting prices to manage parking occupancy, and it appears largely successful. Los Angeles has already adopted a similar program called LA Express Park (see Chapter 41), and other cities are watching the results. After drivers see that prices can decline as well as increase, they may appreciate the availability of open curb spaces and learn to use the pricing information to optimize their parking choices for each trip. Parking prices that seemed unthinkable in the past may become indispensable in the future.

With performance parking prices, drivers will find places to park their cars just as easily as they find places to buy gasoline. But drivers will also have to think about the price of parking just as they now think about the prices of fuel, tires, insurance, registration, repairs, and the cars themselves. Parking will become a part of the market economy, and prices will help to manage the demand for cars and driving.

If SF*park* succeeds in setting prices to achieve the right occupancy for curb parking, almost everyone will benefit. Other cities can then adopt their own versions of performance parking prices. Getting the prices right for curb parking can do a world of good.

This article is adapted from "Getting the Prices Right: An Evaluation of Pricing Parking by Demand," originally published in the Journal of the American Planning Association *70 (January 2013): 67–81.*

38

Market-Priced Parking in Theory and Practice

By Michael Manville and Daniel G. Chatman

One of the first lessons of economics is that price controls lead to short-ages, and shortages lead to queues. Street parking vividly illustrates this principle. Many cities keep valuable street spaces free or under-priced, and as a result they fill up quickly, leaving shortages at busy times. These shortages create moving queues as drivers circle the block searching for spaces—they "cruise." Cruising, in turn, creates conges-tion and pollution.

The textbook answer to this problem is simple: lift the price control and let the market set the price for curb parking. The "right" price will keep one or two spaces open but no more. Just as a private firm wants its inventory to sell briskly without being exhausted, so too should cities keep parking spaces well used but never completely full. With most, but not all, spaces occupied, any driver willing to pay can find a spot, reducing cruising without creating underuse.

This approach to street parking is sometimes called performance pricing, because instead of choosing a price and seeing what happens to occupancy, the city chooses a performance standard (e.g., one or two spaces always open) and lets the price adjust to achieve it.

Performance pricing for parking is similar to congestion pricing for roads: both use prices to "clear the market" and prevent the overuse of scarce infrastructure. Like congestion pricing, performance-priced parking is rare. Most cities prefer to keep roads and parking free, even though cities that have experimented with congestion tolls have seen remarkable results. When London implemented congestion pricing in 2004, the price of driving into central London went from 0 to £5.

Traffic volumes fell 25 percent the very first day of tolling. Results were similar in Singapore, where traffic volumes fell 44 percent in the first year of tolling, and in Stockholm, where traffic fell more than 10 percent. Vehicles in toll lanes on California's performance-priced State Route 91 zip along unencumbered by congestion, even as vehicles in the nearby free lanes sit mired in traffic. In all cases, as the price goes up, congestion goes down. Could market-priced parking do the same thing?

In 2011, San Francisco decided to find out by creating a market-priced parking pilot program in its downtown called SF*park*. SF*park*'s explicit goals were to reduce cruising (its slogan was "live more, circle less"), increase the speed and reliability of transit, and make walking and cycling safer. For researchers, SF*park* provided a real-world test of performance pricing. Would raising the price for parking nudge occupancy down and vacancy up in one of America's densest and most congested cities?

ABOUT SF*PARK*

Prior to SF*park*, meter rates in San Francisco were like those in most cities. They varied by neighborhood, but not by time of day or day of week. Prices were rarely high enough to generate turnover, and often much lower than off-street rates. In downtown, the highest on-street price was $3.50 an hour, while the median off-street price was $10 an hour. This disparity created curb shortages and gave drivers strong incentives to cruise. The San Francisco Municipal Transportation Agency (SFMTA) compounded this problem by rarely changing the rates. And when the SFMTA did raise prices, it usually did so to raise revenue, not to improve parking. There was no fixed timetable for reviewing meter rates, nor any formula for changing them. Increasing the rates was rarely popular and often laborious because most of the meters were older, coin-operated devices.

SF*park* changed these conditions. Using modern equipment, the program made prices more responsive to demand, and made price changes more transparent and predictable. And unlike many public initiatives, which get launched with fanfare and then fade from view before anyone can scrutinize them, SF*park* displayed an admirable commitment to openness and analytical rigor. The SFMTA selected eight "treatment" neighborhoods and four control neighborhoods. In both areas, it replaced thousands of coin-operated meters with digital "smart" meters that allowed credit card and remote payment. The agency also placed magnetic sensors in the pavement to measure parking occupancy. Together the sensors and meters relayed information wirelessly to the SFMTA, allowing the agency to correlate prices with occupancy. All these data were available to the public.

Once the new equipment was installed, the city began gathering data and also relaxed the parking time limits. On some blocks, the city allowed parking for up to four hours, and on the remaining blocks, it eliminated time limits altogether. Finally, in late spring 2011, the SFMTA used its new data to set meter rates in the treatment neighborhoods. The new rates varied by block, by time of day (morning, midday, and afternoon "timebands"), and by day of the week (weekday versus weekend). The price adjustments were based on the average occupancy for each timeband on each block over the course of six to eight weeks of sensor data. Prices for any of the three timebands on a block could rise or fall depending on the calculated occupancy levels (Table 38-1). Thus, if a block was congested in the morning but vacant in the afternoon, the morning rate rose while the afternoon rate fell.

In short, SF*park* replaced an opaque system of rates that changed infrequently and by whole neighborhoods with a more transparent system where prices changed over smaller units of time and space. It also provided something close to an experiment in priced parking. SF*park* gave researchers the classic "before-and-after, within-and-without" research design: we could examine conditions on blocks that received variable priced parking before and after SF*park*, and compare these to conditions on similar blocks that were never "treated" with variable pricing.

DID SF*PARK* WORK?

Performance pricing is intended to reduce cruising, and cruising is notoriously difficult to measure—it is hard to look at a car moving in traffic and know if it is searching for parking. Cruising is caused by a shortage of street parking, however, and shortages *can* be measured through occupancy and vacancy rates—the share of spaces that have vehicles in them and the share that don't, respectively. Thus one way to evaluate SF*park* is to see if shortages became less common on treated blocks; namely, were these blocks more likely to have at least one open space?

Table 38-1 Criteria for parking rate changes, SF*park*

Average Block-Side Occupancy	Rate Change per Hour
Under 30%	−$0.50
30–60%	−$0.25
60–80%	No change
Above 80%	$0.25

Here is where things get tricky. SF*park*'s meters and sensors can measure average occupancy. Drivers, however, can respond to price increases in ways that may not change average occupancy. As prices rise, more vehicles could park for shorter periods of time. This higher turnover could help local businesses, but need not alter average occupancy (and might even increase local traffic). Drivers could also respond to higher prices by carpooling. Carpooling would change vehicle occupancy but not necessarily change parking-space occupancy. And, of course, some drivers might respond to higher prices by choosing not to pay. When subway fares rise, some people pay more, some people ride less, and some people jump the turnstile. Drivers may be no different. If higher prices just encourage meter evasion or double parking, price changes may have little impact on occupancy or vacancy.

SF*park*'s meters and sensors could not track many of these changes. The SFMTA could not rely on its meter and sensor data to calculate vehicle turnover or the parking duration. Sensors also cannot tell if drivers are double parking or carpooling, and cannot distinguish between types of nonpayment. Some nonpaying drivers are simply scofflaws, and others have credentials, such as disabled placards or government tags (acquired legally or illegally), that let them avoid payment.

EVALUATING SF*PARK*'S PRICE CHANGES

In our study of SF*park*, we wanted to observe all of these behaviors. The best way to do so was to pay research assistants to stand on the streets all day and have them watch drivers park. (Yes, it was tedious; we paid well.) We selected about 40 block sides in the treatment zones and 9 "control" block sides nearby. Because we were interested in pricing's impact on cruising, we concentrated on blocks where occupancy was often high. We then observed each block three different times, usually a week or two after SF*park* announced price changes. Student surveyors watched and recorded cars parking while pricing was in effect, typically from 7 a.m. or 9 a.m. until 6 p.m. This continuous observation allowed us to collect not only arrival and departure times for vehicles at individual meters, but also data on vehicle occupancy, double parking, and nonpayment by type. We observed 13,431 parking sessions during three rounds of observation over one year.

We found that when prices rose on a block its average occupancy rate fell. This result was encouraging—exactly as SF*park* had intended. Average occupancy, however, is only one way to measure parking availability and may not be the best one, particularly if the average occupancy gets measured over the course of many weeks (as it did in SF*park*). A potentially better metric is minimum vacancy: the share of

Observed blocks
Control groups

0   0.5
└─┴─┴─┴─┘
    miles

Figure 38-1   Map of pilot zones, rounds 1 and 3

minutes that a block has at least one space open. When we analyzed minimum vacancy rates, we found that price changes had no effect. We also found no statistical association between price changes and carpooling, or price changes and vehicle turnover.

How can we make sense of these results? Nonpayment seems to be part of the answer, but not a huge part. The larger issues, we think, are twofold. First is the crucial difference between average occupancy and minimum vacancy. SF*park* raised prices only if the average occupancy was more than 80 percent. Our favorite way to think about this is as follows: suppose you have a block with 10 spaces and observe it for three hours, meaning there are 1,800 total possible minutes of parking on the block. If 1,200 of those minutes are occupied, the average occupancy rate is 67 percent, and the price should not change. But this figure indicates nothing about how those 1,200 minutes are distributed. They could be spread evenly across the three hours, implying that three spaces are always empty, or they could be two straight hours of zero vacancy followed by one hour of complete vacancy.

Now think about how the disparity between average occupancy and minimum vacancy could widen as occupancy gets calculated over longer periods of time. A block with an average morning occupancy of 67 percent for the month could contain hundreds of hours with no vacancies at all. The pricing mechanism can achieve the "right" average occupancy without attaining a consistent minimum vacancy. This is a problem, because drivers search for vacancies, not average occupancies.

The second problem is that SF*park* was not an example of "true" congestion pricing, in that prices did not closely match changes in demand. Compared to standard approaches for pricing parking, SF*park* was certainly using a market mechanism. Compared to most other markets, however, SF*park* remained tightly controlled. Look back at Table 38-1: the SFMTA limited the size and frequency of price changes. Rates changed once every eight weeks, and rates could neither increase by more than 25 cents per hour nor decrease by more than 50 cents per hour each time. Finally, the agency imposed a price floor of 25 cents, and a price ceiling of $6.00 per hour. So a block that started out $1.00 below its optimum level would take eight months to reach its market-clearing price (assuming nothing else changed) and blocks where the price should have been $6.50, or zero, would never reach their correct prices.

SF*park*, in short, was an example of price-controlled performance pricing. Because the price had a cap, it may not have risen enough to actually create consistent vacancies in some areas. On blocks with high parking demand, rather than "clearing the market," rising prices might have simply attracted drivers who were willing to pay more. As a result, in high-demand areas, rising prices may have changed the composition of parkers rather than created more vacancies. In principle this problem could be solved over time, if the price catches up to demand. But because there are caps on both the price level and the size of price changes, that is a big *if*. We cannot measure the queue on blocks without vacancies, but if they are large, prices may not be able to rise to clear them.

We do not fault the designers of SF*park* for these decisions. It is always easier to criticize a program after the fact than it is to design and deliver that new program in the first place. And trying to overcome the obstacles we list certainly has its own challenges. For example, winning permission to let prices truly float would have been difficult, perhaps even impossible. Nor is it obvious that more frequent or larger price changes would be administratively possible, or even desirable. A price that truly keeps at least one space vacant might fluctuate a lot. With more frequent or larger price changes, the benefits of increased vacancy might be outweighed by the unpredictability such a system could create for drivers. Drivers who arrive at their regular spots and find that the price had doubled might get discouraged and circle the block looking for a better deal—exactly the behavior SF*park* was designed to prevent.

The primary takeaway from our research is that performance pricing will always have to navigate a tension between the effectiveness of a price (does it actually create vacancies?), the stability of a price (how often does it fluctuate?), and the political acceptability of the price (is it so high that the public revolts, leading to no pricing at all?). Because this balance is most difficult to strike in the highest-demand areas, which are the areas most likely to generate cruising, the benefits of pricing programs may not be as large as were originally hoped. Nevertheless, the benefits *are* large, and SF*park* was a beginning, not an end. Policymakers and academics alike should work to expand and improve upon San Francisco's valuable work.

This chapter previously appeared in ACCESS, *Fall 2016, where it was adapted from "Theory versus Implementation in Congestion-Priced Parking: An Evaluation of SFpark, 2011–2012," published in* Research in Transportation Economics *44, no. 1 (June 2014): 1–9.*

39

Cruising for Parking: Lessons from San Francisco

*By Adam Millard-Ball, Rachel Weinberger, and
Robert Hampshire*

Parking management has been a vexing problem for cities since the invention of the automobile. Among the concerns are traffic congestion, air pollution, and greenhouse gas emissions caused by drivers searching for available parking—an activity colloquially known as *cruising*. Cruising for parking in a 15-block business district in Los Angeles has been estimated to produce 3,600 miles of excess travel each day—equivalent to two round trips to the Moon each year.

Many cities try to reduce cruising by increasing the supply of parking. They require private developers to provide off-street spaces to accommodate the expected demand for [free] parking, and they provide public garages to make up for shortages at the curb. These minimum parking requirements have been standard practice in US cities since the 1950s.

Although cities have increased the supply of off-street parking, they have neglected to manage on-street spaces. Because they seem unable or unwilling to properly price scarce curb spaces and enforce restrictions, cities suffer from cruising, double parking, and illegal parking in bus stops and other restricted zones. If the price of off-street parking is higher than the price of parking at the curb, drivers will rationally choose to cruise.

Recently, a wave of interest in more effective curb parking management, particularly through performance-based pricing, has arisen in cities as diverse as Seoul, Mexico City, New York, Seattle, Los Angeles, and Budapest. The movement is exemplified by San Francisco, which introduced variable priced parking to improve space availability and reduce cruising.

Here we evaluate the effectiveness of the pilot San Francisco initiative, SF*park*. We ask whether it succeeded in reducing cruising and examine how to set performance targets to achieve a given level of parking availability.

ABOUT SF*PARK*

One of the defining features of SF*park* is that it adjusts parking meter rates based on occupancy levels observed over the previous weeks or months, with the aim of achieving a per-block occupancy rate between 60 and 80 percent. The city increases meter prices by 25 cents per hour if the occupancy on a block exceeds 80 percent, and reduces the price by 25 cents per hour if the occupancy is less than 60 percent. By adjusting the price, the city expects to redistribute parking demand from very crowded blocks to less crowded ones.

Parking sensors tracked occupancy levels in both pilot areas where meter prices changed, and in control areas where meter prices remained unchanged. The sensors provided detailed occupancy data, which the city used to adjust rates about every six weeks. The six-week frame was selected to allow users to become accustomed to the new prices before making additional changes. The sensors, which have a limited lifespan, were disabled at the end of 2013. Since then, SF*park* has adjusted meter rates using meter payment data to estimate occupancy.

Our study of SF*park* uses the sensor data. We obtained occupancy snapshots every five minutes over a six-week period, and average hourly occupancy rates over a two-year period. We used the five-minute snapshots to model the likelihood that a space would be available, given the block size and an hourly average occupancy. We then developed a simulation model to estimate the amount of cruising by calculating the distance a driver must travel before finding an available space.

SETTING A PARKING OCCUPANCY TARGET

An occupancy target represents a tradeoff. The lower the occupancy, the easier it becomes for drivers to find a space and the less they will cruise to find a vacant spot. A lower occupancy, however, also means that curb spaces are idle more of the time, which wastes the space and deprives the city of revenue from parking meters.

One rule of thumb that has gained wide policy traction is to use an average occupancy rate of 85 percent to eliminate cruising. This rate would ensure that at least one parking space is available on every block at all times. To achieve this 85 percent occupancy rate, parking prices should vary throughout the day and across different blocks. The 60–80 percent target occupancy under SF*park*, by contrast, is slightly lower than the widely accepted rate of 85 percent. The rationale of SF*park* is the variability in parking demand. An occupancy rate of 60–80 percent averaged over a period of time may include moments where occupancy exceeds 85 percent and even reaches 100 percent.

Any occupancy-based goal, however, is somewhat arbitrary. More importantly, it does not relate directly to public policy goals of improving availability and reducing cruising. Driver behavior is not guided by average occupancy on a block. Rather, it is guided by price and availability. Knowing that the *average* occupancy is 85 percent is little comfort if a block is full.

Moreover, more people try to park at high-demand times and are therefore exposed to crowded parking conditions. For example, take a block that is empty half the time, fills up very rapidly, and then remains full. When full, drivers will continue to arrive but be forced to seek parking elsewhere. Objectively, this block has an average occupancy rate of about 50 percent, yet only one user experiences it as 50 percent full. The vast majority of parkers, or would-be parkers, arrive after the block is full and experience it at 100 percent occupancy. While the average occupancy target may thus be met, the user experience still leaves something to be desired.

Therefore, the variable relevant to policy is the demand-weighted *probability that a block is full*. We use the sensor snapshot data to calibrate the relationship between this measure and the average occupancy. We find that block size and the length of the averaging period are important practical factors to consider when measuring the performance of the 85 percent rule of thumb.

The Size of the Block

Figure 39-1 shows the relationship between block size (number of spaces) and the probability of unavailable parking. For a given occupancy level, the probability that a block is full decreases as the size of the block increases. This makes intuitive sense and suggests that a uniform occupancy target across all block sizes may be inappropriate from a policy perspective. For very large blocks, a parker has a good chance of finding a space even when more than 90 percent occupied. In this case, the occupancy target could be increased to 90 or 95 percent.

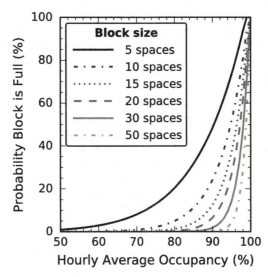

Figure 39-1   Probability of a block being full for different block sizes

Measurement Time Period

The rate of observations and the period over which the average occupancy is measured also matter when selecting an occupancy goal. Consider, for example, a block with 85 percent average occupancy. If the average is based on five observations in a five-minute period (i.e., one observation per minute), then it is highly unlikely that the block is ever full during this time. At the other extreme, if the average is computed over a 24-hour period with one observation made every hour, the chances are much greater that the block was actually full over some periods and quite low during others. Therefore, if a two-week period of averaging is used, as in the case of SF*park*, then a lower occupancy target may be appropriate to ensure parking availability and reduce cruising.

The takeaway message: the fewer spaces on the block and the longer the period of averaging, the lower the occupancy target needs to be to achieve parking availability.

DOES SF*PARK* REDUCE CRUISING?

Our simulations suggest that SF*park* worked. Occupancy levels moved towards the 60–80 percent target range. In addition, cruising fell by more than 50 percent over a two-year period in the SF*park* pilot areas compared to the control neighborhoods.

The two years of our data occurred during a rebounding local economy, when parking pressures would be expected to intensify. In fact, there was little change in occupancy in the pilot areas—reflecting the success of SF*park*—while parking availability and cruising worsened in the control areas.

Success, however, did not happen overnight. On average, each individual rate adjustment brought a block 0.1–0.2 percentage points closer to the 60–80 percent target range (Figure 39-2). It took nearly two years for these small changes to grow into a larger and statistically significant cumulative effect, with an average difference of 1–2 percentage points after ten rate adjustments. For example, a typical block with 84 percent occupancy fell to 82–83 percent occupancy over two years, while a block with 50 percent occupancy rose to 51–52 percent.

That SF*park* took time to influence behavior should come as no surprise. Almost all rate adjustments were just 25 cents, up or down. Drivers are presumably reluctant to forgo the first available space in the hope of saving a quarter and finding a space on a neighboring block. Only when rate differentials between neighboring blocks grew larger over time did the incentive to seek out cheaper parking increase substantially. Moreover, it is unclear how many motorists were aware of the differential rates and the opportunity to save money by choosing a space on a more distant block. Some hold disabled placards and can park for free at

Figure 39-2 Impacts of rate changes on occupancy over time

meters by state law. According to City of San Francisco surveys, about 20 percent of metered spaces are occupied by disabled placard holders.

SF*park* effects on cruising were smaller—but still encouraging— compared to its effects on occupancy. In pre-SF*park* baseline simulations, the average motorist could find parking within just 0.13 blocks—equivalent to about 50 feet, or just a few seconds. (This does not include the distance driven partway along the block where the driver ultimately finds a space.) Our simulations suggest that each rate adjustment reduced the average search for parking in the SF*park* pilot by about a hundredth of a block (roughly four feet) compared to the control areas. The cumulative impact after the tenth rate change was between 0.07 and 0.17 blocks (roughly 30 to 70 feet).

This reduction in cruising seems small but is more than 50 percent less than our baseline. In other words, SF*park* produced a small absolute but large relative reduction in cruising.

DIFFERENCES IN PERCEPTION AND DATA COLLECTION

Almost any resident or visitor to San Francisco can regale you with stories of their parking miseries. Self-reported survey data also indicates that cruising is a major problem. How is it we have data suggesting an average distance cruised of just 50 feet but perceptions of much longer times?

Two separate pieces of data from the San Francisco Municipal Transportation Agency (SFMTA) provide useful points of comparison. Parkers interviewed on the street reported an average search time of more than six minutes (albeit down from more than 11 minutes before SF*park* was implemented). Meanwhile, bicycle surveyors, who followed a predetermined route in certain neighborhoods, found that average search time for an available space ranged from just over 30 seconds in the early mornings, to nearly two minutes at lunchtimes.

The face-to-face SFMTA surveys show markedly more cruising than both the bicycle surveyors and our own results. Thus, cruising may partly be a problem of perception. Differences between the reported cruising times may also arise if some of the interviewees searched for a zero-cost space on a residential street, passing up an available metered space.

The contrast between our results and the bicycle surveys may be due to methodological differences. For example, we do not count the distance traveled on the block where a driver ultimately finds a space. If parking were available on the first block, we would register zero cruising, while the SFMTA surveyors would count up to the length of the block, typically 400 feet. We also sample all blocks in sensor-equipped neighborhoods, while the SFMTA's survey routes tend to start on the busier commercial streets and ignore vacant parking spaces that may be visible on side streets.

METERING: LOCATIONS AND TIMES

Our interpretation is that cruising may indeed be a problem, both before and after SF*park*, but mainly on blocks without meters or in the evenings after meters have switched off. (The analysis described above only considers metered blocks during metered hours.) Motorists cruising for a parking space during the daytime may forgo a readily available metered spot in the hopes of finding a no-cost parking space (or one with a longer time limit) on a residential side street. In the evening, our data show that cruising increases markedly in many neighborhoods around 5 pm, an hour before parking becomes free at 6 pm. A driver arriving at 5 pm will be able to pay for just one hour and park until the next morning.

Figure 39-3 illustrates the patterns of parking and cruising over the course of an average weekday in three distinct neighborhoods. Fisherman's Wharf is a tourist-oriented destination and part of the SF*park* pilot. The Marina is a mixed-use commercial district and an SF*park* pilot neighborhood. Inner Richmond is a similar commercial district, but in a control area where meter rates remained unchanged.

In both commercial districts (the Marina and Inner Richmond), cruising remains low for most of the day, with a small peak around lunchtime. Cruising then rises dramatically around 5 pm as the rush of restaurant customers and returning residents begins, and peaks around 8 pm. The evenings show much less cruising in Fisherman's Wharf, a neighborhood where there are fewer local residents and neighborhood-oriented businesses. Given the apparent effectiveness of pricing, a next step for SF*park* to reduce cruising would be to extend the hours of meter operation to all periods of excess occupancy.

CONCLUSIONS

San Francisco's parking experiment, SF*park*, is the first large-scale experiment with performance-based management of on-street parking. Judged by its impact—improved parking availability and reduced cruising—it has been a success.

Several lessons can be taken from the San Francisco experiment. First, small changes in meter rates, such as 25 cents per hour, are unlikely to have much impact on driver behavior. There is only a discernible effect on occupancy and cruising after individual meter rate changes combine

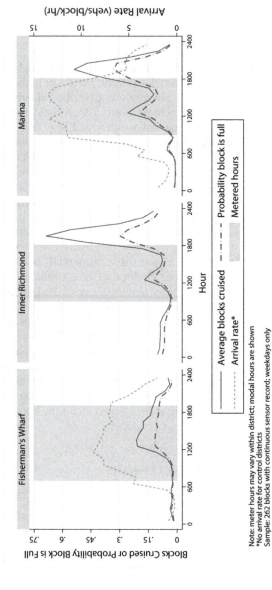

Figure 39-3 Cruising versus probability that a block is full for three selected neighborhoods

Note: meter hours may vary within district; modal hours are shown
*No arrival rate for control districts
Sample: 262 blocks with continuous sensor record; weekdays only

Average blocks cruised ----- Probability block is full
Arrival rate* ▨ Metered hours

Blocks Cruised or Probability Block is Full

Arrival Rate (vehs/block/hr)

Hour

to form much larger price differences between nearby blocks, and after drivers have time to adjust to the patterns of prices. Cities that want to change parking availability or cruising will need to consider more substantial price changes that are immediately noticeable, or have a long-term strategy of small-but-frequent rate adjustments.

Second, few cities will be able to replicate the expansive (and expensive) network of in-street sensors that San Francisco used to monitor occupancy and make rate adjustments. Fortunately, similar results may be possible with simpler methods, such as using transaction data or occasional manual surveys.

Third, sensors provide a precise estimate of average occupancy, but that measurement only loosely relates to cruising, driver frustration, and the probability that a block is full.

Finally, while a performance-based strategy such as SF*park* can succeed, most of the gain occurs simply from pricing parking in the first place. For a city such as San Francisco, extending meter hours into high-demand times in the evenings and on Sundays, or pricing parking on unmetered residential streets, would provide a bigger win than adjusting rates where meters already exist. At least in San Francisco, cruising does not appear to be a major problem when there are meters in operation. Rather, the fabled scarcity of parking in urban neighborhoods results primarily from drivers searching for a *free* parking space.

This chapter previously appeared in ACCESS, *Fall 2016, where it was adapted from "Is the Curb 80% Full or 20% Empty? Assessing the Impacts of San Francisco's Parking Experiment," published in* Transportation Research Part A: Policy and Practice *63 (May 2014): 76–92.*

40

Optimizing the Use of Public Garages: Pricing Parking by Demand

By Gregory Pierce, Hank Willson, and Donald Shoup

Cities are beginning to use demand-based prices to manage their on-street parking. San Francisco, for example, created SF*park*, which adjusts the prices at 7,000 parking meters to achieve a target occupancy rate for on-street spaces. The program has received much publicity for adjusting parking prices based on demand.

While on-street parking management programs receive attention, cities routinely build off-street parking garages at great cost with scant public scrutiny. Other than recovering the cost of building and maintaining the garages, cities appear to have few clear goals for managing their off-street parking supply.

In the same SF*park* program that makes demand-responsive adjustments to on-street prices, however, San Francisco also implements demand-based pricing for public parking garages. The program has experimented with adjusting the prices of 11,500 off-street parking spaces in 14 city-owned parking garages.

OPTIMAL PRICING POLICY FOR PUBLIC GARAGES

Effective parking management presents a challenge because, like airline seats and hotel rooms, parking spaces are perishable goods—they must be used within a short span of time or they become worthless. Effective management of a perishable good has two essential components. First, perishable goods must be sold within a limited time period. Seats on airplanes or rooms in a hotel, for example, are wasted if they go unused, and the time that a parking space goes unused cannot be resold later. Second, perishable goods are optimally managed by charging different prices at different times or for different people. In the private parking industry, price differentiation is already common practice as shown by the lower hourly rates offered to early birds or by validated parking for nearby shop customers.

Cities should treat their public garages as hotels for cars, and parking prices should resemble hotel prices that vary according to demand. Hotel prices vary according to the size of rooms, the day of the week, the season, and other factors, and so can parking prices. Hotels that operated without variable prices would quickly generate all the complaints that are now common with parking.

Effective parking management requires reasonable revenue goals. For off-street parking, cities commonly set revenue goals based on the cost to build and operate garages. A 2014 study in 12 U.S. cities found that construction costs averaged $24,000 per space for aboveground parking structures and $34,000 per space for underground garages (Chapter 3). Low parking prices may not recoup the construction costs and can lead to a financial loss, but prices high enough to recoup the construction costs can leave substantial vacancies.

In public garages, cities must also balance the competing goals of reliable availability and high occupancy. Low occupancy means parking spaces are readily available, but the garage is bringing few visitors to adjacent businesses, schools, and other amenities. Full occupancy means the lot maximizes parking space use, but then it denies service to new customers. The greater the variation in demand during a time period, the more difficult it is to balance the two goals. In order to achieve a balance, a driver's probability of finding an open space upon arrival is a key guide to setting prices.

If the capital and operating costs of a private parking lot are fixed, the owner will attempt to maximize revenue, even if many spaces remain vacant. Figure 40-1 illustrates how a 100-space garage can maximize revenue with only a 50 percent occupancy rate. Price is represented on the x-axis, and the demand curve slopes downward. The garage is full when the price is zero, and has zero occupancy when the price is $1 an hour. Maximum revenue, $25 an hour, occurs at a price of $0.50 an hour ($0.50 × 50 occupied spaces = $25). But leaving half the parking spaces vacant is not optimal for a public garage since its purpose is to make parking available, not simply to make a profit. A parking system accommodates users most efficiently at an occupancy rate between 85 and 95 percent of capacity. At this rate, entering cars don't have to search throughout the

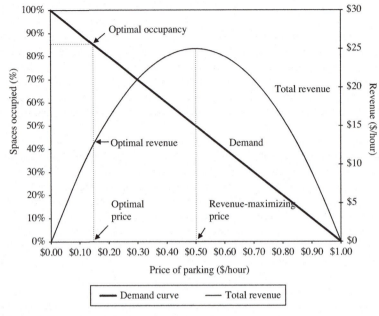

Figure 40-1   Parking prices, occupancy, and revenue

entire system to find a vacant space, yet most spaces are occupied. If a city aims for an 85 percent occupancy rate to manage the parking supply efficiently, the garage would price parking at $0.15 an hour, yielding total revenue of $12.75 an hour ($0.15 × 85 occupied spaces = $12.75). Therefore, in this example, pricing parking to achieve efficient occupancy generates only about half the maximum total possible revenue.

A city should have three goals when setting garage occupancy targets: ready availability, high occupancy, and revenue. By relying on a single target, such as revenue, cities leave the other two goals unfulfilled. No evidence suggests the weight that cities should assign to each of these goals, but cities should manage their parking garages based on explicit concern for each of these goals.

THE STATUS QUO

Private investors rarely build stand-alone parking garages because of their high construction costs and low returns. Cities also make private investment in commercial garages less profitable by underpricing curb parking and requiring off-street parking for residential and commercial buildings.

Cities often provide parking for hypothetical customers and workers who they think would shop or work in the area if cheap, plentiful parking were available. Cities also build off-street parking to satisfy particular merchants or to make redevelopment plans more palatable to local residents. And while public garages nearly always lose money, proponents argue they are necessary to enhance urban growth, with little research to back this claim.

Unlike most other cities, San Francisco controls a substantial portion of its off-street parking supply. City-managed garages account for as much as 60 percent of the publicly available off-street parking spaces in some neighborhoods, and about 16 percent of the city's total off-street parking supply. The San Francisco Municipal Transportation Authority (SFMTA) manages both the city's parking and its extensive public transportation systems—bus, streetcar, and metro.

Before SF*park*, the SFMTA set parking prices in garages to cover costs rather than to manage occupancy, and it charged drivers more to park in off-street than in on-street spaces. This pricing system encouraged drivers to cruise the streets hoping to find a free or cheap on-street space, while commuters and long-term parkers used the garages as all-day car storage. On-street metered parking was usually scarce, while garages had many available spaces most of the time.

THE INNOVATIONS OF SF*PARK* IN OFF-STREET SPACE MANAGEMENT

SF*park* adjusts off-street parking prices every three months based on the parking demand at each garage during five different time intervals in the day. The city aims for each garage to have an average occupancy no lower than 40 percent and no higher than 80 percent at all times. If expected garage occupancy exceeds 80 percent for a particular time period, SFMTA raises the hourly rate for that time period by $0.50. If expected garage occupancy is below 40 percent during a time period, the hourly rate is lowered by $0.50 for the subsequent quarter. SF*park's* rate-setting policies for both on- and off-street parking have brought garage hourly rates equal to—and in many cases below—nearby parking meter rates, giving drivers a financial incentive to go straight to the garages rather than cruise for on-street parking.

In addition to varying hourly prices based on demand, SF*park's* garage policy addresses non-price factors. For instance, rush-hour garage queues cause drivers to lose time. In response, program managers adjusted the time requirements for early bird parking and added off-peak discounts to lessen the peak congestion in and near garages at

Table 40-1   SF*park* off-street parking rate variations

Hourly rates	Based on demand, vary over five time periods: 12 am to 9 am 9 am to 12 pm 12 pm to 3 pm 3 pm to 6 pm 6 pm to 12 am
Off-peak discounts	For drivers who enter the garage before the morning rush hour (8:30 am), commonly called "early birds," or those who leave after the evening rush hour (6:30 pm)
Monthly rates	Vary depending on whether a space is reserved or used for carpooling
Daily maximum rates	Charged for 24 hours of parking
Merchant validations	Reduces or entirely covers a driver's parking cost

rush hour. As a result, fewer cars now enter during the morning rush and exit during the evening rush.

SF*park* has not, however, simplified the hourly rates for parking prices. Pricing based on the time of day and on the level of demand has actually made hourly rates more complicated than they once were. The hourly price, and thus the total parking charge, now depends on when the drivers park, not simply on how long they stay. Drivers may also pay multiple rates depending on when they park. For instance, a driver might pay a daytime hourly rate for the first portion of a parking session, and a lower evening rate for the remainder of the stay.

Consider the variety of price options available to a driver who wants to park in a garage (Table 40-1). For researchers and SFMTA, varied parking rates, price maximums, discounts, and validations make calculating drivers' responses to price changes difficult because parkers each pay different prices and no one price fully describes how much any particular driver might pay.

SF*PARK* RESULTS: PRICE, OCCUPANCY AND REVENUE

Similar to findings for on-street parking under SF*park*, hourly parking prices in individual garages varied widely in response to local demand. Planners will never be able to accurately predict the prices needed to achieve the target occupancy for every garage at every time period. Instead, the best way to achieve a target occupancy goal is to do what SF*park* already does: adjust prices in response to the observed occupancy based on trial and error. Because most garages initially had many vacant spaces on most days and at most times, the average hourly price of parking across all garages fell by 20 percent during the program's first year. During the program's second year, the average daytime hourly prices at SF*park* garages rose, but still remained lower than the average price before the program started.

While prices fell modestly, average weekday occupancy for hourly parkers rose by 38 percent in the first two years of the program. As Figure 40-2 shows, this positive trend remained remarkably consistent across normal working hours, with more erratic responses during the early morning and late evening periods.

The SF*park* program presented a large revenue risk for SFMTA. Total revenue across garages dipped at the outset of the program, but recovered to *surpass* pre-program revenue by the end of fiscal year 2013. By comparison, revenue from non-experimental garages remained flat throughout the period. In the end, SFMTA's experiment clearly paid off.

After SFMTA's first two years of dynamic pricing, drivers paid lower hourly prices. Not surprisingly, drivers facing lower prices are more eager to park in garages, leading to higher occupancy. As a result, San Francisco has slightly increased its revenue yield from the garages with demand-responsive pricing. In other words, everyone wins under SF*park*. The combination of lower prices, higher occupancy, and more revenue benefits drivers, businesses, and the city.

SF*park*'s positive effects are best illustrated by looking more closely at the Performing Arts Garage, which is located near the Civic Center neighborhood in downtown. Before the SF*park* program, garage daytime rates were set uniformly at $2.50 per hour, and peak weekday hourly occupancy averaged only about 25 percent. Under SF*park*, low

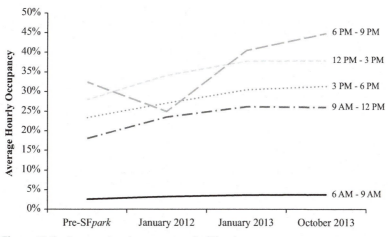

Figure 40-2   Average hourly occupancy in SF*park* garages

occupancy rates resulted in repeated hourly price reductions every three months. By January 2013, hourly rates for the Performing Arts Center had dropped to the statutory minimum of $1 per hour. As prices dropped, the garage's peak weekday occupancy rose to about 85 percent and total revenue increased more than 10 percent.

IMPROVING SF*PARK*'S OFF-STREET PROGRAM

Despite SF*park*'s success in improving off-street parking management, the program can make several further improvements. Garage prices are not reduced unless occupancy falls below 40 percent and are not increased unless occupancy rises above 80 percent. SFMTA reasons that maintaining such a wide range will help to avoid peak occupancy above 95 percent. But since peak occupancy rarely, if ever, exceeds 95 percent in any garage, SF*park* should set the minimum target range at 60 percent occupancy or higher to optimize use, even if this policy leads to revenue loss.

Price changes should also be more transparent. SF*park* maintains explicit criteria for adjusting prices based on observed occupancy, but in practice, it does not always follow these guidelines. Refraining from rule-based price changes distorts the off-street parking market and invites criticism from parking reform skeptics. SFMTA should, at a minimum, publicly explain its rationale if it sets prices to achieve alternative objectives.

The principles of performance-based pricing for municipal garages can also be applied to parking assets managed by other public entities. For instance, universities located in dense urban areas often maintain parking lots and garages on their campuses. These spaces are occupied during the day primarily by those with permits, and many remain vacant in the evening. Reducing the price of parking in the evening to increase occupancy of the garages can increase attendance at cultural events, improve the sense of community, enhance safety, and relieve parking congestion on nearby residential streets.

CONCLUSION

SF*park* reduced parking prices in the municipal garages, increased garage occupancy, and increased parking revenue. The program's results show that cities can more effectively manage their parking assets to maximize public benefits by setting occupancy rather than revenue targets. Thus, small changes to management practices can produce large benefits for cities.

REFERENCES AND FURTHER READING

Barter, Paul. 2010. "Off-Street Parking Policy without Parking Requirements: A Need for Market Fostering and Regulation." *Transport Reviews* 30, no. 5: 571–88.
http://www.tandfonline.com/doi/abs/10.1080/01441640903216958

Pierce, Gregory, and Donald Shoup. 2013. "Getting the Prices Right: An Evaluation of Pricing Parking by Demand in San Francisco." *Journal of the American Planning Association*, 79(1): 67–81.
http://www.tandfonline.com/doi/abs/10.1080/01944363.2013.787307

SFpark. 2014. *Pilot Project Evaluation: The SFMTA's evaluation of the benefits of the SFpark pilot project.* http://sfpark.org/about-the-project/pilot-evaluation

CHAPTER

41

LA Express Park

By Peer Ghent

In 2008, the U.S. Department of Transportation awarded Los Angeles a grant for a pilot project in its downtown to demonstrate the feasibility of an intelligent parking system. Using the latest available technology, the Los Angeles Department of Transportation (LADOT) designed a system to: 1) reduce traffic congestion; 2) increase the availability of on-street parking; and 3) create more travel choices for the public. LADOT was able to draw upon the experience of SF*park,* a similar project that San Francisco began about a year earlier (see Chapters 36, 37, and 38 above).

PROJECT ELEMENTS

The project elements include:

1. vehicle occupancy sensors for each of the 6,300 on-street parking spaces;
2. new technology parking meters that can accept credit card payments, coin payments, and cell phone payments, and that can charge different prices at different times of the day and week;
3. a comprehensive parking guidance system including a website, several parking apps, dynamic message signs, and an interactive voice response system;
4. a sophisticated computer system to integrate all of the parking data; and
5. a pricing engine to determine the desired parking pricing.

LADOT branded the project LA Express Park. It continues to use this brand as it expands the project to other areas of the city.

PARKING POLICIES

LADOT began gathering real-time parking occupancy data for the 6,300 on-street parking spaces in the downtown area in September 2010. Initially the data were limited to approximately 600 spaces to establish a baseline for parking policy decisions before any changes were made and to measure the "before" baseline for subsequently evaluating the effectiveness of LA Express Park.

Operations began in May 2012. Before the project started, most of the parking time limits were one hour between 8 a.m. and 6 p.m. LADOT increased the time limits to two or four hours depending upon the block: predominantly retail blocks were set at two hours, and blocks with less need for turnover were set at four hours. LADOT also extended the meter operating hours to 8 p.m. on blocks where the parking demand warranted.

LADOT implemented demand-based pricing in three phases. Initially it adjusted the prices on all blocks but kept the same price all day. Then, if demand varied during the day, it set different prices depending upon the time of day. Finally, it tested setting the prices in real time based upon current demand. The price changes were in increments of $0.50 or $1.00 per hour. The price points are $0.50, $1.00, $1.50, $2.00, $3.00, $4.00, $5.00 and $6.00 per hour. This approach differed from SF*park*, which elected to make smaller changes, $0.25 or $0.50 per hour. LADOT believed the larger increments would be more likely to achieve the desired changes in driver behavior.

DEMAND-BASED PRICING

In June 2012, LADOT made the initial price changes based upon demand in different locations. By August 2012, it was clear that aligning prices with demand would also require time-of-day pricing on most blocks. LADOT reviewed the demand patterns and divided the weekday enforcement hours into three periods: 8 a.m. to 11 a.m., 11 a.m. to 3 p.m., and 3 p.m. to 8 p.m. On Saturdays, the prices remained constant throughout the day. Parking is free on Sundays and holidays.

By far the biggest challenge is determining the demand-based price that best meets the project goals. After trying several approaches, the LA Express Park team chose an algorithm that compares the share of time more than 90 percent of parking spaces are occupied with the share of time less than 70 percent of parking spaces are occupied. The goal is to set the prices to maximize the time the parking occupancy is between 70 percent and 90 percent.

LADOT made eight price changes in the first year. The number of required price changes declined each year. By 2016, the prices had stabilized, and LADOT is now implementing price changes only one to three times per year. Importantly, most of the price changes moved steadily toward an optimum price. Few prices cycled between increases and decreases.

PARKING GUIDANCE

LA Express Park uses both demand-based pricing and parking guidance to manage on-street parking. The parking guidance system shows the locations for all the off-street public parking. For the publicly owned off-street parking structures, it also shows the available occupancy. Many of the privately owned off-street parking lots have been using demand-based pricing for years. Typically, they have discounted "early bird" rates to ensure that most of their capacity is fully used throughout the day. As a lot fills with cars, the operators will often post a higher price for parking.

While there are no revenue goals for LA Express Park, the project team recognized that to gain the sustained support of the mayor and city council the project had to be at least revenue neutral. If revenue were to increase, that would be a plus. The principal goal, though, was to reduce traffic congestion and the associated pollution. By increasing parking availability in the highly congested areas and guiding drivers to the available parking that fit their requirements for price and convenience, there would be less need to search for available parking. The hypothesis was that reduced search time would reduce the number of cars circling and thus reduce congestion and improve drivers' parking experience.

On-street parking occupancy sensors provide data to support: 1) parking guidance; 2) guided parking enforcement; and 3) demand-based pricing. For parking guidance, the sensor data are sufficient. For guided enforcement, the data must be integrated with the payment status of the parking space. As for demand-based pricing, the sensor data must be analyzed along with the current parking policies to determine the policy changes required to meet the project's goals.

Using sensor data for parking guidance is very straightforward. The sensors indicate whether parking is vacant or occupied, and the parking guidance system communicates that information for new parkers.

Similarly, using sensor data combined with payment data to guide parking enforcement officers to potential violators appears straightforward. Depending upon the local parking laws, however, this task can be very challenging. California allows drivers with disabled parking placards to park at an on-street meter free with no time limit. If few drivers qualified for a disabled placard, this would not cause a problem. In California, however, approximately 12 percent of the licensed drivers have disabled placards. Without filtering the data, parking enforcement officers would be guided to potential violators who were legal because they had a disabled placard. As long as this condition persists, the parking enforcement officer receives many false signals that reduce the incentive to use the guided enforcement system. Thus, the anticipated benefits of more efficient enforcement are lost.

For guided enforcement to be effective, the parking management system must filter the data to eliminate the unpaid spaces that have disabled placards. For example, you could eliminate from the potential violator list all of the spaces for which no payment had been made and target the spaces for which payment had initially been made, but the paid time had expired.

Prior to late September 2012, there was a tow-away, no-stopping policy in effect from 3 p.m. to 7 p.m. on many streets. This policy was strictly enforced, and few cars parked during those hours. LADOT then removed the no-stopping policy on several streets, and parking occupancy from 3 p.m. to 7 p.m. increased as one would have predicted. Somewhat surprisingly, occupancy also increased significantly early in the day before 10 a.m. One possible explanation is that these parking spaces became suitable for all-day parking by disabled placard holders. With the previous no-stopping policy, having to move their cars at 3 p.m. inconvenienced the placard holders.

RESULTS

For the first seven months of the demonstration project in downtown Los Angeles, all the occupancy changes were in the desired direction. Fewer parking spaces were occupied over 90 percent of the time; fewer parking spaces were occupied less than 70 percent of the time; and more parking spaces were occupied between 70 percent and 90 percent of the time.

Beginning in January 2013, there was a gradual increase in total occupancy. In part, this may reflect an improved economy and the impact of economic development in the downtown area. The increase in total occupancy puts upward pressure on the over 90 percent occupied spaces. In addition, the data show a reduction in the number of paying parkers in the higher-price, high-congestion areas. It appears, however, that those who use disabled placards to park free quickly fill the parking spaces made available by higher pricing.

Lower parking prices in the under-occupied areas likely encouraged some drivers to park on-street instead of in more expensive off-street facilities. If true, this behavior would not affect traffic congestion because it is generally very easy to find available parking on the blocks priced at $0.50 per hour.

By August 2013, many of the price changes were up against the limit set by the city council that prices could change from the baseline by no more than plus or minus 50 percent. Therefore, LADOT sought and received city council approval to raise rates by as much as 100 percent of the base rate and to lower rates to $0.50 per hour. LADOT had determined that if the recommended rate were to go below $0.50 per hour, there was not enough parking meter revenue to justify the cost of operating the parking meter (maintenance, collection, credit card charges, etc.).

Total on-street parking occupancy has increased steadily since the project began in May 1012. As shown in Figure 41-1, the total occupancy during parking enforcement hours for the entire project area increased from 57 percent to almost 70 percent in the first three years. Unpaid occupancy rose during the same period from 25 percent to almost 30 percent. Figure 41-2 shows unpaid occupancy as a percent of total occupancy was practically constant at about 43 percent of total occupied hours.

The increase in parking demand over time and the large number of drivers who were not required to pay for parking made it very difficult to influence demand in the congested zones through pricing. After January 2013, the percentage of time the parking spaces were occupied over 90 percent of the time increased despite the increases in the hourly rates for parking. LADOT concluded that as long as the demand from the non-paying parkers exceeded the supply of available parking spaces, it made no sense to increase the hourly rates higher than $6 per hour.

With the new authority from city council, LADOT implemented additional rate changes in February and May 2014. In 2016, more than 3,000 metered spaces have an hourly rate of $0.50 for at least one time period during the week. The minimum rate before the project started was $1.00 per hour. Table 41-1 shows the distribution of the average parking rates before the start of the project (May 2012) and the distribution after two years of operation (May 2014). Not including the revenue from the longer enforcement hours, meter revenue is up 2.5 percent since the start of the project. Paid occupancy is up 16 percent, and the average hourly rate is down 11 percent.

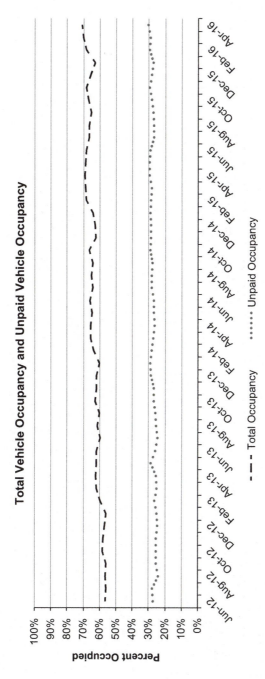

Figure 41-1 Total occupancy and unpaid occupancy as percent of available parking hours

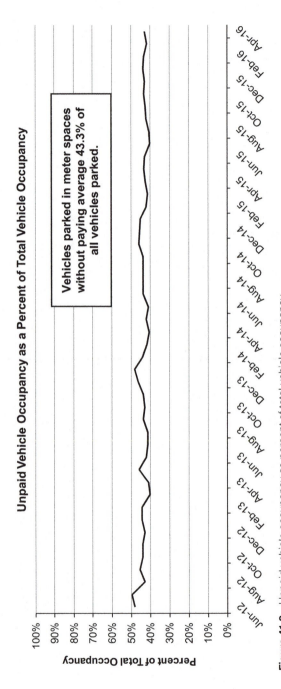

Figure 41-2 Unpaid vehicle occupancy as percent of total vehicle occupancy

Table 41-1 Distribution of average hourly parking rates prior to start of project and after two years of operation

Distribution of Average Hourly Parking Rates		
Average Hourly Parking Rates	May 2012	May 2014
$6.00		30
$5.00		246
$4.00	414	816
$3.00	1,947	840
$2.00	821	430
$1,50		628
$1.00	3,036	1,013
$0.50		2,289

PUBLIC ACCEPTANCE

Thus far, the public has been very accepting of the changes in meter policies. While many are simply not aware of the changes, intercept surveys found that people who do know about the price changes view them as fair. Surveys of parkers in February 2013 revealed that: 25 percent of the respondents knew of LA Express Park and the supporting parking apps; 24 percent knew that some prices change throughout the day; and 37 percent thought time-of-day pricing is the best way to solve parking problems. They are pleased that they have options when parking downtown. For the high-demand areas, there is now a better chance that they will find an available parking space, but they will most likely have to pay a higher price. In most cases, the higher on-street price will be less than the price for nearby off-street parking.

For those seeking a lower-cost parking alternative, the parking guidance system informs them of available parking options. Because each block face is priced independently, it is now possible to find less expensive parking around the block, across the street, or within a short walk. Previously, the pricing was by parking meter zones, and all block faces within the zone had the same price. Furthermore, without a parking guidance system, the parker had no way of knowing where there was lower-cost parking available and, even if he or she did know, it was likely to be a long walk!

REVENUE

The revenue generated from parking meters and parking citations is very important to the city of Los Angeles. Effective parking enforcement is necessary to ensure the public is abiding by the parking policies. For LA Express Park, there were no measureable changes in enforcement activities; therefore the project did not influence net citation revenues either up or down. Although increased meter revenue was not a goal for the project, it was up slightly for comparable enforcement hours. Overall, LA Express Park was essentially revenue neutral.

LA Express Park improved the drivers' parking experience without affecting net parking meter revenue. The increase in revenue was offset by the operating costs associated with the sensors, the parking guidance systems, and the computer systems integrating the data. In other words, taken as a whole, the base rates in place before the start of the project were close to the demand-based rates set by LA Express Park.

To understand this phenomenon, one has to look at the history of the parking meter rates. For 20 years prior to 2008, most parking meter rates in Los Angeles had not increased. Except for downtown, most of the hourly rates were $0.25 per hour. Recognizing that metered parking was severely underpriced, LADOT made recommendations to the city council to raise the rates. The council approved doubling all of the parking rates and set the minimum rate at $1.00 per hour.

For the 6,300 parking spaces in LA Express Park, it appears that the doubling of rates produced reasonable results. Where prices had already increased from $0.25 per hour to $1.00 per hour, however, it appears that many were overpriced. Reducing those spaces back to $0.50 per hour increased the paid occupancy and made the meter spaces more productive.

The new meter technology employed in LA Express Park has had a dramatic impact on meter revenue. By accepting credit cards, the new meters allow the parker to pay the required fees without having to carry a bag full of quarters. Rather than short-pay the meter and gamble that the vehicle won't be cited, the parker tends to buy insurance by over-paying with a credit card. Equally important is the meter management system that reports meter maintenance issues. By texting the parking-meter technician when a meter requires maintenance, repairs are made promptly and meter downtime is less than 1 percent. This compares to an estimated 20 percent down-time for coin-only, non-reporting meters.

Because of the observed performance improvements for new meter technology, LADOT had new meters in place before they began collecting baseline data. New meter technology did not bias the observed data for LA Express Park because the meter technology did not change during the pilot program.

Recognizing the positive net revenue impact of new technology parking meters, LADOT made plans to replace all of its 35,000 on-street single-space meters. These plans were completed in December 2012. Citywide parking meter revenue increased from approximately $25 million per year to over $50 million per year after the new meters were installed. For jurisdictions where hourly meter rates have not kept up with inflation, the introduction of new meter technology and demand-based pricing may significantly increase parking meter revenue.

CONCLUSIONS

Demand-based pricing for parking when combined with effective parking guidance can make the parking experience much more pleasant for drivers. By reducing the time spent searching for available parking, traffic congestion and the associated pollution are also reduced. The consumer is better able to find parking that meets his or her needs for convenience and economy.

As more people become aware of their parking options, demand-based pricing should lead to a better distribution of parked cars. For the high-demand areas, some drivers will be discouraged by the high prices and will park elsewhere or use public transportation. This will increase parking availability for those willing to pay the higher price. For the underused areas, lower parking prices and longer time limits will encourage an increase in paid parking hours and possibly an increase in total parking meter revenue. Parkers who seek lower prices will be willing to walk a bit farther to reach their destinations.

Based upon the experience in Los Angeles, demand patterns for parking during the week in downtown areas are very stable. This observation allows for demand-based prices to be set through sampling techniques; good results may be obtained without having to monitor parking occupancy for all spaces 24/7. The quality of the parking guidance will decline but may be adequate for most situations.

Properly communicated to the public, demand-based pricing will be viewed as being fair to the consumer. Therefore, in cases where price adjustments have not happened in years, demand-based pricing can be a path to increased revenues. This was not the case in Los Angeles because prices had doubled just before implementing demand-based pricing.

The most effective means to increase parking revenue is to install reliable, up-to-date parking meters and revenue control devices. Parking meters must accept multiple forms of payment; coins are not practical for payment of higher hourly parking rates. Sophisticated locks and security systems are necessary to minimize the possibility of pilferage. Credit card payments must comply with Payment Card Industry (PCI) standards. Coin collection, coin counting, and coin transport to the bank must be monitored by effective security measures. In Los Angeles, following these procedures more than doubled revenue from parking meters; demand-based pricing had a negligible effect on net parking meter revenue but has improved a motorist's ability to find available parking.

Accordingly, revenue should be a secondary consideration when planning a congestion pricing program for parking. The real benefit of parking congestion pricing is to make available more parking spaces in high demand areas and to increase parking usage in underoccupied blocks. In addition, the public sees the benefit of the program and believes that the pricing changes are fair. Public acceptance of these programs is much more likely when increasing revenue is not the primary goal.

REFERENCES AND FURTHER READING

Zoeter, Onno, Christopher Dance, Stéphane Clinchant, and Jean-Marc Andreoli. 2014. "New Algorithms for Parking Demand Management and a City Scale Deployment," *Proceedings of the 20th ACM SIGKDD International Conference on Knowledge Discovery and Data Mining*. Pages 1819–28.

42

The Politics and Economics of Parking on Campus

By Donald Shoup

Big universities resemble small cities. They have athletic facilities, concert halls, housing, hospitals, libraries, museums, offices, restaurants, stores, theaters, and—of course—parking. Big universities also have big transportation problems, and to solve these problems, a few universities have reformed their pricing policies for both parking and public transportation. The promising results of these reforms suggest that cities can adopt similar policies to reduce congestion, clean the air, and conserve energy.

Universities have adopted two main approaches to campus parking policy—one political and the other economic. The political approach relies on administered rules and regulations, while the economic approach relies on market prices.

ADMINISTERED PARKING

University of California president Clark Kerr wrote, "I have sometimes thought of the modern university as a series of individual faculty entrepreneurs held together by a common grievance over parking." Earlier, as chancellor of the Berkeley campus, he remarked, "The chancellor's job has come to be defined as providing parking for the faculty, sex for the students, and athletics for the alumni." More recently, UCLA Chancellor Albert Carnesale said, "At UCLA, parking is the most important issue for everyone." UCLA has more parking spaces than all but one other university in the United States—Texas A&M. If parking is so abundant, how did it become more important than sex and athletics? Campus parking problems, I will argue, stem from mispricing, not scarcity.

FEUDAL HIERARCHY

In academia, you are not what you drive so much as where you park. At Berkeley, for example, only Nobel Laureates earn the highest status symbol on campus—a reserved parking space. After Professor Charles Townes won the 1964 Nobel Prize in physics and Berkeley put his name on a space, Townes commented, "It saves me a whole lot of time. The cost is not the big thing—it's the convenience." Shortly after Professor Daniel McFadden won the 2000 Nobel Prize in economics, he received a standing ovation during halftime at a Cal football game. When asked which was better, the adulation of 50,000 people or the lifetime reserved parking space, he replied, "Well, the parking space goes on and on. It's considered slightly more important than the prize itself." The California Institute of Technology also reserves spaces for Nobel Laureates. After Professor Rudolph Marcus won the 1992 Nobel Prize in chemistry and a colleague saw his name on the reserved space outside his office, Marcus remarked, "Well, the Nobel Prize has to be worth something." The University of Groningen in the Netherlands adopted a more sustainable policy when it reserved a special bicycle rack for Professor Ben Feringa, who won the 2016 Nobel Prize in chemistry.

Universities often lead society in advocating social and economic equality, but their complex parking hierarchies make the *Titanic* look like a one-class ship. UCLA has 175 different types of parking permits, carefully ranked according to the status of faculty, staff, and students. Major donors also receive campus parking permits, based on the size of their donations. Parking privileges are cumulative, which means that holders of higher-rank permits can park in the spaces reserved for their own rank as well as in the spaces available to permits of a lower rank. UCLA reserves the best parking spaces for the coveted X permit, whose holders can park in the premium spaces reserved exclusively for X permits and also in the spaces for all other permits. The X permit is the ultimate campus status symbol, equivalent to a knighthood. If UCLA is an ivory tower, the parking system is its moat.

PARKING ANXIETY

Because demand exceeds supply when parking spaces are priced far below their cost, UCLA administrators have devised a "point system" that ranks students' priority for campus permits. A student's chance of receiving a permit is based on a jumble of factors that supposedly measure the "need" for parking. Each factor is assigned a point value, and the points are totaled to decide a student's priority for parking. Yet students' anxiety about the point system extends far beyond the simple issue of *whether* they get a parking permit; point totals also determine *where* they park. As Bob Hope joked, "It takes four years to get through UCLA, or five if you park in Lot 32." Because a permit to park in remote Lot 32 costs the same as a permit to park at the center of campus, students whose point totals put them at a great remove will feel slighted as long as other students pay the same price to park in more central locations. Shoup (2008, 128–135) explores the bizarre methods that UCLA and other universities use to distribute student parking permits.

Parking may seem trivial, but it's a serious problem in the minds of many students. In a 1983 survey of UCLA students, 70 percent reported parking as a problem, while only 28 percent felt their writing skills were a problem, and only 24 percent felt their math skills were a problem. Another survey in 1989 found almost identical results. Sixty-nine percent of students reported that parking was a major problem, while only 12 percent reported "too much school work" as a major problem. Perhaps because of these depressing findings, UCLA has not conducted similar studies in recent years.

PARKING IS A POSITIONAL GOOD

In jockeying for parking, politicians make academics look almost egalitarian. Consider this story told by Christopher Hicks in the Office of Management and Administration during the first Bush administration:

> There are fifteen parking spaces there right next to the West Wing. So I put all the new Assistants to the President ... there so they had the best parking spaces. ... I had one guy ... [he] found me literally ... outside the Oval office ... on inauguration morning and started screaming at me for, (1) I hadn't gotten artwork hung up in his office, and (2) I had the audacity to put him at the end of that line of parking spaces. He didn't want to be number fifteen, closest to Pennsylvania Avenue; he wanted to be number one (Shoup 2005, 26–27).

Parking envy is a perfect example of what Oxford University economist Fred Hirsch termed a "positional good." Because positional goods are valued for their relative status, competition for them becomes a zero-sum game in which one's gain is canceled by another's loss. If the angry person in the fifteenth parking space is promoted to the first position and everyone else is shifted one space down, the gain to one is offset by losses to 14 others.

Parking is even more positional in Hollywood, where status-seeking is also rampant. In the film industry, as Burt Reynolds observed, your parking space knows before you do when your career is in decline— someone else's name is on the sign when you pull into your reserved space at the studio.

AVERAGE-COST PRICING

Since the price of a UCLA parking permit is far below the cost of a new parking space, drivers who park in a new structure pay only a small fraction of the marginal cost of their parking. For example, UCLA opened a $47-million, 1,500-space parking structure in 2003. The capital and operating expenses were $223 per space per month, but the price of a parking permit was only $55 a month. Because the capital and operating costs of parking are so high and the permit price is so low, new parking structures have a long payback period (the number of years before the accumulated cash inflow from operations will repay the initial capital cost). One campus parking structure opened in 2004 had a payback period of 30 years. How does this compare with the payback periods for other campus investments? UCLA's criterion for investing in energy conservation is that the payback period must not exceed three years (the money saved by reducing energy use must repay the capital cost in three years or less). For a campus committed to sustainability, it seems unwise to reject solar power that will take only four years to repay its capital cost but build a parking structure that will take 30 years to repay its capital cost and will also—by attracting more cars to campus—increase energy consumption, traffic congestion, and air pollution. When it comes to promoting sustainability, UCLA seems to focus first on sustaining its Parking Service.

The difference between the high cost of a new parking structure and the low price charged for parking in it creates a substantial deficit. UCLA finances this deficit by raising the prices charged for all the other parking spaces on campus. Because the marginal cost (the cost of adding another space to the parking supply) is so far above the average cost (the total cost of the system divided by the total number of parking spaces), each new space added to the parking supply drives up this average cost. Permit prices that cover the system's average cost increase every time a new parking structure is built, yet the parking shortage persists. Even after spending $358 million (in 2002 dollars) to construct 19,700 parking spaces between 1961 and 2002, UCLA did not provide a parking space for every student willing to pay the system's average cost for a permit. UCLA's most recent underground garage, completed in 2016, cost $84,000 per space to construct, and there is still a waiting list for parking on campus.

Most universities follow this average-cost pricing approach. A professor at the University of Illinois told me that after he recommended charging the users of new parking structures a price that would cover the cost of building them, an astonished administrator responded, "Why, if we did that, we wouldn't build any parking structures!" This objection is unfounded, of course, because parking structures can be built where drivers are willing to pay the cost-recovery price of parking in them.

INCREASED VEHICLE TRAVEL

If you build it, they will come. Parking spaces don't create vehicle travel, but they clearly enable it. Vehicle travel induced by new parking spaces is similar to vehicle travel induced by new roads. Parking-induced vehicle travel is not a problem for UCLA, but it is for Los Angeles, which has the worst traffic congestion and air pollution in the nation. In 2014, the Texas Transportation Institute estimated the annual cost of traffic congestion in the Los Angeles metropolitan area was $13.4 billion. To put this congestion cost in perspective, in 2014 the total tax revenue (property taxes, sales taxes, hotel taxes, utility taxes, and all other taxes) in the City of Los Angeles was only $4 billion. In this congested environment, building garages that increase automobile travel to campus makes a bad situation for the region even worse.

A FAILING GRADE ON CAMPUS PARKING

Campus parking is closer to communism than to capitalism, but it manages to combine the worst features of both systems. Universities distribute parking according to status and purported need but rarely give any preference to low-income staff or students. Providing cheap parking on expensive land inflates the demand for travel by car and does nothing to help those who cannot afford a car. So consider a novel alternative: let prices do the planning.

DEMAND-BASED PARKING PRICES

With all the intellect on campus, one would expect universities to teem with creative ideas about how to solve the parking problem.

Nevertheless, most universities price parking at average cost and distribute permits according to status or assumed need. Research in economics, political science, and urban planning seems to have little impact on parking administrators. Naturally, professors should not expect to decide how to allocate campus parking because universities hire faculty to think and they hire administrators to make decisions. Problems can arise when the faculty try to make decisions and administrators try to think. Nevertheless administrators should not totally ignore academic research in making university policy.

A few universities do charge higher prices for the more convenient parking spaces in high demand. Washington State University, for example, uses a zone system of parking prices. The price in each zone is set according to three criteria: proximity (location with respect to major destinations on campus); quality of the facility (garage, paved surface, or gravel surface); and demand (competition for the zone). WSU sets fees that allow drivers to choose the parking spaces they are willing to pay for. Taking the zone system to its logical economic conclusion, prices for parking can be adjusted to balance demand and supply at each location and time.

Flexible prices can balance demand—which varies over time—with the fixed supply of spaces. We can call this balance the Goldilocks Principle of parking prices: the price is too high if too many spaces are vacant and too low if no spaces are vacant. When a few spaces are vacant, the price is just right. If a parking shortage or surplus regularly occurs at any time in any location, the price can be nudged up or down. If Goldilocks prices keep a few spaces vacant at every location, drivers can always find an available space near their destination.

Universities can set the price of parking to match the demand for the available supply at each location and time. Prices will be lower in less convenient locations and at off-peak hours, and parking can be free whenever and wherever there is excess capacity even at a zero price, such as on weekends and during vacations. Free parking at off-peak hours will encourage students to come to campus during uncrowded times to use the library and athletic facilities, to attend plays and concerts, or to take advantage of the many other resources of the university. Why charge students anything to park when the spaces would otherwise remain empty? Free parking for students at off-peak hours will help to make the campus a livelier and safer place at night and on weekends.

Demand-based parking prices will also reveal where building new parking would be justified. If high prices in some locations produce revenue that would recover the cost of building a new structure, investment in more parking may be warranted. Similarly, low prices will reveal locations where new construction is unwarranted.

CONVERTING FIXED COSTS INTO MARGINAL COSTS

UCLA allocates parking permits to students either for the quarter or the year. Drivers thus pay an upfront cost for the permit and nothing extra for parking on each trip. The zero marginal cost of parking invites permit holders to drive to campus alone, encourages overuse of scarce spaces during peak hours, and leads to shortages that generate demand for even more campus parking. The permit system works well for conventional commuters who drive to campus five days a week and stay there all day. The system does not work as well for students who come to campus only on certain days, who do not remain all day, or who drive to campus only occasionally.

Some universities charge everyone for parking, even those who don't drive to campus. Florida Atlantic University, for example, bundles the cost of a parking permit into tuition payments. Parking is free on every day and, because the cost is hidden, students don't know they pay for parking. Students who are too poor to own a car (or choose not to) subsidize their classmates' free parking.

The structure of parking prices at airports provides an example of what performance-based prices on campus could look like. Everyone expects to pay for parking at airports, and to pay higher prices for parking closer to the terminals. The expensive central spaces encourage short-term parking and carpooling, while the cheaper remote spaces attract long-term parkers and solo drivers. Many passengers use public transportation or shared-ride vehicles to get to and from airports specifically to avoid paying parking fees, which have become a major source of airport revenue. Similarly, once people have become accustomed to campus parking that is priced according to demand, the idea of going back to administered parking will seem as absurd as expecting free parking at airports (desired, perhaps, but understood to be neither realistic nor ultimately beneficial).

Letting prices manage parking will take a heavy burden off university administrators who now devote endless hours debating how to micromanage parking for faculty, staff, and students. Even higher political bodies, all the way up to the president's cabinet in Washington, D.C., waste time talking about parking, as suggested by this description of a cabinet meeting in which Daniel Patrick Moynihan participated: "a cabinet meeting which was mainly bitching about parking in federal buildings—all right, it was supposed to be about office space, but it was also about parking, it always is." What Joseph Schumpeter said about politics in general applies perfectly to the politics of parking in particular: "The typical citizen drops down to a lower level of mental performance as soon as he enters the political field. He argues and analyzes in a way which he would readily recognize as infantile within the sphere of his real interests." If universities let prices allocate parking, everyone can spend more time dealing with academic issues.

PARKING-FEE LEVEL VERSUS PARKING-FEE STRUCTURE

There is a key distinction between the level and the structure of parking fees. The level of the fee refers to the amount, while the structure refers to the way drivers pay it (per hour, day, or month). A fee of $2.50 a day and $50 a month both amount to the same charge for 20 working days a month, but drivers react differently to a daily fee than to a monthly one. Drivers' behavior will respond more to a change in a parking fee's structure than to a change in its level. Imagine, for example, that the price of a parking permit is $50 a month, with no daily option. If a commuter wants to drive to campus twice a week and bike on three days, the rational decision is to buy a parking permit. And with a permit, the marginal cost to park at work on any given day is zero. But once you have bought a car, paid for insurance, and have a parking permit, why not drive every day, since the cost is no greater than riding a bike? If the permit price increases to $60 a month, most commuters will continue driving to work, so the higher prices will do little to reduce vehicle trips.

Suppose the fee level remains $50 a month, but the structure is changed to include the option of paying $2.50 per day (the payments can be automated with license plate readers). In this case, commuters need not buy a permit for an entire month. Instead, they can pay only for the days when they drive to work. On other days, they can ride transit, carpool, walk, or bicycle to work and save the $2.50 daily fee. Offering the option of a daily fee will increase the number of commuters who drive only a few days each month and reduce the number who drive every day. In this way, restructuring the fee without increasing its level can reduce the number of vehicle trips by giving commuters new options.

Another benefit of offering the option of a daily fee is that commuters won't oppose it. Raising a parking fee from $50 to $60 a month can provoke substantial resistance but only slightly reduce solo driving. In contrast, adding the option to pay $2.50 a day can reduce solo driving but arouse no opposition because it does not increase the monthly cost for someone who drives every day.

EFFICIENT LOCATION CHOICES

For parking spaces with hourly prices based on demand and supply, drivers who choose parking locations to reduce their individual costs will park in a pattern that also reduces the total cost of time spent walking to and from the parked cars. Why? Demand-based prices will allocate the central spaces to carpoolers, short-term parkers, and those who place a high value on saving time, for three reasons. First, because carpoolers split the cost of parking among two or more people, they are less sensitive to parking prices and will therefore use the more expensive central spaces. Second, because short-term parkers pay for a short time, they are similarly insensitive to parking prices and will also use the more central spaces. Third, those who place a high value on saving time will use the more central spaces because the time they save outweighs the higher cost (*The High Cost of Free Parking*, Chapter 18).

Drivers may have different destinations on campus on different days, and they can park in different locations on different days. Those who want to spend only a short time on campus—such as for a quick trip to the library—will not have to spend a long time walking from their assigned parking spaces to their final destinations. The faster turnover of the central parking spaces will make them available to more people.

If parking prices increase toward the center of campus, will rich drivers monopolize the central parking spaces? All else being equal, drivers who place a high value on saving time will pay more and walk less, but time value is only one of several factors that determine the optimal parking location. Because parking duration and the number of people in a car also affect location choice, drivers who place a high value on time will not automatically park in the best parking spaces. Many other factors also affect how much drivers are willing to pay to save walking time on any particular trip: whether they are late or tired, whether they are carrying heavy packages, whether they want the exercise, and other circumstances that are unique to each trip. A driver's value of saving time can vary greatly from one trip to another. An old Ford may park in an expensive space at the center of campus if its driver is in a hurry and plans to stay for only a few minutes, while a new Bentley may park in a cheaper space at the periphery if its driver has plenty of time, enjoys walking, and stays all day. To allay equity concerns, any extra revenue that results from higher prices for the central spaces can be used to pay for alternative forms of transportation, such as fare-free public transportation for students, staff, and faculty.

TOP-DECK DISCOUNTS

For administered rather than priced parking, it's difficult to make sure that all the campus parking spaces are well used. The top decks of parking structures pose a special problem. No one, it seems, wants to park on the roof. Cars bake in the sun on hot days, drivers get wet on rainy days, and it's a long drive up and down every day. Spaces on the top decks are the least wanted and the last occupied.

To test whether UCLA's top deck spaces are well used, I took photographs of the top deck of Parking Structure 3 North during Fall 2016 and Winter 2017, and never saw more than four of the 115 spaces occupied. I did once see a skateboarder who said the top deck was his favorite site on campus because it slopes and there are never any cars.

I also used Google Earth to examine historical photos of the campus. Since 2003 24 photos show the top deck of Structure 3 North. Most photos showed no cars on the top deck. The peak occupancy was eleven cars on March 15, 2006, a Wednesday. The lack of oil spots on the top deck also suggests that cars rarely park there. Although there is a long waiting list for students who want a campus parking permit, the chief function of this top deck has been to provide shade for cars parked on the level below it.

After considering the photographic evidence, the UCLA Parking Service sold 160 new permits in Structure 3 to students on the waiting list. Even after selling the new permits, an occupancy count in Structure 3 at the busiest hour of the busiest day of the week found 135 vacant spaces.

Because the top deck of a parking structure is the last place where drivers want to park, some commercial and municipal garages offer discounts for drivers who are willing to park on the roof. These drivers don't hunt through the parking structure hoping to find an open space, but instead save money by heading straight to the top.

Top deck discounts will give drivers who are short of money a new option, and the more convenient spaces they vacate on the lower decks will become available for other drivers. The goal of top deck discounts is to manage the parking system better by using prices to balance the supply and demand for spaces. Parking on campus will become less like a scavenger hunt and more like assigned seating in a theater.

UCLA can afford to charge a bit less for the top deck spaces. At the price of $79 a month for a permit in 2016, the 160 new permits sold in Structure 3 earn $12,640 a month. If UCLA discounts the price for the 115 spaces on the top deck by $10 a month, the discount will cost UCLA $1,150 a month, which is much less than previously empty spaces now earn.

Saving $10 a month for parking on the top deck may not seem important, but students who are barely scraping by may leap at the opportunity. And top deck discounts can ensure that the least convenient parking spaces are occupied, not wasted.

Seats at athletic events, theater performances, and concerts on campus are already priced in proportion to their desirability; charging

Figure 42-1 Top deck discount

less for the least desirable parking spaces will be a small reform with ample precedent. Universities reserve the best parking spaces for top administrators and faculty. Surely they can charge less for students who park on the roof.

FARE-FREE PUBLIC TRANSPORTATION AT UNIVERSITIES

Many U.S. universities contract with public transit agencies to offer fare-free public transportation for their students, staff, and faculty. These programs, with a variety of names, such as UPass and ClassPass, effectively turn university identification cards into public transit passes. The university pays the transit agency an annual lump sum based on expected student ridership, and the transit agency accepts the school's identification cards as transit passes. For every eligible member of the university on any day, a bus ride to campus (or anywhere else) is free. Unlimited access is not free transit, but is instead a new way to pay for public transit. When UCLA established its transit pass program in 2000, bus ridership for commuting to campus increased by 56 percent and solo driving fell by 20 percent during the first year (Brown, Hess, and Shoup 2003).

TRANSPORTATION PRICES TURNED UPSIDE DOWN

Pay-as-you-park pricing for drivers combined with fare-free public transportation will change the price of travel in two important ways. First, the price of parking will switch from a fixed cost per month (with no marginal cost) to a marginal cost per hour or per day (with no fixed cost). Second, the marginal cost per trip on public transportation will fall to zero. The increased marginal cost of parking will reduce vehicle trips, and the reduced marginal cost of using public transportation will increase transit ridership. Taken together, these two price reforms will reduce vehicle travel much more than either one acting alone because in combination they will turn transportation prices upside-down.

In 2016, the Massachusetts Institute of Technology turned its transportation prices upside-down with a new program called Access MIT. It allows the faculty and staff to ride the subway and local bus systems for free, and it also shifts payments for campus parking from annual permits to pay-per-day parking at gated lots. Access MIT makes it easy for commuters to drive to campus on some days and use public transit or bike or walk on other days. Here is MIT's description of the program:

> Access MIT represents the Institute's progressive vision for rethinking the culture of commuting and encouraging sustainable transportation practices. These programs provide commuters with the flexibility to choose, day-to-day, how they would like to commute, and encourage us all to utilize a variety of transportation options over the course of a given week. By connecting the MIT community to flexible, affordable, and low-carbon transportation options, we seek to ease parking demand while positively impacting our campus, community, and environment.

Access MIT caps the total cost of daily parking payments during a year at the current cost of a one-year parking permit, so commuters who drive to campus every day will not pay more than before. This price cap holds harmless all commuters who drive to campus every day, and everyone else gets a new way to save money if they drive on some days but not others. The cap on the annual cost of parking thus removed commuters' opposition to the new daily payments.

By raising the marginal cost of parking, Access MIT reduces the demand for parking on campus, and by reducing vehicle travel to campus it also reduces traffic throughout the city. MIT could reform the system further by providing parking discounts for drivers who arrive before the morning rush hour begins and/or depart after the evening rush hour ends. San Francisco offers these off-peak discounts in its municipal garages, and more cars now enter before the morning rush and depart after the evening rush (Chapter 40).

Pay-by-plate technology makes it simple to use even more sophisticated pricing schemes (Chapter 34). Because cameras read license plate numbers when cars enter and exit each garage, a university can charge for parking by the hour, with prices that vary according to location and time of day. Chapter 40 explains how San Francisco varies the prices in municipal garages according to demand, with lower prices at times of low demand and in less popular locations and higher prices at times of high demand and in more popular locations. Universities can also adopt this variable pricing policy to manage campus parking demand. Rather than pay a flat, daily rate, drivers can pay only for the parking they use. The lower prices during off-peak hours will especially benefit the lower-paid custodial staff who work at night when public transit service is infrequent or unavailable.

By using prices to shave the peaks off parking demand, universities will find that they won't need so many parking spaces to meet the peak demand, and they can convert some of their parking lots to classrooms, research facilities, dormitories, auditoriums, or other uses that better serve academic goals.

CONCLUSION: LET PRICES DO THE PLANNING

In *The Public Use of Private Interest*, Brookings Institution economist Charles Schultze wrote "Harnessing the 'base' motive of material self-interest to promote the common good is perhaps *the* most important social invention mankind has yet achieved. ... [But] the virtually universal characteristic of public policy ... is to *start* from the conclusion that regulation is the obvious answer; the pricing alternative is never considered."

Campus parking policies based on regulations rather than prices are a perfect example of Schultze's argument. Is there a better way to manage campus parking? A lower-cost alternative that is both fair and efficient? A system that relies on incentives rather than on top-down decisions? There is, and some universities already use it: they charge higher prices for the more desirable parking spaces, and they charge users by the hour or day rather than by the month or year. In short, they rely more on the market and less on bureaucracy.

Demand-based parking prices can manage travel demand, but are they fair? At universities, it does not seem unfair that well-paid administrators and senior professors should pay a higher price to park in the most convenient spots in the center of campus, while financially challenged students and staff will pay a much lower price to park at the periphery—especially if the university spends the revenue earned by the higher-priced central spaces to finance fare-free public transportation.

Similarly, in cities it does not seem unfair to charge higher prices for curb parking in the center of business districts than in the more distant spaces—especially if the city spends the revenue to reduce the price of public transportation.

With both demand-based parking prices and fare-free public transit programs, a few universities are leading the way for the rest of society. Some cities already set a goal of about 85 percent occupancy for curb parking in their central business districts and instruct their parking authorities to adjust meter rates to achieve this goal (Chapters 36–41). Similarly, some transit agencies already offer private employers the option to enter into fare-free public transportation contracts that cover all their employees. Demand-priced parking and fare-free transit are appropriate for many different settings, and they can contribute to many important goals of transportation demand management: reduced congestion, cleaner air, energy conservation, and sustainable cities. Few other transportation reforms contribute to so many goals, produce such easily quantifiable benefits, and have such low costs. And all these benefits accrue simply by following the age-old axiom in public economics: get the prices right.

REFERENCES AND FURTHER READING

Brown, Jeffrey, Daniel Hess, and Donald Shoup. 2003. "Fare-Free Public Transit at Universities: An Evaluation," *Journal of Planning Education and Research* 23, no. 1: 69–82. http://shoup.bol.ucla.edu/FareFreePublicTransitAtUniversities.pdf

Brown, Jeffrey, Daniel Hess, and Donald Shoup. 2001. "Unlimited Access." *Transportation* 28, no. 3: 233–67. http://shoup.bol.ucla.edu/UnlimitedAccessUCLA.pdf

Shoup, Donald. 2005. *Parking Cash Out*. Chicago: Planning Advisory Service. http://shoup.bol.ucla.edu/ParkingCashOut.pdf

Shoup, Donald. 2011. *The High Cost of Free Parking*. Revised edition. Chicago: Planners Press.

This chapter is condensed from "The Politics and Economics of Parking on Campus," in The Implementation and Effectiveness of Transport Demand Management Measures: An International Perspective, *edited by Stephen Ison and Tom Rye. Aldershot, UK: Ashgate Publishing, 2008, pp. 121–49.* http://shoup.bol.ucla.edu/PoliticsAndEconomicsOfCampusParking.pdf

43

Cashing Out Employer-Paid Parking

By Donald Shoup

A thing which you enjoyed and used as your own for a long time, whether property or opinion, takes root in your being and cannot be torn away without your resenting the act and trying to defend yourself, however you came by it.

—OLIVER WENDELL HOLMES

Employer-paid parking is an invitation to drive to work alone. It is also the most common tax-exempt fringe benefit offered to employees in the United States. Evidence from a variety of sources shows at least 90 percent of American commuters who drive to work pay nothing to park (Shoup 2005, 3). Tax exemptions are usually justified on grounds that they promote a public purpose, but the tax exemption for employer-paid parking increases traffic congestion, air pollution, and greenhouse gas emissions.

Employer-paid parking subsidizes many commuters who would have driven to work anyway, but it also persuades more commuters to drive to work alone instead of carpooling, riding public transit, biking, or walking to work. A survey of 5,000 commuters and their employers in downtown Los Angeles showed that, on average, employer-paid parking stimulated a 34 percent increase in the number of cars driven to work (Shoup 2005, 8).

THE U.S. INTERNAL REVENUE CODE ENCOURAGES
SOLO DRIVING TO WORK

The U.S. Internal Revenue Code classifies an employer's payment for an employee's parking as a tax-exempt fringe benefit for the employee. But if the employee pays for parking at work, the code does not allow the employee to deduct the parking charge as a work-related expense. Therefore, to take advantage of the tax-exemption for commuter parking, the employer must pay for the employee's parking.

The code exempts employer-paid parking from more than just the federal income tax. The exemption is automatically extended to Social Security taxes, state income taxes, unemployment insurance taxes, and all other payroll taxes. When these related exemptions are taken into account, $1 of employer-paid parking is worth more than $2 in taxable cash income for many employees. Therefore, the asymmetrical tax exemption for employer-paid (but not for employee-paid) parking is a clear and strong financial incentive that has shifted the responsibility for paying for almost all commuter parking from employees to employers, and has thus reduced the commuters' cost of parking to zero. The tax exemption for employer-paid parking is a targeted tax subsidy that has the unfortunate, unintended, and largely unnoticed effect of increasing the number of commuters who drive to work alone.

PARKING CASH OUT

Public transportation advocates have tried for years to end this tax bias because it reduces transit ridership, increases gasoline consumption, and aggravates traffic congestion and air pollution. But eliminating a tax exemption that benefits so many workers—at all income levels—is politically difficult. Thus, it seems quixotic to try to eliminate the special tax exemption for employer-paid parking, no matter how much harm the subsidy does.

Given the general popularity of employer-paid parking subsidies, a short step in the right direction would be to amend the Internal Revenue Code's definition of "qualified parking" that is tax exempt as follows. The text in roman type is the existing definition of tax-exempt "qualified parking" in Paragraph (5), Section 132 (f) of the U.S. Internal Revenue Code, and the italic text is the proposed amendment:

QUALIFIED PARKING. The term "qualified parking" means parking provided to an employee on or near the business premises of the employer ... *if the employer offers the employee the option to receive, in lieu of the parking, the fair-market value of the parking, either as a taxable cash commute allowance or as a mass transit or ridesharing subsidy.*

To qualify for a tax exemption, the parking would have two requirements. First, it is paid by the employer, and, second, the employee has the option to take cash instead of the parking subsidy.

This amendment retains the popular tax exemption for employer-paid parking but requires that employers who subsidize parking must offer commuters the option to take an equivalent cash payment or a mass transit or ridesharing subsidy in lieu of the tax-exempt parking. The proposal has several important benefits:

1. *Commuters have a new choice.* Transportation economists often recommend congestion tolls and parking fees to reduce solo driving, but they are politically unpopular. In contrast, parking cash out doesn't require drivers to pay anything; instead, it rewards commuters for choosing an alternative to driving to work alone. Parking cash out is a buy-back, not a take-away.
2. *Free parking will have an opportunity cost.* When commuters are offered the choice between free parking and nothing, the parking has no opportunity cost. But offering commuters the option to choose either free parking or its cash value makes it clear that parking has a cost, which is the cash not taken. The new "price" for taking the "free" parking increases the perceived cost of solo driving to work.
3. *Parking cash out will benefit employees.* Offering employees the option to cash out their parking subsidies avoids the intractable problem that voters don't like new taxes and motorists don't like to pay for parking. Employers can continue to offer tax-exempt parking subsidies, so long as they broaden the offer. Cashing out adds a new alternative to the typical take-it-or-leave-it choice between a parking subsidy and nothing. Commuters who choose the cash and cease driving to work are clearly better off or they wouldn't make this choice. Commuters who continue driving to work are no worse off, although the foregone cash means that drivers in effect pay for their "free" parking.
4. *Parking cash out will cost employers little or nothing.* The cash-option requirement is a small intrusion in employers' decisions about employee compensation. The requirement is only that if an employer offers to subsidize commuting, the subsidy cannot be confined to parking (and thus driving to work). The only added cost for an employer occurs in the case of commuters who are now offered free parking but do not take it. These commuters would have to be offered the cash value of the parking subsidies

they have not taken, so they will receive the same subsidy as drivers.

5. *Parking cash out will especially benefit low-paid, female, and minority commuters.* Because they are in the lowest tax brackets, the lowest paid workers gain the most after-tax cash from a taxable cash allowance. The cash allowance is also larger in proportion to a lower income, so the cash option would clearly improve the relative wellbeing of the lowest paid workers. Low-income, female, and minority employees are also less likely to drive to work and more likely to take public transit. In the United States, 58 percent of black commuters drive to work alone and 16 percent ride public transit, while 78 percent of white commuters drive to work alone and only 2 percent ride public transit (Shoup 2005, 77).

6. *Parking cash out will increase transportation equity.* Because parking cash out provides an equal benefit to all commuters regardless of their travel choices, it removes discrimination by age, gender, ethnicity, income, or any other demographic variable that may be related to work travel. Avoiding discrimination against non-drivers is simple transportation justice.

7. *Parking cash out will strengthen Central Business Districts.* Employer-paid parking equalizes the cost of parking between downtown and suburban work sites (by making it free to drivers in both places) and does nothing to make downtown superior to a suburban location. Because downtown employers must pay more than suburban employers to provide parking, however, downtown employers can offer more cash in lieu of a parking space without any increase in their cost. This higher cash option for downtown commuters makes downtown work sites relatively more attractive than suburban work sites. Downtown commuters can more easily take advantage of the cash option by shifting to mass transit. Because a high density of employment implies a high density of potential fellow carpoolers, downtown commuters can also more easily shift to carpools. Finally, parking spaces vacated by new carpoolers will become available to shoppers, business clients, and tourists.

8. *Parking cash out will create a tax revenue windfall.* In choosing between a parking subsidy and its cash value, commuters have to consider that the cash is taxable but the parking subsidy is not. When a commuter does voluntarily choose taxable cash rather than a tax-exempt parking subsidy, federal and state income tax revenues increase. This increased tax payment does not result from higher tax rates or from taxing previously tax-exempt parking subsidies. Rather, it results from voluntary action: cashing

out an inefficient parking subsidy that costs the employer more to provide than the employee thinks it is worth. Cashing out an inefficient parking subsidy converts economic waste into increased tax revenue and increased employee welfare, at no extra cost to the employer. This tax revenue windfall is an additional benefit above and beyond the reduced air pollution, traffic congestion, and energy use (Shoup 2005, Chapter 6).

PARKING CASH OUT IN CALIFORNIA

The U.S. Internal Revenue Code creates a strong incentive for employers to pay for employee parking and thus a strong incentive for commuters to drive to work alone. States and localities are then left with the enormous problem of dealing with the resulting traffic congestion and air pollution. In 1992, California enacted legislation that directly addresses the problems caused by employer-paid parking and that serves as a model of how the federal government could address the same problems. Briefly, California requires employers of 50 or more persons who provide a parking subsidy to employees to:

> provide a cash allowance to an employee equivalent to the parking subsidy that the employer would otherwise pay to provide the employee with a parking space. ... "Parking subsidy" means the difference between the out-of-pocket amount paid by an employer on a regular basis in order to secure the availability of an employee parking space not owned by the employer and the price, if any, charged to an employee for the use of that space (Section 43845 of the California Health and Safety Code).

The employer must offer an employee the option to take cash in lieu of a parking subsidy only if the employer makes an explicit cash payment to subsidize the employee's parking. Therefore, the employer saves the cash paid for the parking if the employee takes the cash allowance instead. The employer's avoided parking subsidy directly funds, dollar for dollar, the employee's cash allowance, so there is no net cost for the employer when an employee forgoes the parking and takes the cash. The employer must offer the cash allowance only to each employee who is offered a parking subsidy. And each employee's cash allowance is equal to the parking subsidy offered to that employee, so if some employees are offered smaller parking subsidies than other employees, their required cash allowance is smaller. Thus, the law is tightly written to avoid imposing a net cost on employers.

Giving commuters a choice between a parking subsidy and its cash value reveals that free parking has a cost—the foregone cash. Commuters who forego the cash are, in effect, spending it on parking. Employers can continue to offer free parking, but the new option to take cash instead of parking will increase the share of commuters who walk, bike, or ride the bus to work.

PARKING CASH OUT REDUCES TRAFFIC

Case studies of firms that have complied with California's cash-out law found that for every 100 commuters offered the cash option, 13 solo drivers shifted to another travel mode. Of these 13 former solo drivers, nine joined carpools, three began to ride public transit, and one began to walk or bicycle to work. Overall, the share of commuters who drove to work alone fell from 76 percent before the cash offer to 63 percent afterward (Figure 43-1).

The large shifts away from solo driving reduced vehicle miles traveled and vehicle emissions for commuting to the eight firms by 12 percent (Shoup 2005, Chapter 4). This reduction in vehicle travel is equivalent to removing from the road one of every eight cars driven

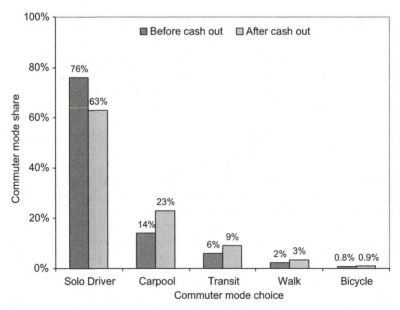

Figure 43-1 Commuter mode share before and after parking cash out

Source: Shoup 2005, p. 66

to work at the case-study firms. The larger shift to carpooling than to transit shows that parking cash out can work even in places with limited public transit.

A few commuters who shifted away from solo driving moved into more expensive apartments closer to their worksites and began to walk, cycle, or ride transit to work. In these cases, parking cash out allowed commuters to convert a parking subsidy for driving to work into a housing subsidy for living closer to work.

The eight firms, considered together, reduced their payments for parking almost as much as they paid in cash to commuters. The firms' average commuting subsidy per employee rose from $72 before cash out to $74 a month afterward, or by only 3 percent (Shoup 2005, 29–31). A simple, fair, and almost costless reform of employer-paid parking significantly reduced vehicle travel.

Beyond reducing traffic congestion and air pollution, parking cash out increases tax revenues without increasing tax rates. Suppose an employer pays $100 per space per month to provide free parking. A commuter in the 25 percent marginal tax bracket who chooses a taxable $100 payment instead of the free parking will receive $75 after tax. The $25 a month in tax revenue results from voluntary action: a commuter who cashed out values $75 a month in after-tax cash more than a parking space that costs the employer $100 a month to provide. The $25 a month in tax revenue comes from reducing the inefficiency that occurs when, faced with the typical choice between free parking and nothing, commuters take free parking they value substantially less than what it costs the employer to provide.

In the case studies of firms that offer parking cash out, employees' taxable wages increased by $255 per year per employee offered the cash option. Federal income tax revenues increased by $48 per year per employee, and California income tax revenues increased by $17 per year per employee. Therefore, federal and state tax revenues increased by $65 per year per employee offered the cash option (Shoup 2005, 55).

In addition to what the firms spend for parking subsidies and for cash payments in lieu of parking subsidies, there is also the cost of administering parking cash out. When interviewed, the firms' representatives all said that parking cash out is simple, easy to administer, and almost automatic.

- It's very simple. It's not difficult at all. (Case 2)
- The cash-out program is really simple. It is very easy to administer. (Case 4)
- Cash back doesn't cause a problem—it helps you. It's the biggest single help. I give it to payroll and they put it on a computer. It's automatic. (Case 6)

When asked to estimate the cost of administering parking cash out, one firm's transportation coordinator said she spends approximately two minutes a month per employee on the cash-out program. The other firms' representatives reported the cost is imperceptible, and one likened it to the cost of making changes in the number of exemptions for employees' income tax withholding.

The firm's representatives also mentioned that parking cash out helps to recruit and retain workers:

- The employees think it's fair. (Case 2)
- It's a good hiring incentive for us. (Case 4)
- Since we moved to cash out, we've always received a good response. (Case 4)
- I would definitely recommend [parking cash out]. We've always found that cash works. Cash is always a good incentive. (Case 4)
- People like the idea, they like the cash in hand, and it does add to their paycheck. (Case 5)
- [Employees] love it. The ones that qualify love it. And the ones who drive alone don't care because they get free parking. (Case 6)
- [Cash out] made employees happy. It became a benefit we were offering to employees. We emphasize it in our new employee orientation. (Case 8)
- If we decided to scratch the program, we would probably end up with at least 50 or 60 more employee cars, with no place to park. (Case 8)
- Cash works very well for us. (Case 8)

ENFORCING THE LAW

Unfortunately, although some employers comply with California's cash-out law, most employers have never heard of it. Enforcing the law was formerly impossible because the law did not include any penalty for noncompliance. Fortunately, however, the state now authorizes cities, counties, and air districts to establish a penalty for failing to comply with the cash-out law.

Cities can now use parking cash out as a cost-effective and fair way to reduce traffic congestion, air pollution and greenhouse gas emissions. A penalty for failing to offer cash out is like a ticket for failing to pay at a parking meter. The chance of receiving a citation may be enough to induce most employers to comply with the law. Commuters will also be in a much stronger position to ask their employers to comply with the law. Cities don't have to establish a new policy to reduce traffic congestion and air pollution. They only have to establish a penalty for violating an existing state law.

Santa Monica is the only city that now enforces the state's cash-out law. Thirty-three employers in Santa Monica are subject to the law, and for some of them more than half of their employees choose cash rather than free parking. Cities that follow Santa Monica's lead can reduce traffic congestion and improve air quality without increasing employers' costs.

IMPLICATIONS FOR FEDERAL ACTION

Sooner or later, when traffic congestion and air pollution become even more intolerable, when we run out of room for new freeways, and most people recognize the threat of global warming, we will ask ourselves why the U.S. Internal Revenue Code strongly favors free parking and solo driving. The only real question is the magnitude of the mayhem we create before we slightly amend the tax code to include parking cash out.

California's cash-out legislation shows that employers who pay for parking if a commuter drives to work can offer to pay the same amount if the commuter walks, bikes, or rides the bus to work. Some employers will undoubtedly encounter problems in adjusting to the cash out requirement, but the real challenge for many employers will be to abandon the outdated notion that the best way to help commuters get to work is to pay for their parking.

California's experience suggests that, at the federal level, it is sensible to proceed cautiously, beginning first with the requirement to offer cash in lieu of a parking subsidy only in the clearest "win-win" case where the employer pays out-of-pocket cash to a third party to subsidize parking. Later, after employers have been given sufficient advance notice to adjust to the emergence of a parking market where prices rather than subsidies allocate parking spaces, the cash-out requirement could be extended to all employer-paid parking. To repeat, however, the proposed amendment to the Internal Revenue Code does not prohibit, tax, or discourage employer-paid parking. Rather, the proposal is simply that an employer who offers to pay for parking if a commuter drives to work alone must also offer to pay the same amount if the commuter doesn't drive to work alone.

Because cash is taxable and a parking subsidy is tax exempt, offering employees the option to cash out parking subsidies will reduce solo driving to work by less than would ending parking subsidies altogether. The research on commuters in Los Angeles, however, suggests that the taxable nature of cash does not greatly diminish its attractiveness.

Requiring employers to offer employees the option to cash out their parking subsidies will reduce traffic congestion, improve air quality, conserve gasoline, enhance employee welfare without adding to employers' costs, and increase tax revenue without increasing tax rates. All these benefits will derive from subsidizing people, not parking.

REFERENCES AND FURTHER READING

Shoup, Donald. 2005. *Parking Cash Out*. Planning Advisory Service Report No. 532. Chicago: Planning Advisory Service. http://shoup.bol.ucla.edu/ParkingCashOut.pdf
Parking Cash Out. 2010. StreetsblogLA. https://tinyurl.com/ycbjx2e

Part III

Parking Benefit Districts

The money you put into a parking meter seems to vanish into thin air. No one knows where the money goes, and everyone wants to park free, so politicians find it easier to require ample off-street parking than to charge fair market prices for scarce curb parking. But cities can change the politics of parking if they return curb parking revenue to pay for public services in the neighborhoods that generate it. If each neighborhood keeps all the parking revenue it generates, a powerful new constituency for market prices will emerge—the neighborhoods that receive the revenue. If nonresidents pay for curb parking, and the city spends the revenue to benefit the residents, charging for curb parking can become a popular policy, rather than the political third rail it often is today.
—DONALD SHOUP, THE HIGH COST OF FREE PARKING

44

Parking Matters in Old Pasadena

By Douglas Kolozsvari and Donald Shoup

Charging the right price for curb parking makes perfect sense theoreti-cally, but it is tough to sell politically. Paying for parking is a "grudge purchase" in marketing terminology—a purchase the buyer does not want to make, like paying baggage fees to an airline. After all, taxes have already paid for the streets, so why should drivers have to pay to park on them?

Opposition to paid parking extends across the political spectrum. With hostility to markets from the left and to governments from the right, it is hard to convince either side that cities should charge market prices for curb parking. No one wants to pay for parking, and few people realize that free parking does any harm. The left often under-estimates how prices affect individual choices, and the right often underestimates how individual choices create collective consequences. As Niccolò Machiavelli wrote in *The Prince* in 1532,

> There is nothing more difficult to take in hand, more perilous to conduct, or more uncertain in its success, than to take the lead in the introduction of a new order of things. Because the innovator has for enemies all those who have done well under the old conditions, and lukewarm defenders in those who may do well under the new.

To create the necessary political support for parking meters, some cities have established Parking Benefit Districts that use the resulting meter revenue to pay for neighborhood public services.

PARKING BENEFIT DISTRICTS

The money you put into a parking meter seems to vanish into thin air. No one knows where the money goes, and everyone wants to park for free, so politicians find it easier to require ample off-street parking than to charge for scarce curb parking. But cities can change the politics of parking by spending the curb parking revenue to pay for public services in the metered neighborhoods. If each neighborhood keeps its curb parking revenue, a powerful new constituency for parking meters will emerge: the communities that receive the revenue. If visitors pay for curb parking and the city uses the revenue to benefit the metered neighborhoods, charging for curb parking can become a popular policy that unites the interests of the city, the business community, and the residents.

Charging the right price for curb parking will manage curb spaces efficiently so that drivers (and their passengers) who are willing to pay for parking don't have to waste time cruising for it. Right-priced curb parking can therefore improve the customer experience and attract more visitors who spend more money while shopping. The purpose of charging the right price for curb parking is to maximize efficiency, not to maximize meter revenue. Although efficient use of curb space is the primary aim, the resulting revenue can produce a surprising array of benefits.

To see the benefits of parking meters with local revenue return, consider an older business district where most stores have no off-street parking and vacant curb spaces are hard to find. Cruising for free curb parking congests the streets, and everyone complains about a parking shortage. Charging for curb parking will increase turnover and reduce traffic congestion, and the convenience of a few vacancies will attract customers who are willing to pay for parking if they don't have to spend time hunting for it. Nevertheless, merchants fear that charging for parking will keep customers away. Suppose in this case the city creates a Parking Benefit District (PBD) in which all the meter revenue is spent to clean the sidewalks, plant street trees, improve store facades, sponsor events, put overhead utility wires underground, and ensure public safety. The meter revenue will help make the business district a place where people want to be, rather than merely a place where everyone can park free if they can find a space. Residents, merchants, and property owners are more likely to support the idea of demand-based prices for curb parking if the city spends the resulting revenue to improve the neighborhood. People will see their meter money at work.

Curb parking revenue needs the right recipient to generate political support for demand-based prices. In commercial areas, Business Improvement Districts (BIDs) are logical recipients of this revenue. Their legality is well established and their operating principles are familiar to public officials and business owners. BIDs are therefore ready-made recipients for curb parking revenue. Parking revenue can either reduce the taxes businesses pay to the BID or increase the district's services. This arrangement can encourage local businesses to form BIDs, and thus elicit self-help efforts from the benefitted businesses. Earmarking curb parking revenue to fund BIDs and giving the BIDs a voice in shaping parking policies for their area will encourage businesslike management of the parking supply.

Pasadena, California, is the leading example of how a Parking Benefit District can revitalize an older business center. Pasadena's experience shows how parking meters with local revenue return can help improve public services, the built environment, and the visitors' experience.

YOUR METER MONEY MAKES A DIFFERENCE IN OLD PASADENA

Pasadena's downtown declined between the 1930s and the 1980s but has since reinvented itself as Old Pasadena, one of Southern California's most popular shopping and entertainment destinations. Dedicating parking revenue to finance public services has played a large part in this revival (*The High Cost of Free Parking*, Chapter 16).

Old Pasadena was the original commercial core of the city, and in the early twentieth century was an elegant shopping district. In 1929, Pasadena widened its main thoroughfare, Colorado Boulevard, by 28 feet, which required moving the building facades back 14 feet on each side of the street. Owners removed the front 14 feet of their buildings, and most constructed new facades in the popular Spanish Colonial Revival or Art Deco styles. A few owners, however, moved back the original facades in an early example of historic preservation. The result is the handsome, circa-1929 streetscape in Old Pasadena.

The area sank into decline during the Great Depression. After WWII, the narrow storefronts and lack of parking led many merchants to seek larger retail spaces in more modern surroundings. Old Pasadena became a commercial skid row with wonderful buildings in terrible condition. The area was known mainly for its pawn shops, porn theaters, and tattoo parlors, and by the 1970s much of it was a retail slum slated for redevelopment. Vacant stores lined the streets, and property owners let their buildings decay because the low rents did not justify repairs. Pasadena's Redevelopment Agency demolished three historic blocks on Colorado Boulevard to make way for Plaza Pasadena, an enclosed mall with ample free parking. New buildings clad in then-fashionable black glass replaced other historic properties. The resulting

"Corporate Pasadena" horrified many citizens and led the city to reconsider its plans for the area. In 1978 the city published the *Plan for Old Pasadena*, which stated, "if the area can be revitalized, building on its special character, it will be unique to the region." But the plan did not minimize the problems:

> The area is commonly perceived as undesirable and unsafe. Comments heard about West Colorado include the following: "The area's been going downhill for years." "It's a bunch of dirty old buildings." "It's filthy." "It's Pasadena's sick child." "The area is unsafe."

Although the city listed Old Pasadena in the National Register of Historic Places in 1983, commercial revival was slow to come, in part because the lack of public investment and the parking shortage were intractable obstacles.

PARKING METERS AND REVENUE RETURN

Old Pasadena had no parking meters until 1993. Curb parking was free with a two-hour time limit. Customers had difficulty finding places to park because merchants and their employees parked in the most convenient curb spaces, moving their cars periodically to avoid citations. The city's staff proposed installing meters to regulate curb parking, but the merchants and property owners opposed the idea. They understood that their employees occupied many of the most convenient curb spaces, but they feared that meters, rather than freeing up space for customers, would discourage customers from coming at all. Customers, they assumed, would go to shopping centers that offered free parking. Meter proponents countered that drivers who would stay away because they refused to pay for parking would make room for drivers who are willing to pay for parking if they could find a space. Proponents also argued that people who pay for parking probably spend more money in Old Pasadena than people who will come only if they can park free.

Debates about the meters dragged on for two years before the city compromised with the merchants and property owners. The city offered to dedicate all the meter revenue to pay for public investments in Old Pasadena. The business and property owners quickly agreed because they saw that the meters would directly benefit them, and the desire for public improvements outweighed the fear of driving customers away. "The only reason meters went into Old Pasadena in the first place," said Marilyn Buchanan, a prominent business leader and chair of the Old Pasadena Parking Meter Zone (PMZ), "was because the city agreed all the money would stay in Old Pasadena."

Merchants and property owners began to see the parking meters in a new light—as a source of revenue. They agreed to charge $1 per hour for curb parking and to operate the meters in the evenings and on Sundays. The city borrowed $5 million to finance the city's ambitious plan to improve Old Pasadena's streetscape and to convert its decayed alleys into attractive walkways with access to shops and restaurants. In effect, Old Pasadena became the first PBD in the country.

ADDED PUBLIC SERVICES AND LOCAL CONTROL

Local control and the added public services provided by the program contributed greatly to its success. The city worked with Old Pasadena's BID (the Old Pasadena Management District) to establish the boundaries of the Old Pasadena Parking Meter Zone (PMZ) where the parking meters were installed, ensuring that only the metered blocks would benefit directly from the meter revenue. The city also established the Old Pasadena PMZ Advisory Board, consisting of business and property owners to recommend parking policies and to set spending priorities for the zone's meter revenue. Many of the board members have also been active members of the BID.

In 2009, the city adjusted the prices for Old Pasadena's 690 parking meters to better manage curb parking. The prices changed from $1 per hour everywhere to $1.25 per hour in the core area and 75¢ per hour in the periphery. After this price adjustment, the resulting revenue

Figure 44-1 The new Old Pasadena

Photo credit: Donald Shoup

was $2,025 per meter in 2012 (Table 44-1). The PMZ earned additional revenue from valet parking services that use meter spaces, from investment earnings on the meter fund balance, and from miscellaneous sources (for example, the use of metered spaces for filming and construction projects), resulting in a total revenue of $2,208 per meter. The total capital and operating expenses for collecting the revenue amounted to $471 per meter (21 percent of gross revenue). Old Pasadena therefore received net parking revenue of $1,737 per meter. Therefore, in one year, the 690 meters provided $1.2 million in total revenue to fund additional public services.

The first claim on this revenue was the annual debt service of roughly $415,000 to repay the $5 million borrowed for the sidewalk and alley

Table 44-1 Old Pasadena parking meter revenues and expenditures, FY 2012

PARKING REVENUE			
Meter charges	$1,397,470	$2,025	per space for 690 metered spaces
Valet at meter spaces	$107,628		Valet use of metered spaces
Investment earnings	$7,723		Interest on fund balance
Miscellaneous revenue	$10,484		Use of metered spaces for filming, etc.
Total parking revenues	$1,523,305	$2,208	per metered space
PARKING EXPENSES			
Operating expenses			
Personnel	$128,716		
Cash handling	$72,083		
Parking meter repair	$18,910		
Materials and supplies	$6,050		
Rent	$7,400		
Merchant banking fees	$52,724		
City abatements	$8,581		
Total operating expense	$294,464	$427	per metered space
Capital expenses			
Parking meter lease payments	$29,462		
Parking meter replacement	$1,129		
Total capital expenses	$30,591	$44	per metered space
Total parking expenses	$325,055	$471	per metered space (21 percent of gross revenue)
NET PARKING REVENUE	$1,198,250	$1,737	per metered space (79 percent of gross revenue)

EXPENDITURES IN OLD
PASADENA
  Operating expenditures
  in Old Pasadena

Old Pasadena Management District	$425,796		
Security in Old Pasadena	$325,425		
Lighting services	$28,923		
Contract services	$12,464		
Internal services	$21,888		
Total operating expenditure	$814,496	68%	of net parking revenue
Capital expenditures in Old Pasadena			
Traffic mitigation	$6,364		
Debt service for streetscapes and alleys	$415,189		
Total capital expenditure	$421,553	35%	of net parking revenue
TOTAL EXPENDITURES IN OLD PASADENA	$1,236,049	103%	of net parking revenue

Source: City of Pasadena Fund Appropriation Report, Old Pasadena Parking Meter Fund, FY 2012

improvements. Of the remaining revenue, $815,000 was spent to increase public services in Old Pasadena. The city provided some of these services, such as additional police foot patrols, at a cost of $325,000. The parking enforcement officers who monitor the meters until 2 a.m. on the weekends and 11 p.m. every other day are official "eyes on the street" with radios connected to the city's dispatch center, which further increases security. The area's BID received $426,000 of meter revenue for added sidewalk and street maintenance and marketing (maps, website, brochures, etc.). The BID also uses parking revenue to fund events that attract visitors. Drivers who park in Old Pasadena finance all these public services that enhance their experience, at no cost to the businesses, property owners, or taxpayers.

    Old Pasadena has done well compared with the rest of the city. Its sales tax revenue increased rapidly after parking meters were installed in 1993 and is now higher than in other retail districts in the city (Figure 44-2). In 2009, South Lake Avenue, which was formerly the city's premier shopping district and which has an ample supply of free off-street parking, requested the city to establish a PMZ similar to Old Pasadena's and to install meters for all its curb parking spaces.

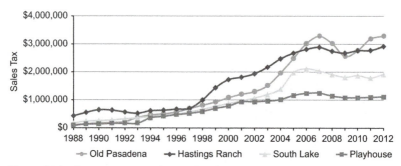

Figure 44-2 Sales tax receipts for the city of Pasadena

A VIRTUOUS CYCLE

As Old Pasadena began to attract more visitors, the sidewalks and public spaces needed more maintenance. This would have posed a problem when the area relied on the city for regular cleaning and maintenance, but now the BID has meter money to pay for the added services. The BID has arranged for daily sweeping of the streets and sidewalks, trash collection, removing graffiti, and twice-monthly pressure washing of the sidewalks. Returning the meter revenue to Old Pasadena has thus created a virtuous cycle of continuing improvements.

Figure 44-3 Your meter money makes a difference

Photo credit: Donald Shoup

The meter revenue funds public improvements, the public improvements make the area more attractive to customers, and more customers generate additional meter revenue that is then available to pay for further public improvements. Giving the BID the responsibility for spending the meter revenue reassures business and property owners that the city does not use the funds for any other purpose. As signs on the meters say, "Your meter money makes a difference in Old Pasadena."

Parking meters with revenue return do not, by themselves, explain Old Pasadena's revival, but they contributed to the city's other efforts to improve the area. Skillful planning, lower minimum parking requirements, and the construction of public parking structures also contributed to the success. As a result of these coordinated efforts, Old Pasadena is now a place where everyone wants to be, rather than merely another place where drivers can park free.

In an interview with the *Los Angeles Times* in 2004, Marilyn Buchanan explained how parking meters helped turn Old Pasadena around:

> We've come a long way. This might seem silly to some people, but if not for our parking meters, it's hard to imagine that we'd have the kind of success we're enjoying. They've made a huge difference. At first it was a struggle to get people to agree with the meters. But when we figured out that the money would stay here, that the money would be used to improve the amenities, it was an easy sell.

Interviews with shoppers confirmed this shift in how people perceive Old Pasadena and its parking. Drivers are willing to pay for parking in proportion to the quality of the destination, and as Old Pasadena improved, so did the drivers willingness to pay for parking. Consider this shopper's statement reported in the *Los Angeles Times*:

> This place, it's perfect, really. They've kept the buildings and the streets well. That makes it so attractive. People are walking around because they like the way it looks and feels. It's something you just don't see in Los Angeles. As a driver, I don't mind paying more for what you have here. I tell you what: For this, I will pay.

Old Pasadena has become not just pedestrian friendly, but pedestrian seductive, so that thousands of people enjoy strolling around and spending money.

The success has even accelerated in recent years. In a 2010 interview, Marilyn Buchanan said about the use of meter revenue: "Our public-private parking management situation works because of the knowledge we [the Old Pasadena business community] bring to it. ... We have the passion for Old Pasadena and the business sense to recognize long-term good."

Parking Benefit Districts are even more important for the downtown and other commercial districts in a big central city than they are for the commercial districts of small suburbs. The main competition for a central city is not with other central cities, but with its own suburbs. The city of Los Angeles competes more with Pasadena and Santa Monica than with Chicago or New York. If Los Angeles copied the successful PBDs in Pasadena, for example, it could begin to repair some of its 4,600 miles of broken sidewalks, which would help Los Angeles to compete not only with its suburbs but also with other central cities.

CONCLUSION: PARKING MATTERS

Suppose U.S. cities at the beginning of the twentieth century had chosen the parking policies that Pasadena adopted in the 1990s. The merchants and property owners benefitting from the parking fees would have been less inclined to recommend free parking. Market-priced parking would have discouraged store employees from occupying scarce curb spaces, making them available to customers. By creating a few vacancies, market prices would also have eliminated cruising for parking on downtown streets, thereby reducing traffic congestion. Public transit would have run faster, and the higher speeds would have reduced both operating costs and fares, making public transit more competitive with the automobile. Less congestion and better transit would have increased the appeal of the central city shopping district relative to the suburbs. Instead, cities began to require off-street parking everywhere, and we now expect to park free at both ends of every automobile trip. We live with the resulting traffic congestion, urban sprawl, and air pollution.

The free-parking policies that cities adopted in the early twentieth century are understandable because neither parking meters nor BIDs had been invented. But both exist today, and the challenge is to use them so they work well together. If BIDs receive the meter revenue, every parking meter will resemble a cash register at the curb, and all businesses will see the advantages. Charging market prices for curb parking and dedicating the revenue to BIDs will help solve transportation, land-use, and economic problems that plague many central cities.

Older business districts are like shopping malls without ample free off-street parking. Merchants may fear that charging for curb parking in these business districts will drive customers away, but earmarking the revenue to pay for increased public services can mitigate these concerns and create the necessary political support for parking meters.

The area's constituents will have an incentive to support demand-based prices for curb parking. Charging the right price for curb parking will reduce the transportation problem by opening a few curb vacancies and will make the business district an attractive place to shop, not merely a place where drivers can park free after they cruise long enough to find a space. Customers will know that they can find convenient spaces to park, without the parking uncertainty that can deter some people from visiting. Spending the meter revenue to finance public amenities that draw customers will help solve the economic problems that plague many older business districts, with no new taxes. Like Old Pasadena, older business districts can literally pull themselves up by their parking meters.

REFERENCES AND FURTHER READING

Arroyo Group. 1978. *A Plan for Old Pasadena*, Pasadena: City of Pasadena, California.
Old Pasadena Management District Annual Reports: http://www.oldpasadena.org/about.asp
Salzman, Randy. "The New Space Race." *Thinking Highways*, June/July 2010.
Shoup, Donald. 2011. *The High Cost of Free Parking*. Revised edition. Chicago: Planners Press.
Streeter, Kurt. 2004. "Old Pasadena Thanks Parking Meters for the Change." *Los Angeles Times*, March 2.

This chapter is adapted from Douglas Kolozsvari and Donald Shoup, "Turning Small Change into Big Changes," ACCESS 23, Fall 2003, pp. 2-7.

Revitalizing a Downtown with Smart Parking Policies

By Dan Zack

One of the most dramatic downtown comeback stories is taking place in Redwood City, California. This dynamic district, once ridiculed as Deadwood City, has seen an amazing turnaround due to zoning reform, effective investments in public spaces, and smart parking strategies.

At the turn of the millennium, Redwood City's downtown was charming, but it had struggled economically since the 1960s. In the late 1990s, the city and its redevelopment agency launched a concerted effort to turn its downtown around. Revitalization plans included a 4,200-seat cinema, a restored courthouse with a Courthouse Square Plaza, thousands of new apartments, hundreds of new hotel rooms, and hundreds of thousands of square feet of new office, retail, restaurant, and entertainment uses.

At the time these plans were being created, parking was already considered tight. So, where would all of these new people put their cars? As the downtown development coordinator, I was given the task of figuring it out.

ADVENTURES IN PARKING MANAGEMENT

As revitalization efforts began to move forward, the downtown parking system was a mess. Despite the area's sluggish activity levels, prime on-street parking spaces were consistently crowded. Meanwhile, the only public parking garage in the neighborhood was operating well under capacity. At the peak activity period, the occupancy rate for the entire

Figure 45-1 Parking on unmetered Broadway; metered parking on side streets. Photos taken within minutes of each other.

Photo credit for both: Dan Zack

district was just under 70 percent, yet the public was convinced that the city needed to build more parking.

Downtown Redwood City installed parking meters in 1947, but they were still thought of as foreign invaders by many locals nearly 60 years later. Neighboring cities, such as San Carlos, Menlo Park, and Palo Alto, didn't have meters, and citizens were convinced that this put Redwood City merchants at a competitive disadvantage.

There were also peculiar gaps in the metering system. Meters had been removed here and there over the years in response to complaints. Broadway, the city's main street, was completely unmetered due to an earlier attempt to attract customers to the area. Spaces on Broadway and other unmetered spots were usually unavailable even during the calmest hours. Nearby metered areas would often be completely empty; after all, why pay when you can get a good spot for free?

Whenever there was nighttime or weekend activity due to special events, another peculiarity would emerge. Prime curbside parking would become completely jammed, but desirable parking spaces in nearby private lots, most of which belonged to banks, sat empty. Fearsome *Keep Out* signs guarded the entries, warning that unauthorized cars would be towed. The city would occasionally attempt to coax these businesses into opening their lots to the general public during off hours, but they refused, usually citing liability concerns.

The most dysfunctional part of the parking system, however, was enforcement. The chaos consisted of a simple two-phase process. During Phase One, I would receive angry calls from merchants. "Your parking enforcement officers are monsters! All of my customers are getting tickets! They're killing my business! You need to tell them to back off!" At first I obliged; I certainly didn't want to be responsible for killing businesses. I requested that enforcement be lightened up. Then came Phase Two. After a brief period of calm, the angry phone calls would resume. This time, the pleas were for stricter enforcement. "My neighbor's employees are parking in front of my business all day, and they aren't getting tickets! My customers can't find parking! You need to step up enforcement!" Back to Phase One we went. Lather, rinse, and repeat. Clearly, this wasn't working; how could I break the cycle?

ZONING MADNESS

Like most cities, Redwood City requires private development to provide on-site parking. The zoning ordinance listed 36 separate uses, each of which had its own parking requirement. A 2,000-square-foot ground-floor storefront would need 10 spaces for an ordinary retail shop, but only four spaces for a furniture store. If a restaurant wanted to move into this spot, it would need 30 or more spaces. In reality, more parking would not be added; a new business with a higher parking requirement simply wouldn't open. These requirements undermined our revitalization efforts.

The parking requirements were problematic for residential uses too. Two parking spaces were required for each new dwelling, regardless of size. Since downtown was entirely built out with low-rise buildings, new parking spaces would need to be located in expensive parking structures, at a cost of $20,000 or more per space. Requiring too much parking wasn't just wasteful and inefficient; it made the infill housing that we desired completely infeasible.

Parking requirements were one of the reasons that unsubsidized housing had not been built in Downtown Redwood City in decades, even though the area was a prime location for housing. The city has a perfect climate, the downtown Caltrain station allowed car-free commuting to San Francisco and Silicon Valley, and the zoning code allowed new buildings to rise to a healthy 100 feet. Despite all of these advantages, nothing was built, not even during the frenzy of the late 1990s dot-com boom.

TAKING THE METER BY THE HORNS

With construction of the cinema project underway, the effort to improve the public parking system began early in 2005. We knew we couldn't afford to build our way out of the problem. Our redevelopment agency had taken on all of the bond obligations that it could in order to get downtown on track by improving streetscapes, constructing a garage under the cinema, restoring the courthouse, and creating Courthouse Square. Building more public parking wouldn't be possible. We would have to be creative.

We pored over parking occupancy data to understand when and where parking problems existed. We looked at expected future patterns based on parking demand projections done for the cinema's environmental impact report. We examined public parking management programs throughout the region and across the U.S. We studied academic research. We knew effective options were out there.

To solicit good ideas from people who knew the area and to rally public support, we held a series of workshops with downtown stakeholders. We showed maps that plotted parking occupancy, block-by-block, for various time periods. We challenged the public to identify what was presently working and what wasn't, and to brainstorm solutions. As we parsed the current activity patterns, it became obvious that unmetered areas were the most congested, and people began to suggest that the best parking spots should be priced the highest. At the final workshop, we unveiled our recommended public parking management strategy.

The first and most important part of the plan was the meter pricing strategy. We established base meter rates, block-by-block, for the entire downtown area in accordance with the current and projected demand. The busiest area, Broadway, was priced the highest; the first block of side streets was a little cheaper, and off-street facilities and curb parking on the outskirts received the lowest prices. Prices were to be adjusted based on demand, with a target occupancy rate of 85 percent, as recommended in Donald Shoup's book, *The High Cost of Free Parking.* Staff would be empowered to adjust prices up to four times per year in $0.25 increments in response to occupancy, as long as an hourly rate of $1.50 was not exceeded. We would meter parking during all busy hours: 10 a.m. to 10 p.m., seven days per week.

During the workshops, we learned that people really disliked time limits. If prices ensure an acceptable vacancy rate, why bother with time limits? We decided that removing them would make the system much friendlier.

Another step toward creating a system that would be easy to follow was upgrading the meters. In the busiest areas, coin-operated single-space meters were replaced with multi-space meters that accepted coin, bill, and credit card payment. For many people, being required to pay is bad enough; why add to the insult by forcing them to travel with a pocketful of quarters?

Finally, a Parking Benefit District was established. This meant that any surplus funds generated by the new system could be spent on other needs, such as security, lighting, or extra janitorial services in downtown. The merchants saw this as an important part of the plan.

The ordinance language took months to craft. I worked carefully with our city attorney to make sure that we were within the parameters of California's Vehicle Code and case law. In July 2005, we took the plan to the city council. People who had attended the workshops packed the council chambers and spoke in favor of the plan they had helped to create. Only one person spoke against the plan. After some deliberation, the city council adopted the ordinance unanimously.

ZONING SANITY

Redwood City also needed to change the way its zoning ordinance dealt with parking for private development. A new form-based code, known as the Downtown Precise Plan (DTPP), was expected to bring thousands of apartments and hundreds of thousands of square feet of office space to the area, and our downtown parking requirements were not designed to deal with this kind of development boom. After getting the public parking management plan adopted, we began working on these off-street parking requirements. A group of us on city staff met for months in order to develop a strategy.

While removing off-street parking requirements is an excellent strategy when combined with effective management of public parking, some in the group were reluctant to do so. Everyone involved, however, agreed that lowering and simplifying the requirements was essential and that parking rules had to be modified in order to encourage dense, mixed-use development.

Prior to the revitalization program we had a moderate surplus of parking, so we did not need to use our zoning ordinance to dig our way out of a parking deficit. We wanted to require just enough parking to ensure that the parking supply grew proportionally to new development but not so much that it would inhibit growth.

We discovered the Urban Land Institute's shared parking model and realized that encouraging shared parking could reduce the amount of parking that we needed. Downtown was developing a diverse range of land uses, all with differing peak activity periods. Rather than calculating the maximum need of each use individually, we decided to calculate the maximum need of all nonresidential uses together at any given time. We plugged our expected development numbers for retail, restaurant, office, and theater uses into the model. If all new commercial buildings shared their parking, they would only need an average of three spaces per 1,000 square feet of space. This was less parking than the zoning code required for most commercial buildings.

At first we struggled with the best way to translate this into a code, but eventually we settled on this: We merged all uses except for residential and hotels into a single category and gave it a single requirement. This "blended" commercial requirement would allow the use of buildings to change without any unnecessary regulatory burdens. To strongly encourage shared parking, we set the commercial parking requirement at six spaces per 1,000 square feet, and then allowed for a by-right discount of 50 percent if parking is shared, which would lower the requirement to three spaces per 1,000 square feet. This was far lower than most of the previous requirements, some of which were as high as 20 spaces per 1,000 square feet, but it was much closer to our actual needs. Residential requirements were reduced to 1.5 spaces per unit for large units, and as low as 0.75 spaces per unit for studios. Previously, all housing had required 2.25 spaces per unit. We also created an in-lieu parking fee program to further enhance flexibility for tough projects. This allows developers to satisfy their parking requirement by paying a fee, which can then be used by the city to create public parking.

Downtown Parking Requirements: BEFORE

Use	Parking Requirement
Residential Uses	
Single-Family, 4 Bedrooms or Less	2 covered spaces
Single-Family, More Than 4 Bedrooms	2 covered spaces, plus 0.5 covered space for every bedroom in excess of four
Accessory Units	1 space
Duplex	2 spaces per unit
Multiple Family	2 spaces per unit (1 of which must be covered) plus 1 space for every 4 units for guest or visitor parking
Rooming or Boarding Houses	1 covered space for each bedroom, but not less than 3 spaces
Commercial Uses	
Automobile service stations, auto repair, or machinery sales and services garages	1 space per 500 square feet, or 3 spaces per bay, whichever is greater
Financial services, professional, business or administrative offices	1 space per 250 square feet
Financial services, professional, business or administrative offices, within 1,500 feet of train station or generating 100 or more PM peak period trips	1 space per 300 square feet
Bowling alleys	5 spaces for each bowling lane plus additional spaces for other uses such as restaurants, pool or billiard parlors, if present, according to the requirements for such other uses
Dance, assembly, or exhibition halls without fixed seating	1 space for each 50 square feet of floor area used for dancing assembly, or exhibition space
Funeral homes and mortuaries	1 space for each 5 seats in the chapel, plus 1 space for each parlor room, plus 1 space for each employee
Furniture or appliance stores, including repairs	1 space for each 500 square feet
Hotels and motels	1 space for each living or sleeping unit, plus additional spaces for other uses such as restaurants, lounges, if present, according to the requirements herein for such other uses
Medical or dental offices and clinics	1 space for each 200 square feet
Personal services, such as beauty shops and barber shops	1 space for each 200 square feet
Pool or billiard parlors	2 spaces for each table
Restaurants, but not including fast food restaurants, lounges, and night clubs	1 space for each 3 seats
Restaurants, fast food	1 space for each 3 seats, or 1 space for each 50 square feet of floor area, whichever is greater
Retail stores and shops	1 space for each 200 square feet
Theaters, auditoriums, and assembly halls with fixed seating	1 space for each 3.5 seats

Figure 45-2 Downtown Redwood City parking requirements before code revision

Downtown Parking Requirements: BEFORE

Use	Parking Requirement
Commercial Uses	
Health/fitness facilities, Small (2,000 square feet or less)	1 space for each 250 square feet
Health/fitness facilities, Large (over 2,000 square feet)	1 space for each 200 square feet
Live/work unit	2 spaces per unit
Industrial Uses	
Industrial or manufacturing plants	1 space for every 2 employees on the maximum working shift, but in no case less than 1 space for each 600 square feet of floor area
Warehouses	1 space for each 2 employees on the maximum work shift, plus 1 space for each 1,000 square feet of floor area
Research and development	1 space for every 250 square feet of gross floor area devoted to office and administrative use; plus 1 space for every 2 employees on the maximum work shift (but in no case less than 1 space for each 600 square feet of gross floor area) for areas devoted to laboratory, manufacturing or assembly use; plus 1 space for every 1,000 square feet of gross floor area devoted to warehouse use
Miscellaneous Uses	
Churches, synagogues, houses of worship, with fixed seating	1 space for each 3.5 seats in the main meeting room; or if no fixed seats, 1 space for every 50 square feet; plus if classrooms are present, 1 space for every 15 classroom seats
Hospitals, but not including out-patient clinics	1 space for each patient bed, plus 1 space per employee on the largest shift
Sanitariums, convalescent homes, nursing homes, and rest homes	1 space for each 6 patient beds, plus 1 space for each staff or visiting doctor, plus 1 space for each employee
Schools, 10th Grade and Below	1 space for each classroom and administrative office, plus 1 space for every 100 square feet in the auditorium
Schools, 11th Grade and Above	1 space for each student over 16 years in age
Emergency Shelters	1 space for each 5 beds and 2 additional spaces
Mixed-Use, Studio and One Bedroom Residential Units	1 space per unit
Mixed-Use, Two Bedrooms or Larger Residential Units	1½ spaces per unit
Mixed-Use, Commercial Uses	A minimum of 75 percent of the normally required commercial parking as otherwise required, if residential spaces are made available to the commercial tenants and customers

Figure 45-2 *continued*

Downtown Parking Requirements: AFTER

Use	Parking Requirement
Residential Uses	
Studio	0.75 spaces per unit
One Bedroom	1 space per unit
Two Bedrooms or More	1.5 spaces per unit
Non-Residential Uses	
Hotel	Restricted: 1 space per guest room
	Shared: 0.5 spaces per guest room
All Other Non-Residential Uses	
	Restricted: 6 spaces per 1,000 square feet
	Shared: 3 spaces per 1,000 square feet

Figure 45-3 Downtown Redwood City parking requirements after code revision.

These changes were adopted into the Redwood City zoning ordinance in March 2006. The final improvement to Redwood City's parking requirements came in 2011 with the adoption of the DTPP, which added rules for the physical form of new parking lots and garages. Parking facilities were required to be wrapped with shops, offices, and apartments, and auto entrances were to be located on secondary streets or alleys.

LESSONS LEARNED

Overall, the parking strategy was successful, although some aspects did not work as hoped. The new meters and prices debuted in March 2007 during an economic slump. Without the expected throngs of visitors, the increased parking prices were hard for people to accept. The new meters were also a sticking point. While the tech-friendly crowd liked the advanced features, many citizens found the machines difficult to use and they were not eager to learn a new system. To complicate matters, the machines sometimes didn't operate well, such as when heavy rains caused coin jams or when Wi-Fi connectivity was slow for credit card authorizations. The technology caused a backlash.

In the face of complaints, the city council's commitment to the occupancy-based price-changing scheme wavered, and prices were not adjusted. This limited the success of the system, but the base meter rates that we put in place proved to be fairly effective. Before the new meters and prices, the average occupancy on Broadway was nearly 100 percent. During the first year of the new system it fell to 83 percent even though the total number of visitors to downtown rose slightly. People generally redistributed themselves away from crowded core areas and out to the periphery as we had hoped. In the first month after the debut of the new meters, the sale of monthly parking permits increased by 50 percent as employees sought cheaper options. Some areas were still crowded at certain times, but the base meter rates sufficed and the lack of time limits didn't cause any problems.

Surprisingly, the average duration of parking space usage on Broadway fell from over two hours to about one hour after the one-hour time limit was removed and the street was metered with appropriate pricing. In 2007, Conor Dougherty of the *Wall Street Journal* described how the elimination of time limits made it more convenient to do business in downtown. "In the past, Cheryl Angeles has had to jump up in the middle of a coloring treatment, foil in her hair and a black-plastic cape around her neck, to pop more quarters into the meter. Twice the self-storage company regional manager got $25 parking tickets when she didn't make it in time. Now that the time limits have been removed, she can pay once and return when the appointment is over."

I handed off management of the parking system in January 2008 in order to lead the completion of the DTPP. For the next couple of years, my successors understandably focused on easing the complaints, ironing out the kinks in the new technology, and getting downtown through the recession. Prices were lowered, and metering hours were scaled back. With the strengthening economy, the city began to re-embrace the original pricing strategy, raising rates in the core to $1 per hour in 2014.

Our innovations with public parking resulted in some struggles, but reforming our parking requirements was easier. Changing to a single parking requirement for all commercial uses no longer discouraged new businesses from opening up in old buildings. Downtown's ground-floor vacancy rate was 30 percent during the darkest years of the recession, but it dropped to 6 percent by 2013. An improving economy, thousands of cinema patrons, and new residents brought the new businesses, and the reformed parking requirements made sure we didn't have to turn them away.

Mandaloun restaurant, for example, applied for permits as we were finishing up our work on the new parking requirements in 2006. They intended to move into a space previously occupied by a Western-wear shop. According to the old code, the change in use would have triggered a huge parking shortfall, and the restaurant was initially told that it would not be approved. When we got the new single parking requirement for all uses adopted soon thereafter, the restaurant was able to open.

The in-lieu parking fee has also been successful. It made several small projects feasible that wouldn't have worked previously, including the restoration of the historic Mayers Building that had been boarded up for years. The restoration was challenging because the facade had been

Figure 45-4 The restoration of the Mayers Building was made possible by the in-lieu parking fee program

Photo credit for both: Dan Zack

decimated by an earlier modernizing project and there were major structural issues to attend to. The addition of a third floor made the project pencil out, and the parking requirement for the new square footage was satisfied with an in-lieu payment.

The DTPP was adopted in January 2011, and within a year the Silicon Valley economy began to warm up. Soon, Redwood City was in the midst of the development boom that it had hoped for. By the summer of 2014, nearly 1,500 units of housing and 300,000 square feet of office space were under construction. None of these projects would have met the old parking requirements, but they had no problem meeting the new ones. Our shared parking incentive worked, too. All of the commercial developments share their parking in order to reduce their parking requirement. One project brought 900 spaces into public use during nights and weekends.

Form controls in the DTPP keep new garages hidden and streetscapes lively, comfortable, and safe. The garages for new buildings are lined with live/work units, shops, and offices, and the auto entrances are kept away from the most important pedestrian streets. The new buildings look like places for people, not warehouses for cars.

The days of Deadwood City are over. New residents and employees fill the pubs and coffee shops. The cinema is one of the busiest in the Bay Area, and events at Courthouse Square draw tens of thousands of people to downtown every year. Today, rather than hearing that Redwood City is losing business to neighboring cities, you are more likely to hear the old refrain: Nobody goes there anymore, it's too crowded!

46

Paid Parking and Free Wi-Fi in Ventura

By Thomas Mericle

Ventura, California, is leading the way in rethinking how parking policies can better serve U.S. cities. In 2010, Ventura took the first steps towards implementing its new comprehensive parking management program by charging for on-street parking. Its historic downtown had not seen paid parking since the early 1970s. The Downtown Parking Management Program was approved in 2007 as a part of the broader Ventura Downtown Specific Plan, which proposes ambitious policies, programs, and strategies to support economic growth and redevelopment opportunities. The program leverages the basic economic concept of supply and demand to make parking available to customers when and where they need it.

To create a new vision for how parking is managed, the city arranged a public-private partnership for each phase of the overall program from planning to ongoing implementation. Dedication and support among staff, management, and elected officials was key to the program's success.

CREATING THE PROGRAM

In 2007, Ventura conducted an in-depth data survey of existing parking in the downtown core area. The survey included on-street, off-street, public, and private parking. At the same time, the project team and city staff examined land uses and vacancy rates to determine whether new parking requirements might be appropriate for the downtown area.

There was a perceived parking shortage in the city's downtown. Though it was relatively easy to find on-street and off-street parking throughout most of downtown, the 274 on-street parking spaces on Main Street were full eight out of the 11 metered hours per day, reaching 93 percent occupancy on Saturday nights. Unfortunately, most of the curb spaces were occupied by merchants or their employees.

In early 2008, the project team distributed a Parking Intercept Survey to more than 600 downtown merchants, employees, and customers. This qualitative assessment gathered data on the perceptions, attitudes, and habits of people who parked downtown. Business owners responded that most customers were not willing to walk more than one block or, at most, up to two blocks to their intended destination. Contrary to merchants' perceptions, customers were willing to park a short distance away (on a side street, for instance) and walk to the store of their choice. Interestingly, 86 percent of business owners believed that most customers find it difficult to find an on-street parking space, while 74 percent of customers said that it was not difficult to find an on-street parking space. Although 57 percent of employees parked in an off-street lot or parking structure, 23 percent parked in the prime on-street spaces on Main Street and California Street. In some cases, employees were permitted to park on the street in front of other businesses and move their cars every two hours. Overall, the survey results confirmed the need to give priority to parking for customers and move employees into secondary spaces.

GUIDING PRINCIPLES

Based on the results of these studies, the city developed a parking program to better manage the existing parking supply and reduce or control the parking demand. The city proposed the following goals for the program:

- Customers first
- Business and city partnership
- Increase share of employees commuting by alternative modes to increase available customer parking
- Improve all modes of access
- Comprehensive on- and off-street system
- Reinvest on-street parking revenue into the project area
- Begin analysis of the feasibility of a parking structure

PROGRAM CREATION

First, the program identified Main Street as priority parking area for customers, and established a paid parking system to encourage turnover.
The city also established on-street time limits on adjacent streets and
a residential parking permit program. Lighting, wayfinding, and new
marketing materials helped people use the surrounding municipal off-
street lots and increased walkability throughout the entire downtown.
Off-street public parking lots changed time limits from a combination
of one-hour, two-hour, four-hour, or all-day parking to either four-hour
or all-day parking, thus allowing some turnover for longer-term visitors and day-long parking areas for employees and commuters.

The program created a residential parking permit program for downtown residents in older buildings without off-street parking facilities
and a special event-parking program to serve a number of downtown
events.

The city built demand-responsive pricing into the program. Parking
data were used to identify areas with greater than 85 percent parking
occupancy. Then, parking management tools and strategies were used
to reduce the occupancy of on-street spaces and increase occupancy
in off-street lots with excess parking spaces. These strategies included
paid parking coupled with removal of parking time limits, an increase
in short-term parking on streets surrounding the downtown core, and
consistent time limits for core off-street lots. The price of on-street parking would be set to achieve an 85 percent occupancy.

The program considered demand, location, time, price, and supply
strategies to give priority to customer parking. Using these strategies,
the program can take care of residential parking issues and better
manage employee parking. The most sought after parking spaces were
priced with multi-space pay stations. Time limits on surrounding on-
street parking encouraged turnover and made off-street municipal
parking lots more attractive to both customers and employees.

Signage and wayfinding systems were crucial components in making
parking spaces easier to find and helped create a more pedestrian
friendly environment. To encourage "park-once" behavior and to add
flexibility for customers, the city removed the on-street two-hour time
limits as the system transitioned to paid parking. Since customers can
add time at any of the pay stations, they can stay as long as they want.

IMPLEMENTATION

The city, the Downtown Ventura Organization, and the merchants
organized community discussions to: 1) create an Ordinance Code that

established a Downtown Parking District; 2) define the role of the proposed Downtown Parking Advisory Committee; 3) fund a police officer and cadets for enforcement; and 4) establish publicly available Wi-Fi. A few businesses opposed the program, but key property and business owners took partnership roles in the program to help it reach successful implementation.

One issue discussed for many years was the desire for free Wi-Fi for customers visiting downtown. Both the city and the downtown business and property owners supported the idea, but it lacked funding. In an early meeting of the Downtown Parking Advisory Committee, however, everyone agreed that using the pay stations to provide free Wi-Fi for the public would create popular support for the program.

The Wi-Fi issue was a major component in searching for a pay station vendor. The city chose the Digital Payment Technologies (now known as T2) Luke pay station because of its ability to use Wi-Fi communications rather than the typical cellular communications. The Motorola Mesh system allowed for Wi-Fi to cover the downtown core area where the pay stations were located. By setting up a two-channel system (a secure one for communications and an open one for the public), free public Wi-Fi was provided at no additional cost to the city or the merchants.

In 2010, Ventura installed pay stations in downtown Ventura covering 318 paid parking spaces along Main Street, California Street, and five other side streets, and demand-based pricing began in September of that year. Figure 46-1 shows the downtown core area and the parking that was in place in September 2010. On the first day, lunchtime customers turned quickly onto Main Street and found ample parking in front of the shops and restaurants. They were not stuck in traffic caused by drivers cruising for parking. Customers who wanted free parking could now park in either on-street spaces with time limits or in longer-term off-street municipal parking facilities.

Employees no longer parked free in front of the shops; they could choose between paying for on-street parking or using the free off-street parking facilities nearby. That morning, Ventura Mayor Bill Fulton enthusiastically wrote in his personal blog, "The paid parking portion of our downtown parking management program had gone into effect at 10 a.m., and it was already showing results."

Despite initial success, the program experienced some growing pains. A few business owners pushed back, claiming they did not know anything about the paid parking and that their businesses were now losing sales. "Our volume has gone down since the parking meters have been put in," said one local businesswoman. However, she also acknowledged "people just don't like to change." Nevertheless, when the Downtown Ventura Partners, which is the Business Improvement District (BID) for the area, surveyed downtown businesses, 83 percent supported the meters, 13 percent were neutral, and only 4 percent did not support the meters.

In 2009 and again in 2010, Ventura conducted on-street parking surveys to monitor changes in the downtown parking area. These surveys, and an analysis of both metered and nonmetered on-street parking found reduced occupancy on Main Street and increased occupancy on nonmetered streets and off-street parking lots in the downtown area. Over time, this has increased pressure on the city to provide more off-street parking to serve those customers who are willing to walk longer distances to park free.

The city aimed to make some changes before the first holiday season, Christmas 2010. The meters were removed from one underoccupied block. The price on less frequently used side streets was reduced from $1 per hour to $0.50 per hour. Moreover, in order to adhere to the "customer first" philosophy, the city eliminated variable pricing ($1.00 for first two hours and $1.50 for every additional hour). This move was also based on customer and business-owner feedback that variable pricing was too complex and slowed down the payment process. Instead, the city switched to a consistent 10 a.m. to 9 p.m. time-of-day scheme (previous paid-parking limits lasted until midnight on Friday and Saturday nights) and offered free parking coupons. A customer simply needed to ask any downtown merchant to receive a coupon. Almost 15,000 coupons were used during the first four months of initial paid parking implementation. The coupon program ended on January 2, 2011. During the 2010 holiday season a coupon code was used in online and print advertisement promoting the downtown area. Following these changes, Board Chairman of the Downtown Ventura Partners BID said a majority of merchants and property owners supported the program.

While the program initially did not generate the amount of revenue anticipated due to a variety of factors, including a reduction in the number of paid spaces and reduction in the hours that meters operated, for the first time in years there were now prime parking spaces available for patrons, a reduction in cruising for parking, and a movement of employees into more remote off-street spaces. Even though there were some initial hiccups, the program was going well. After all, the goal of the program was to manage parking, not generate revenue.

The BID's Executive Director, Kevin Clerici stated, "As downtown's popularity has grown, parking demand has grown with it. Yet we have not constructed a single additional space. Our parking management system had led to the results we were seeking—with employees using outlying all-day lots, and customers willing to pay a small price for premium parking. Those who don't mind walking a block or two can still find free spaces. No one loves paying for parking, but complaints have diminished."

A SURPRISING REDUCTION IN THE FEAR OF CRIME

Ventura uses police cadets to enforce parking regulations throughout the city. These cadets generally work fewer than 20 hours per week and have expressed an interest in becoming police officers. Usually between 18 and 24 years old and attending college, the cadets work in uniforms with light blue shirts, which differentiates them from the sworn officers who wear dark blue shirts. When the city started charging for parking in downtown, the cadet program was expanded to enforce the new meters. There were several sensible reasons for utilizing police cadets for enforcing district parking.

- Police cadets are under the direction of, and in constant communication with, the police department.
- They are a reliable labor source with future desire to be hired as full-time police officers.
- They provide a uniformed presence that deters crime in the district.

The downtown parking cadets work under the direction of a police corporal. The corporal position, which is funded by the district, also provides additional benefits to the Ventura's Safe and Clean efforts in the downtown area to reduce crime and improve security.

Police Chief Ken Corney reported that the program produced a "reduction in the fear of crime and increase in quality-of-life issues. The uniformed presence of the cadets and their ability to immediately contact the police dispatch and sworn officers using their portable radio has had a tremendous impact on the perception of crime and disorder in the areas they patrol. Reductions in calls for service for non-parking related incidents during parking enforcement hours and public and merchant comments are the strongest indicator of the success of the program."

CURRENT STATUS

The Program has performed well. Since paid parking was implemented in 2010 through October 2016, the pay stations have generated $3.3 million in parking revenue. This revenue is used to operate, maintain, and manage the program as well as pay for all enforcement activities and the full-time police corporal and cadets assigned to the downtown area. Net revenues are being collected for downtown enhancement projects. For instance, in 2014 the program started paying for increased downtown restroom and sidewalk cleaning, and in early 2016 replaced a 30-year-old payment system in its downtown beach-front parking structure.

The Downtown Ventura Partners BID has been working with the city and merchants to ensure that the program is still serving their parking needs. The BID's executive director recently stated, "some of our most vocal proponents of the meters had been our merchants, who have now come to appreciate that their customers can usually find a stall in front or near their store for little more than a dime or quarter." Looking forward, he says "our next step is implementing a pay-by-cell system where merchants and shop owners can pay for people's parking, allow-ing them stay longer and building goodwill." Due to downtown busi-nesses' success, the city and the BID are beginning to think about how to build more parking spaces to accommodate the increase in visitors, residents, and employees.

In late 2015, due to changes in Payment Card Industry (PCI) data security compliance standards, the city converted all of the 59 pay stations to cellular communications. The existing Wi-Fi system has remained in place for providing the public with free Wi-Fi. The advan-tage of now having separate systems is improved public Wi-Fi because the primary use of pay station data transmission is no longer necessary, further benefiting visitors.

LESSONS LEARNED

Ventura used a systematic approach based on extensive data regarding parking demand, location, time, price, and supply strategies. It used the newest technology and program techniques, while carefully customiz-ing the program to meet local conditions. The city staff worked closely with stakeholders and elected officials throughout the process. The program gave priority to customer parking and recognized the need for protecting residential parking. The importance of communication and partnership cannot be underestimated.

Ventura installed parking meters that adjust meter prices in response to parking demand and return the meter revenue to pay for public services. The commercial streets now have open parking spaces, traffic congestion has declined, public services have improved, the downtown is cleaner and safer, business has prospered, and everyone has access to free Wi-Fi. These results were not achieved easily and they didn't happen overnight, but the benefits far exceed the costs.

47

A Parking Benefit District Grows in Houston

By Maria Irshad

It's Saturday night. The streets are teeming with people streaming out of nightclubs and bars at the end of a raucous night. Partiers ramble down residential streets, searching for their cars, yelling and sometimes fighting in yards along the way. Meanwhile, valets are running back and forth setting off car alarms to quickly identify customers' vehicles.

Residents watch the mayhem from their bedroom windows and wonder if they will ever be able to sleep through the night on a weekend. They dream of waking up in the morning without finding empty cans, bottles, and pizza boxes in their front yards.

Sound familiar? A burgeoning entertainment district can deliver great economic gains to a formerly sleepy area, but those gains come with a lot of pain.

BACKGROUND

The Washington Avenue Corridor in Houston began to become an entertainment district around 2005. The four-mile corridor runs east-west, sits right outside of downtown, and is surrounded by residential neighborhoods to the north and south, including the historic Old Sixth Ward.

Houston is synonymous with sprawl, but density along the Washington Corridor has recently increased dramatically. Between 2000 and 2010, the population in the corridor increased by 47 percent, significantly outpacing growth in the rest of the city.

Washington Avenue's parking supply, however, did not grow as fast as the economy. Buildings whose use has not changed since 1989 were grandfathered, so although a bar frequented by a few regulars suddenly drew large crowds, it was not required to provide more parking. In the case of the Washington corridor, most of the existing bars and night-clubs had little or no off-street parking. Eventually, longstanding local bars and small music venues were replaced by nightclubs and bars that drew a different—and much larger—clientele. By 2011, Washington Avenue had morphed into a thriving nighttime economy—with the parking problem to prove it.

The transitioning commercial landscape of Washington Avenue coincided with a residential boom. Developers tore down bungalows on large parcels of land and replaced them with three-story townhomes on narrow streets that lacked sidewalks and curbs. This new development multiplied the number of vehicles and increased the demand for parking in the neighborhood. Not only were residents battling each other for limited on-street parking, but they also had to contend with the weekend bar and nightclub patrons, who were provided little off-street parking.

The private sector ruffled feathers while adapting to demand. Valet services charged drivers $20 and parked the cars for free in front of houses. Residents complained that valet operators brazenly placed cones on residential streets to save spaces for their customers.

Conflicts between residents and businesses multiplied. Residents complained about the noise, parking, traffic, and public intoxication to the mayor, city council members, and city officials. A few sentiments pulled from a 2011 survey include: Developers need to be held accountable. … [They] destroyed our neighborhood"; "No more bars in the Washington Avenue corridor"; and "How many bars are too many? Well, it's too many when you have to do a parking study, and all the neighbors are complaining." Residents were almost always at odds with the business owners.

Business owners were unsympathetic. The right-of-way was public. As far as they were concerned, anything not designated as a Residential Permit Parking (RPP) district or a no-parking zone was fair game. While there were business owners in the corridor who made attempts to address residential concerns, it was rarely to the residents' satisfaction.

LET'S TALK

As early as 2009, discussion forums and task forces were being formed to resolve the growing parking problem. Outcomes included surveys of all off-street parking requirements in the district, validation of occupancy permits, improved and increased signage, frequent meetings with the police department to address noise issues, and a better management plan for free on-street parking in commercial areas.

In 2009, the city's first step to mitigate the parking issue was to implement RPP districts in neighborhoods surrounding the corridor. While RPPs alleviated the problem to some extent, many of the residential streets did not qualify for the program because the ordinance required blocks be composed of at least 75 percent single-family housing. To date, nine RPP zones have been established near the corridor, including about 300 parking spaces.

The Houston-Galveston Area Council conducted a Livable Centers study of the area, and the study confirmed that parking problems challenged the residents' quality of life. The study recommended improved management of the on-street parking supply via a Parking Benefit District (PBD). A PBD includes on-street metered parking for visitors, provides permits for residents, and returns a portion of the meter revenue to the community for public improvement projects. The mayor and the area's newly elected city council member, Ellen Cohen, became champions for this policy in the Washington corridor.

Stakeholder meetings were followed by town hall meetings, where plans and a timeline for the implementation of the PBD were made available to anyone interested. Fourteen different entities representing various neighborhoods, homeowners, and businesses in the corridor participated in a total of 27 stakeholder meetings. Online surveys solicited feedback and answered questions. Transparency was key, and the goal was to provide relief to the residents while also protecting the interests of business owners. A website, www.houstonpbd.org, was set up so stakeholders could provide feedback and review maps, FAQs, and presentations from past meetings.

On December 5, 2012, the Houston City Council unanimously approved an 18-month pilot program to test the viability of the PBD. "People that go out to restaurants and are prepared to spend a significant amount of money want to find a place to park," District C Councilmember Ellen Cohen said. "They're certainly prepared to spend a little bit more to find a place and pay for it."

The PBD's supporters believed that it would bring parking relief and new revenue to pay for public services, while some business owners feared the prices might deter patrons. The ordinance required a formal report on the program within 18 months after the meters were installed.

The pilot program required the deployment of 54 parking pay stations to manage about 350 parking spaces seven days a week, 7 a.m. to 2 a.m., although much of the district had no parking from 6 a.m. to 9 a.m., and again from 3 p.m. to 6 p.m. to ease traffic flow during rush hour.

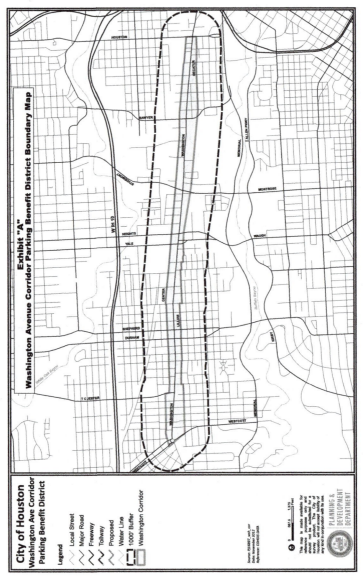

Figure 47-1 Map of Washington Avenue Parking Benefit District

Photo Credit: Maria Irshad

To provide relief for the streets not eligible for existing Residential Parking Permit (RPP) restrictions (because of an insufficient proportion of single-family housing), PBD Permit Parking zones were designated within the PBD boundary map and in the ordinance. This protection restricts parking for residents or businesses only, and was able to provide the same protection as RPP on streets that did not qualify under the existing RPP ordinance.

DOLLARS AND CENTS

The ordinance committed 60 percent of net meter revenues to public improvement projects and the remaining 40 percent was allocated to the city. As the project was in a test stage, the council wanted to ensure that the program could operate and generate sufficient revenue. Therefore, before allocating funds to public improvement projects, the pilot PBD had to accumulate at least $250,000 in net revenues. Projects were to be initiated within 18 months of the pay stations going live.

Because the area lacked a Business Improvement District (BID), the city managed the project. An advisory committee was put in place to monitor performance and to develop and to rank the project list. Residents and area businesses would have representation on the advisory committee, but the majority of committee members represented business interests.

The meter revenue projections were based on parking occupancy studies conducted in 2011 that reflected, on average, 70 percent occupancy (about 270 of 350 parking spaces). At 70 percent occupancy, projections indicated that the meters would amass $256,000 in net revenues in the first 12 months.

POST-DEPLOYMENT

Pay stations and new parking signs in the corridor went live in May 2013. Stickers on the pay stations let customers know that much of the revenue would go back to improvements in the district. All the local news channels, blogs, and the daily newspaper covered the story and, in some cases, editorials voiced support. For the 18-month pilot period, the advisory committee met monthly in a public setting to review the program.

Some parking behaviors unexpectedly changed after the meters were installed. A few off-street pay parking lots became free, allowing daytime parkers to move off-street. Employees and patrons would drive up to a half-mile to find free parking in the neighborhood and walk to their destination. The parking problems residents had long lamented persisted. Nevertheless, of the 17 streets eligible for RPP, only one street submitted an application. Residents were unwilling to request an RPP even though the price of a permit was only $25 per year.

The number of vehicles parking on the metered streets declined significantly. After installation, about 100 vehicles parked on the street on any weekend night, compared to 270 before the meter deployment. Residential streets with no parking restrictions within walking distance of the corridor continued to demonstrate high parking occupancy.

Due to the lower-than-expected meter revenue, the PBD was reevaluated. The initial revenue projections did not take into account the meter citations issued in the corridor. Looking at the program holistically—what it cost and what revenue it generated—the committee recommended that the new revenue earned from meter citations should also be credited to the PBD.

Because 80 percent of the meter transactions were by credit card, the city was able to reduce the expense of maintenance and collection activity in the corridor, as compared to other metered areas where the credit card use hovered around 57 percent.

Without the increased revenues and reduced expenses, the PBD would have failed to accumulate sufficient revenue to cover the debt service for the meters. The program's setup burdened the district with all the expenses, but it returned only a portion of the revenues. The city, on the other hand, had no expenses but enjoyed revenue from both meters and expired meter citations.

In June 2014, at the end of the 18-month pilot, the advisory committee unanimously voted to send the PBD ordinance back to city council with two changes, which were unanimously approved. First, the city would be responsible for a share of the capital, maintenance, and operational costs based on the revenue generated by the number of meter citations. Second, the city reduced the project hurdle amount from $250,000 to $100,000 to allow for projects to be initiated sooner.

THE ART OF METERING

As the program evolved, new challenges emerged. Parkers in the PBD overstayed their paid time at the meters, in some cases because they were not aware that the meter operated until 2 a.m. instead of 6 p.m. like many other parts of the city. The number of citations issued for expired meters exceeded the number of citations written for no payment at all by 57 percent, suggesting that more education was needed in order for the corridor to benefit from the program's full potential.

To highlight the evening hours and to bring attention to the corridor, the city partnered with the Houston Arts Alliance to initiate an "Art Meter" project. A local artist transformed three meters in the Washington Corridor into functioning art pieces that incorporate lighting to draw attention to the need to pay at night.

The city also commissioned a local artist to create sculptural, cut-steel structures enveloping the parking meter with a light fixture inside the meter. Each piece represents one of Houston's three seasons (spring, summer, and fall). The Art Parking Meters displayed a "fun and unique twist to traditional parking meters," said Mayor Annise Parker. Especially in the city's arts community, the project showed there could be more to parking than just paying a meter.

TEAM WORK

By September 2014, the Washington PBD met its goal of raising at least $100,000 in net revenues, and the advisory committee started vetting and ranking its project list. Having banked about $70,000 for projects, the committee elected to focus on smaller projects offering the most immediate impact on the corridor. The committee revised the project list to focus on projects that encourage alternative modes of transportation, including bike racks, marketing efforts, or improved bus shelters.

Thus far, the committee has approved expenditures for the Washington Parking Benefit District to sponsor bike racks that were installed in 2016. The bike racks serve two goals: promotion of an alternative method of transportation as well as raising public awareness of the Washington Parking Benefit District.

Although parking occupancy was below the original projections, the PBD pilot is considered a success. Occupancy rates and meter revenue continue to grow in the corridor. Most importantly, complaints have decreased significantly. Since the meter deployment, the Washington Corridor has continued to experience growth with new restaurants and residential developments.

Perhaps the PBD's greatest benefit is the culture of collaboration that it promotes. Businesses and residents now work together to improve their community. The art meter project let parking officials, artists, and the community collaborate to marry fun with function. In the fall 2015, the advisory committee worked with the Mayor's Office and the Health Department to launch "Sunday Streets," an annual event allowing the public to bike, walk, roller skate, hula-hoop, or do any other physical activity in the street without cars. Residents and businesses continue to provide the city with potential meter locations and identify areas where additional enforcement is required.

The PBD advisory committee, through its ongoing discourse and engagement with the community, has come to represent a unified voice speaking on behalf of the Washington Corridor stakeholders. The committee continues to hold public meetings, which provide a venue for residents and businesses to voice concerns. Their website is frequently updated to include meeting agendas and minutes so that the general public is kept aware of the happenings in the district. Other materials, such as permit applications, governing ordinances, and media coverage, are also posted on the site so that residents have a one-stop shop for civic information.

We often talk about the unintended harm from government actions, but we rarely mention the unexpected benefits. What started as a plan to manage curbside parking has grown into a unified voice for businesses and residents who seek to promote economic development while maintaining a sense of community. This new culture of collaboration is certainly an important benefit of the Washington Avenue Parking Benefit District.

REFERENCES AND FURTHER READING

Website for the Washington Avenue Parking Benefit District: *www.houstonpbd.org*
Parking Benefit District Ordinance: http://www.houstontx.gov/parking/
washingtonavenue/pbd_ordinance_20140611.pdf

48

Parking Benefit Districts in Austin, Texas

By Leah M. Bojo

For a moment, set aside your assumptions about people's overwhelming distaste for parking meters. Imagine a magical place where the residents of a busy mixed-use area take it upon themselves to formally propose that meters be installed to manage their bustling streets.

This scenario is difficult to imagine in most cities. Though we know parking meters can solve operational problems, we also know they can create political problems. In our car-reliant culture, residents feel entitled to free on-street parking, particularly in residential areas. When parked cars crowd a neighborhood, the residents often advocate for resident-only parking as the remedy. Unfortunately, these residents don't see any connection between charging for parking and their own goals of achieving safer, tidier streets.

Parking Benefit Districts (PBDs) can address the political friction that comes with a proposal for parking meters. A PBD is a geographically bounded area in which parking meter revenue is dedicated to infrastructure improvement projects within its boundaries (Figure 48-1). The political goal of a PBD is to help residents see their streets as assets by turning high parking demand into revenue to improve the immediate area. Attitudes change when the city sets aside a portion of meter proceeds to spend on local streetscape improvement projects.

Austin, Texas, created a successful PBD program in 2011, describing it as a way "to improve availability of on-street parking while promoting walking, cycling, and transit use." A three-part process first explored a pilot program, then created a citywide program for neighborhoods to opt into, and finally allowed the first official district to opt into the

Figure 48-1 A two-way cycle track installed on Rio Grande Street using revenue from the Parking Benefit District pilot

program. Through this process the high-demand pilot area eventually became the first PBD in Austin. The success of the pilot program supported the creation of a citywide PBD policy.

The 25-block pilot area that now comprises Austin's first PBD is located just west of the University of Texas campus, about 1.5 miles from the heart of downtown. It covers a rapidly growing, mixed-use area serving pedestrians, cyclists, and transit users. Full of students, the neighborhood includes a mix of multifamily and retail uses near single-family homes. Tensions between long-time residents and students had grown as the neighborhood became more popular among student renters. In 2005, the area was upzoned as part of the University Neighborhood Overlay. The overlay included an option to allow new development to decouple parking fees from leases as a condition to increase density. City officials hoped that some students—persuaded by lower rents—would ride transit, bike, or walk to campus instead of drive. Unfortunately, free on-street parking undermined the effects of separating parking costs from rents. Why lease a parking space if you can park on the street for free? Students stored their cars on the streets, sometimes without moving them for months at a time. On-street parking was completely unmanaged and overcrowded. People parked too close to intersections, cars blocked driveways and fire hydrants, and parking spaces were hard to find. At the same time, the area was in great need of infrastructure improvements (Figure 48-2). The extremely high demand for parking in a politically engaged residential area inspired the city to seek an innovative new approach to parking management.

INITIATING THE PILOT

Austin began exploring a PBD program in 2006 by securing a $43,000 grant from the Environmental Protection Agency. This allowed the city to test a PBD by metering the West Campus area, a sizable area outside of downtown. The grant covered meter operating costs, ensuring sufficient revenue would be available to fund area infrastructure projects. During the pilot's development, the city also assured nearby neighbors that the meters could be removed after the grant money was exhausted if the pilot was not deemed successful. This gave residents and city staff a trial period and the promise of an evaluation before the meters became permanent.

City staff considered the pilot a success. In addition to managing the parking, the meters generated considerable revenue. Though the pilot included only 96 metered spaces—compared to thousands downtown—it collected almost $300,000 over four years, proving that a small area with high parking demand can create a sizable revenue stream. The city combined this revenue with other capital funding to widen sidewalks and add benches, street trees, bicycle racks, trash receptacles, and a cycle track along two key streets through the area (Figures 48-3 and 48-4). Bolstered by this success, city staff brought forward an ordinance in 2010 to create a permanent PBD program with the goal that the West Campus pilot area would become the city's first official PBD.

Figure 48-2   The West University Neighborhood is full of missing sidewalks that the PBD can help fund

Figure 48-3   A West University Neighborhood street, complete with pedestrian-scale lights and bike racks

Figure 48-4   The streetscape along 23rd Street funded in part through the PBD pilot

CHALLENGES OF MOVING FROM PILOT TO PROGRAM

The well-received pilot was a very real success, but when the city first proposed the permanent PBD program, some nearby residents and university students raised concerns. In response, city staff assembled a stakeholder group made up of these residents and students to vet the proposal and work through the issues.

Nearby single-family resident stakeholders challenged almost every aspect of the proposed PBD program. They began with the following questions:

- What share of revenue from the metered area should go to the Parking Enterprise Fund (PEF) to be spent citywide?
- What share of the expenses from a PBD should be covered by revenue from the metered area?
- What will the program cost?

After much deliberation, the stakeholders agreed that the revenue from each PBD should cover the program expenses for that district. Program expenses included credit card fees (75 percent of parkers paid by credit card), parking enforcement costs, meter service and maintenance, program administration, receipt production and supplies, street signs and markings, and debt service on the meters.

City staff also insisted that some portion of the revenue go to the citywide PEF so that differences in parking demand among neighborhoods would not create investment inequalities. Acknowledging this, the residents requested that, after program expenses were deducted, 51 percent of the revenue go to the district and 49 percent to the PEF. Staff agreed to the proposed revenue split.

Parking revenue, however, was only one of many concerns voiced by the residents. For example, residents asked how the city would prevent the parking meters from making neighborhoods feel more like business districts.

City staff worked to ameliorate this concern by using multi-space kiosks rather than individual meters. The kiosks not only reduced the total number of meters in neighborhoods, but also provided the opportunity to place them on street corners in single-family areas instead of directly in front of homes.

Residents also questioned how spillover parking would be addressed in the areas adjacent to PBDs. To address this concern, city staff added that all neighbors living adjacent to a proposed PBD, as well as residents in the PBD, had to be notified of the district's creation. All potentially affected residents would then have the opportunity to weigh in. This gives adjacent residents the opportunity to provide input about the appropriate boundaries in order to minimize parking spillover.

Students also voiced one main concern: the loss of free on-street spaces around older apartment complexes that lack off-street parking. Many of these apartment buildings pre-date parking requirements, and their residents parked on the streets. Staff met this concern by allowing residential parking permits for qualifying multifamily residents.

OVERCOMING COMMUNITY DISTRUST

Both residents and students in the stakeholder group asked questions that expressed a lack of trust in city processes:

- How will we know that earmarked revenue is spent in the district as promised?
- Will that revenue be enough to build anything useful?
- Could a district be foisted on a large area by a small group of neighbors, business owners, or by the city itself?

Staff met each of these concerns with small but significant changes to the proposed program requirements. To ensure that PBD revenue was spent in the district, the city was required to hold an annual meeting with the district stakeholders and to share monthly profit and loss reports. To show that sufficient revenue would be generated to build useful projects, city staff shared sidewalk construction cost analyses and added the requirement that a list of potential projects accompany a district's application. By analyzing the project list alongside the revenue projections for a proposed district, city staff could ensure that the proposed improvement projects could realistically be built with projected revenues. Staff also specified that other funding programs could be used in conjunction with the parking revenue, which allowed leveraging the parking revenues to create opportunities to build bigger projects.

Finally, the PBD ordinance was revised to address residents' concern that a small minority could impose a PBD against the will of the majority. The ordinance stipulated that a PBD application may be initiated only by a registered neighborhood organization at least partially located within the proposed district. Once the application is submitted, precise requirements for public engagement mandated resident notification, a community meeting, multiple public hearings, and, ultimately, approval by the city council for each individual district.

Though the process was long and at times arduous, gaining community trust was crucial to the success of the PBD ordinance. Generally, these trust-related issues were easy to remedy through changes to the application process and program requirements. Because city staff took the time to listen and take input, they gained the stakeholders' trust.

STAFF CONCERNS

Through public outreach, city staff also handled some internal concerns. Austin's Transportation Engineer must maintain the ultimate right to install meters wherever he or she sees fit, even in the face of political difficulty. Therefore, staff clarified that PBDs would not be the only method of installing meters going forward. The program is intended to provide a mechanism for areas to get ahead of the curve, installing meters earlier than the city may have otherwise, in exchange for a share of the revenue. There is no legal way—nor should there be—for the city to relinquish the authority to manage its streets.

City staff did not want to include existing meters into PBDs. In the pilot area, a few streets already had meters, and the stakeholder group wanted revenue from those meters to be included into the new PBD. Staff, however, did not want meter revenue that had been budgeted for citywide projects to suddenly be diverted to a small area. This issue was remedied with an agreement to look at districts case by case. In some cases, only incremental revenue from existing meters could be included in the PBD so as not to disrupt those existing revenue streams.

After all the stakeholder concerns were addressed, the city council easily passed the revised PBD program in 2011. The program included the provisions discussed above, plus a 96-space minimum requirement per PBD to warrant the fixed-costs required for operation. The program also required: an occupancy study to make sure that the parking demand was sufficient; an agreement between staff and stakeholders to record district specifics; and the provision that an underperforming PBD could be removed. Though PBD program stakeholders were mostly from the original pilot area, the stakeholders and staff had made an active effort to create a program that would be appropriate and applicable anywhere in the city.

PROGRAM TO PBD

In 2012, about a year after the PBD ordinance passed, the city council approved the West University PBD proposed by area residents. This process went smoothly because most of the community's questions had been answered during the extensive process to create the citywide PBD program. To convert the pilot area into an official PBD, the West University stakeholders gathered the required petitions, notified the area, and held the requisite community meetings. Almost immediately upon approval of the overall program, the West University area stakeholders began working to create their list of priority projects for the district—all of which had to support bicyclists, pedestrians, or transit users. They drew the district boundary outside the metered area to allow future expansion and increased the number of meters from the pilot's 96 to over 300 (Figure 48-5). They drafted their agreement with

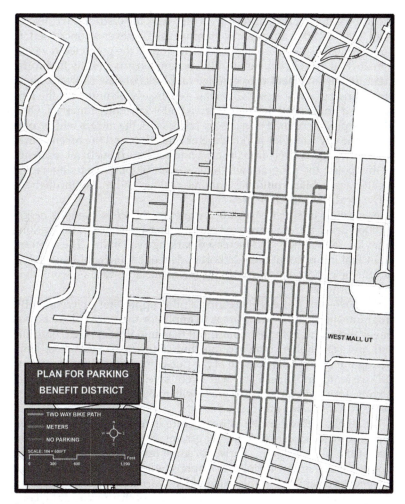

Figure 48-5 Map of the West University Neighborhood parking benefit district

Source: Austin, Texas, Transportation Department

city staff and proposed the West University PBD to the city council, where it was easily approved.

BENEFITS TO AUSTIN

The West University PBD's revenue has increased each year since its formal implementation. Even though the program was not operational during the entirety of its first year, the district still collected more than $95,000 through September 2013. Revenue increased to almost $150,000 the following fiscal year, double the predicted revenue.

In 2016, the West University PBD began constructing its first infrastructure improvement project—several blocks of new sidewalk along a pedestrian priority street. City staff are already planning for the next project—a linear park through an area that is currently unpaved. Once all of the predetermined projects are completed, the meters will become part of the city's regular parking meter collection, and the revenue they produce will go entirely into the citywide coffers to benefit all residents. At this point, the program will have served its purpose by managing street spaces while promoting walking, cycling, and transit through the PBD's local infrastructure projects.

In addition to streetscape improvements, the West Campus neighborhood benefits from improved parking management—better parking behavior, safer streets, and increased parking availability. The concerns about making residential neighborhoods feel commercial have faded, and the neighborhoods are reaping the financial rewards of consistent vehicle turnover.

The three-step process of creating a pilot, approving a citywide PBD program, and then allowing areas to apply for their own districts took longer and required more public input than initially expected. Both city staff and stakeholder patience ran thin at times. Nevertheless, hammering out an overall program at the outset made the West University PBD easier to implement and will likely save time and staff resources moving forward. That consistency will make future PBDs easier to create, forecast, and enforce.

The public interest in the infrastructure investment process and the opportunity to educate stakeholder groups emerged as two added benefits of the pilot program. Early on, some opponents argued that the program was merely passing city responsibility to neighborhoods. That perspective dissipated as the stakeholders learned the particulars of the PBD program's costs and revenues, as well as the bureaucratic complexities of its drafting and implementation. This transparency instilled trust in the program and in the city overall. The PBD program created value above and beyond that of conventional paid parking. It created a shared interest in metering and set an example of how successfully managed parking can improve a mixed-use area.

LESSONS FROM AUSTIN

The West University PBD has exceeded staff expectations and is considered a great success. Nevertheless, there are lessons to be learned.

While no additional neighborhoods have applied for PBDs since the program was approved, two very similar metered districts, called Parking and Transportation Management Districts (PTMDs), have recently been installed in Austin. The PTMD program is conceptually the same as the PBD program: newly installed meters will generate revenue to benefit the areas where the meters are located. The PTMD program has slightly different rules and application processes, which were needed to overcome the narrowness of the PBD application and funding requirements. As a concession to stakeholders, the PBD program allows applications only from resident organizations. Therefore, a new program was required to allow for different applicants and revenue splits. In hindsight, the language for PBDs could have been broader. Had the language in the PBD program been less strict, a parallel program with only slightly different application and spending requirements would not be needed. So far, a mixed-use developer and a group of area merchants have requested PTMDs. Like the PBD program, an overall PTMD program was created first, and then specific areas were able to apply for their own district.

EVIDENCE OF SUCCESS

Austin is already seeing tangible benefits from the pioneering efforts of the PBD and PTMD programs. The West University stakeholders have expanded the metered area within their PBD, and there are multiple places in Austin where the streets are safer for bicyclists, pedestrians, and transit users as a result of the meters. Residents are more aware of parking meters as a viable management tool and more trusting of their city government to implement them. Consequently, other cities can look to Austin's success and feel confident moving forward with their own parking programs. They can also see where Austin could improve by streamlining the PBD and PTMD programs. The creation of the PTMD program, however, points to the success of sharing meter revenue with neighborhoods.

Though perhaps not quite magical, the resident-proposed parking-meter-area scenario is no longer so difficult to imagine. It's happening in Austin and can happen in any city that seeks the benefits of Parking Benefit Districts.

REFERENCES AND FURTHER READING

Austin's Parking Benefit District Program ordinance, 20111006-053: https://austintexas.gov/department/city-council/2011/20111006-reg.htm#053
Austin's West University Parking Benefits District ordinance, 20120927-75: https://austintexas.gov/department/city-council/2012/20120927-reg.htm#075

49

Parking Benefit Districts in Mexico City

By Rodrigo García Reséndiz and Andrés Sañudo Gavaldón

Few transportation policies have been more controversial in Mexico City than ecoParq, which is the city's name for Parking Benefit Districts (PBDs) where the city charges for on-street parking and uses the revenue to improve local public space. Although the city allocates 30 percent of the meter revenue to pay for local public benefits in the metered areas, many people think charging for on-street parking is radical and unfair. Residents want to park free in front of their homes, workers and visitors want free or cheap parking in front of businesses, and operators of the informal on-street parking market want to keep charging for the on-street spaces they have appropriated as their own private property.

Despite early opposition, ecoParq now manages 26,000 of Mexico City's parking spots. The benefits of charging market prices for parking include less traffic congestion, cleaner air, and better public services in the neighborhoods where parking meters were installed.

EcoParq isn't perfect; several features of the program must be refined and polished in order to provide a better experience to users, such as greater transparency and more efficient use of revenue in the affected neighborhoods. The initial results of pricing curb parking, however, have been mostly positive, making it difficult to oppose expansion of the program.

BEFORE ECOPARQ

Early attempts to charge for on-street parking in Mexico City began in the 1990s, when residents of two popular commercial areas, Cuauhtémoc and Juárez (also known as the *Zona Rosa*), wanted to address the over-crowding of their streets with commuters' cars. Residents and business owners, in partnership with the local government, approved the instal-lation of parking meters operated by a private concessionaire. As a part of the agreement, 84 percent of the net revenue went to the conces-sionaire to operate and maintain the parking meters. Only 16 percent of the net revenue was set aside for public improvement in these areas. Although well intentioned, corruption, lack of enforcement, and opacity in how public funds were allocated and spent undermined the benefits of this effort. Consequently, other neighborhoods were discouraged from charging curb parking.

After the early efforts to regulate on-street parking were abandoned, weak on-street parking enforcement and more driving have increased traffic congestion. Weak enforcement has also promoted a robust infor-mal private market. Parking in unregulated business and commercial areas is impossible without paying a fee to *franeleros* (named after the red rags they use to attract customers), who illegally manage public space. *Franeleros* appropriate public space with the help of buckets, traffic cones, wooden crates, and the like. Needless to say, their goal is not to improve parking and mobility but to maximize their profits

Figure 49-1 Illustration of a street before the implementation of Parking Benefit Districts in Mexico City

by parking as many cars as possible on the streets and sidewalks. This creates a hostile environment for pedestrians and limits their mobility.

IMPLEMENTATION AND GROWTH OF ECOPARQ

The early attempt to charge for on-street parking in the 1990s was not a success, leaving the city with no more than 5,000 single-space parking meters. In 2011, the government of Mexico City explored the concept of Parking Benefit Districts (PBDs) with the understanding that a different strategy was needed to produce the desired results.

The new strategy included the participation of three public agencies. The Mexico City Department of Urban Development and Housing designated the areas where the PBDs were implemented. The Mexico City Department of Finance was in charge of receiving the revenue collected by the private companies overseeing the parking meters. Finally, the Mexico City Public Space Authority was tasked with supervising the installation, operation, and maintenance of the parking meter system. With the goal of recovering, reclaiming, and managing public space, this authority was also in charge of creating a public input process for determining how the funds would be reinvested. The new strategy also included a financial plan, allotting 70 percent of the parking meter net revenue to the private operator and 30 percent to public space improvements within these areas. The PBDs more than doubled the number of metered curb spaces in Mexico City from 11,315 in 2012 to 26,378 in 2014.

The recently implemented PBDs should be only the beginning of an ambitious target to meter more than 100,000 parking spaces in the city. When completed, the program could serve as a model for parking policy throughout Latin America.

BENEFITS

The quality of life and public space has improved in the ecoParq neighborhoods. The program demonstrates that the overcrowded curb parking was not due to a lack of supply but rather to a lack of efficient management. For example, in Polanco, an upscale area in Mexico City, on-street parking was 100 percent occupied (and more than 100 percent when taking into account illegal parking) before ecoParq was introduced. After ecoParq, although some streets were still saturated, average occupancy rates declined to levels between 65 and 90 percent. Figures 49-3 and 49-4 show the on-street occupancy rates in Polanco before and after the implementation of ecoParq.

Figure 49-2   Illustration of a street after the implementation of Parking Benefit Districts in Mexico City

The number of blocks with high occupancy (ranging from 86 to 100 percent) fell almost 75 percent, while those with an occupancy rate ranging between 51 to 85 percent increased more than 600 percent. The increased number of open parking spaces suggests a lower number of cars circulating through this neighborhood while searching for a parking space. The parking meters in Polanco reduced the average cruising time from 13 minutes to three minutes. This reduction in cruising led to fewer emissions, less illegal parking, and a more livable city.

The collective benefits of PBDs have proved to be bigger than the individual benefits of free parking. In addition to reducing congestion and emissions, PBDs generate more than $16 million annually for public space improvements, which translates into benefits for the majority of the population and not only motorists. Parking meter revenues pay

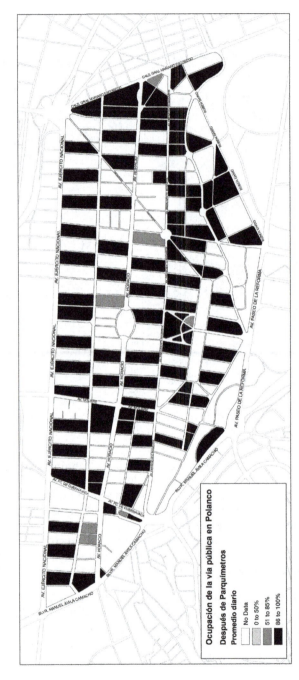

Ocupación de la vía pública en Polanco

Después de Parquímetros

Promedio diario

☐ No Data
☐ 0 to 50%
▨ 51 to 85%
■ 86 to 100%

Figure 49-3 Average daily on-street parking occupancy percentages before ecoParq

Source: ITDP, 2012

for better sidewalks, graffiti removal, new landscaping, and more pedestrian spaces.

Changes to on-street parking policies commonly generate side effects. Mexico City experienced two major unintended consequences. Historically, public officials had made transportation policy behind closed doors, with little transparency or accountability. Because parking meters are a highly controversial subject, however, the city knew it had to sponsor outreach events to inform the public about the benefits of charging for on-street parking, and the stakeholder meetings were highly politicized. So, the first unforeseen side effect was that some neighborhoods refused to implement a PBD. Nevertheless, some PBDs moved forward. Opposition may subside as the newly implemented ecoParq districts become established and improve their neighborhoods.

A second unforeseen yet desirable outcome occurred when setting the "right" price for curb parking, which triggered a review of Mexico City's minimum parking requirements. Advocates of better parking policies, such as The Institute of Transportation and Development Policy, knew that to implement comprehensive parking reform in the city, it would be necessary to eliminate, or at least reduce, the minimum parking requirements. Thus, the benefits of better on-street parking regulation have stimulated discussion about reducing off-street parking requirements (see Chapter 15).

ROOM FOR IMPROVEMENT

EcoParq can definitely be improved. Beyond the improvements related to technology, such as payment options, real-time information, and demand-responsive pricing strategy, proposed changes must come from local public officials, such as the creation of a parking management department, a new contract scheme between the private operators and the government, and a long-term plan to finance public space improvements.

Because the city is attempting to create one of the largest paid on-street parking systems in the world, it should create a specific parking management department. Controlling on-street parking necessitates a strong and qualified public agency, regardless of whether the meters are operated by public authorities or private companies. This department should be in charge of setting the official guidelines for every stakeholder with the vision of providing a minimum quality of service for every neighborhood. Therefore, it should also be in charge of planning and evaluating the private operators' management of eco-Parq. Periodic evaluations are essential to identify areas for improvements to address mobility and public space objectives. The agency

Ocupación de la vía pública en Polanco
Antes de Parquímetros
Promedio diario

- ☐ No Data
- ☐ 0 to 50%
- ☐ 51 to 85%
- ■ 86 to 100%

Figure 49-4 Average daily on-street parking occupancy percentages after ecoParq

Source: ITDP

Figure 49-5   Sidewalk and a parking meter in Polanco, Mexico City
Source: ITDP

should also push for a large share of meter revenue destined to public projects.

To increase efficiency, competing concessionaires should bid for the contract to manage the parking spaces. Money collection should be centralized in a trust account, instead of going to a general government account, to pay the legitimate recipients for intended uses. This will increase transparency and public confidence, and will also reduce implementation risks and complaints. Perhaps most important, independent accountants should audit ecoParq's revenues and expenditures, and publish the results.

EcoParq should also adopt more convenient payment options, such as credit and debit cards, prepaid parking, and pay-by-phone technology. These changes should include the introduction of a mobile app that provides real-time information to users about availability and pricing. In recent years, technology used to manage curb parking and measure occupancy has advanced rapidly. The existing parking meters in Mexico City are programmed to charge a flat rate, regardless of the demand for curb parking. Setting different prices at different times of day could help to manage on-street parking more efficiently.

Finally, the city should adopt a long-term plan to finance public space improvements with parking revenue. Public officials should start a participatory process for developing a five- or 10-year vision of public spaces in the area. The parking benefit districts will allow the city to achieve this vision.

CONCLUSION

There was a time when drivers controlled every inch of Mexico City's streets, and those who walk were second-class citizens. Now, in some parts of the city, PBDs have left those times behind. In fact, not only have pedestrians benefited from the PBDs, but so have residents, business owners, and the vast majority of citizens. If PBDs expand throughout the city, Mexico will be famous not only for its great size, its rich history, its food, and its culture, but also for its livability. Automobile drivers who pay their fair share for using public land will finance this enhanced livability.

REFERENCES AND FURTHER READING

Díaz, R. 2012. "Políticas Públicas Destinadas a Reducir el Uso del Automóvil: Manual de Implementación de Sistemas de Parquímetros para Ciudades Mexicanas." Instituto de Políticas para el Transporte y Desarrollo México. http://mexico.itdp.org/documentos/manual-de-implementacion-de-sistemas-de-parquimetros-para-ciudades-mexicanas/
Medina, S., A. Sañudo, X. Treviño, and J. Veloz. 2013. "Impacts of the ecoParq Program on Polanco: Preliminary Overview of the Parking Meter System after One Year Running." Institute of Transportation Development and Policy. https://www.itdp.org/impacts-of-the-ecoparq-program-on-polanco/
Medina, S., and X. Veloz. 2012. "Planes Integrales de Movilidad: Lineamientos para una movilidad urbana sustentable. Instituto de Políticas para el Transporte y Desarrollo México. http://mexico.itdp.org/archivo/documentos/manuales/?tdo_tag=reduccion-del-uso-del-automovil
Sañudo, A. 2012. Implementación de Parquímetros en Polanco: Estudio de Línea Base.: Instituto de Políticas para el Transporte y Desarrollo México. http://mexico.itdp.org/documentos/implementacion-de-parquimetros-en-polanco-estudio-de-linea-base/

50

Parking Benefit Districts in Beijing

By Donald Shoup, Quan Yuan, and Xin Jiang

Many low-income neighborhoods have two serious problems: overcrowded on-street parking and undersupplied public services. One policy can address both problems: charge for on-street parking to manage demand and use the resulting revenue to finance local public services.

Charging the right price for on-street parking is the best way to manage demand, and the right price is the lowest price that will produce one or two open parking spaces on every block. This is the Goldilocks Principle of parking prices: the price is too high if many spaces are open, and the price is too low if no spaces are open. If one or two spaces are open on each block, drivers can reliably find a curb space at their destination, and the price is just right. Goldilocks prices will ensure that curb parking is both well used (most spaces are occupied) and yet readily available (new arrivals always see a convenient place to park).

New technology has solved the practical problems of charging demand-based prices for curb parking. Meters can charge different prices for parking at different times of day, and occupancy sensors can report the availability of curb spaces in real time. The remaining problems of charging for curb parking are political.

PARKING BENEFIT DISTRICTS

To solve the political problems of charging for curb parking, some U.S. cities have made parking meters popular by forming Parking Benefit

Districts (PBDs) that spend the meter revenue to pay for public services within the metered areas. If all the meter revenue disappears into a city's general fund, few businesses or residents will want to charge for on-street parking. Dedicating the revenue to pay for neighborhood public services, however, can create local support for priced parking. Prices manage the parking, and public services improve the neighborhood. Everyone who lives, works, visits, or owns property in the district can then see the benefits paid for by parking.

Old Pasadena, a historic business district in Pasadena, California, illustrates the potential of PBDs (see Chapter 44 above). Parking meter revenue in Old Pasadena helped convert a former commercial skid row into a popular destination. In 1993, the city installed parking meters in Old Pasadena and committed the resulting revenue of more than $1 million a year to rebuild the sidewalks, plant street trees, add historic street furniture, increase police patrols, and provide other public services. Following the example of Pasadena, several other U.S. cities, including Austin (Chapter 48), Houston (Chapter 47), and San Diego, have committed parking revenue to finance public services on the metered streets.

Will PBDs work in other countries? To help answer this question, we examine the case of a historic neighborhood in Beijing, China. Although our case study focuses on one neighborhood, the findings should be relevant for any neighborhood where: (1) on-street parking is overcrowded; (2) public services are undersupplied; (3) most residents park off-street or do not own a car; and (4) residents who do own a car have higher incomes. Many cities, especially in Asia, Africa, and Latin America, have neighborhoods that fit these four criteria.

PARKING SPACES AND PUBLIC SERVICES IN HUTONGS

The Chinese word *hutong* refers to narrow alleys in historic neighborhoods in Beijing, and they are similar to streets in low-income parts of many older cities around the world. Figure 50-1 shows a hutong before cars arrived.

Regularized Parking

Hutongs are typically between three meters (10 feet) and nine meters (30 feet) wide. Beijing prohibits parking in alleys that are narrower than six meters, and permits parking in wider alleys only in legal spaces that are marked by lines painted on the roadway. Nevertheless, because drivers have nowhere else to park, illegal parking has become a widespread practice tolerated by the authorities (Figure 50-2).

Figure 50-1 A hutong before cars arrived

Figure 50-2 Unregulated parking and resulting traffic in a hutong

Many drivers avoid using their cars because parking will be difficult when they return. Some drivers have devised ingenious tricks to preserve their parking spaces when they leave, such as erecting temporary sheds to prevent anyone else from parking. In effect, car owners privatize public land by encroaching on the streets.

The share of cars parked illegally in Beijing has been estimated to be as high as 45 percent. Cars often block traffic and occupy much of the space planned for cyclists and pedestrians. Because so many drivers now park illegally, enforcing the regulations is politically difficult. The best solution may therefore be to regularize and charge for some of this illegal parking, taking into account urban design, the competing needs of different road users (pedestrians, cyclists, delivery vans, emergency services), and the residents' demand for parking spaces.

Regularizing informal on-street parking implies marking the boundaries of spaces and assigning rights to their use. This process has two main benefits. First, it makes parking more convenient and reduces the traffic chaos caused by illegal parking. Second, it creates the opportunity to charge for on-street parking and thus produce revenue to improve public services.

Better Public Services

If cities spend the revenue from on-street parking to pay for desired public services, many residents, especially those who park off street or do not own a car, may support charging for parking in their neighborhoods. While most hutongs in Beijing have running water, electricity, and even internet access, many do not have sanitary sewer connections. The residents must therefore use public toilets. Because many alleys have overcrowded parking and unsanitary public toilets, we examine whether charging for on-street parking can yield enough revenue to provide clean public toilets. More convenient parking for drivers and better toilets for everyone may create the popular support necessary to regularize and charge for on-street parking.

A PILOT PROGRAM

Fortunately, we have an example where Beijing piloted a program to regularize parking and provide public services. Xisi North 7th Alley is a typical hutong with 247 households and about 660 residents. The regularization part of the program aims to prevent illegal parking, remove obstacles used to secure vacant parking spaces, and reserve parking spaces for alley residents (Figure 50-3).

Figure 50-3 Regularized parking spaces in Xisi North 7th Alley

The pilot program also improves public services. Government employees clean the public toilets (Figure 50-4). Surveillance cameras and 24-hour patrol officers increase security. Private firms provide other services, including street cleaning, trash collection, and landscape maintenance.

FINANCIAL ANALYSIS

Capital and Operating Costs

Parking is free in the pilot program and a subsidy from the subdistrict government pays to provide the public services. We can, however, estimate whether parking charges could replace the subsidy for the pilot program. The capital costs for 7th Alley, which were mainly for sanitation, landscaping, and parking regularization, totaled about $62,000 (¥380,000). The operating costs, which are mainly for the salaries of toilet cleaners, trash collectors, and patrol officers, are about $24,600 (¥150,000) a year.

Other neighborhoods with chaotic parking and poor public services would like to see similar improvements, but government subsidies are not available to subsidize the pilot program everywhere. Can charging market prices for on-street parking yield enough revenue to finance

Figure 50-4 Public toilet in Xisi North 6th Alley

the capital and operating costs of similar programs in other neighborhoods? To answer this question, we examine the potential parking revenue in 7th Alley.

Revenue from On-Street Parking

Cities can use several non-price ways to distribute parking permits among residents (for example, by lottery), but charging for the permits is the only way to produce revenue to pay for public services. Auctioning the permits is the simplest way to discover the price that will equate the supply and demand for parking in a neighborhood. Beijing auctions land for residential, commercial, and office uses, and Shanghai auctions license plates. Therefore, auctions for parking permits have well-established precedents.

Uniform-price auctions are often used when selling a large number of identical items. Consider how a uniform-price auction could allocate the permits in 7th Alley, which has 52 parking spaces. Suppose each resident can submit a bid for one permit. After the bids are ranked in descending order, the highest 52 bidders receive permits. All the winning bidders then pay the same price: the lowest accepted bid. All but the lowest winning bidder thus pay less than what they actually bid. Uniform-price auctions encourage people to bid the highest price they are willing to pay because the high bidders do not risk paying more than the lowest accepted bid. Your bid determines whether you receive a permit but not what you pay for it.

The auction prices for on-street parking will presumably relate to the market price of nearby off-street parking. For example, if residents can rent parking in a nearby garage, that price could put a ceiling on what residents are willing to bid for a permit to park in the alley. Because the prices in the nearest garages are around $80 a month, this seems a reasonable estimate for the auction value of the 52 parking spaces in 7th Alley. If the auction price is $80 a month, the 52 permits will yield total annual revenue of about $50,000 ($80 × 52 permits × 12 months) to pay for added public services.

Although $80 a month may seem a lot to charge for a permit to park on the street, car owners will receive guaranteed parking spaces, which are valuable assets where parking had previously been a big problem. Because the parking revenue will pay for public services, the combination of guaranteed parking and the new public services may entice even residents who park on the street to support market-priced parking. If most residents park off street or do not own a car, they can provide strong political support for PBDs.

The Payback Period

At a price of $80 per space per month, the potential parking revenue in 7th Alley is about $50,000 a year, which is double the program's operating cost of $25,000 a year. Because the net operating revenue is about $25,000 a year ($50,000 – $25,000) and the capital cost was about $62,000, the payback period for the capital investment is 2.5 years ($62,000 ÷ $25,000). In this case, the parking revenue should more than cover the operating costs and quickly repay the capital costs of the alley improvements. This result suggests that the program can be self-financing and is replicable in other neighborhoods.

POLITICAL PROSPECTS OF RESIDENTIAL PARKING BENEFIT DISTRICTS

Residential parking permits are usually free or cheap because influential car owners resist paying a market price to park in front of their own homes. Residential Parking Benefit Districts resemble conventional Residential Parking Permit Districts but differ in three key ways. First, the number of permits is limited to the number of curb spaces. Second, drivers pay market prices for the permits. Third, the permit revenue pays for neighborhood public services. In neighborhoods where most residents park off street or do not own a car, the desire for better public services can outweigh the desire to park free on the street.

To examine the political feasibility of charging for parking to finance public services, we examined the demographics of people and cars in 7th Alley (Table 50-1). Only 35 percent of households own a car. The other 65 percent who are carless will receive better public services without paying anything, and they outnumber the car owners almost 2-to-1. If the carless majority prefers public services to free parking, a PBD may be politically feasible.

EQUITY IN RESIDENTIAL PARKING BENEFIT DISTRICTS

A lottery that gives every household an equal chance to win a parking space might seem fairer than an auction. A lottery, however, would not provide any revenue to pay for public services. A lottery would instead give valuable land to a few lucky car owners and nothing to everyone else. Randomly giving free parking to a few car owners and nothing to many more people who cannot afford a car is hardly fair.

If charging for parking can earn $50,000 a year to pay for public services, free parking subsidizes car ownership by $50,000 a year. Is providing free parking for 52 cars more important than providing better public services for the 660 people living in the alley? If the city were already charging market prices for parking and spending $50,000 a year to provide extra public services, few would argue that the city should remove the public services to provide free parking.

Parking Benefit Districts are bottom-up governance, not top-down regulation. But will charging for parking place an unfair burden on lower-income residents? In Beijing, car-owning households have more than twice the income of carless households (Table 50-2). In 7th Alley, they have almost three times the income of carless households. Charging for parking and spending the revenue for public services will therefore transfer income from richer to poorer households. Because richer households who park their private cars on public land will finance public services not only for themselves but also for many poorer people, it is hard to argue that charging market prices for on-street parking will be unfair.

When both equity and efficiency are considered, PBDs should be most appropriate where car owners have higher incomes and most residents do not own a car, so the poorer, carless majority will receive public benefits at no personal cost.

Parking Benefit Districts can efficiently manage on-street parking and equitably finance public services, but do they privatize public land?

Table 50-1 Automobile ownership in Beijing

	Beijing	XiSi 7th Alley
Number of households	8,358,893	247
Number of households who own cars	3,510,735	86
Number of households without cars	4,848,158	161
Share of households who own cars	42%	35%
Share of households without cars	58%	65%

Source: 2013 Beijing Statistical Yearbook
 2013 Beijing Economic and Social Development Statistical Reports
Time of the data: at the end of 2013

Table 50-2 Average annual income per household in Beijing

	Beijing ($/year)	XiSi 7th Alley ($/year)
All households	13,150	9100
Households who own cars	16,600	15,600
Households without cars	8,000	5,600
Income ratio of owners/nonowners	208%	279%

Source: North 6th Alley Community Residents Committee; Beijing Traffic Management Bureau

The government owns the land, charges market prices for parking private cars on it, and spends the revenue to provide public services. PBDs thus resemble market socialism, not privatization.

CONCLUSION: TURNING PROBLEMS INTO OPPORTUNITIES

Streets belong to the community and PBDs can monetize on-street parking to pay for community benefits. Our case study of a pilot program in Beijing found that on-street parking can finance important public investments with a payback period of less than three years. Most households do not own a car, and the car-owning households' average income is almost three times that of carless households. PBDs will therefore transfer income from richer drivers to poorer nondrivers, while rich and poor alike will benefit from regulated parking and better public services.

Parking Benefit Districts are most appropriate in dense neighborhoods where: 1) on-street parking is overcrowded; 2) public services are undersupplied; 3) most residents park off street or do not own a car; and 4) residents who do own a car have higher incomes. Where these criteria are met, any city should be able to offer a pilot program to charge for parking and use the revenue to finance public services. If residents don't like the results, the city can cancel the program. If residents do like the results, however, the city can offer this self-financing program to other neighborhoods. Because neighborhoods will have money to spend and decisions to make, residents will gain a new voice in governing their communities. Residential PBDs may turn out to be a fair, efficient, and politically feasible way to improve the world, one parking space at a time.

REFERENCES AND FURTHER READING

Shoup, Donald, Quan Yuan, and Xin Jiang. 2016. "Charging for Parking to Finance Public Services," *Journal of Planning Education and Research*, Vol. 37, No. 2, June, pp. 136–149. https://www.dropbox.com/s/lgrzggpz1r3myr2/ChargingForParkingToFinancePublicServices.pdf?dl=0

51

Residential Parking Benefit Districts

By Donald Shoup

When the music changes, so does the dance.

HAUSA PROVERB

Charging drivers for parking on a residential street may seem like charging children for playing in a public park. But if curb parking is free and all the spaces are occupied, drivers who want to park will circle the block hoping to see a car pulling out. This search for hard-to-find free parking congests traffic, pollutes the air, and wastes fuel. Free curb parking on a crowded street gives a small, temporary benefit to a few drivers who are lucky on a particular day, but it creates large social costs for everyone else every day.

If cities charge the right price for curb parking—the lowest price that will produce one or two open spaces on each block—no one will need to hunt for parking. All drivers will suddenly have great parking karma.

To create political support for right-priced curb parking in commercial areas, some cities have created Parking Benefit Districts that spend the meter revenue for public services on the metered streets. These cities offer each district a package that includes both priced parking and better public services such as clean sidewalks and free Wi-Fi. Everyone who visits, works in, or owns a business in a commercial district with a Parking Benefit District (PBD) can see their meter money at work. But will PBDs also work in residential neighborhoods?

RESIDENTIAL PARKING BENEFIT DISTRICTS

In residential neighborhoods, Parking *Benefit* Districts resemble conventional Parking *Permit* Districts (neighborhoods where a permit is required for on-street parking) but differ in three important ways. First, the number of permits in a PBD is limited to the number of curb spaces. Second, drivers pay market prices for the permits. Third, the permit revenue pays for neighborhood public services.

Consider a neighborhood where most residents either do not own a car or, if they do own a car, park it off-street. Only a small minority store a car on the street. In this case, the prospect of better public services—a cleaner and greener neighborhood—may persuade a majority of residents to support charging market prices for on-street parking.

Charging market prices for curb parking doesn't mean that only the rich will be able to park on the street. Because cities are segregated by income, the rich will compete mainly with each other for on-street parking and will drive up permit prices in their own neighborhoods. Higher prices for residential parking permits in richer neighborhoods will act like an income tax on motorists who park on the street.

UNIFORM PRICE AUCTIONS

How can cities set market prices for residential parking permits? A uniform-price auction, which is often used when many identical items are sold, is the simplest way to discover the market price for the limited number of residential parking permits. Limiting the number of permits to the number of available spaces is important. A district with more on-street parking permits than on-street parking spaces would be like a theater that sells more tickets than it has seats.

Consider how a uniform-price auction would work on a block with 20 on-street parking spaces reserved for residents. Any resident can bid for a permit. The bids are ranked in descending order and the highest 20 bidders receive permits. In a uniform-price auction, all the winning bidders then pay the same price: the lowest accepted bid. All successful bidders except the lowest bidder thus pay less than what they bid. A few curb spaces can also be reserved as metered parking for drivers without permits.

Auctioning permits to park on residential streets may at first feel as repugnant as auctioning kidneys to transplant recipients. But if the revenue pays to repave the streets, clean the sidewalks, plant street trees, and provide other public services, critics may change their minds. Few will pay for curb parking but everyone will benefit from the public services. Because cities do not now charge for parking on residential streets, Parking Benefit Districts provide a new source of public revenue and won't take resources away from any other public program.

Residents who don't store a car on the street may begin to eye crowded curb spaces as a potential revenue source for public services and view free parking the way landlords view rent control. Free curb parking *is* like rent control for cars. Randomly giving free parking to a few drivers and nothing to people who cannot afford a car, or choose not to own one, is unfair.

At first glance, skeptics may think that auctions for parking permits will privatize public land, but the government owns the land, charges market prices for parking private cars on it, and spends the revenue to provide public services. PBDs thus resemble market socialism, not privatization.

Nevertheless, some critics may say market prices for parking will be too high for drivers to pay. There are four responses to this criticism. First, the price will be high only if drivers are willing to pay a high price for parking they previously got free. Second, with a uniform-price auction, all permit holders except the lowest successful bidder are willing to pay an even higher price than what they do pay for a permit. Third, if the price is high, more money will be available to pay for better public services. Fourth, any price lower than the market price will create a shortage of curb parking, which will lead to cruising that congests traffic and pollutes the air. These are good reasons to refute any claim that market prices for curb parking will be too high. If, for example, market-priced curb parking on a block can produce enough revenue to pay for free Wi-Fi and free transit passes for all residents, who would say the market price is too high?

Everyone wants to park free, but for a driver there's not much difference between free curb parking that's not available and market-priced curb parking that's not affordable. There is, however, a huge difference for cities. Free curb parking on a busy street increases traffic congestion and air pollution, while market-priced curb parking produces revenue to pay for public services.

Residential PBDs could be tried on one side of each block. They would earn only half as much revenue as charging for parking on both sides of the street, but they would give residents the choice between either free or paid parking. Residents could then directly compare the benefits of free parking that is hard to find and paid parking that is guaranteed. If the residents later decide to price both sides of the block, they would double the money available to pay for neighborhood public services.

RESIDENTIAL PARKING BENEFIT DISTRICTS IN MANHATTAN

Manhattan would be a good place to test the benefits of residential
PBDs because only 22 percent of its households own a car (Table 51-1).
Despite its low car ownership, Manhattan may generate more cruising
in its residential neighborhoods than in any other city on Earth (*The
High Cost of Free Parking*, 277–278 and 285–288).

Elected officials know the parking problem. New York City Council
Member Mark Levine said in 2017, "As anyone who's ever looked
for a parking spot in Manhattan knows all too well, it is a brutal
and time consuming process." People who complain about parking
naturally sees it from the view of drivers, but cruising for parking
is also hard on everyone else. It slows all other traffic, including
public transit and goods movement. It endangers cyclists and pedestrians, and it pollutes the air everyone breathes. By reducing cruising
for parking, residential PBDs can improve life for almost everyone in
the city.

Cities can treat their valuable on-street parking as a public
endowment to finance public services, and the revenue will be
impressive. Condominium parking spaces have been sold for up to
$1 million in Manhattan and $300,000 in Brooklyn, so curb parking
spaces should bring high prices at auction (*The High Cost of Free Parking*,
513–519).

Governments are good at making major public investments like highways and subways, but not so good at maintaining them (Figure 51-1).
Revenue from on-street parking can pay to keep public infrastructure
clean and in good repair.

In Manhattan, a large majority will benefit from the public services
while a small minority will pay for on-street parking. Because the average income of households in Manhattan who own cars is 88 percent
higher than that of carless households, charging for curb parking and
spending the revenue for public services will redistribute income from
richer to poorer families (Table 51-2).

Table 51-1 Automobile ownership in New York City

	New York City	Manhattan
Number of households	3,063,393	738,131
Number of households without a car	1,699,976	577,967
Number of households who own a car	1,363,417	160,164
Share of households who own a car	45%	22%

Source: 2008-2012 American Community Survey 5-Year Estimates

Figure 51-1   Subway station at West 4th Street in Manhattan
Source: Eric Goldwyn

Table 51-2   Average annual income per household in New York

City	New York City	Manhattan
All households	$77,060	$120,091
Households who own a car	$96,472	$191,389
Households without a car	$61,836	$101,554
Income ratio of owners/nonowners	156%	188%

Source: 2008-2012 American Community Survey, Public Use Microdata Sample

GUARANTEED EQUALITY

If richer neighborhoods have higher parking prices, they will earn more money to pay for public services. To avoid this inequality, cities can use what in public finance is called *power equalization*. Suppose the city's average permit revenue per curb space is $2,000 a year. In this case, the city can spend $1,000 a year per space for added public services in every PBD and spend the other $1,000 a year for citywide public services. Neighborhoods that charge market prices for parking will receive equal revenue to improve their public services and all neighborhoods will benefit from the improved citywide public services.

With power equalization for parking-financed public services, neighborhoods that earn the most revenue will subsidize neighborhoods that earn the least revenue. This sharing arrangement retains the local incentive to install parking meters (every PBD gets revenue to pay for public services) but the revenue is distributed equally among all the metered neighborhoods (every PBD gets the same revenue per parking meter). Distributing meter revenue with power equalization seems fairer than the usual policy of installing parking meters in neighborhoods that have a parking problem and then spending all the revenue anywhere in the city.

TOTAL REVENUE

The total revenue PBDs can earn depends on the number of parking spaces in a city. San Francisco is the only American city that has conducted a complete census of its on-street spaces (San Francisco Municipal Transportation Agency 2014). San Francisco has 275,450 on-street spaces, or about one curb space for every three residents. Laid end-to-end, San Francisco's on-street parking spaces would stretch about 1,000 miles, which is longer than California's 840-mile coastline. If each on-street parking space is 160 square feet, San Francisco's on-street parking would cover about 1.6 square miles, the size of Golden Gate Park. The land value must be immense; since 90 percent of San Francisco's on-street parking is unmetered, the parking subsidy must be immense.

Although New York does not have an exact count, experts have estimated that the city has at least three million on-street parking spaces, about one curb space for every three residents. If laid end-to-end, these parking spaces would stretch almost halfway around the earth and would cover about 17 square miles of land, 13 times the size of Central Park. Because 97 percent of New York's on-street parking is unmetered, the parking subsidy must be astronomical. Land is expensive for housing but free for parking cars on the street in front of the housing.

If only half of New York's three million on-street spaces were in Parking Benefit Districts and they earned an average revenue of $2,000 per space per year (only $5.50 per day), the total revenue will amount to $3 billion per year. Half could go to improve neighborhoods and the other half could pay for citywide public services, such as renovating the subway system. With power equalization for parking finance, this tsunami of money will flow from richer to poorer neighborhoods and from Manhattan to the outer boroughs. Planners and politicians can let money and public services persuade citizens to charge market prices for on-street parking in their neighborhoods.

LOCAL OPTION

Cities can offer neighborhoods the choice between free curb parking or better public services. For example, if a block has 20 curb spaces and each space can earn $2,000 a year, free parking subsidizes drivers by $40,000 a year ($2,000 × 20). If the city already charged market prices for curb parking and earned an extra $40,000 a year to pay for public services on a block where most residents don't park a car on the street, few would say the city should spend $40,000 a year less for public services to subsidize hard-to-find parking for 20 cars.

PBD revenue can finance a wide array of public services in residential neighborhoods. Examples of the services already being provided by PBDs in business districts include nightly street and sidewalk cleaning; free public Wi-Fi for everyone in the district; and free transit passes for all workers in the district (Chapters 44-50). Providing these new public services financed by curb parking will also create new jobs in the neighborhood. In contrast, free curb parking doesn't employ anyone.

PBDs can also eliminate the need for on-street parkers to move their cars from one side of the street to the other on street-cleaning days. Permit revenue can pay for vacuum equipment to clean around and under parked cars so drivers won't have to move their cars for street cleaning and won't get tickets for street-cleaning violations.

PBDs are a bottom-up rather than a top-down policy because each neighborhood will decide whether to adopt one. Only the neighborhoods where a majority of the residents want a PBD will get one. Even the neighborhoods that choose not to have a PBD will benefit from the citywide services financed by neighborhoods with PBDs. This local democratic choice is impossible with most other transportation policies, such as whether to build rail transit or impose congestion tolls.

Any city can offer a pilot program to charge for on-street parking in a few densely populated neighborhoods with scarce curb parking and use the revenue to finance public services (*The High Cost of Free Parking*, 447–50). If residents don't like the results, the city can cancel the program. If residents do like the results, however, the city can offer this self-financing program in other neighborhoods.

TRANSITION POLICY

If a neighborhood already has a Residential Parking Permit District with free or cheap permits, residents will probably resist shifting to market-priced permits. Cities can solve this problem by allowing current permit holders to continue paying the old price for their permits but charge market prices for new permits. If the existing permits are "grandfathered" at the old low price, current residents will not be priced out of the neighborhood and market prices will phase in as old residents move out. The original residents will enjoy the new public services without paying more for parking.

Vancouver, British Columbia, intends to use this transition policy to introduce market prices for residential parking permits in the West End of the city. The transition to market prices should be fast because many households do not keep their parking permits for long. Only 20 percent of the permits in Vancouver remain active more than five years.

Protecting current residents to gain political support for a transition has good precedents. Rent control often applies to current residents but rents reset to market rates when properties turn over. This transition policy may seem more expedient than fair, but reforms must start from the status quo. As Supreme Court Justice Benjamin Cardozo wrote, "Justice is not to be taken by storm. She is to be wooed by slow advances."

AFFORDABLE HOUSING

Parking Benefit Districts can increase the supply of affordable housing. Almost every proposal for new housing in an old neighborhood now comes bundled with a dispute over scarce curb parking. Current residents fear that new residents will compete for the free on-street parking and make their already difficult parking situation worse. As a result, cities require new housing to provide enough off-street parking to prevent crowding the on-street parking. Free curb parking is thus a tail that wags two dogs—transportation and housing.

If on-street parking is free, the only way to limit the number of cars parked on the street is to limit the number of new housing units and require them to have ample off-street parking. These parking requirements increase the cost and reduce the supply of housing. But if permits restrain the demand for parking to fit the available curb supply, new housing will not lead to overcrowded curbs. Cities can then remove their off-street parking requirements and allow developers to provide less parking and more housing. If a developer provides little or no off-street parking, the developer takes a risk, not the city or the neighborhood. Cities that use PBDs to manage on-street parking won't need to require off-street parking.

PBDs can further increase the supply of affordable housing by allowing homeowners to convert their garages into granny flats. Homeowners who convert their off-street parking garages into housing may be able to surrender their former curb cut and convert it into a new curb parking space, which will increase the on-street parking supply. Cities could encourage garage conversions by rewarding homeowners who surrender their curb cuts. For example, a city can offer a permanent free transit pass in exchange for closing a curb cut, and the cost would be financed by the curb parking revenue from the new parking space.

Figure 51-2   Garages converted into housing

Source: Donald Shoup

Figure 51-2 illustrates how second units can improve the urban design of residential façades when it replaces a garage door that formerly dominated the front of a house. (The entry door to the second unit can be in the side setback.)

By creating new affordable housing, garage conversions can reduce the demand for the existing affordable housing by increasing both the number of small units and their geographical availability. If reformed parking requirements allow it, garage apartments can create income-integrated communities not only in the sense of income diversity within a neighborhood but also of people with different incomes living on the same piece of property. The garage apartments will be what has been called naturally occurring affordable housing (NOAH): units that are affordable without being supported by public subsidies. Because the residents of the new garage apartments will not be competing for the existing supply of affordable housing, the benefits of the new NOAH units will trickle sideways and lower the rent of all other housing.

Most residents probably won't ask for a PBD because they want to increase the supply of affordable housing, but they may ask for a PBD because they want to improve their neighborhood. As a byproduct, removing off-street parking requirements will remove a major barrier to affordable housing.

EMPLOYMENT EFFECTS OF PARKING BENEFIT DISTRICTS

PBDs will increase public spending, but paying for parking will reduce private consumption. How will this affect local employment? Public services are produced locally but much of private consumption is imported from outside the region and the only local jobs created are for Amazon truck drivers. On balance, shifting spending from private consumption to public services will increase the demand for local labor (Shoup 2010, 230-31). We can import cell phones but can't import clean sidewalks, so shifting spending from new cell phones to cleaner sidewalks will increase local employment.

PBDs are not a make-work program, but politics are often more important than economics in public policy, and creating jobs is politically important. If spending for private consumption declines slightly, the resulting job losses may be invisible in an economy that creates and loses many jobs every month. In contrast, most of the jobs created by new public spending are easily seen, especially if they are for union members. Improving neighborhoods will benefit almost everyone in the city, but the jobs created by providing new public services are another benefit of Parking Benefit Districts.

TURNING PROBLEMS INTO OPPORTUNITIES

I have used New York City to suggest how PBDs can work in densely populated neighborhoods with scarce parking, but many other cities around the world are as dense as New York, and many older American cities have some very dense neighborhoods. Dense neighborhoods in any city can benefit from PBDs.

Policy is driven by politics, and diverse interests across the political spectrum can find things to like in a PBD. Liberals will see that it increases public services. Conservatives will see that it relies on market choices. Drivers will see that it guarantees curb parking and freedom from moving their cars for street cleaning. Residents will see that it improves their neighborhood. Environmentalists will see that it reduces energy consumption, air pollution, and carbon emissions. And elected officials will see that it depoliticizes parking, reduces traffic congestion, and pays for better public services without raising taxes.

Cities that manage their curb parking as valuable real estate can stop subsidizing cars, congestion, and carbon emissions. Instead, they will improve transportation, reduce the cost of housing, and provide better public services. Parking Benefit Districts with power equalization can fairly and efficiently manage public land used for private parking. They may turn out to be a politically popular way to improve cities, the economy, and the environment, one parking space at a time.

REFERENCES AND FURTHER READING

Brown, Anne, Vinit Mukhija, and Donald Shoup. 2018. "Converting Garages into Housing," *Journal of Transportation and Economics*.

City of Vancouver. 2017. "West End Parking Policy." http://vancouver.ca/streets-transportation/west-end-parking-strategy.aspx

San Francisco Municipal Transportation Agency. 2014. "On-street Parking Census Data and Map." http://sfpark.org/resources/parking-census-data-context-and-map-april-2014/

Shoup, Donald. 2010. "Putting Cities Back on Their Feet," *Journal of Urban Planning and Development*, Vol. 136, No. 3, September, pp. 225–233. http://shoup.bol.ucla.edu/PuttingCitiesBackOnTheirFeet.pdf

Shoup, Donald. 2011. *The High Cost of Free Parking*, Chicago: Planners Press.

Shoup, Donald Shoup, Quan Yuan, and Xin Jiang. 2017. "Charging for Parking to Finance Public Services," *Journal of Planning and Education Research*, Vol. 37, No. 2, June, pp. 136–149. https://www.dropbox.com/s/lgrzggpz1r3myr2/ChargingForParkingToFinancePublicServices.pdf?dl=0

Epilogue

Doing More with Less

If I'd a knowed what a trouble it was
to make a book, I wouldn't a tackled it,
and ain't a-going to no more.

MARK TWAIN, *HUCKLEBERRY FINN*

When the American Planning Association published *The High Cost of Free Parking* in 2005, half the planning profession thought I was crazy and the other half thought I was daydreaming. But attitudes toward our current parking policies are beginning to shift from thoughtless acceptance to skeptical criticism, and many planners now agree that parking reforms are both sane and practical. Cities can do more with less parking.

Chapters 1–3 in *The High Cost of Free Parking* explain how cities began to require off-street parking in the 1930s and how parking requirements spread around the country and the world. Nevertheless, urban planning education provides no instruction on how planners set parking requirements, and textbooks offer no help. The index of a book on urban planning typically skips from "Paris" to "participation" with no entry for parking. Most textbooks in transportation and urban economics also fail to mention parking. Studying city planning without noticing parking is like studying the motion of planets without noticing gravity. Nevertheless, the land use with the single biggest urban footprint has been almost invisible to scholars in every discipline (*The High Cost of Free Parking*, 25–26).

The American Planning Association's monumental 1,514-page *Growing Smart Legislative Guidebook: Model Statutes for Planning and the Management of Change* missed the opportunity to draw attention to the problems with parking requirements. The APA published the 11-pound *Guidebook* in 2002 as the culmination of its seven-year, $2.5-million "Growing Smart" project. The goal was to offer reforms for outdated planning laws. The *Guidebook's* editor explained:

> Our planning tools date from another era. They are shopworn and inadequate for the job at hand. … Reform of planning statutes is a serious contemporary concern that affects every state, region, and community in this nation (Meck 2002, xxx–xxxi).

The *Legislative Guidebook* suggested reforms for almost every planning issue except parking. Its 72-page index has five pages for words that start with 'P,' but parking is not one of them.

Parking doesn't just have *something* to do with city planning. It has *everything* to do with city planning. Allan Jacobs (Berkeley professor of city planning and former director of the San Francisco City Planning Commission) explained:

> Automobile parking is a pervasive issue. Prepare a plan for an individual street or neighborhood, or for a central area, and parking is certain to be a major subject—a bone of contention—more time and energy consuming than housing (Jacobs 1993, 305).

Minimum parking requirements are an outdated practice unmoored from theory, data, and current objectives. Planners cannot fix parking requirements by trying to update them. Instead, planners should try to repeal them. Buffalo repealed all parking requirements citywide in 2017 and replaced them with a single sentence: "There are no provisions that establish a minimum number of off-street parking spaces for development" (Chapter 23). Mexico City removed all its minimum parking requirements in 2017, and replaced them with maximum parking limits (Chapter 15). London did the same thing in 2004 (Chapter 16).

PARKING AND PLANNING THEORY

Most planning students don't learn anything about parking in graduate school, but they do take courses in Planning Theory. A rapid succession of planning theories blossomed in the 20th century. The names of some evoke images of what planners would like the city to be (city beautiful, garden city, and radiant city). Names of others optimistically describe what planners do (communicative planning, comprehensive planning, participatory planning, rational planning, and strategic planning). Several names reflect the planners' politics (advocacy planning, critical planning, equity planning, and radical planning). All these names are somewhat self-congratulatory, as if to reassure everyone that planners do good things. When outsiders observe what urban planners do, however, the names they give to planning theories are more modest (incrementalism) and less flattering (muddling through).

What theory of urban planning best explains how planning for parking went wrong? Advocacy planning, incrementalism, and muddling through, with a veneer of rational planning, are the best candidates. First, everyone wants to park free, so advocacy planners would support parking requirements, especially since developers seem to pay for the parking. Second, planners have assembled parking requirements incrementally over decades, with a new one added whenever a new land use, such as a nail salon, emerges. Each new parking requirement seems logical on its own, but the cumulative effect is devastating. Third, muddling through also explains how planners set parking requirements. Limited information, limited consideration of alternatives, political pandering, and groupthink increase the muddle. Finally, the parking requirements are disguised in an elaborate camouflage of rational planning, with many tables of precise numbers and ratios that suggest careful calculations. For future planning theorists, minimum parking requirements will be a planning disaster to remember (*The High Cost of Free Parking*, Chapter 5).

Planning theories and policies are always a work in progress. What a previous generation believed right often looks wrong today, and what we believe right today may seem wrong to future generations. For example, urban renewal programs once seemed to be the best hope for rescuing downtowns but most cities have abandoned them. We attribute each new failure to the mistakes of previous generations and make U-turns so fast we forget we were formerly headed in the opposite direction.

My three recommended reforms are the exact opposite of the conventional wisdom about parking. First, cities require ample off-street parking while I recommend removing these requirements. Second, cities keep on-street parking free or cheap while I recommend charging market prices for it. And third, cities put parking meter revenue into the general fund while I recommend using it to pay for local public improvements. But some cities are already making U-turns. Some have reduced or removed off-street parking requirements (see Chapters 16–23). Some charge market prices for on-street parking (see Chapters 35–41). Some have established Parking Benefit Districts to spend the meter money locally (see Chapter 44–51). Future planners may condemn off-street parking requirements and free on-street parking as severely as we condemn the urban renewal disasters of the twentieth century. Future planners may also marvel at how their predecessors could have been so wrong for so long.

THE HIDING HAND

Planning theorists have not yet discovered a theory with explanatory power comparable to Adam Smith's "invisible hand" in economics. Perhaps the nearest analogy to the invisible hand in economics is the "hiding hand" in planning. Politicians and planners can pursue public goals by hiding the cost of reaching these goals. For example, cities use inclusionary zoning to require affordable housing, hiding its cost in the cost of market-rate housing. Cities don't have to subsidize the affordable housing and no one knows who really pays for it. Cities also hide the cost of parking by requiring buildings and businesses to provide an ample supply of parking spaces.

How big is the hidden cost of parking? Chapter 7 of *The High Cost of Free Parking* estimates that the subsidy for off-street parking in the United States is between 1.2 percent and 3.6 percent of the national economy. In Chapter 11, Gabbe and Pierce estimate that hiding the cost of parking in the cost of housing increases rents by about 17 percent, even for those who are too poor to own a car. Hiding the cost of parking in the cost of housing also increases car ownership and driving (*The High Cost of Free Parking*, Chapter 20). As with most hidden costs, it isn't clear who pays for the required parking, but someone must—residents, investors, workers, developers, shoppers, and all users of real estate. The cost of parking doesn't go away just because drivers park free. Given the high cost of required parking spaces and their harmful consequences, planners should not uncritically assume that the demand for free parking automatically justifies off-street parking requirements. Demand depends on price, but planners rarely think about what drivers pay for parking or what the required spaces cost.

THE SPEED OF REFORM

Minimum parking requirements have persisted so long that they can't be called a crisis; they are a chronic condition. They may seem permanent but I suspect they will wither as a new generation of planners loses respect for them. As Max Planck explained, "science marches on, funeral by funeral."

Paradigm shifts in urban planning are often barely noticeable while they are happening, and afterward it is hard to tell that anything has changed because few planners remember the abandoned pieties. Cities don't need off-street parking requirements, the Earth can't afford them, and we won't miss them if cities begin to charge fair market prices for curb parking and spend the revenue on local public services.

Off-street parking requirements are a house of cards and may be surprisingly easy to sweep away. In 2004, London replaced its minimum parking requirements with maximum parking limits (Chapter 16). In 2015, Fayetteville, Arkansas, removed all off-street parking requirements except for residential uses. In 2016, Buffalo removed all its parking requirements (Chapter 23). In 2017, Mexico City replaced its minimum parking requirements with maximum parking limits (Chapter 15). Removing all parking requirements at once is not only more effective than reducing them one at a time but is also easier because planners don't have to invent each new lower parking requirement, justify it to a planning commission and city council, and then administer it.

But cities can't remove off-street parking requirements without also charging the right prices for on-street parking. When you are walking along a busy street with crowded curb parking, imagine how much the curb could earn if all the cars paid market prices that produce a few open spaces. Imagine what public improvements the parking revenue could finance. And imagine how the open curb spaces could reduce the demand for off-street parking requirements.

CONCLUSION

In 1862, Abraham Lincoln wrote, "As our case is new, so we must think anew, and act anew." These words are as apt now as they were more than 150 years ago. In planning for parking, our case is new, so we should think anew and act anew. Cities began to require off-street parking in the 1930s when traffic congestion and air pollution were less severe and global warming was not a concern. All these are now important problems and parking subsidies magnify them.

In his 1961 Farewell Address to the nation in which he famously warned of the military-industrial complex, President Eisenhower said, "We—you and I, and our government—must avoid the impulse to live only for today, plundering, for our own ease and convenience, the precious resources of tomorrow." Our parking-industrial complex is now plundering the resources of tomorrow at a rate Dwight Eisenhower could not have imagined.

Planning professors rarely end a book or lecture with quotes from two Republican presidents but I hope most people will agree their advice applies to the need for parking reforms. Pioneering in parking reform may not be the safest strategy for city planners, but closely following successful pioneers is a smart strategy. I hope the 51 chapters in this book have provided enough evidence to show that parking reforms can produce major benefits for cities, the economy, and the environment.

Trying to reform your own city's parking policies may feel like paddling a canoe to tow an aircraft carrier but if enough people paddle, the ship will move. I hope *Parking and the City* will encourage planners, politicians, and citizens to begin paddling. Reform depends on leadership from all of you.

REFERENCES AND FURTHER READING

Jacobs, Allan. 1993. *Great Streets*. Cambridge, Mass: MIT Press.
Meck, Stuart, ed. 2002. *Growing Smart Legislative Guidebook: Model Statutes for Planning and the Management of Change*. Chicago: American Planning Association. Available at: www.planning.org/guidebook/Login.asp
Shoup, Donald. 2011. *The High Cost of Free Parking*. Chicago: Planners Press.

Index

collective benefits, 42
command-and-control planning, 16
commercial areas, 43–5, 172; Mexico
City, 186–7. *See also* office buildings;
shopping centers
commons problem, 308
community goals, 227, 234
community parking resources, 218
commuting, 129
concert halls, 76–7
condominiums, 143; ARO, 208–10
congestion, 2, 76, 101–8, 129, 261; LA
Express Park project, 380; London,
354–5; Los Angeles, 178; parking as
automobile-enabling infrastructure,
102–3; parking induces driving,
distorts markets, 103–7, **105, 107**;
Residential Parking Benefit Districts
and, 483; SF*park* and, 334–5
congestion tolls, 39
conservative and liberal viewpoints,
53, 242
cooperative capitalism, 46
Corney, Ken, 443
corruption, 14–5, 35
Costanza, George, 137
cost of parking requirements, 5–6
credit card payment, 30, 225, 284, 324,
355, 387, 458; pay stations, 440–9
crime, 241, 280, 443
cruising, 22–4, 31, 76, 270, 354; Berkeley,
317; choosing, 264–5; exponential
costs of, 24–5; familiarity with
area and, 319–20; lessons from San
Francisco, 361–9, *368*; Los Angeles,
265–6; Manhattan, 486; measuring,
356–7; psychological changes, 23;
studies, 262. *See also* on-street parking
Cuauhtemoc area (Mexico City), 464

dark energy metaphor, 6
de Blasio, Bill, 152–3
demand-based pricing, 3, 18, 25–8
demand for cars, 2, 10, 15, 20
density, 1, 153–4; European cities, 19–20;
London, 194, *195*, 197; Los Angeles,
74–5; of parking, 78–9; planning
process for parking, 70, *71*; within
and between regions, 75

developers, 146, 148–9, 201; Adaptive
Reuse Ordinance (ARO), Los
Angeles, 206–12, *208, 209*; big-box
retailers, Mexico City, 186; Buffalo,
251–2; unbundled parking, 158–9
Dhaka, Bangladesh, *168*
Digital Payment Technologies (T2),
441
digitized parking lots, 133–4, *134*
disabilities and parking, 34, 279–80, 286,
309, 365–6, 381–2
disabled placard abuse, 34–5, 289–306,
352–3; logic of priced parking, 290–2;
two-tier solution, 35, 301–6, 352;
unfunded mandate, 302–3
Disney Hall (Los Angeles), 76–7
doormen, informal parking and, 277
double parking, 286, 329, 336, *337*
Dougherty, Conor, 435
Downs, Anthony, 10
driverless cars, 39, 94
dynamic (demand-responsive) pricing,
22, 28, 30, 225, 236, 268–73, 289–90,
320–1, *345, 346*, 354, 473; caps, 358;
garages, optimizing use of, 370–7; LA
Express Park, 379–80; price elasticity,
349–50, *350*; Redwood City, 430;
SF*park*, 322–43, 326–8, 342, 344–5;
time periods, 29–30, 32–3, 67, 69, 180,
217, 321, 351, 373–4, *374*, 382

early bird rates, 316, 324, *333*, 371, 380
ecological service valuation, 137
ecoParq, Mexico City, 189, 464–72
ecosystem services, 133
Eisenhower, Dwight, 499
elderly, housing and parking
requirements, 141, 153
electric cars, 255
Emanuel, Rahm, 304
emissions, tailpipe, 255, 312–3, 334
emissions costs, 171–6
employer-paid parking, 403–12; cash
out, 404–7; cash out and traffic
reduction, *408*, 408–10; cash out in
California, 407–8; enforcing law,
410–1; implications for federal action,
411–2; Internal Revenue Code, 404–5,
407, 411

Made in the USA
Middletown, DE
14 November 2021